THE PEOPLE I LOVE

A Biography of Luigi G. Ligutti

Vincent A. Yzermans

THE LITURGICAL PRESS
Collegeville, Minnesota

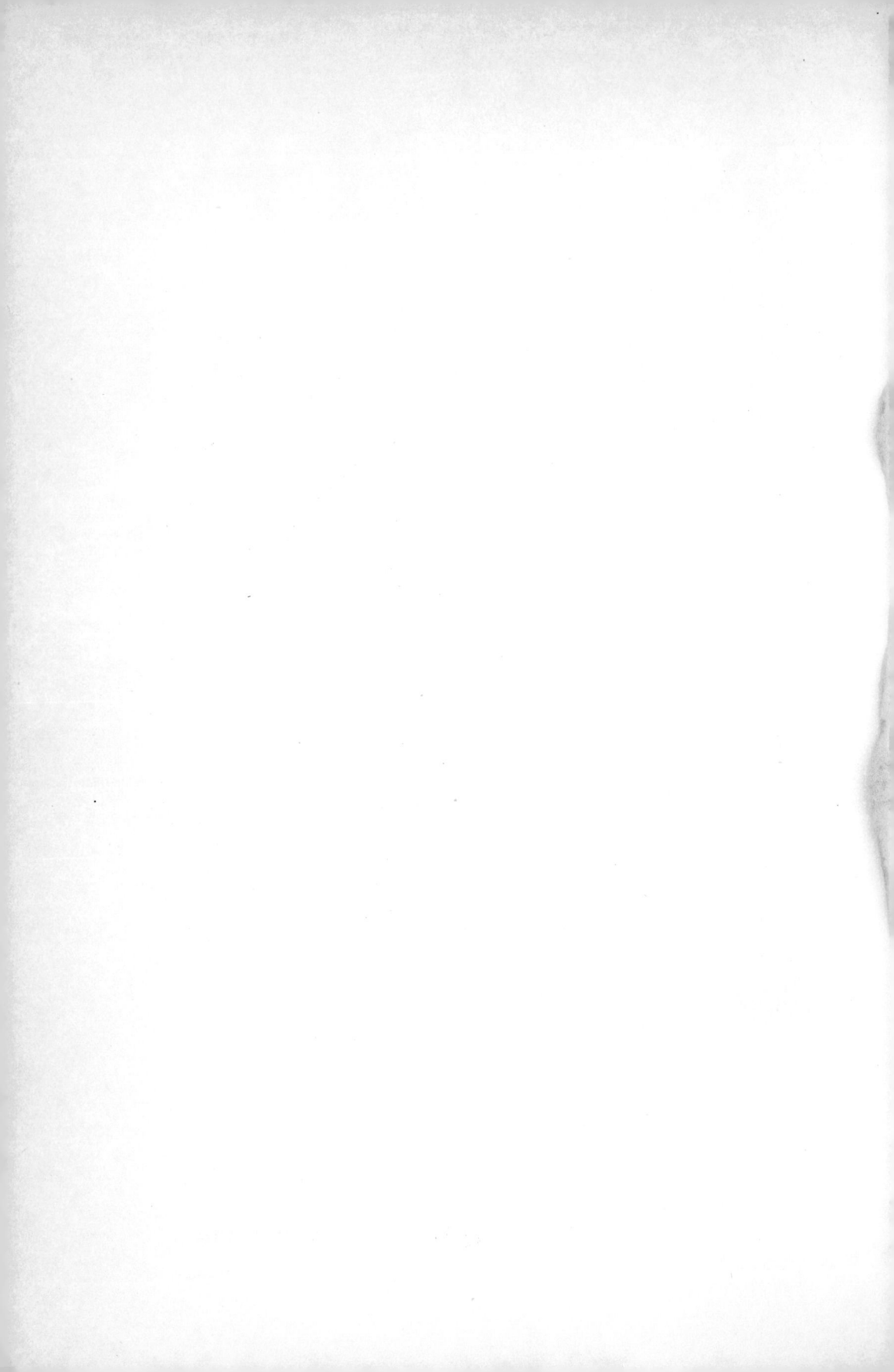

BV
4374
.L538
Y94

THE PEOPLE I LOVE

196609

Nihil obstat: Rev. Msgr. John George Weber, *Censor deputatus*. *Imprimatur*: ✠ George H. Speltz, D.D., Bishop of St. Cloud, Minnesota, January 19, 1976.

Photo credits:
National Catholic Rural Life Conference, pp. 47-48; Chicago Photographers, top p. 171; Associated Press, bottom p. 171; Shields, bottom p. 173; Giordani, Rome, top p. 174, top p. 261, top and bottom p. 265, p. 266; Des Moines *Register* and *Tribune*, bottom p. 174; Felici, Rome, bottom p. 262; Sheraton Photo Service, top p. 263.

Cover by James McBride.

Copyright © 1976 by the Order of St. Benedict, Inc., Collegeville, Minnesota. Printed in the United States of America. All rights reserved. ISBN 0-8146-0895-7.

DEDICATION

To the people I love of St. Rose of Lima Parish

TABLE OF CONTENTS

Page		
Page	ix	FOREWORD
	xiii	INTRODUCTION
	1	NEW TIMES DEMAND NEW MEN
	11	DIOCESAN APPRENTICESHIP
	23	THE YOUNG PASTOR OF GRANGER
	49	MAN'S RELATION TO THE LAND
	76	TIME OF TROUBLE
	85	TRAVELING WITH A PURPOSE
	117	SHARING WITH THE POOR
	149	UNDER THE SOUTHERN CROSS
	177	LONELY GUARDS WHO WATCH
	206	COUNCIL CONSULTANT
	231	VATICAN OBSERVER TO FAO
	267	STILL GOING
	294	EPILOGUE
	297	APPENDIX
	314	INDEX

FOREWORD

A biography of any man is difficult. A biography of a man of the stature of Msgr. Luigi G. Ligutti is exceptionally difficult because he was involved in so many critical and sometimes crucial issues throughout the fifty-five years of his priestly service. Priestly life, rural ministry, immigration, world peace and hunger, international organizations, and countless other activities always kept him "a man on the go." First, last, and always, however, he was a priest.

I have attempted to weave these strands of Ligutti's life into the framework of his priestly dedication and service. It is not only the story of one priest's life but in many ways the story of American Catholicism during the middle years of this century. In so many ways, as the following pages attempt to recall, Ligutti was part of the growing-up phase of our national and Catholic experience. Ligutti's concerns were our concerns; his observations should provide as much wisdom for future generations as they have for all those with whom he dealt in his busy life.

This biography was inspired by Fr. Frederick McGuire, C.M., former director of the Latin American Bureau of the National Catholic Welfare Conference. He was the first to present the idea and throughout the past five years continually offered me support, advice, and encouragement. Due appreciation must also be acknowledged to the following for their helpful suggestions and advice: Most Rev. George H. Speltz, D.D., bishop of St. Cloud; Fr. Colman J. Barry, O.S.B., Fr. Robert Trisco, Fr. Wilfred A. Illies, and Msgr. John Tracy Ellis. A special debt of appreciation is owed Most Rev. Peter W. Bartholome, D.D., former bishop of St. Cloud. Also, a special thanks of friendship and assistance is owed Most Rev. Mark J. Hurley, D.D., bishop of Santa Rosa, for his assistance and counsel in the progress of this work.

In many ways this work is more autobiographical than biographical. It could not have been written without the many hours that Monsignor Ligutti himself spent in advising and encouraging me. To him must go the credit for whatever good; to me must go the responsibility for any errors or omissions.

I have attempted no more no less than to recount the life of a man from the available sources. Admittedly, the evidence might be prejudicial, but it was the only documentary evidence available. A future historian must evaluate these judgments in the light of further evidence. Here footnotes and scholarly references have been eliminated. The reader must trust that this information comes chiefly from the personal files of Monsignor Ligutti and interviews made with him between 1971 and 1975. I have tried to be as objective and impartial as possible. There must be some few lines that I might make. This is the place.

Ligutti is a loyal son of the Church, as many documents in his files attest. He did not seek honors, power, or influence. He wanted nothing more than to serve the Church. In this regard he was very much like Pope John XXIII.

Ligutti is truly a great man, a respected leader and forceful spokesman for "the little people of the world." His present ordinary, Bishop Maurice Dingmann of Des Moines, perhaps best described Ligutti as "Iowa's greatest contribution to the Catholic Church." Although he traveled the world and spends his remaining days in Rome, his heart remains in Iowa. He left Granger, but Granger never left him.

With all his charming simplicity, Ligutti was not a simple man. His complexities in many ways were astounding. He loved the land and he loved academe. He always wanted to be a professor and ultimately became a foremost teacher outside the halls of the university. He loved life and the living, yet few men had a deeper respect for the dead. He would become almost poetic when a tulip shot its sprout above the ground or when wheat promised a good yield. At the same time, he would drive fifty to a hundred miles out of the way to visit the grave of a relative or friend. He transpired time; eternity was as real as history.

Ligutti was a "driver." Work for him was as important as the air he breathed. He rose early — about four-thirty — for prayers, meditation, and Mass. By seven o'clock he was prepared for the work of the day. He also retired early; by ten o'clock the day was done. If he was forced to linger at a dinner, a speech, or seminar, he was obviously anxious to return home. When an associate rebukingly said that he missed the more interesting discussions after ten o'clock in the evening, Ligutti replied, "If it can't be said before nine o'clock, it isn't worth listening to after twelve o'clock."

His love for people was more than exceptional. He could visit with Pope Paul VI as familiarly as with a Drake University sophomore. Monsignor Ligutti was loved and respected by members of the Food and Agriculture Organization because he was a living witness of the goodness and willingness of the Church to serve all men.

This biography is, then, prejudicial. It is a testament of one midwestern priest to an older, wiser, and great midwestern priest. I trust that the reader will consider this fact.

Feast of the Assumption, 1975
St. Rosa, Minnesota

MSGR. VINCENT A. YZERMANS

INTRODUCTION

It was in the early thirties that I first met Msgr. Luigi Ligutti. He had come to the office of Catholic Charities in Brooklyn to meet with Msgr. J. Jerome Reddy, its executive director, with whom I was just beginning my own association in the work of that diocesan agency. Little then did I realize how that introduction would someday blossom into a deep and abiding personal friendship and affection, nor did I realize the influence this kindly, stalwart man would have on my own life and labors, just as it has had on the lives and labors of thousands of others.

I like to believe that when the history of our time and the influence of the Church upon it in the mid-half of the twentieth century is written that the names of two men will loom large in that account. I link them together because they spearheaded two great movements within the Church, the depth of whose great influence on the accomplishments of the Church it would be almost impossible to measure adequately. I think, naturally, of Monsignor Ligutti who, as executive secretary of the National Catholic Rural Life Conference, and Msgr. John O'Grady, as executive secretary of the National Conference of Catholic Charities, labored so diligently to weave the work of these two great movements into the structure and programs of the Catholic Church in America and, most particularly, in the field of social action, both nationally and internationally. I also link together the names and lives of these two great men because they labored hand-in-hand and their programs mutually influenced one another.

By the end of the thirties, thanks to the influence of these leaders, diocesan organizations of these two great movements were rather firmly established throughout the United States. It was not surprising, then, that in the early forties it was to the leaders in these movements throughout the country that War Relief Services — NCWC, the newly-established agency of the American bishops for the relief of the victims of the war that was then raging throughout the world, should turn to spread the need for its propagation, development, and support among the people of our country. I have said publicly many times that down through the years the men who lead and make up these great institutions of our Church have been, and continue to be, the "backbone" of what is now known as Catholic Relief Services — USCC.

Having assisted War Relief Services to establish a broad program of relief for victims in every area affected by the great war, it was only natural for the organization to turn again to Monsignor Ligutti to establish a program for the resettlement of thousands of the more than a million displaced persons that the war had left in its wake in western Europe. He not only helped to set up the National Catholic Resettlement Council, with its vast network of diocesan resettlement committees, but self-sacrificingly he joined a group of six Rural Life and Charities' men in a visit to the displaced persons' camps in 1948 to bring back the story of their suffering and hardship to Americans. He lent his full strength and influence to the promotion of legislation that ensured their entry into the United States by the hundreds of thousands. With the exception of Monsignor O'Grady, with whom I have already linked him, few, if any, priests in the United States have as deeply left their imprint on the accomplishments of Catholic Relief Services as has Ligutti.

As I look back on it, it was his concern for the crucial issues of humanity — human misery, hunger, and starvation — that shaped Monsignor Ligutti's life. From my personal experiences and contacts with this marvellous man, I realized in later years that he was at his best in the problems of environment, hunger, immigration, and development. His speeches of the 1940's and 1950's were only heeded in the majestic assemblies of Church and State in the 1960's and 1970's. In this sense he was a man at least a generation ahead of his time. It is consoling to note that his biographer brings this matter to our attention.

Ligutti, as I know him, was never an organized man. He could effectively present the challenge, outline broad goals to be achieved, get the work under way, and then go on his way to another program or project. He left behind him, however, a sense of dedication, a spirit of inspiration that was infectious.

He was never, however, a headstrong man. He was gentle, gracious, and convinced of his position. This, perhaps, was the secret of his success as executive director of the National Catholic

Rural Life Conference, as an organizer of rural congresses, as a Vatican observer to FAO. He was a "universal man" long before Americans came to respect men for this universality.

These words, however, are not meant to be a paean of praise of Ligutti. No one would appreciate or respect them less than Ligutti himself. Throughout the past three years he kept telling his biographer to write more about his faults and failings and less about his triumphs and successes. His biographer might be a good historian, but he was not a good servant to Ligutti's words. Each man, in the secret recesses of his soul, knows more of his faults than the world can ever expose.

One item stands out in bold relief throughout these pages. Both the biographer, a good friend of mine, and the subject of this biography, a close friend of both of us, reveal the generous heart, the magnanimous soul, the undaunted spirit of a priest of God. Whether in Iowa, Washington, Rome, or any place in the world, Ligutti was first, last, and always a priest of God.

We should not, we know, canonize the living. But that does not mean that we cannot praise the living for their good works. We praise Monsignor Ligutti in this biography, which is not only a record of his work but an inspiration to the many who will come after him.

It is coincidental and at the same time fortuitous that the subject of this biography has spent his life in the cause of rural life and its author spent the four years in research and writing while serving as a rural pastor in the central Minnesota diocese of St. Cloud. Both Monsignors Ligutti and Yzermans, as priests of God's Church, are dedicated to assist people in any possible way. This biography reveals many — but not all — of the facets of the assistance Ligutti, though now in his eightieth year, continues to render people. Yzermans has by this work shown all of us how we can serve God's people wherever we might be.

We congratulate Monsignor Yzermans for writing this biography of a man so richly deserving to be long remembered. More than that, we congratulate Monsignor Ligutti for being an inspiration, guide, and collaborator with the countless people he knew throughout the rich and bountiful eighty years that God has given him.

☩Edward E. Swanstrom
Auxiliary Bishop of New York and
Executive Director, Catholic
Relief Services — USCC

THE SONG OF THE PLOW
by Harry Kemp

It was I who built Chaldea and the Cities of the Plain;
I was Greece and Rome and Carthage and the opulence of Spain.
When their courtiers walked in scarlet and their queens wore chains
    of gold,
And forgot 'twas I that made them, growing godless old and bold,
I went over them in judgment, and again my corn fields stood
Where empty courts bowed homage in obsequious multitude . . . .
For the nation that forgets me, in that hour her doom is sealed
By a judgment as from Heaven that can never be repealed!

THE PEOPLE I LOVE

CHAPTER ONE

NEW TIMES DEMAND NEW MEN

It was not the best of years, nor was it the worst of years. The United States was struggling to recover from the economic depression of 1893. Pope Leo XIII was writing encyclicals and trying to restore the spiritual and moral leadership of the Vatican. Nicholas and Alexandra were engaging the mysterious monk of Siberia and in the process losing not only the Tschovich but also the throne. Grover Cleveland was serving his second term as President of the United States. Latin America, as usual, was in rebellion with puppet dictators and military juntas. It was 1895. The world, then as now, was in turmoil; not the best of years and not the worst of years.

Our story begins in a neatly tucked-out-of-the-way village called Romans in the Province of Udine, Italy, on March 21, 1895. Aloysius Domenico Ligutti was born on that day, the fifth and youngest child of Spiridione Ligutti and Teresa Ciriani. His parents were married in 1873 and had been previously blessed with four children: Francesca, born December 7, 1879; Antonio, born September 24, 1881; Teresa, born June 6, 1883; and Napoleon, born May 28, 1886. The parents took their youngest child to the small parish church on April 1, 1895 to be baptized by the pastor, Don Justiniano Tonini. The family was religious, unscarred by the anti-clericalism of late nineteenth-century Italy.

On his father's side the child could trace his family back to 1260 to a certain Tonolino di Clauzetto of the minor nobility. The name Ligutti first appeared in 1325 as a proper name for one of the sons of Giacomo di Tonolino. His mother numbered two distinguished churchmen on her side. Her uncle, Giuseppe Cardinal Callegari, bishop of Padua and classmate of St. Pius X, died in Padua on April 14, 1906. Her brother, a priest of the archdiocese of Udine, was Msgr. Cio-Batta Ciriani. He died in 1923.

The family was not wealthy, but even though by present standards, it would be called poor, it was rich in the abundance of many good things. Its home, not unlike the home of Pope John XXIII in Sotto il Monte, was blessed with the affection of devoted parents, close family ties, and many friends and neighbors. The parish church was the center of its social and religious life. Christian values were cultivated and prized as highly as the vineyards and wheat fields surrounding the village, providing sustenance and life to the close-knit villagers. There was a pleasant, peaceful rhythm to the daily routine of the Ligutti family. The home was across the road from the village school where "Gino," a name Ligutti received during his infancy, first came in contact with the world of books and learning.

The lad lived as any other Italian boy in the area. He studied his lessons, being fond of school, fished in the stream that flowed through the village, served Mass in the parish church, helped in the fields during harvest time, and with other boys of the village engaged in a hobby called "digging." The area was steeped in history. Caesar's legions camped in the area; medieval lords and dukes waged battles throughout the countryside; Napoleon's army tramped across the fertile plains and trudged along the dusty roads. An enjoyable Sunday afternoon was searching for the remnants of wars and artifacts of bygone civilizations. From these early years Gino developed not only a love of history but an historic sense that would leave its mark on his mind throughout his life.

Sundays were special days for this growing Italian boy. He loved to stand in the fields, breathe the fresh mountain air washed by the salt whiffs that came from the nearby sea, and listen to the ringing of the bells from the campaniles of the churches in the surrounding villages. Later in life he fondly recalled how when the wind was right he could hear as many as six bells chiming from as many villages. On Sundays, too, after assisting at Mass in his own village church, he and his brothers walked three miles to the neighboring village of St. Martin to assist at the high Mass where the liturgy was performed with greater solemnity and the choir was more impressive than in Romans.

A major event in the life of the young Gino was a trip to Udine. With his parents, an older brother or sister, he rose before dawn. Mother packed a lunch and father strapped to the wagon whatever humble wares he hoped to sell in the market. The lad was filled with wonder as their peasant cart rumbled into the city, which at the time numbered no more than twenty-five thousand people. He was filled with admiration by the magnificent palace on the hill, awed by the ancient cathedral with its invaluable paintings by Tiepolo, and, no doubt, had more than second thoughts when his parents pointed out the majestic palace of the archbishop and the nearby seminary.

In later life he recalled how his mother never went to Udine without visiting the popular shrine-church of Our Lady of Graces. Less than a block away from the majestic shrine was a small Methodist church. His mother never passed in front of that church. Instead, with an instinctive fear of Protestants, she grabbed her small son's hand and took a circuitous path behind the Methodist church in order to find her way to the pure, clean air of the Catholic shrine. In later years as the housekeeper in Woodbine, Iowa, she was the warm-hearted friend of many Protestant women and children. "You know," she said to her son on many occasions, "they are also good people!" At the time, however, the incident left a profound impact on the lad who later would become one of America's first and foremost ecumenists.

Ligutti grew during these years in the instinctive wisdom of the Italian peasant under the watchful eyes of devoted parents, schoolmasters, and parish priest. He was an exceptionally good pupil and enjoyed school very much. At that time primary education was limited to three grades, but with the help of his brother he completed the work in two years. At age nine he entered the secondary school and a year later began to study Latin.

During this period events were happening in the Ligutti home that profoundly changed the course of the bright young student's life. When twenty-three years old, Gino's sister Francesca, following her marriage, emigrated to the United States. His two older brothers, Antonio and Napoleon, one an agriculturist and the other a terrazzo worker, followed shortly thereafter. Finally, his father joined his three children in search of a happier and more abundant life in the United States. Unlike his children, however, the elder Ligutti was unhappy in America and shortly returned to Romans. When Gino was fourteen years old a tearful mother, a proud father, and a happy parish priest enrolled the promising young student in that magnificent minor seminary in Cividale. Two years later, on April 25, 1911, Gino received the last letter from his father, who died within the month.

The following summer his sister Francesca, who was then living in Des Moines, Iowa, which already numbered a substantial colony of Italian immigrants, returned with her seven children to visit her mother and brother in Romans. Francesca persuaded her mother to return with her to the United States, and the mother, in turn, insisted that Gino come along in order to keep the family together. The young seminarian was reluctant to go because of his strong desire to be a priest, but out of filial devotion he fulfilled his mother's wish. In later years Ligutti referred to his own mental attitude and anguish by quoting Dickens' opening sentence of *The Tale of Two Cities*: "It was the best of times, it was the worst of times, it was the age of wisdom, it was the age of foolishness, it was the epoch of belief, it was the epoch of incredulity."

The long arduous journey from the northeastern corner of Italy to the southwestern corner of Iowa was astonishingly undertaken by a mother and son who could not speak a word of English and a courageous daughter with seven young children.

Much later, when he sought American citizenship, no record of his entry into the United States could be found. Only after a diligent search did he discover that he had entered the country under the name of his brother-in-law as Luigi Romano. Unlike most Italian immigrants of this period, however, the family wasted no time in New York or the eastern seaboard. Immediately, they boarded a train for Des Moines and passed through the Empire State. The only significant incident of the journey that the young Ligutti remembered was that the train moved onto a ferryboat at Buffalo and crossed Lake Erie.

The wearied and worried little group of immigrants changed trains in Chicago, and as it clickety-clacked across the farmlands of Illinois and Iowa, the mother and son felt the biting cold weather. This was a new experience. The train chugged into the depot in Des Moines on a mid-January day in 1912 with the thermometer reading 36 degrees below zero — the coldest day in history for Des Moines. Immediately the group was bundled off to Francesca's home. The one thought that overwhelmed the young Ligutti for several days was the stark realization: "Now we are really poor...."

Such a thought, however, did not daunt his spirit. He had secured his mother's promise that she would let him continue his studies for the priesthood. He declined the insistence of his mother, sister, and brother-in-law that he continue his studies in the public schools of Des Moines. He found assistance in Father Romanelli, pastor of the Italian parish in Des Moines. Before the month was out he was enrolled in the fifth year at St. Ambrose

College in Davenport, Iowa. With the financial assistance of his brothers and sister, young Ligutti enrolled at the college on February 1, 1912, took the six-hour trip from Des Moines to Davenport by train, and began a new adventure in the United States. Strangely enough, his first impression of the college was seeing the Mississippi River, solidly covered with ice, and viewing the old brewery wagons bringing beer across the ice from Rock Island, Illinois, to Davenport.

His memories of St. Ambrose College were happy ones. For the two and a half years he spent in these pleasant surroundings, he earned straight "A" grades. When he enrolled he could speak only a few words of English. On his own time and with firm determination he started with Baldwin's *School Reading by Grades.* By sheer effort he quickly learned his adopted tongue. Later in life he recalled that one of the first words he learned was "jiggers," the signal given by mischievous students when the dean of discipline was approaching. It amused him greatly because he neither then nor later understood the origin of the word. Philology was his life-long hobby.

Later, too, he recalled the food; like most students he found it to be an easy and ready scapegoat for all complaints. "I remember, of course," he said, "that I could not eat the food they served. It was tasteless. The meat was what we called 'bull's neck.' All I ate for the first months was bread, butter and sugar on top. The tea was abominable." For a youth from sunny Italy transplanted to the Upper Midwest, the weather "was just so damn cold." With affection he recalled Fr. William Shanahan, the president of the college, who helped re-instate the Italian youth and his two friends, "Lizzy" Welsch and Ambrose Burke, after one of their midnight escapades.

On June 10, 1914 Ligutti graduated from St. Ambrose College in the company of such classmates who would remain life-long friends as John Cash, William J. Hynes, Leo Kerrigan, Leo S. Roling, Edward Rosenthal, and others. At this early stage in life, Luigi developed one of his most endearing and attractive characteristics, the ability of making and keeping friends.

Twenty-five years later Ligutti returned to his alma mater to receive an honorary degree and deliver the commencement address. He asked his audience to forget the sheepskin he received and look upon him as a "humble shepherd of God's flock lost somewhere in the midst of Iowa."

During the two and a half years that Ligutti spent at St. Ambrose, ecclesiastical life was taking on new vigor in southwestern Iowa. On August 12, 1911, about the time Ligutti was leaving Romans, Pope Pius X established the new diocese of Des Moines, comprising 12,446 square miles of southwestern Iowa. Austin Dowling (1868-1930) of Providence, Rhode Island, ordained a priest four years before Ligutti's birth, was named first bishop of the new see and was installed as ordinary on January 31, 1912, one day before Ligutti left the city for the college.

The new bishop faced trying circumstances. It was not only the economically poorest part of the state but also the weakest in the Church. The young Ligutti heard many sad stories about lapses and scandals created by the clergy of the area. In those days it was more than common that a priest in trouble was moved further and further west, based on the all-too-human-adage practiced even among some bishops, "Out of sight, out of mind."

Ligutti summed up his estimation of his first ordinary in the direct sentence, "Dowling was a very great man and he liked me very much." After graduating from college the young seminarian called upon this new bishop of the new diocese. Bishop Dowling gave him a small book entitled *The Works of Horace*. On that occasion Ligutti learned a lesson he never forgot. In presenting the book to the new graduate the bishop said, "Translate this ode." When Ligutti came to a passage he was unable to translate, he skipped over it.

"You're bluffing," the bishop chided.

"Yes," replied the young translator, "but that is the American way."

"No," the bishop said, "Americans who are good scholars never bluff. We have good scholars in America" (Dowling himself was one). "Doctor Kirk at Drake University is a good Latin scholar and he would never bluff."

Later in life, when purchasing the headquarters for the National Catholic Rural Life Conference, Ligutti discovered that his next-door neighbor was Arthur Kirk, son of the Latin scholar. They became life-long friends. Many years later Ligutti would clip from an unknown magazine a translation from Book 3, Ode 9, of Horace. He chuckled more than once as he read the last two verses:

Horace:
Listen, Lyd dear, concentrate
Suppose I give Chloe the gate?

Could you love your Horace, kid,
And kiss him like you used to did?

Lydia:
Oh now, dear Quintus, you're so wild,
And my nice boy is sweet and mild —
But you — your wildness — oh, so sweet! —
Come — love me! Sweep me off my feet!

Dowling told his erring translator never be a bluffer, study Latin, and go to St. Mary's Seminary in Baltimore in the fall. The bishop had been a schoolmate of Fr. Francis Havey, a Sulpician priest and a professor at the Baltimore seminary. The bishop, Father Havey, whom the students called "Pop," and Fr. James A. Walsh, later a bishop and a founder of the Maryknoll Fathers, were together at St. John's Seminary, Brighton, Massachusetts. Needless to say, the young seminarian was delighted with the opportunity.

Ligutti's family, however, was still miffed by his decision to become a priest; they wanted him to be a doctor or a lawyer. For this reason he left his sister's home the first Christmas in Des Moines, returned to St. Ambrose College for the term, and the next summer earned his livelihood as a handyman around a boarding house for Italian laborers that was operated by a kindly family from Florence, Italy. His last summer as a student in Des Moines he spent doing odd jobs around the elegant Victorian-style home of the McDonnells, a prominent Irish Catholic family. Although disappointed by the temporary estrangement of his own family, he did not lose courage. His sentiments were those from the "Ballad of Sir Andrew Barton," whose words he copied in his notebooks:

"Fight on my men," Sir Andrew says,
 "A little I am hurt, but yet not slain;
I'll but lie down and bleed awhile
 And then I will rise and fight again."

During these years the pastor of Visitation parish, Fr. Joseph Nugent, took a special interest in the immigrant-seminarian. A good friend of the eloquent populist, William Jennings Bryan, Nugent was also a distinguished speaker and preacher. The elderly priest made frequent use of the psalms in his sermons and thereby instilled in the young Ligutti a love for the psalms and an ability to use simple, homey illustrations in his sermons and addresses.

Father Nugent was later both proud and pleased to preach at his former seminarian's first Mass.

The next three years, from 1914 to 1917, were among the happiest and most peaceful of Ligutti's life. He loved his studies and again proved himself more than an ordinary student. He found himself in an entirely new and different orbit of friends and thrilled by the experiences he encountered each day. He was going through the process of Americanization. With a twinge of regret he recalled that for three years at St. Mary's Seminary he was the only Italian among the student body.

"That was the time," he recalled, "when Italians just did not exist as far as vocations were concerned." Doubtless, he was hurt by not finding any of his own countrymen or their descendants among his fellow students. In his notebook he wrote a verse by James Lowell that expressed his own philosophy of life:

> New times demand new measures and new men,
> The world advances and in time outgrows
> The laws that in our fathers' day were best,
> And doubtless, after us, some purer scheme,
> Will be shaped out by wiser men than we,
> Made wiser by the steady growth of truth.

Ligutti's favorite subjects were the classics, history, and canon law; he was not too much drawn to philosophy and theology, although he earned superior grades in these and all his subjects. His love for history continued throughout his life, and one of his great heroes was the zealous Dominican missionary of Iowa, Samuel Mazzuchelli. Not surprisingly, Ligutti joined the Iowa State Historical Society. He desired to join the Sulpicians and devote his life to academe, a thought he seriously entertained for several years. Bishop Dowling, however, refused him permission because of the priest-shortage in the diocese of Des Moines.

During summer vacations during World War I he worked either in a camp established by the seminary to aid the war effort or for the noted Catholic family, the Shrivers, whose plantation was not far from Westminster, Maryland. There he met Cardinal James Gibbons, friend of the Shrivers and sometimes his companion on afternoon walks in Baltimore. One day the young Ligutti (an Italian immigrant and victim of much Irish-German Catholic prejudice) heard the cardinal state in a casual conversation at the Shrivers that he would never ordain a Negro. This cut deeply into the soul of the young man who was already developing a strong social sensitivity and a deep-seated hatred of prejudice of any kind. "This remark jolted me," Ligutti later recalled, "because there was a Negro in our class, although he left before ordination. The cardinal's biographer, Msgr. John Tracy Ellis, found it difficult to believe when I told him of this incident."

At St. Mary's Seminary, Ligutti again demonstrated his innate ability to make friends. Throughout his life he kept in contact with his classmates and numbered them among his closest associates. Two of them, Fr. Joseph P. Morrison of Chicago and Fr. Louis A. Arand, S.S., the highly-respected superior of graduate priest-students at the Catholic University of America for many years, were among his most intimate friends. Rarely would he pass through Chicago or stop in Washington, D.C., without calling upon them.

His ordination class of fifty-six priests represented twenty-seven dioceses and eighteen states. Among them were Fr. John K. Sharp of Brooklyn, "a writer of note," said Ligutti; Thomas K. Gorman of Los Angeles, the editor of the *Tidings* and future bishop of Reno, Nevada, and Dallas-Fort Worth, Texas; Arthur Belknap of Lead, South Dakota, who died in 1921. Ligutti noted in the class annual: "The shooting of Father A. Belknap in Lead, S.D., is a mystery. He was called out on a night sick-call and his body found next day. Many rewards were offered but no solution of the mystery to date, July, 1923." The murder of Father Belknap remains one of the mysteries surrounding the coloful diocese of Lead, now Rapid City, South Dakota.

In February, 1916, the young seminarian delivered his first sermon in the refectory. It was entitled "Anger and Revenge." Although it might never be included in any anthology of great sermons, it revealed a style that would be polished and refined in the coming years. Its simplicity of language, use of illustrations, and directness would mark future addresses and sermons. Its subtle humor escapes the reader today, but his listeners knew well that he was speaking not only to but also about several faculty members. It opened with a florid sentence, typical of the style of that period: "Towering one of those beautiful hills at the foot of the Alps, mirroring itself in the wavy vineyards of the plain, projecting itself out from a canvas of snow capped mountains, undercover of the everlasting blue sky of Italy there stands a ruined castle." The speaker recounted the tragedy that befell a noble Italian family because of the anger of the lord of the castle. He pointed out the great harm that anger causes Christians.

Through a series of "ifs" he showed how little acts of impatience can grow into the voracious vice of anger.

Time passed swiftly during these happy years of 1914-1917 in Baltimore. Studies were completed and ordination approached. The young deacon was faced with the impediment of age, for normally a priest is not ordained until he reaches his twenty-fourth year. Bishop Dowling pointed this out to the young man, but already Ligutti was beginning to realize that obstacles are made to be overcome and not to stop one from attaining the final goal. In canon law he remembered that a bishop could dispense from the impediment of age. He called this fact to the attention of the bishop and received permission to be ordained at the age of twenty-two and six months. He arrived at the magic date on September 22, 1917 and was at the time and for several succeeding years the youngest priest in the United States.

On September 22 he entered St. Ambrose Cathedral in Des Moines, and with the laying on of hands by Bishop Dowling was ordained a priest. With his mother and members of his family proudly seated in the front pews, with the choir singing *Tu es Sacerdos in Aeternum*, Luigi Domenico Ligutti fulfilled the wish he had expressed as a boy in Romans, "I want to be a priest." After a long and arduous journey from his native to his adopted land, after overcoming obstacles of language, family, prejudice, and age, the farm boy from northern Italy had become a priest of the diocese of Des Moines, Iowa.

This man casually remarked in June, 1972, "Plants have to have roots, you know, and people also have to have roots, if they are going to produce any lasting, valuable results."

These were the roots of this "shy man . . . deeply sensitive man . . . a man with much humanity." He was about to embark upon one of the most exciting and adventurous careers of an American priest in the mid-twentieth century. His life has been in many ways a microcosm of the macrocosm of the Catholic Church of the United States during one of its most exciting and challenging periods. Ligutti was part of the excitement and the challenge.

CHAPTER TWO

DIOCESAN APPRENTICESHIP

The day of Ligutti's ordination was, as it should be, one of jubilation. The first Mass dinner was served in the elegant Victorian home of the McDonnells, for whom he had worked as a seminarian. Family, friends, and neighbors streamed through the house and across the lawn that he once tended, extended good wishes, and received the first blessing of this promising young priest. The following day was more intimate — a private dinner in his sister's home with only the immediate family and his mentor of St. Ambrose College, Father Shanahan, who had served as the assistant priest at the first Mass.

The young priest's vacation was brief. Within ten days he was on the train returning east to pursue graduate studies at the Catholic University of America. He enrolled on October 1, 1917 in the department of Greek and Latin. Dowling had told him as a seminarian that he wanted him to study the classics and he did so. He also took courses in philosophy under Edward A. Pace, in canon law under Filippo Bernardini, and educational pedagogy under Thomas Edward Shields.

Bishop Dowling had planned to establish a central Catholic high school in Des Moines, called then the Des Moines Catholic Academy and later Dowling High School. He was preparing a faculty for the institution. (Fifty years later Ligutti returned to the school and rummaged through the library to see if the books he had catalogued as a young priest were still there. They were.) The bishop had picked Ligutti to be one of the four priest-members of the first faculty.

Two significant events stood out in Ligutti's mind during this year of graduate studies. He was entertained as a guest in the Shriver home where he had once worked as a farmhand. More importantly, he became an American citizen in Baltimore on

June 17, 1918 at age twenty-three. Frequently in later life, when appearing before state and national legislative hearings or in replying to attacks against the Church by bigoted groups such as the Klu Klux Klan, he would proudly point out that he was an American citizen, not by accident of birth but by free and happy choice.

At the Catholic University of America he threw himself into his studies and thoroughly enjoyed the experience. He again demonstrated his love for history and the classics. Here, too, he showed his huge capacity for friendship and the friends he made during this year became his collaborators and associates in later life. He was delighted to find his friend Fr. Louis Arand, S.S., among his classmates. He came to be a close friend also of the future director of the National Conference of Catholic Charities, John O'Grady. The genial Irishman lived in St. Thomas Hall, but after O'Grady lived there it was called "O'Grady's flats." Dr. George Johnson, later one of the nation's leading Catholic educators, was a fellow student. Luigi's neighbor in Caldwell Hall was Fr. Virgil Michel, O.S.B., who became the principal leader of the liturgical movement in this country.

Little did Ligutti and Michel realize at the time how their studies and experiences would ultimately make them close collaborators in both the liturgical and rural life movements. In his own idiom Virgil Michel expressed his interest in rural life when he wrote in a 1938 issue of *Orate Fratres*: "I know now that it is indeed very often a misfortune to be born in a larger city; and subsequent experience and contacts have convinced me that it may become almost an irreparable spiritual calamity to be born in some of our largest metropolitan areas." In the same article the Benedictine monk of St. John's Abbey bemoaned the filling-station atmosphere of too many big city parishes when he said:

> There is no question primarily of turning as many city dwellers as possible into "dirt" farmers.... The question is first of all one of decentralization of the present artificial city congestions, of bringing people back closer to nature, regardless of their professions in life. It is not first of all a question of city or farm, but of unnatural life as against a normal life close to nature.

At the time Dom Virgil was writing these thoughts, the subsequent pastor in Iowa expressed the same thought in different words. "The artificiality of modern life," Ligutti wrote, "is a greater impediment to Christianity than the primitiveness of the jungle." Fifty years later he recalled that the Benedictine's master of arts thesis had been entitled "The Critical Principles of Orestes A. Brownson." Another graduate colleague was his former classmate at St. Mary's Seminary, Thomas K. Gorman, who received his licentiate in canon law with a dissertation on "The Diocesan Curia." These were among the men who received their M.A. degrees with Ligutti on June 12, 1918. Fifty years later the Catholic University conferred upon Ligutti an honorary doctor of letters in recognition of his contributions to Church and country since he left what was at time referred to as Washington's "Vatican hill."

Recalling his interest in the classics, deepened during these years, Ligutti commented:

> I fell in love with the classics. I still take the book of Virgil with me when I travel. It is all worn. I read it for pleasure. I think it is a most wonderful book. I read Cicero and Aristotle, too. Of course, I have a translation where they have the Greek on one side and the English on the other side. I became interested, very interested, in the origin of words, in semantics.

His notebooks and addresses reveal this love of the classics. One of his favorite and most quoted verses is Kemp's "The Song of the Plow" because it is studded with classical references. His library consists of many books of the classics and philology. "Even now," he said, "when I find a word that I want to get the origin of, I put it down and look it up because I have all the books." He continued:

> When I was in Des Moines editing the rural life column every week, once a month I explained the origins of agricultural words, such as how certain words in agriculture got started and developed. Once someone wrote to me and said, "The hell with this kind of stuff. The thing we want is better prices." But I knew then and know now that there is more to rural life than better prices.

His love of the classics and semantics enabled him to create a simple, direct style in writing and speaking:

> I can't do anything else. I don't have a curial style. Like today when I wrote a report for the secretariat of state; it was very direct and very harsh and very, very tough. It is just me. I don't want any curial style. English is direct, not like Italian. But even my own personal style is more direct.

With his customary value of the sacredness of time the new master of arts wasted little before registering at Columbia University, New York, for the 1918 summer session. There he enrolled in two education courses before returning to Des Moines later in the summer. The following summer he returned to Columbia and enrolled in two Latin courses and one education course. He received two "B's" in Latin and a "C" in educational theory. One paper he wrote for the Latin course was entitled "The Arch of Septimius Severus." During the summer, 1920, he enrolled at the University of Chicago where he took three courses: Introduction to the Study of Language, Caesar's Gallic Campaigns, and Modern Italian Literature. In each he received an "A."

Although he was aiming at receiving the doctorate of philosophy in classics, the shortage of priests and other circumstances in the diocese prevented him from ever fulfilling that ambition. He was once a poor boy; now he was a poor priest-student. He paid his own train fares and tuition out of his meager monthly salary of $30. He earned his board and room in New York at St. Joseph's German parish, and when he could, he volunteered for "door duty" in order to receive an extra fifty cents an afternoon. With justifiable apprehension he occupied the room of the notorious Fr. Hans Schmidt who had been electrocuted a short time previously. The wretched priest had procured an abortion for a girl with whom he had been intimate and who died during the abortion.

Ligutti recalled how before going to class at Columbia University he would go to Morningside Park and change his collar, for priests in those days were looked at askance in secular universities. He did the same at the University of Chicago. Some fifty years later, when conducting a seminar at Columbia, he told his hosts that he was registered there as a student for two summer sessions, and before he enrolled his bishop had warned him to watch out lest he lose his faith at such a godless institution. "But that," he said with a smile, "was fifty years ago!"

After his first summer session he returned to Des Moines and joined the faculty of the academy. His duties consisted of teaching Latin and serving as registrar and librarian. He recalled the hustle and bustle of the days before the academy opened its doors to eight students in the freshman class and the return of the three upperclasses who had been transferred from the former parochial St. John's High School:

> I will never forget the day before we opened. The old auditorium and gymnasium was in the back of the building

and was the dirtiest, filthiest, lousiest place you ever saw. Two of the boys and myself went there and started to sweep out the place in preparation for the people who would be coming the next day. Then there was the question of downstairs. The toilets were in the basement and they were even dirtier than the gymnasium. The trio went down, took one look, turned up their noses, and fled for the purer air outdoors. Less than an hour later they found Bishop Dowling cleaning up the toilets. One of the pupils, Jack Boylan, and Ligutti ushered the bishop aside. "Bishop, you get out of here," Ligutti said. "We will clean this up." The bishop left. Ligutti recalled, years later: "That is one of the memories of Dowling that I will never forget. Throughout my life I have never hesitated to do any work whatever it might be, no matter how dirty it might be, because Dowling could clean up the dirtiest and filthiest toilets that I have ever seen." The pupil, Jack Boylan (1889-1953), became the third bishop of Rockford, Illinois, on February 17, 1943.

When the academy opened Dowling took more than an ordinary interest in its operations. When an instructor was ill he acted as substitute teacher. He came to the school every day he was home and audited one or the other classes. He took a back seat, told the instructor to continue the lesson, and acted as an alert and interested pupil. The neophyte instructor recalled how this induced the teachers to prepare their classes with more diligence than they would have done. Many an afternoon after school Ligutti walked with the bishop to the corner of Twentieth and Grand Avenue. Recalled Ligutti:

> He used to walk from the hip. His steps were not from the knees. He was a short man, but he took longer strides than I would, even though I was much taller than he was. He always carried on an interesting conversation on a variety of subjects. He was a great and learned man.

By this time the ecclesiastical scene in the diocese had changed. The seven years of Dowling's administration witnessed a remarkable growth and deepening spiritual awareness among the Catholics of southwestern Iowa. When he arrived the 25,000 Catholics were administered by 61 priests in 54 parishes and 25 missions. On January 19, 1919 the bishop was privately notified by the apostolic delegate that he had been appointed successor to John Ireland, the recently deceased archbishop of St. Paul. On January 31 the appointment was made public. During Dowling's seven years in Des Moines the Catholics in the diocese had increased to 35,000, served by 80 priests. A Catholic college and four high schools had been established. The Holy See did not lose time in appointing Fr. Thomas W. Drumm (1871-1933) to succeed Dowling. Father Drumm was consecrated the second bishop of Des Moines on May 21, 1919.

The following year changes in the Ligutti household altered the course of the young instructor's life. His mother was living with Anthony, the bachelor brother. Anthony courted an American girl, fell in love with her, and entered into the bonds of matrimony. In the diocese many older priests were dying, causing vacancies in many parishes. The combination of a mother who did not care to live with newlyweds and many parishes without pastors prompted Ligutti to approach Bishop Drumm and request a parish in order to provide a home for his mother who would also serve as his housekeeper.

The bishop readily granted his request and appointed him pastor of Sacred Heart Church, Woodbine, with the mission of St. Bridget of Erin Parish, Magnolia (an Irish settlement), and later, St. Ann's Parish, Logan, the Harrison County seat. He assumed these new duties the day after Thanksgiving, 1920. Thus by the strange alchemy of an episcopal letter the man who wanted to be a Sulpician, who loved the halls of academe, and who was a popular high school teacher became a country pastor. Years later, when asked how he became interested in rural life, Ligutti replied, "My people were farmers and I was interested in my people."

Woodbine and Magnolia were chiefly farming centers. On the first Sunday in Woodbine the offertory collection amounted to seventy-five cents. Upon his arrival, he numbered 100 people in Woodbine, 40 in Magnolia, and 19 in Logan. Even though he had received only $25 a month as a teacher, that sum appeared as a gold mine compared with the poverty he now faced in his parish and missions.

Magnolia afforded the opportunity of working among Irish people who possessed a deep faith. It was the oldest church in western Iowa, the mother church of most of the stronger and larger parishes in the area. It once possessed a parish priest who commuted to Omaha to offer Mass. Magnolia always had a special claim on Ligutti's affection, just as so many Irish and Italian immigrant people have an affinity for each other because of their common faith, mutual sufferings, and the nativist antipathy they experienced.

"The old Irish settlement," Ligutti said, "was the poorest of the poorest of God's poor. The people were still primitive. The Irish lived in the hills and were just about as primitive as anybody could be in the United States. They were good people, though, good to the core with their prayers and Christian faith." In spite of what he called "those terrible roads" he went out to Magnolia on Saturday afternoons and evenings — a distance of seventeen miles — on his motorcycle in summer and in a horse and buggy during the winter months.

Logan presented another distinct problem. He began his apostolate there by offering Mass in the Shield's home. Nothing, perhaps, demonstrated so visibly the status of Catholicism than the church building. The parish was in charge of a former army chaplain, Fr. Patrick McDermott, who wisely undertook the building of a church and then left with only the four bare walls erected and no windows. This did not discourage Ligutti. He scraped together what money he could ("God only knows where it came from!"), and by the following July 26, the feast of St. Ann, the church was dedicated. "One of my altar boys there," he said with more than a glimmer of pride in his eyes, "is today a prominent surgeon in New York. His father was a fallen-away Catholic but came back to the Church before he died."

Since most of the people in the Woodbine area were of Scandinavian and English descent, Ligutti considered that the entire community was his parish. He entered enthusiastically into every aspect of community life. He took a particular interest in the school and continually strived to upgrade the quality of education. He joined the Lions Club and associated freely with the business people. When a golf course was being planned, he was among its most active supporters. He practiced grass-roots ecumenism by making friends with the Protestant clergymen and extending his warmth and friendship to Catholics and Protestants alike.

There were also consolations. His mother had been very happy bustling around the house and singing in her kitchen. Although she never learned to speak English fluently, she made friends with many women in the parish and considered her years in Woodbine among the happiest of her life. The young pastor found refreshment in two hobbies that he took up during this time, hunting and fishing. They remained hobbies for the rest of his life, and whenever he could squeeze a day or two into his schedule he would sneak out to the nearest lake in the summer or hide behind a duck blind or tramp through the cornfields in the autumn.

He learned this love of the outdoors from his friend and neighbor, Fr. Declan Dower, an Irishman who loved to hunt. Many a pleasant day Dower spent with Ligutti and his mother in a hunting expedition that would sometimes drag out for two, three, or four days. Ligutti admitted, however, that he was not very good with the rifle because of his weak eyes.

In late autumn and winter he especially enjoyed coon hunting with his beloved coon dogs. In Woodbine the priest became very attached to his dogs. He especially enjoyed hunting at night, for, as he remarked, "In Woodbine I could go out at night and sleep during the day." When he was moved five years later and the press of duties became heavier, he could no longer engage in coon hunting and thus supplanted his coon dogs for two dashing greyhounds. His love for his dogs was revealed in a note he wrote in 1927 as a tribute to "Brownie" on the occasion of his death. "You have died, faithful friend, while the white wind-driven snow was swirling in the air. With your passing there goes from my life a love – perhaps more elevating than many a human love." Nonetheless, he did more than hunt and fish during these years. The spiritual and material renewal in his parish and missions attest to that fact. He also enrolled in a correspondence course in Greek (those classics again) from the University of Chicago.

Coon hunting provided the young pastor the opportunity of getting to know Bishop Drumm better. In 1922 he asked the bishop for $100 from the diocesan mission fund to sponsor a parish mission. The bishop replied, "I am not sending you $100. I am coming out to give the mission myself." Mrs. Ligutti outdid herself in her culinary arts and other services for the bishop. After the mission the bishop stayed on for another week and went hunting each night. He had never been coon hunting before, so the pastor, assisted by Dower and a few boys of the parish went out one cold December night with the two coon dogs and an Airedale. Bishop Drumm wore high boots and kept up with the party as it climbed gullies and followed the banks of a winding creek. The dogs barked when they had a coon treed. Hearing the barking, the party judged the dogs were about a mile ahead of them and started running. The pastor was carrying the lantern. As soon as they began running the bishop stumbled, fell on a briar patch, and scratched his hands and face. Happily he took the fall in good grace. "Drumm was an extremely good shot," said Ligutti, and then added as an afterthought, "He was Irish."

The energetic young pastor, however, undertook other activities in his first parish that he would continue and expand throughout his life, such as the problems of rural life, the religious education of young people, the promotion of tithing, and the personal apostolate of sending letters to local and national publications. The rural pastor in Iowa followed with enthusiasm the work of an Eugene, Oregon, pastor named Fr. Edwin Vincent O'Hara, who was implementing in his far-flung rural parish the directives of Pius X on the Confraternity of Christian Doctrine. Little then did either realize how their thoughts and paths would intertwine in the coming decades.

In 1925 Ligutti drew up "a few suggestions from the practical experience of a very successful 'one-horse' religious vacation school." He chose St. Bridget's Parish in Magnolia as the example, for there, under the branches of a huge elm tree, the first religious vacation school was held in the state of Iowa. "At that time," he wrote, "there were thirty families in the parish with fifty-four children under twelve years old. No child lived closer than a mile and a half from the church. Magnolia was centrally located to the towns of Logan, Mondamin, Modale, Pisgah, and Little Sioux." From July 6-25 two Dominican sisters from the neighboring convent of Missouri Valley were, with the pastor, the entire faculty. The latter who lived seventeen miles away picked up many of the children in what was described as "his prancing steed, a Harley-Davidson, with the speed of a Stutz, the comfort of an Essex, and the cheap-running qualities of the lamp that burns 98 percent air."

The curriculum was rigorous by today's standards. The day began at nine o'clock with Mass and an instruction by the pastor, followed by catechism lessons, a half-hour recess, singing, more catechism, and recitation of the Rosary. Lunch, which the children brought, was at noon followed by recreation until one o'clock. The afternoon began with Bible history, a fifteen-minute recess, health and first aid instructions, altar boys' practice, girls' work in the church, and the day was concluded at three-fifteen with the Way of the Cross. Every moment had been used to instill Christian principles.

Recreation periods, when the sisters had charge of the girls and the pastor the boys, were more than baseball, boxing, tree-climbing, egg hunts, and races. They were also a means of instilling the lessons of obedience, fairness, charity, and generosity. The results of this one year's vacation school showed an attendance of seventy-one with an average daily attendance of fifty children, seventeen first communicants, and eight altar boys trained. That the parents not only paid all the expenses but also gave the sisters $75 attests to their appreciation. Throughout the years as a pastor Ligutti continued to conduct religious vacation schools. Although they became more elaborate with more teachers, including seminarians, and better facilities and techniques, the basic format was established under the spreading elm in Magnolia.

The religious education of children was not the only concern of Father Ligutti during these years. He followed with interest the development of the correspondence courses in religion for adults which Msgr. Victor Day of Helena, Montana, conducted in his far-flung parish.

Ligutti followed O'Hara's lead in rural life and religious education, but he himself was the pioneer in another area that only in recent years has become of growing national and international concern in the Church. He was one of the first — if not the first — Catholic pastors in the United States to promote tithing. He came upon the practice through his reading, his congenial contacts with Protestant clergymen, and his own deep conviction that tithing and its spiritual benefits were the only truly effective means willed by God to support the Church. In 1922, both in Woodbine and Magnolia, he delivered his first sermon on the subject. During September, 1922, again in these communities, he delivered four sermons on tithing, stressing that we are but stewards of God's gifts and that the Catholic concept of giving derives from the Jewish laws of the Old Testament. At this time he wrote:

A Tither's Creed

I believe in God the creator of heaven.
I believe God created the earth and all that dwell therein.
I believe He created man and endowed him with a soul — free and immortal.
I believe God retains the ownership of the earth and of all that grows and dwells therein.
I believe that we men are merely the stewards of anything we may legally possess.
I believe that God is not only the owner of the earth by the right of creation but also by right of His continual care which He bestows upon it.

> I believe that the sources of material wealth — Land — Labor — Capital — are God's and that which is produced by them is God's directly or indirectly.
> I believe I am a steward for a brief period of time — till the Lord shall say: "Thou shalt be steward no longer."
> I believe the Son of God became man and died for our sins to regain for us God's friendship.
> I believe the Son of God preached a doctrine and established a Church which was to continue till the end of the world.
> I believe God is still interested in the doctrine He preached and the Church He established.
> I believe that in order to acknowledge in a practical way these my beliefs, I must return to God a share of what He has given to me for the establishment and development of His works in this world.

During these formative pastoral years Ligutti undertook an apostolate that all too many clergymen say they should but too seldom carry out. He became an avid, almost incessant letter-writer to editors of Catholic and general publications. He took advantage of the letters-to-the-editor columns in order to praise, correct, or explain. Throughout his life he carried out this apostolate with his name consequently appearing countless times in such publications as the *Farm Journal,* the New York *Times,* the Des Moines *Tribune,* and *Register, Commonweal, America* — to name but a few. It is impossible to estimate his services to religion and rural life rendered by his life-long attention to sending a letter here, a reply there, and a note of praise elsewhere.

One of the earliest of such letters appeared as an advertisement in the Woodbine *Twine.* It was "A Reply to the Klan" in which he took to task a lecturer in the city park sponsored by the local Klu Klux Klan. The speaker cast aspersions upon "the character and patriotism of the Roman Catholics." Apologetical in tone, Ligutti's letter respectfully asked the speaker, or any member of the local Klan, to prove that no 100 per cent American would employ a Catholic to teach in the public schools and that Catholics think more of the pope than the American flag. "Where is the proof for these statements?" Ligutti asked. "Facts and not bombastic statements are needed to satisfy an intelligent audience even though they may be listening to a 'fluent' speaker." Another letter, published in the January 7, 1939 Des Moines *Register* began with a clever statement Ligutti would use many times in ensuing years. "Sometime ago a friend of mine wrote me," he said, "saying that there should be less religion in politics. I replied promptly by stating that there should be *more* religion in politics."

Five years as a country pastor had filled Ligutti with a dominant conviction that shaped the personal thinking and action of the remainder of his life. He expressed that philosophy in a simple sentence, "I was interested in the problems of rural life because my people were farmers." This he would extend and refine in the coming years through further study and research. By 1925 his convictions were firm and his ambitions were determined by the needs of country people. He had learned his lessons well from the book of life that he read and lived in Woodbine, Logan, and Magnolia. He was ready to move on, but he would leave part of his heart among the people of Harrison County, Iowa.

CHAPTER THREE

YOUNG PASTOR OF GRANGER

Dates and places are not mere statistics; they are events. People make places as much, and even more than, places make people. A date is but a number on the calendar. For a man a date can be the turning point in his life. So it was with Fr. Luigi Ligutti when he was appointed pastor of Assumption Parish, Granger, Iowa, on January 1, 1926, effective the following April 8. His life was never to be the same again. Both places and people changed the course of his life.

Ligutti was then thirty-one years old. The joyful experiences of Woodbine, Logan, and Magnolia were soon to end. He knew at the time he had reached a milestone, for on January 15, 1926 he began a diary. His first three entries are significant. On that day he took his mother to the nursing home of the Sisters of Mercy in Council Bluffs. On January 17 he noted his desire to remain at peace and full of composure the rest of his life. The following day he wrote, "As a priest I resolve in favor of poverty and struggle for a priest." He went hunting again several times, tried smoking again but without too much pleasure, picked up reading his beloved classics, and noted as "good news" that his classmate Fr. Thomas Gorman had been named editor of the Los Angeles *Tidings*. By the end of the month he simply noted, "I am glad that I have three dogs."

He was very much at home among his parishioners. He wrote that Jake Weiss was shaving hogs; he attended a meeting to form a golf club in Woodbine; he spoke to a local group of farmers on Fascism and Masonry. "The fun it is to see and talk to people in a small town on Saturday night," his diary noted. By the end of February he observed, with obvious reference to his new parish, that he would be satisfied with even a little success.

He arrived in Granger, preaching his first sermon on the first Sunday after Easter. The first few days were a whirlwind of meeting new families such as the Costellos, the Morans, the Campanis, and the Schultes. With the help of Joseph Biondi and Michael Grugiono, young men of the parish, he measured off the places for planting trees. He continued to meet his new parishioners throughout the first month and, typically, planted trees and flowers around the parish grounds. On May 2 he was delighted when his mother joined him in Granger as his housekeeper, and four days later a Passionist priest, Fr. Malcolm Lavalle, preached the annual Forty Hours devotion services. (In later years, Father Lavalle became the superior general of that order.) This was the first of his many happy associations with the Passionists in Des Moines. So life would spin its thread for the new country pastor. The day-to-day activities would be very much the same — serving people, loving people, helping people. Against this backdrop his zeal prompted him to be an innovator and creator that would bring prominence to Granger, Iowa.

If Sinclair Lewis had not chosen Sauk Centre, Minnesota, as the locale of *Main Street,* he might well have chosen Granger. A local history of Granger begins with words typical of many midwestern towns:

> Before the town of Granger was built, there was a railroad station and post office one and one-half miles north of the present site of Granger. This place had two names. The railroad name was Kelsey and Hatton was the post office name. Hatton is listed as a post office in Polk County from 1882 to 1891.... The first store was a frame structure. The lumber was hauled from Des Moines on the railroad.... The Genesers bought two lots from Sieberling, of Mitchellville, Iowa, and built the brick store and a house south of the store, which is now Lamberti's beer parlor, [1936].... Francis Geneser, father of John and George, laid out and named the streets of Granger. The first street running north and south, west of the railroad is Main, then Walnut, Locust, and Sycamore. The town of Granger was named for Ben Granger, an official of the railroad. The railroad company wished to call the new town Geneser, but Francis Geneser did not care to have it so named.

Shortly after Ligutti arrived, he wrote the following notes about his new parish:

> Granger was opened for settlement on midnight, April 30, 1843. The land was ceded by the Fox and Sac Indians on October 11, 1842. By 1846 all the Indians had left the county.

First to stake claims were in Van Meter township in the fall of 1845. In 1848 John Sullivan staked his claim in Washington township, but later sold it for a shotgun. According to local tradition, Hugh, John and Mrs. Radigan settled in 1848; later, Tom, Martin, Mike, William and Simon joined them. In 1852 the little Morans came — settled where Little Willie now lives. The big Morans came next — they settled where Jim Carroll now lives.

The Catholic Church came to Dallas County with the appointment in 1874 of Fr. Edward Gaule as resident pastor of Dallas Center. Funds were collected for the priest's residence wherein Mass was offered until 1879. In 1894 Granger came into being. Fr. H. W. Malone, pastor of Dallas Center, established Assumption parish on August 15, 1900. In 1904 Father Malone was succeeded by Father Moron who remained until Ligutti came in 1926. Shortly after his arrival the latter noted the following about the Granger parish:

> Assumption Church — Granger, Iowa — Dallas Co., Des Moines Diocese. Twenty square miles of territory — Granger is about centrally located. Farmers and coal miners. Farmers live near Granger, mostly Irish-American. Coal miners live in small mining "camps," towns and villages where there is no Catholic church. Nationality — Italian and Slav, (mostly Croatian). Distances from Granger to mining camps and towns — Dallas — 3 miles; Gibbeville, 4; Moran, 7; Grimei, 7; Woodward, 10; High Bridge, 8; Zookspur, 10. Parish church in Granger with two masses on each Sunday. Mission chapels in Moran and Zookspur — one mass in each place every Sunday.

Such was the locale of this Italian-American priest, the portion of the Lord's vineyard committed to his care. The problems were those of every pastor during this period: poverty, poor housing, distance, broken homes, lack of religious education, all aggravated by the growing depression and drought throughout the Midwest. He faced them. The depression was making its inroads in Granger. The miners were living in extreme squalor. About them Ligutti wrote, "To work 150 days for a whole year is considered exceptional, less than 80 days a year is very common. The result is much leisure and no way of employing it in useful pursuits." There was, also, the gnawing necessity for religious instructions and Catholic education.

Set in the context of the present parish ministry, Ligutti's approach in 1926 may seem heavy-handed and dictatorial. Given, however, the nature of parochial administration then, his approach was democratic, sensible, and realistic. Once again he became the promoter of tithing and sought to introduce the practice among his Granger flock. On June 12, 1927 he wrote his parishioners this letter:

> On the first Sunday of July the new financial year will begin for this parish. New envelope-sets and pledge cards are distributed during June.
>
> Weekly tithing is the accepted and commanded system of financing the Church in the Des Moines diocese.
>
> The income from tithes in our parish from July, 1926, to June, 1927, was very revealing and surprisingly disappointing. The majority of the 190 who did make pledges actually fulfilled them, some did not and a few did not make any pledge. But the amounts pledged were out of proportion with the means and incomes of about 90 per cent of the parishioners.
>
> I said in my letter of June, 1926: "Let your conscience be your guide," and when I looked over the pledge cards I was really amazed as a very peculiar situation was then revealed to me. Men and women of faith, so I thought, men and women of means, I knew, men and women with intelligence and education, I presumed, making such small returns in weekly tithing, in such a serious, self-satisfied fashion, was more than I could understand.
>
> I said nothing, however, as I realized that during 1926 the special repair fund appeal had been answered, on the whole, very nicely.
>
> During 1927 we plan on no special appeals, and at no future time shall we rely upon special appeals to meet the ordinary expenses of our parish.
>
> The weekly tithes must be raised to a level more in keeping with the means and needs of this parish. The $3,600 estimated amount that the yearly tithes are at the present must be DOUBLED, because of actual needs and because $7,200 would be nearer to a proportionate return in this parish....
>
> My mother and I have been returning $3.50 per week during 1926-27. We will return $4.00 per week during 1927-28. That is more than a tenth of our income, but we thank God we are able to return that much. How many parishioners

are willing and ready to match this proportion? If your pledge card is returned to you, it will be because we consider your pledge as an insult to your faith and a disproportionate return.

Well did Ligutti then know the poverty of many of his people, but he also knew that many who could contribute more, did not. Never did he tire, however, of preaching the gospel of tithing. Subsequent achievements in Granger proved the success of his zeal. He took a two-pronged approach, the elaboration of the Confraternity of Christian Doctrine classes that he had successfully carried out in Woodbine and the establishment of a truly Catholic rural school. Both projects brought national attention to Granger.

At the 1935 Convention of the National Catholic Rural Life Conference in Rochester, New York, Dr. George Johnson of the department of religious education of the Catholic University of America (and a former graduate student with Ligutti), read a paper entitled "The Professional Preparation of Teachers for Catholic Rural Schools." There Johnson enunciated the following principle that Ligutti had already applied in establishing Assumption High School in 1929:

> Precious little attention has been paid by Catholic educators to the problems of education in rural areas. As far as rural education is concerned there have been a few voices crying eloquently in the wilderness. They have refused to allow apathy to discourage them and they have not been rebuffed by the polite boredom that so frequently greeted their attempts to get a hearing for the case of a Catholic School outside of the city.

Johnson might well have penned these words about Ligutti and his work in Granger. As early as August 12, 1931, James E. Cummings, the assistant to Msgr. George Johnson, had asked Ligutti for information about the "outstanding work in the religious instruction of Catholic children not in Catholic schools."

Ligutti replied to Cummings' inquiry in a report on the status of the religious-instruction work in Granger, giving due acknowledgement to his assistant, Fr. Paul Marasco, who was the driving force behind the project. He reported that the Catholic school in Granger consisted of four years of high school and the fifth to eighth grades inclusive. In 1930 seventy-three pupils were enrolled. "All the other children," he wrote, "attend public schools in towns, camps or country. Distance and lack of transportation facilities keep the children from attending the Catholic school." There were 222 children enrolled for Saturday classes and religious vacation school, which was held on a three-term basis: September to November and March to May, thirteen Saturdays of two hours each; three weeks in July and August of five days a week with four hours a day. This amounted to approximately 112 hours of religious instruction a year. The division of the hours was very similar to the program previously inaugurated in Woodbine. Throughout the years the religious education program in Granger employed seminarians and sisters from various surrounding communities. It also attracted some national attention in Catholic circles inasmuch as it showed what could be accomplished in a rural parish with the effort, perseverance, and goodwill of parents, teachers, pupils, and priests.

Assumption High School was another innovative concept in Catholic education. The late Emerson Hynes, at the time professor of sociology at St. John's University, Collegeville, Minnesota, wrote an article about the Granger high school in *The Catholic School Journal* of May 1, 1939 entitled "A Rural School That is Rural." Rightly did the school succeed in blazing the way as an experiment in Catholic rural education. Its success can be measured by the hundreds of letters Ligutti received over the years from former pupils acclaiming their years at Assumption High School as the most formative and enriching of their lives. Its purposefulness can be gauged by the leadership instilled during these years in the students who went on in life to become priests, religious women, doctors, lawyers, business leaders, and, especially, successful farmers and farmers' wives in the hill country and plains of southwestern Iowa. A report issued in 1937 gave a glimpse into the agriculture courses the school offered. It read in part:

> The fundamental principles of Catholic Rural sociology and economics should be stressed. Here are some of the subjects that will be taught:
> I. Animal Husbandry, with the sub-titles, Poultry production and management, dairying, hogs and other animals.
> II. Crops and Soils: With the study of production and management of crops and a detailed study of local soils.
> III. Vegetable Production and Management: With special emphasis upon raising all that is needed for the home and using the scientific knowledge and methods of commercial producers.

IV. Landscaping and Floraculture: Both for bettering living conditions around the farm and even for a possible small cash income.
V. Fruit Growing: With emphasis upon home needs, using again proper methods and increasing the knowledge of the narrow one crop farmer.
VI. The most interesting of all subjects: Bee Culture. If it were only to become acquainted with one of God's most charming creatures, the noble bee, but also to secure at a small investment and a minimum of work a supply of honey for home consumption.

The girls were not overlooked. The same 1937 report outlined the program the girls followed in becoming good homemakers. It stated:

> In the afternoon the girls will take up the study and the practice of home-keeping and the proper employment of leisure time by knowledge of Arts and Crafts.
>
> It will be the chief aim of the course to prepare young women to conduct a home in the country as it should be conducted. To secure such knowledge as necessary and useful to acquire a sense of appreciation of home life in the country and to prepare themselves in the art of being mothers of families.

Here follow the general objectives and the detailed parts in the two-year course:

1. An interest in family life and a desire to be a part of a home in which every member may develop to his maximum ability, mentally, socially and physically.
2. Ability to assist in the organization and management of a home so as to reduce the expenditure of time, money and energy to its minimum and yet maintain the standards desirable for the homes within the community.
3. Ability to contribute to health by applying the principles of nutrition in the feeding of the family.
4. Ability to plan, buy food for, prepare and serve adequate, inexpensive, attractive meals, in a reasonable length of time.
5. Ability to assist in the care and training of children.
6. Ability to perform the manipulative skills necessary for the successful maintenance of a home of the desired standard.

7. Ability to select and combine material, garments, and accessories that are becoming to an individual, suited to an occasion, and within the family budget.
8. Ability to select suitable furnishings for the home and to arrange them attractively.

Assumption High School, however, was much more than a curriculum. It was a unique experiment in Christian living. One incident, perhaps more than many others, best illustrates the educational experience of this truly rural Catholic school.

One day, while walking on the outskirts of Granger, Ligutti came upon an old fence post. He took it home and gave it to his assistant priest, Fr. John Gorman, who at the time was teaching woodworking in the high school. Ligutti pointed out that from the most abysmal, outcast, and neglected piece of nature a work of beauty and art could be resurrected through man's labor. Father Gorman took the fence post to his woodworking shop. The boys worked on it. Out of it came a chalice! A work of art and beauty. Ligutti showed the chalice to audiences around the world, proving a simple point: Man is a beggar sitting on a chair of gold! And this came from Granger, the work of a young priest and group of boys in the woodworking class of Assumption High School. This Father Gorman would succeed Ligutti as pastor of Granger in 1940.

There is, of course, more than a bit of nostalgia when Ligutti recalls the exciting days of Assumption High School. No records can even begin to contain the sentiments of a pastor towards his young people. He was always interested in "life," a gift he inherited from his Italian ancestors. County fairs, athletics (he was particularly interested in boxing to teach sportsmanship and settle playground arguments), and homemaking contests also attracted his interest. Surprisingly enough, he kept track of the scores of local athletic contests and published them year after year in the high school annual. In an article written for his students in 1937, he summarized his philosophy:

> Today in many ways is an ideal day. There is more real joy and happiness today because:
>
> Religion and the family come to the fore and hold the center of the stage.
>
> Today the love of neighbor is carried within the realm of what we get because of what we give.

Let me speak to you of ideals, of dreams perhaps, and of visions of the future:

It is good to dream dreams, it is most wholesome to see visions. To you boys and girls of the country-side, to you young men and women on the farms I address this question today: What are your dreams of the future? What are your ideals?

Ligutti himself was growing during these early years in Granger. He was coming to know America, to be sure. But that was not all. He was slowly, imperceptibly, being molded by the needs of his own people, developing a social consciousness. No one can recall the date when he became interested in such magazines as *Free America,* such books as Herbert Agar's *Home of the Free* or Ralph Borsoldi's *Flight from the City* and the essays of Chesterton and Belloc on distributism. During the long Iowa winter nights he was developing a social consciousness, forced upon him by the poverty of his people and the message of the social encyclicals of Leo XIII and Pius XI. He was not only the pastor of Granger, but also a student of social justice. At this stage he was even so adventurous as to take up and read the radical socialist prophets of the turbulent thirties.

One verse he quoted from time to time was Wilbur D. Nesbit's "The Reserved Section." Nesbit wrote the verse after reading the following words of George F. Baer, head of the coal trust, who said at the time of the great anthracite coal strike in 1902, "The rights and interests of the laboring man will be protected and cared for . . . by the Christian men to whom God in his infinite wisdom has given control of the property interests of this country." Two of Nesbit's verses were:

In the prehistoric ages, when the world was a ball of mist —
A seething swirl of something unknown in the planet list;
When the earth was vague with vapor, and formless and
    dark and void —
The port of the wayward comet — the jibe of the asteroid —
Then the singing stars of morning chanted soft: "Keep out
    of there!
Keep off that spot which is sizzling hot — it is making coal
    for Baer!"

The carboniferous era consumed but a million years;
It started when earth was shedding the last of her baby tears,
When still she was swaddled softly in clumsily tied-on clouds,

When stars from the shop of nature were being turned out
   in crowds;
But high o'er the favored section this sign said to all: "Beware!
Stand back of the ropes that surround these slopes — they
   are making coal — for Baer!"

Perhaps one of the most revealing documents of his own spiritual life was tucked away in his papers for the year 1931. It shows a deeply sensitive and spiritual priest, striving for holiness in the midst of the business of a country pastor. It also records his firm resolve to pursue perfection in the midst of daily preoccupations. His life was centered upon community, parish, school, and home. He resolved to be more considerate, more open, more understanding, especially to the poor and oppressed. It is a deeply spiritual testament of a priest who was not too much unlike so many of his brother priests at the height of the depression in the United States.

Both his social awareness and spiritual life prompted Ligutti to exert an influence beyond Granger. He had already become active in the National Catholic Rural Life Conference and was beginning to be recognized as a Catholic rural life leader. In 1932 he was invited to address the convention of the National Conference of Catholic Charities in Omaha. Msgr. John O'Grady, his friend from his days in Washington, invited him to speak to the delegates. The paper Ligutti read was significant in showing the signs of an emerging country pastor. In the light of future developments within the American Church, Ligutti's address was even more significant. He said, "The farm is the ideal place to raise children; it furnishes ideal home surroundings for mutual love and help. It avoids close neighborhood quarrels. It affords opportunities for developing personal tastes in beautifying the surroundings of the home."

Unfortunately, Ligutti was not heeded by the delegates to the Omaha convention. It would take another decade before his voice would be respected. He returned to Granger, to the work at hand. It was 1932. Roosevelt had come to power and the following year Ligutti wrote an article entitled "The New Deal Comes To Granger." This was the work at hand in the midst of the Great Depression. There were the mining camps, out-of-the-way hamlets where people lived in the most squalid and oppressed conditions. They were the victims of an economic system that had no right to exist in mid-twentieth-century America. Nor was it to be overlooked that future Secretary of Agriculture Henry Wallace operated a farm within the boundaries of this parish. Ligutti was ready for the most popular enterprise of his pastorate in Granger.

Opportunity knocked with the passage of the National Recovery Act of June 16, 1933. Section 208 created the Substistence Homesteads Division within the United States Department of the Interior. Six months later, December 16, the petition for the Granger Homesteads was filed. In that interval Ligutti breathed life and hope into the lives of hundreds of people. A local corporation was formed consisting of Mr. Flack, Dr. Smith, Mr. Johnson, Mr. Furman, and Mr. J. S. Russell, farm editor of the Des Moines *Register* and *Tribune*. Ligutti later recalled that when he submitted the names of the board members to an official in Washington, D.C., the latter quipped, "I suppose they are all Roman Catholics." Ligutti's reply was quick and to the point. "Yes," he said, "they are all devout thirty-third degree Masons!"

In later years Ligutti recalled these early days of the Granger Homesteads:

> The Granger situation presented an ideal locale for the application of Section 208 of the N.I.R.A. It seemed most adapted to the fulfillment of the principles and the needs expressed in the philosophy of the Popes. We sought encouragement from sundry sources, first among Catholic editors, sociologists and economists, then among non-Catholics. From all we received encouragement and promises of help....

A special committee had been appointed at the Iowa State College, with Mr. Paul Taff as chairman and Professors Davidson, Elwood, Wakely, Erwin, and others as its members. The hearing was granted and a kindly reception given to the explanation of the project. Professor Davidson was particularly interested in the project and, being a personal friend of M. L. Wilson, administrator at the Subsistence Homesteads Division within the Department of the Interior, his words of approval bore much weight. An initial petition was forwarded to this office. It was well received, but it fell among the thousand others.

The petition outlined the Granger Homesteads project of building fifty houses on approximately 225 acres of farmland one-half mile outside Granger. The houses ranged in size from four to six rooms, each with a basement, hot air furnace, hot water heater and tank, and an automatic pressure tank connected with the electric well pump. The average land per home was about four acres, making the average available ground for cultivation about three and a half acres. The purpose of the homesteads was to move families from the shacks surrounding the nine mining camps in the area and provide them decent housing with enough land for cultivation. It would also bring these families closer to town with its ready access to stores, school, and church.

The need for the subsistence homes, apart from the poverty in which most families lived, can be seen from two glaring facts. In 1933 the average working days per year by the miners was about 150 — leaving about 200 days without gainful employment, chiefly during the late spring and summer. The average annual income of the miners was $800 per year. It was obvious that neither God nor man ordained such abominable working and living conditions.

Ligutti, however, was not content at this time to leave the Granger Homesteads petition in a pile with a thousand others. In early January, 1934, he boarded a train for Washington, and "armed with data, arguments, and courage," he called upon Mr. M. L. Wilson (the two subsequently became close and life-long friends). Officials within the department graciously received him and informed him that he should draw up a new petition. Quoting a phrase of Dickens, Ligutti called these days the hours of waiting in the "Circumlocution Office." His patience was tried and to his credit he practiced the virtue to an heroic degree. One night he burned the candle at both ends until four o'clock in the morning in his room at the Sulpician Seminary of the Catholic University, "pounding away at Exhibits B, C, D, X, Y, Z, and answering the barrage of questions."

Subsequent events he recorded in these words:

> During this Washington visit, we left no one unseen who could have helped the cause in any way; high ecclesiastics, ambassadors, politicians, cabinet members, the National Catholic Welfare Conference and many others were enlisted in the hastening of the approval.
>
> We felt that much had been accomplished by the personal visit. We continued to correspond with M. L. Wilson and to answer questions. In the meanwhile, the local Democrat, who votes Republican in the Primaries, Mr. Sidney Johnson, secured a Memorial from the State of Iowa Legislature to

the President of the United States recommending the approval of the Project.

March 4, 1934 was an historic day for Granger. By telegram from Washington, Wilson informed Ligutti that "the Secretary of the Interior has approved Granger Project but nothing can be said about it until announced here." On March 15 Secretary of the Interior Harold L. Ickes announced the subsistence homesteads project at Granger. In a news release issued the same day Wilson said:

> The project which we are undertaking at Granger, Iowa, should be one of the most effective demonstrations of the advantages of subsistence homesteads to part-time workers. The seasonal nature of the coal industry means that the miners are not employed during much of the spring and summer.
>
> Two features make this project of particular value. The coal mines in this part of Iowa, unlike many of those of the Appalacian fields, should continue to provide employment to the miners for fifty years or more at least. Moreover, the homesteads will be located on a tract of fine Iowa soil, so that a most auspicious combination of favorable agricultural and industrial conditions is provided.

All of Wilson's observations were correct except one. By mid-century the mines had ceased to operate. His other observations were dead center.

In February, 1935, contracts were signed with the J. E. Lovejoy Company of Des Moines. Wells were dropped and basements were dug in April. By October 3, 1935 the fifty homes were built and turned over to the federal government for final inspection. By snowfall fifty happy families moved into their new homes. The "homesteaders" — as they came to be called — were a cross section of the area: forty-two were mining families, seventeen were of Italian extraction, thirteen of Croation descent. There were twenty Catholic families, fifteen Protestant families, and fifteen mixed marriages. The families had thirty years in which to pay for the land and home at an interest rate of 3 per cent. Ligutti wrote, "The low interest rate and long amortization period are the keys to acceptability and desirability of the whole program." When completed the entire project cost the federal government approximately $200,000 and within twenty years the homesteaders had paid back most of that amount.

Throughout the years Ligutti kept in touch with the homesteaders and they, in turn, never forgot his work for them. In 1970 one of the homesteaders, Virgil Biondi, wrote Ligutti in Rome:

> I always recall many things about my childhood days. They were good and happy and pleasant days. I will never forget those memorable years with you, Monsignor Marasco and the good, kind Sisters of Mercy....
>
> I always do think about the little village of Granger, the Homestead, and they will always remain in my heart.

Virgil Biondi was but a lad of twelve when Granger received its most prominent visitor on June 8, 1936. Mrs. Franklin Delano Roosevelt (who personally intervened on behalf of the Granger Homesteads with her husband) came to view the dream come true herself. She congratulated the energetic pastor, met with the board who had created the homesteads, and was the guest of the fourteen-member Joseph Biondi family. Ligutti served as the first lady's official tour guide. Upon her return to the nation's capital she penned a letter of praise and commendation to the pastor and people of Granger.

More and more people were taking an interest in the Granger Homesteads. Church and Government officials from throughout the United States and foreign countries marked Granger on their maps to see if what was written about so successful an undertaking could possibly be true. Vatican officials made Granger a stopping place during their travels through the Midwest. Rural life leaders from Australia, Europe, and Latin America came to behold a housing project that fulfilled the needs of people. Government officials and representatives stopped by to see what could be done with courage, imagination, and industry. One such was Representative John G. Alexander of Minnesota who praised the success of the project on the floor of the United States House of Representatives on June 30, 1939. At the time he incorporated into the *Congressional Record* an article concerning the Granger Homesteads that originally appeared in *Free America,* a publication promoting Jeffersonian democracy and edited by George Weller in New York City. Congressman Alexander said:

> If Father Ligutti can do this at Granger, Iowa, we as a nation certainly can do it all over the country, and we would probably cut our relief load to one-third of its present amount. What a saving, not only in money but in the morale of our citizenry reflected in the happiness, lives, and contentment which they could not help but enjoy when moved

from the slums, huts, and hovels in which a great majority of our poverty-stricken people are forced to dwell today.

Congressman Alexander was not alone in his praise. Miss Frances Perkins, secretary of labor in the Roosevelt cabinet, herself viewed the Granger Homesteads on February 28, 1939. Upon returning to Washington, she wrote Ligutti, praising his work:

> Among the experiments which have grown out of this last depression, I know none of more constructive economic and social value than the Granger Homesteads project. It is a challenge to other areas where employment is seasonal or irregular. Your leadership and persistency in developing this project has won the admiration of all who know about it. On my part, I offer my sincere congratulations.

For Ligutti such words were more than sufficient satisfaction for a work so close to his heart. He looked upon the project, however, from a different perspective in later years. Recalling the countless hours and seemingly ceaseless activities involved, he felt it was no more than a part of the pastoral ministry. "No matter where a priest is stationed," he said, "there is always work to do. A good priest will see the work before him and go ahead and do it. That is all that I really did in Granger."

One of the more personal and revealing accounts of Ligutti's activities during these years was written by a former associate and friend. Professor Ray Wakely, then on the faculty of Iowa State College and a member of the planning committee for the Granger Homesteads, wrote:

> Although we worked from different stations in life, he in the church and I in the university, we had many common interests and, especially, *basic* in rural development and a deep concern for the welfare of rural people.
>
> I can tell you only some of my more vivid recollections of our common involvements, vivid not because we were often together . . . instead because of his genuine humanness, his sparkling wit and constant good humor, together with the remarkable electric quality of his contacts with me and others as I observed them.
>
> I do not remember when I first met Father Ligutti but it must have been during the depression of the 1930's because I joined the staff in economics and sociology at the (then) Iowa State College in 1930. I remember well that Professor P. M. Elwood called me to say that he was working with a Catholic priest down in Granger who was developing a

project to put out-of-work coal miners on the land where they could live in decency and subsist in part from their own labor on a small homestead. So was born a practical demonstration of the subsistence homestead idea in Iowa. This was an ideal which was promoted earlier by Henry Ford and, now, by Eleanor Roosevelt. The Subsistance Homesteads Division had been established in the U.S. Dept. of Agriculture to help finance and manage worthy projects.

Professor Elwood suggested that I go down to Granger and see for myself what was developing there. So I went. Father Ligutti took me to visit the little "technical high school" which he had developed in a town where the people could not, at that time, support a good public school. I was impressed by the girls who were learning to sew but I do not remember what the boys were doing! Father Ligutti took me to see the abandoned mines at Freeman Spur and the attendant desolation which resulted for the miners. These were prime prospects for the homestead project at Granger. On this visit I was educated concerning the family life of the miners and the importance of the kitchen ranges (cookstoves) as a status symbol which was cherished and cared for by the Italian mothers.

Prof. Elwood, who was Head of the Dept. of Landscape Architecture at Iowa State, developed an artistic layout for the homesteads, each on 5 acres of land. He planned to locate the homes on the plots so that 4 homes would be close to each other to promote sociability but Father Ligutti wanted them located as far away from each other as possible, "So the women wouldn't be fighting all the time." Father Ligutti won, as usual. We decided that he knew his womenfolk.

We were asked to help select the homesteaders. This task was assigned to Prof. Will Harter and myself. We developed a questionnaire, which Father Ligutti called "The Inquisition," to aid us in selecting families that were *in need* and also *likely to succeed* in the Homestead situation.

Imagine our surprise when a widowed mother with 10 or a dozen children was placed in the homestead. She was not one of our prospects, but she was in *great need* and Fr. Ligutti knew she was deserving of help and, if he met peoples' needs, the project would succeed on the basis of that criterion alone. Eventually this family became *exhibit number one*. The mother raised grapes, made wine, and sold it. When neighbors complained and Fr. Ligutti "took her to task" (we always suspected he did it kindly if not sympathetically), she said, "This is the way I know how to make a living. If you know of a better way, I'll do it." If I remember correctly, no better way was suggested.

Year after year the Granger homesteaders held a banquet. Ligutti took the occasion to award prizes, sponsor competitions, promote land development, and give the people a pride in their land, homes, and work. An esprit de corps was established and it soon became a badge of honor to belong to the Granger homesteaders. In more recent years two footnotes were added to the history of the project. In February, 1951, the Homestead Cooperative Association was dissolved. Ligutti's plan for aiding family security had come to a successful conclusion. The pastor of Assumption parish in 1951, a former pupil and assistant pastor of Ligutti's, Fr. John Gorman, served as manager of the cooperative. Time changed the shifting sands. Thirty-two of the original families still lived in their homes on the Granger project. The mines closed, but most of the men worked in the John Deere factory in neighboring Des Moines. "The success of the project," said Father Gorman at the time, "proves that families with small incomes can achieve a high degree of security through cooperative action under good leadership."

The second footnote occurred on December 8, 1955 when ninety-six homesteaders gathered in the American Legion Hall in Granger for the twentieth anniversary celebration. Ligutti, unfortunately, was unable to attend, being at the time a participant in the All-Asian Apostolate of the Laity in the Philippines. In Ligutti's home in Rome is a copper plaque that the homesteaders presented to him as a token of their appreciation. So the busy pastor of Granger left another piece of his heart among the good people he called then, and still calls, his homesteaders.

Luigi Ligutti was not a man to rest on his laurels. The homestead project was one endeavor, Assumption High School another, the religious vacation schools another, the building of a new rectory still another. But the pastor of Granger was not parochial. He was taking a more and more active role in the National Catholic Rural Life Conference. He was on the lecture circuit, speaking before seminarians, priests, sisters, and university audiences throughout the United States. He was writing articles for *America, Commonweal* (whose editor, Edward Skillin, he numbered among his closest friends), *Our Sunday Visitor,* diocesan newspapers, and other general and Catholic publications. His interests were universal. One week he would review Willa Cather's *Death Comes for the Archbishop;* another week an article in *Commonweal* on "The Popes and Agriculture"; another week a letter to the editor of the Des Moines *Tribune* and again a piece for *Extension* magazine. Another letter to the White House which drew a brief reply from Mrs. Roosevelt: "Mrs. Fickel has sent me your letter of September 30, (1944) with the suggestions on the Italian situation. I have given it to the President." In 1935 he was lecturing in Duluth, Minnesota, and was subsequently quoted in the November 2, 1935 *New Yorker*: "For two generations Duluth has been called 'The Zenith City of the Unsalted Sea.' Father Ligutti has given the city a new title recently as, 'The Air Conditioned City of America.'" Ligutti's reference has stuck, for Minnesota's third largest city is still called the same today.

During the late 1930's, Ligutti was also becoming involved with two important Iowa state commissions, one on land tenancy and the other on unemployment. He was involved, first, because of his noticeable concern for the poor and oppressed and, second, because he was recognized by legislators and officials of Iowa as a responsible and judicious spokesman on both subjects. He was, too, always a man who did his homework, knowing facts and figures and confident that his evaluations were accurate. As early as 1937 he was concerned with the problem of the farm-laborer and his living conditions — at least a generation before the problem came to the attention of national leaders and the American public. In a radio address over WHO Radio in Des Moines on November 14, 1937, Ligutti said:

> The farmhand farms for the clean boot farmer who represents the farmer class on commissions. We see him as the cotton picker dragging the sack along the long rows in the southern fields. We find him in the onion fields of Hardin County, Ohio, and in the pea fields of Idaho. The apples and hops give him work in the Pacific Northwest; the lettuce and cauliflower in the Imperial Valley, the citrus in Florida, the tobacco in Kentucky and Tennessee. He husks corn and stacks oats and wheat in Iowa, Illinois and Indiana. He sprays the orchards and picks the fruit in the Great Lakes region. He is a dairy worker in the cities' milksheds and a harvest hand in the Dakotas....
>
> When pay day comes he is a piece worker or a by-the-hour or week or month hireling. He has no collective bargaining

power when he hires on or he is pushed off. It's take what you get and do what you're told.

At the Tenancy hearings in San Francisco last winter a veritable barrage of pleas was made by the farm laborers' group. At the end of the hearings a gentleman stood up and stated that California farm laborers were the best paid in the United States. ($2.18)

The joke of the tragedy is: the gentleman was right!

We must find a common denominator that will apply to such a variety of human types of work as furnished by the farm laborer problem. It does exist.

The fractions of this common denominator may be found scattered but if we have a will they can be brought together. We shall find them in: employers, government, society and employees.

One of the great searches of Ligutti's life was launched to find this "common denominator," be it among the farm workers of the United States, the *campesinos* of Latin America, the peasants of Asia, or the exploited of Africa. To his credit, he never gave up the search. One of the great puzzles of his life was his contemporary and sometime-colleague, John A. Ryan. He could never comprehend how the man who rightly deserved to be called by his biographer, "Right Reverend New Dealer," a son of the rich soil of Dakota County, Minnesota, could advocate so effectively the cause of the laboring man in the city and be so consistently silent on the plight of the working man in the country. The words Ligutti uttered in that historic radio address in 1937 became the motto he espoused the remainder of his life: "It can be done; it must be done; it is our individual and collective fault if it is not accomplished." To his undying credit, he never gave up the battle.

Land tenancy, as we shall see, would always be a major Ligutti preoccupation. He saw its ravages in Iowa during the Great Depression; he saw its harmful effects year after year in nation after nation throughout the rest of his life. His innate love for the land prompted him always to view with indignation any abuse of the land and the people who lived on it. He was, thus, in fullest agreement with President Franklin Roosevelt, who, in addressing the United States Senate Special Committee on Farm Tenancy on February 16, 1937, said:

The American dream of the family-size farm, owned by the family that operates it, has become more and more remote. The agricultural ladder, on which an energetic young man might ascend from hired man to tenant to independent owner, is no longer serving its purpose.

A problem of such magnitude is not solved overnight, nor by any one limited approach, nor by the Federal Government alone. While aggravated by the depression, the tenancy problem is the accumulated result of generations of unthinking exploitation of our agricultural resources, both land and people. We can no longer postpone action. We must begin at once with such resources of man-power, money, and experience as are available, and with such methods as well can be called forth from the cooperative effort of local, State, and Federal agencies of government, and of landlords quite as much as tenants.

Ligutti promptly responded to this call by serving on the Iowa Land Tenancy Commission from November, 1937, until June, 1938. The commission presented its report to the governor of the state on June 29, 1938. The foreword, written by Ligutti, expressed not only his own philosophy but that of the other members as well. Also Ligutti spoke over WHO Radio in Des Moines on the subject in a series of weekly addresses during the last three months of 1937. "Ownership of productive property," he said on that occasion, "is an innate desire of humans." He then quoted Pope Leo XIII who wrote in his encyclical *Rerum Novarum*:

> Men always work harder and more when they work on that which belongs to them. Nay, they learn to love the very soil that yields in response to the labor of their hands, not only food to eat but an abundance of good things for themselves and those who are dear to them.

In this same address Ligutti proposed four solutions to the problem of land tenancy, and these solutions he would continue to propound throughout the world the rest of his life. In reply to the question about what can be done concerning land tenancy, he cited these four findings of the commission:

1. Widespread credit facilities to permit land purchase by tenants.
2. Revision of the system of lease-hold to promote landlord-tenant relationship.

3. Broader conceptions to stabilize rural civilization and give to farmers advantages of city life, and none of its disadvantages.
4. Land purchase by the government, particularly in the South, for the purpose of creating large communities of sharecroppers and other tenants working upon a communal basis.

He concluded his remarks with a homey example:

> We have gone from a spirit of saving and the need of sacrifice to the practice of spending faster than we are earning. They have been telling us that the first rung in the ladder of farming is farm labor; the second, tenancy; the third, proprietorship; but most young men prefer an old secondhand car, and it cannot be denied that the running board of a car can never be the first rung in the ladder to proprietorship.

Ligutti was becoming, unwittingly, a national figure. He was moving more and more into a leadership role within the National Catholic Rural Life Conference. He was more and more in demand as a public speaker. He was in a quandry as he knew he was not giving his undivided attention to his people in Granger. He knew also that there were other commitments and needs that he could, if possible, fulfill. He was a torn man by the end of the decade. He was, however, nationally recognized and, although it meant little if anything to him, it was a distinct honor to the people of Granger.

On June 17, 1938 has was recognized by his Church as a domestic prelate with the title of right reverend monsignor. He did not seek the honor; it came to him through the good graces of his superior, Most Rev. Gerald T. Bergan, the new bishop of Des Moines. The National Catholic News Service reported the event:

> Father Ligutti, who is Des Moines Diocesan Director of the Rural Life Bureau, has become nationally known for the establishment in this community of the now famous Granger subsistence homestead project. For years he has been a leader in movements to better the conditions of rural communities and peoples.

It was a fine tribute.

The celebration of his being made a monsignor was a major event in the history of the diocese and community. Of course, his people were both pleased and proud. Bishop Bergan presided and his friend Bishop Aloisius Muench preached the festive sermon. He was surrounded by people and friends; he was at home with the people he loved. His former schoolmate and friend Fr. Newman Flanagan composed a "second nocturn" for the occasion. It read in part:

> Aloysius (better known to us as Luigi Gino Ligutti), born in Udine, Italy of pious and honest parents in the year 1895, at an early age could recite by heart all the works of Karl Marx. At the age of five he could sing the "Internationale." At the age of sixteen he migrated with his pious mother to the United States to live in Des Moines. He studied at St. Ambrose College in the city of Davenport where he became acquainted with the encyclical of Leo XIII, *Rerum Novarum.* Truly, here in Iowa his conversion took place.

The Des Moines *Tribune* devoted a special editorial to mark the event — a truly exceptional occurrence in these days before ecumenism. It read:

> . . . in his devotion to the welfare of the human order, Monsignor Ligutti's enterprise has by no means been circumscribed by his own parish nor his own church rolls.
>
> Of course this broad vision of modern society's needs has contributed to his recognition as a domestic prelate by the Pope himself.
>
> The other determining factor is that Father Ligutti has not been satisfied with the passive preachment of social idealism that he has successfully sponsored in a very tangible expression in the Granger homestead project and in numerous other ways.
>
> Those who seek earnestly to give religion a new meaning in the modern world can do no better than to review the efforts and accomplishments of this Italian immigrant boy, who sought but a small niche in which to serve his fellows and is filling it magnificently.

Almost thirty years later Ligutti returned to Granger for another significant event when he was honored by dignitaries of Church and State. Here he marked the golden jubilee of his ordination to the priesthood on September 27, 1967. In so many ways it was a day of simplicity and interior joy, just the sort of day he would desire. He was, to be sure, honored once again. But in many ways the honors were hollow. He rather preferred to look back on the religious vacation schools, Assumption High School, the homesteaders, the Iowa commissions. These were the golden days. He was happy to be home with the memories he cherished, the people he loved. If ever there was a home, Granger was home, and Ligutti was happy to be back home.

There is a little hill in the parish cemetery on the outskirts of Granger. On this spot someday the former pastor of Granger will be laid to rest. Over his grave will be the testament of his life. On a simple slab, inscribed with a Celtic cross, will be carved the words this pastor chose himself:

AT PEACE WITH THE PEOPLE I LOVE.

The parish church in Romans, Italy, where Ligutti was baptized, made his First Communion, was confirmed, and from which he left to enter the seminary.

A castle in Spilinbergo, Italy, still owned by the Ligutti family.

In the fall, 1935, fifty Iowa families became the "Granger homesteaders" and moved into homes located on four-acre plots near Granger.

A 1974 view of the Granger Homesteads area.

The National Catholic Rural Life Conference headquarters in Des Moines was "home" to Monsignor Ligutti.

CHAPTER FOUR

MAN'S RELATION TO THE LAND

In 1973 a reporter of the Des Moines *Tribune* interviewed Monsignor Ligutti in Rome. The reporter asked how he had ever become interested in rural life. Ligutti's reply was, as usual, simple and direct, "My people were farmers and I was interested in my people."

In typical, down-to-earth fashion, Ligutti continued to explain to the reporter, Mr. Donald Muhm, the precise incident that caused him to become involved in rural sociology. In Woodbine he hunted at night with his beloved dogs. During one outing his favorite hunting dog fell into a deep gully which had appeared almost overnight in the hills around Woodbine. Ligutti lowered himself with ropes into the gully to rescue the dog. As that gully had not been there the previous year, the experience made the priest realize that soil erosion ruined the land. He then resolved to do something about the problem. Thus he became concerned about rural life.

"Every spoonful of earth," he said to the reporter, "is full of gold. God Almighty must be laughing at us because we do not know how to use it better." He then cited a dramatic example:

> What is the richest country in the world? Switzerland. But what is the poorest country in natural resources? Switzerland. On the other hand, what is the poorest country in the world? Bolivia. But what is the richest country in natural resources? Bolivia. When you use the soil — the great gift of God — you not only develop these natural resources but you also develop man. If you develop man to be reasonable, then there is no reason to go to war. You use the plow in place of the sword.

It was as simple — and complicated — as all that! A son of the soil, Ligutti was always fascinated by the land; not just the land as soil, but the land as a molder of men. Even before his contact with the National Catholic Rural Life Conference, he was a student of rural ecology and sociology. During his years in Granger he was reading his beloved classics; he studied both covenants of the Bible; he gathered from papal documents every help he could to form a philosophy of rural life. He was a pastor, first, to be sure; but he was also a scholar who taught himself. Years later he would say:

> No parish is too small; no assignment is too insignificant. No matter where a priest is, he can always find the way and the means to serve the Church. I have a feeling that many young priests today are looking for "where the action is." I always found the action is where you make it.

In these early days in Granger he was accustomed to quote a poem entitled "Farming," the first two stanzas of which read:

> 1880
> Farmer is at the plow,
> Wife milking the cow;
> Boys threshing in the barn,
> Daughters spinning yarn —
> All happy to a charm.
>
> 1920
> Farmer's gone to see a show,
> Daughter is at the piano;
> Wife is dressed in satin,
> All the boys learning Latin;
> And a mortgage on the farm.

Ligutti was pleased that one of his own boys from the parish, Fr. Jacob Weiss, added the following stanza in later years:

> 1940
> Farmer's tinkering with tractor,
> Daughter made beautiful by Max Factor;
> Mother is busy cooking from a can,
> Sonny at tavern discussing Sally Rand.
> No wonder father is renting land —
> Soon he'll be a hired hand.

The pastor of Granger expressed his personal philosophy in two placards he hung on the walls of his office during these years. Both revealed a way of life that he followed then and still does. The one read:

> To avoid criticism: Do nothing — Say nothing — Be nothing.

The other read:

> The man who is worthy of being a leader of men will never complain of the stupidity of his helpers, of the ingratitude of humankind, or of the lack of appreciation of the public. These things are all a part of the great game of life and to meet them and not to go down before them in discouragement and defeat is the final proof of power.

Ligutti, however, was no armchair philosopher. Once he perceived the need he immediately set to work to solve the problem, be it personal, parochial, or national. From his first contacts with the National Catholic Rural Life Conference (NCRLC) in 1924, he continually kept casting his own thinking in new molds and brought with him numerous friends and collaborators in the United States and throughout the world. He became president of the NCRLC in 1937 and was thus thrust upon the national scene as a leader of rural sociology for the remainder of his life. He could not escape this destiny. It was not a position he created; rather, it was a position created for him. There would be no NCRLC without Luigi Ligutti and the considerable gifts he brought to the office. Well might it be said that the office sought him more than he sought the office.

One cannot overlook the problems and tempo of the world in the 1930's. Roosevelt had launched the "New Deal" in the midst of the greatest depression the United States had ever witnessed. Stalin was carrying out the purges that led hundreds of thousands either to death or Siberia. Hitler was making noises in Munich and planning a totalitarian state. Mussolini was currying favor with the Vatican by creating the Vatican City State and subsequently subjugating Ethiopia. The Church and other civilized agencies and organizations were waging an all-out war against totalitarianism and Communism. And a young Jesuit priest, Fr. Miguel Pro, was shot by a firing squad in Mexico City. They were not the best of times; nor were they the worst of times.

There is no need here to recount the founding of the NCRLC by the former Fr. Edwin V. O'Hara of Eugene, Oregon. That story has been admirably written on the occasion of the organization's silver jubilee by Br. Raymond Witte in his book entitled *Twenty-Five Years of Crusading*, which appeared in 1948. That history was updated by Ligutti in 1950 at the national convention of the NCRLC in Belleville, Illinois. The succeeding twenty-five years of the NCRLC's history deserves another chronicler; the subject lies beyond the scope of this narrative.

No account of the NCRLC and Ligutti's leadership between the two decades spanning the mid-years of the present century would be complete without mentioning the leadership and thinking of five prelates who were the intellectual and moral force as guiding mentors of Ligutti's many projects during this time. Indeed, Ligutti would not have accomplished the undertakings he espoused without the support and assistance of these midwestern prelates. In more than an ordinary manner, Ligutti's accomplishments were a tribute to their approval, wisdom, and counsel. No one realized this better than Ligutti himself.

Two facts should be recorded concerning the late bishop of Kansas City. There is documentary proof that Ligutti personally intervened to have the National Catholic Rural Life Conference's founder named as a personal archbishop. In a letter to his friend Archbishop Romolo Carboni, at the time apostolic delegate to Australia, he interceded on the behalf of Bishop Edwin O'Hara, and within a year the bishop of Kansas City received the personal title of archbishop.

It is not surprising that in later life Ligutti would recall the outstanding men whom he knew. The three prelates whom he called "truly great" were Archbishop O'Hara, Archbishop Daniel Mannix (1864-1963) of Melbourne, Australia, and Don Luigi Sturzo (1871-1959), founder of the Italian Christian-Democratic Party.

The most effective and unique leadership contributed to the NCRLC came from a small diocese in the Upper Midwest. The man had been the young, vigorous rector of St. Francis Seminary, Milwaukee, by name, Aloisius Joseph Muench (1889-1962), who was appointed bishop of Fargo, North Dakota, on August 12, 1935 — at the time the youngest member of the American hierarchy. He arrived in Fargo during the height of the Great Depression, in the midst of the dust storms that were causing havoc throughout the plains states, and on the hottest day ever recorded in North Dakota history.

A city boy by birth, a scholar by choice, and a seminary professor by assignment, Muench came to a diocese struggling for economic and social survival. From the beginning he vigorously applied the principles of social justice that he learned at the University of Wisconsin. These he refined through his friendship and close collaboration with Mr. Frederick Kenkel and other leaders of the Central Verein of the United States. He captured the imagination of priests and people and brought to them a sense of strength and hope. He was beloved by all who knew him and who served the Church with him.

Muench became the champion of the Catholic rural life movement, admirably filling the role of O'Hara who by this time had moved on to other work in the national apostolate of the Confraternity of Christian Doctrine and the Catholic Biblical Association. Muench became, and remained throughout his life, the innovator, the inaugurator, the idea-man of the National Catholic Rural Life Conference. Even when called to serve the Church in post-war Germany as apostolic visitator, and later as papal nuncio, he continued to support the NCRLC. Pope John XXIII, in a congratulatory letter to Muench on his silver anniversary as a bishop in 1960, singled out the cardinal's interest and service to the Conference: "When for a number of years you were president of the National Catholic Rural Life Conference, you accepted the challenge with noteworthy wisdom, diligence, and zeal."

Upon coming to Fargo, Muench drew to himself two priests of the diocese who shared his interest in the rural life apostolate. The three became known, in Ligutti's words, as the "Fargo trio," and exerted a lasting influence upon the aims and goals of the Conference, chiefly through the *Manifesto on Rural Life* that was published in 1939. One of these was Vincent Ryan who was born on the family farm in Columbia County, Wisconsin. He volunteered to serve as a priest in a western diocese and was accepted for Fargo by Bishop James Shanley. For twenty-two years he served as secretary to the bishop, chancellor of the diocese, and pastor of St. Anthony's Parish, Fargo. His interest in social welfare prompted him to organize and become the first director of the diocesan Catholic Welfare Bureau. Throughout North Dakota he was recognized as a leader in the field. In 1939 the University of North Dakota awarded him an honorary doctor of law degree in recognition of this leadership. The following year he was appointed bishop of Bismarck, North Dakota, the first priest of the diocese of Fargo to be elevated to the episcopal dignity. As bishop he launched a vigorous building campaign, crowned by the dedication of the stunningly beautiful Cathedral of the Holy Spirit in 1945. In the eleven years he spent as bishop, Ryan raised over $10,000,000 for new churches, rectories, schools, convents, and hospitals. For two years, from 1939 until 1941, he served as the first episcopal president of the NCRLC. He died of heart failure in his sixty-seventh year on November 10, 1951.

The third member of the "Fargo trio" was William T. Mulloy. If it could be said that Muench was the brains and Ryan the writer, it was surely true that Mulloy was the spokesman. He was gifted with a stentorian voice that enraptured audiences throughout the country. He was, as Ligutti stated at the time of Mulloy's death, "the salesman of Christ's doctrine in all its phases . . . . Things have never happened in the NCRLC. They have been done and Bishop Mulloy was a doer."

As pastor of St. John's Church, Grafton, Mulloy had been an ardent advocate of the NCRLC from its beginning. Through his friendship with Msgr. James Byrnes of St. Paul he became the friend of Ligutti. In January, 1945, he was consecrated bishop of Covington, Kentucky, and brought his zeal and rural life experience to that diocese. He was Ligutti's closest friend among the hierarchy; the three score letters between the two of them reveal him as an intimate friend and supporter in good times and bad. He died of a heart attack in June, 1959. Ligutti wrote, "A product of the good earth of North Dakota, he now rests on a Kentucky hillside. His great and noble soul lives on — a light and a guide even in death."

One of the earliest friends of the NCRLC and one of Ligutti's staunchest supporters was Joseph H. Schlarman. A priest of the diocese of Belleville, he was appointed bishop of Peoria on April 16, 1930 and served that see until his death on November 10, 1951 — the same day, incidentally, that his friend Bishop Ryan of Bismarck died. During his twenty-one years as bishop he paid off a $2,000,000 diocesan debt and left his mark through the expansion of the Catholic school system, the intensification of the spiritual life in the parishes, the inauguration of religion classes for children in rural areas, and an increase in the vocations to the religious life and priesthood. At his death, he left one of the most vigorous dioceses in the Midwest.

Schlarman was more than an exceptional administrator. He was a man of countless interests and the author of books and brochures on historical subjects. As president of the NCRLC from 1943 to 1945, he translated the popular NCRLC booklet *Prayers and Blessings of the Church* and delighted to speak before rural audiences. One of his more famous sermons was delivered in Westphalia, Iowa, at a rural life day. He entitled his sermon "St. Paul Speaks to the Galatian Farmers." His interests in such causes as prison reform, international development, ecumenism, ecology, and rural sociology made him in his thinking a man many years ahead of his time. On the day Schlarman died, as Ligutti was leaving for the Near East, he wrote:

> He was thorough and systematic in all his undertakings. In spite of his advancing years he traveled extensively and always with a purpose. He underwent almost any inconvenience to visit the birthplace of an historical villain or hero. His interests were varied and always catholic. The liturgical movement had in him a monitor and a Maecenas. The National Catholic Rural Life Conference conferred upon him the distinguished service plaque for 1950. He had been its president, its advisor, its benefactor.

Another farm boy from Bellechester, Minnesota, followed closely in the steps of O'Hara and Muench. He was Peter W. Bartholome (1893-), for twenty-five years the coadjutor and ordinary of the diocese of St. Cloud. Throughout these years his three principal interests were Catholic family life, rural life, and education. For many years he served as episcopal moderator of the Family Life Bureau of the National Catholic Welfare Conference, and under his leadership marriage preparation courses were introduced in dioceses throughout the country. From his early days as a priest in the diocese of Winona he developed a strong attachment to the land and became an abiding friend and counselor of the NCRLC. He served as its president from 1955 to 1957 and was continually in demand as a speaker at national, state, and regional meetings of farm organizations.

Bartholome was firmly convinced of the need of the family farm for the spiritual and economic welfare of the nation. He believed that the strength of America was found in the heartland of the Midwest where both national and supernatural virtues were nurtured in the sacred circle of the family-owned-and-operated farm. One of his favorite quotations was taken from the writings of James J. Hill, the railroad empire builder: "Land without people is a wasteland; people without land is a mob."

Although at times Bartholome and Ligutti differed on procedures, they never disagreed on goals. In spite of differences, they were always congenial and close friends. It is of more than passing significance that one of the bishops Bartholome consecrated, Henry J. Soenneker of Owensboro, Kentucky, also served as president of the NCRLC, and Bartholome's successor in St. Cloud, Bishop George H. Speltz, later also served as president of the Conference.

These were some leaders that Ligutti would be closely associated with in the early years of his NCRLC leadership, and later years would introduce other associates and collaborators. These men were his monitors, support, and sustenance. All would enthusiastically subscribe to the statement made by Bishop Vincent Wehrle, O.S.B., at the first meeting of the NCRLC in St. Louis in 1923: "There is something almost sacramental about the life of the rural family."

During the late 1930's, Ligutti was passing through the valley of doubts and discouragements. As president of the NCRLC from 1937 to 1939 he knew that he could not adequately fulfill the demands of both the Granger parish and the rural life apostolate. He was in a quandry. He faced another bitter sadness three months after being named a monsignor with the death of his beloved mother in September, 1938. He wrote in his diary, "It is awful lonesome in this world without a mother." He noted that Bishop Bergan offered to pay the cost of $330 for his monsignorial robes, and he added, "Varieties in church dress — piffle!" The closing months of the year brought another sadness, for his friend and colleague Dom Virgil Michel, O.S.B., died on November 28. During December Ligutti and the executive secretary of the NCRLC, Fr. James Byrnes, were discussing the possibility of securing a young priest of the diocese of Winona as executive secretary of the Conference. The young priest was Peter W. Bartholome.

At this stage Ligutti was plagued with doubts. The new year, 1939, found him wondering whether or not he should not have persisted in his early thoughts of joining the Sulpicians. He resolved "to set aside three days a week for reading and thinking," unfortunately a luxury he could never enjoy as much as he would have liked. In March he was considering moving to a small parish where he could fulfill both the pastoral ministry and the directorship of the Conference. The following month he was asking himself how much longer the hustle and bustle could last — and then he went off to Europe on his first return to his native land since he had left it as a young man. Upon his return in September he attended the NCRLC convention in Spokane where Bishop Ryan was elected president. He noted in his diary, "Happy at getting out of office." He returned to Granger and before the year ended he had drafted an outline of a statement on rural life that he and Muench discussed on the train westward.

His problems did not end, however, for the new year found Bishop Ryan asking him about the feasibility of becoming executive secretary of the Conference since Father Byrnes was resigning. He gave the matter serious thought through the coming months. At the same time he was busy correcting page-proofs of the book *Rural Roads to Security,* a work on which he was collaborating with Fr. John Rawe, S.J., a professor at Creighton University, Omaha. In the end they produced a work on rural sociology, the likes of which has not been duplicated. Death claimed Father Rawe in the full bloom of manhood and cut short a promising career. The obituary notice stated:

> Associated with many of the stalwarts who made rural life into a National Catholic Movement, Father Rawe was the author of pamphlets, assisted in outlining the "Rural Life Manifesto," and was co-author of *Rural Roads to Security.* His untimely death at the age of forty-six in 1947 was a great loss to the National Catholic Rural Life Movement. A man of great vision, he was constantly giving retreats and lectures to such groups as the ladies of the Grail and the students at Boystown, Nebraska. The late Father Flanagan of Boystown called him "the outstanding man in this field."

Rural Roads to Security, in time, became the companion volume to the *Manifesto on Rural Life,* and both remain to this day basic documents of the Catholic rural life movement.

At the end of March, 1939, Ligutti wrote the new bishop of Bismarck concerning his dilemma about the NCRLC executive secretaryship and his Granger pastorate. He knew, too, that the executive secretary of the National Catholic Welfare Conference wanted the NCRLC located within the national headquarters in Washington, D.C. Ligutti also knew that Msgr. Michael J. Ready wanted the NCRLC but *not* Ligutti. At this stage Ryan, Muench, Mulloy, and others insisted that Ligutti become the executive secretary, and they were more than happy to forego the NCRLC moving to Washington. It was the almost unanimous thinking among the Conference leaders that it should remain in the Midwest.

While Ryan and Ready were discussing this matter, Ligutti was again thinking of taking a small rural parish. He consulted his friend Fr. Francis Gilligan of St. Paul, who advised him to remain in Granger. As Ligutti was deeply involved in the rural-life apostolate, Gilligan, professor of moral theology at the St. Paul Seminary, St. Paul, was dedicated to the work of the National Catholic Interracial Conference in Minnesota's Twin Cities, and the two men became close friends through their mutual friend Fr. James Byrnes.

On May 7, 1939 in the Hotel Lowry in St. Paul the die was cast. Ligutti was elected executive secretary of the NCRLC, and that night he asked himself in his diary, "I wonder if I made a mistake." He continued as pastor of Granger and fulfilled the office of executive secretary by traveling between Des Moines and St. Paul by train about once monthly. On October 23 he called upon his superior, Bishop Gerald Bergan, for advice. The bishop advised him to undertake one or the other task, but he did not think he could adequately carry out both. On November 13 he wrote in his diary, "This is the day when I fully decided to move to Des Moines. *Quod Deus adjuvet.*" He closed the last day of the year with four short words in his diary: "Roasting chestnuts. *Deo Gratias.*"

Ligutti resigned his parish on January 1, 1941 after fifteen happy and successful years as a country pastor. He lived simply and poorly in Des Moines until he finally received approval from the executive board of the NCRLC to purchase the present NCRLC headquarters at 3801 Grand Avenue. The NCRLC began to grow with Ligutti, who, at age forty-five, breathed flesh and blood into the organization. He immediately became propagandist, preacher, crusader, public relations director, and spiritual father of the Conference. He took to the road to spread the gospel of Catholic rural life. No high school, college, seminary, motherhouse, or clergy conference was too large or small to announce the good news. His message was simple and direct. He would capture the attention of his audience with an opening folksy verse:

> A garden and a cow
> A smokehouse and a sow
> Twenty-four hens and a rooster
> And you'll have more than you usta'.

Audiences began to listen. He enunciated the philosophy of the NCRLC in a simple phrase: "Christ to the Country — the Country to Christ." On this theme he would elaborate repeatedly, developing three central points of his message: First, "Farming has to develop in accord with overall development, economic and social, of a country or a region." Second, "The center of all welfare and the center of all planning should be the family." Third, "Production will come when purchasing power of the poor is increased. Agricultural production went up only when purchasing power of the poor had gone up." And, at times, he would inject a note of earthly philosophy, such as he did before an audience in Fargo, North Dakota, in 1941, when he said, *"Ora et labora* — and use a lot of fertilizer!"

One would need a computer to itemize the number of speeches and the places the energetic priest visited throughout the next twenty years as a "circuit-rider" of the gospel of rural life. He advocated all that was good, true, and beautiful about Christianity and the United States — a good share of which he learned from his experience as pastor of Granger. In one of his diaries — long before the ecumenical era — he recorded, "Spoke at Drake University. Received $100.00. Largest fee I ever received in my life!" He did not care about the fee, for him the audience was always more important.

During these early years he was constantly plagued with a problem that would nag him as long as he was executive secretary, and later, executive director, of the Conference. He knew his abilities in the realm of ideas and planning, just as he knew his weakness in the area of management and office structure. He was constantly searching for someone to help direct the office. His overriding problem was the inability to secure the right man for the office job. This would always be Ligutti's Achilles' heel. The central problem was caused by the nature of operating a national office. He did, however, succeed during this period in attracting the genius of Fr. William Gibbons, S.J., a professor of economics at Fordham University. Gibbons, an excellent research scholar, became an associate of the Conference and presented some of the finest documentation that has ever been produced by the Conference. His most notable contribution was the organization and successful completion of the Blue Ridge Summit Conference that drafted the blueprint for the NCRLC's subsequent efforts and projects. Few people recognized and appreciated better Ligutti's labors during the 1940's. In a 1973 letter Gibbons stated:

> The current breed of social-activists and protestors who use some church-related groups as cover for their demonstrations and protests, and on occasion for definitely illegal and/or uncanonical behavior, could learn much from men like Monsignor Ligutti. He especially long worked patiently, and frequently behind the scenes, to improve man's lot on earth as well as hereafter. If the Church has better relations with certain international organizations and some govern-

ments today than it did three decades ago, much of the credit is due to him and to those he encouraged to work quietly, at times in the face of misunderstanding from fellow Catholics....

The current problems in world agriculture and food supply, which are being noted by FAO as well as by authorities here [Washington, D.C.], forcefully draw attention to the timeliness of the efforts made by Monsignor Ligutti to further rural development and to improve farming practices everywhere.

One of the prayers Ligutti frequently used during these years revealed his compassion for his brother-man. He used the prayer of Reynolds at many banquets, convocations, and conventions. It read:

Dear Lord:

Be kind to Little People everywhere,
They are so lost, so herded here and there;
They stumble blindly along war-torn roads,
Bewildered, docile, sometimes carrying loads
Of household goods, more often a small child
Who has forgotten he once played and smiled;
They stand on piles of rubble, once their homes,
And burrow in dark caverns like old gnomes;
They never have expected much of life,
Some bread, a hut, freedom from fear and strife;
Not theirs the blame of war, and yet they pay
With everything they have, day after day;
Oh God, the Little People are so thinly worn,
Their shoulders sag, for too long they have borne
The yoke of war. Speak to the hearts of men
That Little People may not pay again.

During these early years as NCRLC executive director, Ligutti was also forced to deal with the question of what was coming to be called the population explosion — a problem he would face the rest of his life. His travels throughout the world convinced him that the lack of knowledge of proper land-use created a world food shortage and thus aggravated the population problem. In one speech, delivered during the Jefferson City, Missouri, convention of the Conference, he bluntly asked: "Can science prove that God is not provident, omnipotent? Or are pseudoscientists the ones who are ignorant?" On the same theme, speaking before five hundred Protestant clergymen in Des Moines in 1946 and pointing out that more than 50 per cent of rural America was unchurched, he said:

> Let the Church in America take a greater interest in America's nursery, that is, in the countryside. Farming must become more and more efficient but the path of efficiency is not that which dumps more and more people into cities. Trends are not inevitable and we must know them and we must try to shape them to the best interest of human beings.

He did more than speak, however, during these years. The Conference published over forty booklets, pamphlets, and leaflets under his supervision; these sold well into the millions of copies. Perhaps the most successful was the beautiful *Rural Life Prayerbook,* published in 1956 and edited by Fr. Alban J. Dachauer, S.J. Ligutti also began a monthly paper for the conference called the *Christian Farmer,* a worthy successor to Bishop O'Hara's original newsletter entitled *Saint Isidore's Plow*. Ligutti also wrote many articles on rural life, poverty, land tenure, and related subjects for daily newspapers, religious magazines, professional publications, and journals of opinion. Between 1937 and 1960 he assisted in planning and executing twenty-one NCRLC conventions, most of which were centered in the Midwest but some were as distant as Richmond, Virginia, and Boston.

"Rural-lifers," Bishop Bartholome once remarked, "always have an exciting time at their conventions. There is always a great deal of discussion and argumentation. They are an 'alive' people." Ligutti, needless to say, was always at the center of each discussion and argument. He made the conventions vibrant with his knowledge, wit, and intellectual stimulation.

Ligutti used two other principal means of propagating Catholic rural life, the radio and congressional hearings. Apart from his own distributist leanings that he developed in Granger, he was also an avid student of papal documents, as his speeches and writings reveal. At all times he was vitally concerned with what we have come to call in later years, "the quality of life."

Speaking before a joint congressional committee in 1949, he described the "hookworms" of the American family:

> Sales pressure has created an artificial demand for keeping up with the Joneses. Lack of proportion in spending, inability to manage one's income and to plan for future needs and emergencies, are hookworms of the low-income group. Beautiful radio and television sets may be found in homes

where the diet is woefully deficient. Purchases on time at high interest rates are not healthy for any family.

In 1951 he took his message to the press in response to a charge that Catholics were maneuvering and planning to push Protestants off the land:

> The Catholic population in the United States is only six per cent rural-farm whereas eighteen per cent of the general population is rural-farm. We Catholics desire to become normal Americans. In our democracy we have every right to seek and achieve a normal rate of rural constituency. The plan to strengthen Catholics in rural America does not call for pushing Protestants off the land.

Few social issues escaped his grasp. Again appearing before a joint congressional committee on the economic report of Congress in Washington on October 21, 1949, he pointed out two types of human production, one spiritual and the other material. Then he continued:

> Unless a balanced production is achieved at the same time in both fields, poverty is the result. No person, family or nation is rich if it possesses only material goods and no person, family or nation can be said to be spiritually rich unless a fair basis of material wealth is present. Working for the attainment of either material or spiritual wealth while forgetting the other makes the final attainment an empty victory. Minimizing or underrating the importance of either results in a lopsided social structure ready to crumble at the slightest disturbance. It is not necessary, as some claim, to lose social freedom in order to gain material freedom. Material efficiency will not be affected by a recognition of the need for concomitant spiritual efficiency.

In another address, delivered at the Fordham Mission Institute in January, 1955, Ligutti returned to the theme that was the cornerstone of his life's work:

> The problems of the world today are the problems of the land and of the people on the land. Actually, if we examine the problems of the world today, whilst undoubtedly we have ideological problems, problems of philosophy.... in the final analysis the problems of people and of nations are related very closely to the land; access to the land on the part of people, no matter where that land might be; land use; land conservation; the proper cultivation of the land for the production of the things that human beings

need on a fundamental basis, and then, the problems of the people on the land.

During these years of Ligutti's ceaseless activity as executive secretary of the NCRLC, events were taking place in his native diocese that would ultimately have an influence on future decisions. On February 9, 1948 Bishop Bergan, his close friend and supporter, was appointed archbishop of Omaha. A month later Edward C. Daly, O.P., was appointed bishop of Des Moines. This change had a profound influence on Ligutti's life and work. In spite of the difficulties he endured with his new superior, Ligutti continually manifested a truly Christian respect for life and living, for superiors and subordinates. This faith shone through in a homily he delivered at the NCRLC convention in Davenport, Iowa, in 1954. He said:

> All works of man, personal or social, physical or intellectual, must be guided in their concept and execution by Christian principles, i.e., by the natural and divine positive law, written in the hearts of men or proclaimed by revelation. The results of human action must also be measured by these same standards. The basic reasons for this are the two fundamental facts: God is God and His divine nature is immutable. Man's relation to God and man's relation to man in their essential relationships extend from eternity to eternity.

During 1948, his fifty-third year, Ligutti delivered over two hundred lectures in the United States, Canada, and other parts of the world. This was the barometer of the pace he was keeping throughout the decade. His energy knew no bounds; his zeal prevented him from saying no. Some selections from these many addresses give an insight into the expanding horizons that this midwestern priest was not only grasping himself but with him other leaders and members of the NCRLC. At times a new thought, a new approach, flashed through his remarks, revealing the insights that he himself was developing as the NCRLC executive director. At the seventh annual meeting of the Soil Conservation Society in New York City in 1948, he said:

> Present day *homo sapiens* is not to consider himself the first or last step in the human ladder. We owe much to the past and to the future. All we have today is not all for today. What tomorrow will have should be partially built today. This applies to culture and agriculture, to soil and souls.... Only an adolescent mentality looks upon soil conservation as a discovery of the twentieth century.

He was, in a word, an ecologist long before the problem reached national attention. He continued the same thought in an address entitled "The Land of Golden Opportunities" delivered at the NCRLC's Boston convention in 1951. He said, "The secrets of making good in the countryside are: Vision — willingness to work, long term views, desire to serve church and state.... I contend that the countryside where there is space, light and air helps you rear a better family." He repeated the same philosophy at the Sioux Falls, South Dakota, NCRLC meeting on October 26, 1956. There his words were marked with pathos: "I am one of a fading number of people in the United States, from eight to six to three millions. We farmers may eventually be as scarce as the buffalo on the prairies. I hear, so many things, and I even worry about prices of what I have to sell and cost of what I have to buy, about taxes and schooling."

In another undated speech delivered during this period, he returned to his attitude toward the land and to the people of the land when he declared:

> Christianity does not exist in a vacuum. It is found in the minds and hearts of the faithful and, through them, in their environment. Rural people live a different way of life from that of their city cousins. It is necessary, therefore, to attend to the peculiar features of the rural way of life and to bring that way of life completely under the benign influence of Christ and His grace. This is a particularly rewarding task because country people have long been especially responsive to Christian ideals. Once thoroughly Christianized, the rural way of life is truly magnificent.

Nothing, perhaps, so openly exposed the soul of Ligutti during this period than his remarks before the Iowa Nurserymen's Association:

> If I were to choose another profession other than the one I am engaged in, I certainly would want to be a gardener. I love to work with my hands in the good earth. I feel every exhilaration when I kneel among my garden, weeding or just admiring a blossom or a fruit.... I look upon the good earth as the greatest material gift of God to mankind. We urge soil conservation and proper use of the land as a duty in conscience. We believe that God blesses the farmer and the nurseryman as a special mission because they are the direct partners with God in creation.

In 1948 Ligutti published a pamphlet entitled "What, Where and Why of the National Catholic Rural Life Conference?" It not only spelled out the underlying aims and objectives of the Conference but also set his own thinking in perspective. In this he was faithful to his mentors O'Hara and Muench. He wrote, "The object of this Conference shall be to strengthen and develop Catholicity in the rural districts and to promote the general welfare of the rural apostolate." This remained his personal aim and ambition throughout these years.

Another significant event occured earlier in 1938. Ligutti was among the half-dozen speakers invited to address the first annual convention of the American Catholic Sociological Society. In his address entitled "The Rural Problem," he approached his audience with the broad spectrum of American culture. He said:

> I would say that American sociological problems are not only exclusively urban or all exclusively rural. I am sure we all agree in stating that the problems are inter-allied and that any attempted solution should take into consideration that which both rural and urban life have to offer.

He then presented the problems of that time as he viewed them — so similar to present problems — as follows:

1. Loss of the ownership of productive property by the many.
2. An increase in proletarian mentality.
3. The selfish materialism of an unregulated capitalistic system.
4. The hopeless mental attitude of the ones who believe that a system of rich and poor is a necessity in the United States.
5. The pharisaical pride of the *post hoc ergo proper hoc* gang who say: "The American system has made us prosperous."
6. The self-satisfied belief that our standards of living are so superior.
7. The human biological decadence occurring in the United States at the present.
8. The vanishing freedoms of the individual, family, and civic body.

Ligutti was not content, however, only to pose questions. He continued to seek answers from professionals in related fields. During these years he wrote a distinguished professor at a university agricultural school, asking for a definition of the "family farm." He received this reply:

Man's Relation to the Land

I have found the *definition* I think you want...: "A *family farm* is a socio-economic institution in which the capital, labor is distributed among the members of the family and community. Size of the farm is not important; relationship to the community is the determining factor."

The executive director of the NCRLC stuck to that definition. In 1954 he advised farm youth to "work for yourselves." He praised the independence that accompanies farming and its united-family possibilities. "Too many young people," he said, "do not hold up the idea of independence." In 1950 he urged a group of farmers in Kansas City, Missouri, to support by investments their own consumer, producer, and service cooperatives. "The farmer," he said, "who shows himself completely capable of handling crops and livestock too often feels completely helpless when it comes to investing his cream check or surplus capital." In 1955 he returned again to the subject so close to his heart when he said that the nation needed more Catholic farmers and less farmers who were Catholic:

> The Christian farmer looks on farming as a good life in this world and preparation for an eternal good life in the next. Even if someone in my parish gave generously to the Church and was kind and good, I would not consider him a Catholic farmer unless I found him ready to help anyone in the community, Catholic or not.

Luigi Ligutti used not only the press, radio, congressional hearings, and the public platform during these years. He also used his pen in personal correspondence to make friends for the rural apostolate. His correspondence was voluminous. Few details, few references of rural life escaped his attention. A birth or death in a former parishioner's family occasioned a note. An attack against the Church evoked an immediate letter to the editor. Friends and associates received his treasured "travel letters" and his observations on the changing conditions of Church and State throughout the world. Reports of these conditions were duly and dutifully dispatched to the Vatican through the office of the then Msgr. Giovanni Battista Montini.

One particular letter Ligutti treasured was from Senator Robert Taft of Ohio. He wrote the distinguished senator that he was praying for his recovery in June, 1953. The senator's administrative aide informed him on July 3 that the letter he received in reply was the last that Taft personally signed before his death.

The senator wrote, "I received your letter of June thirtieth and I am most grateful for your interest in my health and your prayer for my recovery. I am grateful for the kind words you use about my course in public life."

Another letter he treasured came from the office of the Vice-President of the United States, dated January 17, 1961. He wrote the defeated presidential candidate that year and offered his continued support and encouragement. In return Richard Nixon replied:

> A message of congratulations after winning an election, is, of course, always appreciated. But nothing could have meant more to Mrs. Nixon and to me than to receive such a warm and thoughtful message after losing. In the years ahead as we look back to 1960, the disappointment of losing the closest election in history will fade into the background. But your act of thoughtfulness will always remain close to our hearts.

Nothing, perhaps, so pleased Ligutti during these years than the statement, "Man's Relation to the Land." It was the first ecumenical statement in the United States, drafted and agreed upon by religious leaders of the Catholic, Protestant, and Jewish faiths; signed by twelve Jewish, thirty-five Protestant, and thirty Catholic leaders in rural sociology. It remains to this day a charter of principles and aims of religious teaching concerning the land and the people on the land. For Ligutti it was a permanent landmark in the rural apostolate, for he was one of the chief architects of the document. It was widely distributed and published and received favorable comments in the general and religious press.

The statement was in the area of ecology at least two generations ahead of its time. It stressed not only man's stewardship of the soil as a servant of God but emphasized man's use of the land for future generations. Another principle enunciated in the document still remains to be implemented, even though the words were written in 1945: "Emphasize a special program of enlistment and training in secondary, liberal arts, technical and professional schools for professional service to the rural community." Generations yet unborn will come to realize the wisdom of this far-ranging and far-sighted statement.

During these productive years Ligutti was actively engaged in organizing and sometimes directing rural life institutes for pastors and seminarians throughout the county. Several of the more successful of these were held at St. John's University, Collegeville, Minnesota, under the able leadership of Fr. Martin Schirber, O.S.B. Such institutes brought together hundreds of rural life leaders, clerical and lay, from at least forty states and Canada. One young man present at such a workshop proved to be a constant friend and supporter of the NCRLC as well as, for some time, a member of the executive board. He was Msgr. George G. Higgins, the successor of Msgr. John A. Ryan and Fr. Raymond A. McGowan in the Social Action Department of the National Catholic Welfare Conference.

The initial institute was the brain child of Father Schirber and served as a prototype of similar institutes throughout the Midwest in the coming years. Ligutti was as grateful to Schirber for his efforts as Schirber was cognizant of the benefits that accrued to the NCRLC and area rural life leaders. These institutes aided not only the participants' spiritual needs but also their pressing temporal needs. Fr. Colman Barry, O.S.B., historian of St. John's Abbey, wrote:

> The first real rural life summer school for priests and leaders was held at St. John's in 1939. Father Martin Schirber, O.S.B., of St. John's, assumed directorship of these schools, and sessions were held throughout the country in the 1940's. At St. John's, rural life schools were held from 1941 to 1944, in 1946 and 1953. Agricultural leaders from the fields of government, education and state agencies participated, and the sessions served as a rallying point for all groups concerned with rural problems.

In regard to his own thinking concerning these institutes, Ligutti expressed his philosophy in an article entitled "Cultural Erosion" that appeared in 1950. He wrote:

> It would be well for any group to take stock, to survey, to examine the causes, to face the facts and decide on a course to pursue.... It is high time to state again the aims of education, to redefine what constitutes education. It would also be well to survey the results achieved by our Catholic colleges for the rural districts where they have had their beginning.... Now that changes in orientation will not be deemed too scandalous or revolutionary, we make a plea for a small share in the facilities of our Catholic colleges in rural districts. Give our rural people a break.

Along the same line he was on the defensive in the public eye. In answer to the question that there were too many American farmers, he took to KSO Radio in Des Moines in February, 1948:

Yes, there are too many farmers, but there are not too many or even enough farmers in America today — if farming is defined as a noble Christian profession and the farm home as the natural and best place for a family to live. At once I hear a storm of protesting words — not realistic, uneconomic, against the trend, one who would turn back the clock of civilization. I am swamped, but I emphatically proclaim: I believe there should be more farm families in the United States on a full-time and part-time basis because of economic, social, and religious reasons.

He emphasized the same point before a joint congressional committee in Washington on December 21, 1949. He said, "Production is not an end in itself. Unless human beings benefit thereby it is void of real significance. In order to achieve human dignity they must be self-sufficient."

These years of activity sometimes reached a feverish pitch and yet, in keeping with the sermon he had delivered as a seminarian at St. Mary's in Baltimore, Ligutti managed to "keep cool." He was also practicing ecumenism long before most American Catholics even knew how to spell or pronounce the word. He was speaking in Methodist and Lutheran churches; he was addressing Protestant students on university campuses; he was inviting Protestant clergymen and their wives to the national conventions of the NCRLC. At a luncheon given in honor of Protestant clergymen during the 1942 NCRLC convention in Peoria, he brought down the house by opening his remarks, "My dear fellow heretics!" At Grailville he conducted a retreat for Protestant clergymen and their wives in the late 1940's. In Des Moines one of his closest friends, Arthur Kirk, was the son of the same Protestant divine whom Bishop Austin Dowling cited as one of the best classical scholars.

On one occasion he asked a friendly bishop whether or not he could speak in a Protestant church in the latter's diocese. The wise and learned prelate — Archbishop Joseph Schlarman — replied, "Why do you ask the question? If you ask, you force me to answer. It is so much better when you simply act and do not ask questions." During these years one finds such entries in his diaries: "We Catholic priests are too narrow; we must be more open and broadminded," or "There is a great deal that the Catholic clergy can learn from our Protestant brothers."

Ligutti's ecumenical spirit manifested itself also through his interest and collaboration with rural life agencies of other Churches.

He assisted them financially with the meager funds at his command; he helped in their organization and planning, as more than one would attest. "Christ to the Country" was more than a slogan; it was his way of life. Nothing exemplified this concern better than his association with CROP, a program initiated by the Church World Service, Division of Overseas Ministries of the National Council of Churches. CROP was founded by the Rev. John D. Metzler in 1948. From its inception Ligutti was actively engaged in its program of distributing nutritional food to underdeveloped countries. In its twenty-five year history CROP has distributed over $60,000,000 in aid to the poor and oppressed. Through the efforts of Ligutti a fair share — more than a fair share — of these funds were distributed to suffering Catholics. By such activities Ligutti not only built bridges and made lasting friends among other religious leaders but he also aided his fellow Catholics.

At this time, in the early 1950's, Ligutti's ecumenical activities were better known and appreciated among Christians of other Churches than among his own. One of the best testimonies this writer received came from Dr. Stanley Hamilton, a retired minister of the Church of the Brethren. In July, 1973, Dr. Hamilton wrote:

> I first met Msgr. Ligutti in August, 1938 at Antigonish, N.S., while watching the Highland Games. My wife and I were there as members of a tour visiting St. Francis Xavier Univ., their extension studies and the cooperatives.
>
> I was leaning against our old Chevy when a tall, well set up priest came along, put out his hand and said, "My name is Ligutti."
>
> "Ah," I replied, "Granger, Iowa." I had read about his work with housing and community development at Granger. We have been friends ever since. Finding that we were rural minded and favored the family farm we began to correspond and exchange ideas.
>
> In October, 1942, along with some other Quakers I attended the annual meeting of the National Catholic Rural Life Conference, in Peoria, Ill., at the invitation of Msgr. Ligutti. While there several of the Protestants got together in a small group and the idea of forming a Rural Life Association was explored.
>
> Msgr. Ligutti agreed with us, and helped. On December 11-12, 1942, a conference was held at Earlham College, Richmond, Indiana. Representatives of the Church of the Brethren, the Society of Friends, the Mennonite Church and

others interested attended, some 125 in all. Msgr. Ligutti attended, spoke forcefully and helped get the group going. There followed frequent exchanges of ideas and encouragement by correspondence.

In October, 1943, at Wm. Penn College, Oskaloosa, Iowa, during a regional conference of the Rural Life Association, Msgr. Ligutti spoke at a session in the college chapel. He said, "Whether you are Catholic, Quaker or whatever, you may attend church regularly, say your prayers faithfully; yet if you go out the other six days, shove people around, use your elbows and claws to get ahead... that's the kind of person you'll be. *You become what you do.* Then you build a philosophy to explain it and a theology to defend it."

Seldom do such tributes come to a man in his lifetime. By a strange coincidence, however, similar words were used by a later collaborator with Ligutti in 1974. Speaking with this writer at the Ramada Inn in Washington, D.C., on February 26, 1974, Fr. James Vizzard, S.J., said, "I have known many men and women in high places. I would count Ligutti as one of the ten greatest men that I have ever known."

Ligutti's ecumenism was well known outside the Catholic Church during these early days. Before a rural life meeting of pastors in Vermont in January, 1951, Dr. Charles McConnell of Boston University said about Ligutti:

> I am proud of the great Roman Catholic Church for its interest in the soil, and I count it one of my privileges to be a friend of Father Ligutti. I have had him in our theological seminary. He stands up there and pounds the desk and says, "If you Protestants leave the country, what are you yelling about if we come in." That's what he said; exactly what he said. And I am for him. I agree with him one hundred per cent. As for the Catholic Encyclicals and Manifesto of Country Life — why, we teachers have got them on our shelves.

Another letter Ligutti treasured came from the then Msgr. Giovanni Montini, Undersecretary of State of the Vatican, who asked him to draft a speech that Pope Pius XII would deliver to the First International Congress on Rural Life in 1951. It was but one of over a hundred letters that would pass back and forth between Montini and Ligutti in the coming years. Ligutti's response to Montini's request reveals his thinking as executive director of the NCRLC. On June 3, 1951 Ligutti forwarded four suggestions to Montini:

1. Greater consideration must be given to the economic-social and religious problems of the most neglected group of people in the world, i.e., the agricultural population. In the Far East and in Latin America particularly they form a depressed proletariat that may lend an ear to false promises. The Church may well take the leadership at the present as she did in the days of the early missionaries.
2. Each country and even various parts in each country present special problems due to physical, traditional and cultural conditions; therefore no one solution can be applied universally. Evident injustices in land tenure, or standards of living, etc., must not be continued just because they happen to exist and happen to be deeply entrenched in the economic and social structure of a country.
3. Soil, water and forest conservation are greater needs today because of the increasing world population.
4. The devotion to St. Isidore, patron of farmers, should be encouraged among farm families. Seminarians destined to work in rural territories should be made conscious of the problems, needs and possible solutions in their future pastoral work. In dioceses where there is a rural population it would be well to designate a priest specifically trained for this task.

Perhaps no tribute brought more joy and satisfaction to Ligutti than a letter from a young lady written in 1951. It manifested the lasting results of his words and efforts, and so he interpreted it. She wrote:

> I remember you, Monsignor, from the times you came down to the Co-operative League that used to be on 12th Street in New York. I wasn't a Catholic then. Something about you touched me and it, though undefinable, was one of the things that I think helped bring me into the Church, and since my conversion I have tucked you into my evening prayers for the Church.... The excuse for writing is that I am entering the convent. The Missionary Sisters of Our Lady of Africa.

Ecumenism, however, was not his only interest during this period of his life. There always existed a strong affinity between the NCRLC and the Liturgical Conference and this Ligutti promoted as best he could. For several years he served as a member of the executive committee of the Liturgical Apostolate. He kept in the closest contact with its officers and directors, dating back to the days of Dom Virgil Michel, O.S.B., and numbered among his friends Virgil's successor, Fr. Godfrey Diekmann, O.S.B. He was saddened when he learned that Cardinal Samuel Stritch of Chicago had forbidden his priests to attend the Evanston meeting of the World Council of Churches. Ligutti was even more grieved when he learned that the cardinal had severely reprimanded his friend Msgr. Joseph P. Morrison for an address the latter delivered in favor of the vernacular in the liturgy.

Such opposition, however, did not daunt Ligutti. His love for the liturgy grew out of his love for the land. During the years of his directorship, the NCRLC published more than a dozen leaflets and brochures concerning the relationship between liturgy and the land. Schlarman was one collaborator; Emerson Hynes was another, along with others throughout the Midwest. He grasped every prayer or thought that would identify land and liturgy; these he collected as a busy bee his honey. One such prayer from the Byzantine liturgy he found during his travels in Jerusalem:

> Blessing of Grain and Sowing
>
> O Lord our God, we have asked and received of thy most rich and pure hand this grain now before thine eyes. We beseech thee that it be put in thy care, O Lord. For we would not risk burying it in the bosom of the lifeless earth, if we did not look to the command of thy might telling the earth to give birth, and send forth sprouts and give the farmer a crop and bread to eat. So now, we implore thee, O our God, hear our suppliant prayer: open to us thy great treasury, heavenly and good, and pour out upon us thy blessing, till we say: enough — according to thy truthful promises. Drive away from us all insects which eat the fruit of our land and remove all the punishments which we have justly deserved by our sins, sending the abundance of thy mercies upon all thy people, by the grace and compassion of thy only Son and his love for human kind; Who together with Thee and thy all Holy Spirit, the Good and Giver of life is blessed: now and forever and unto ages of ages. Amen.

About this time he also became a friend of the Lutheran theologian Dr. Jaroslav Pelikan through their mutual interest in the Church's liturgy. Pelikan, subsequently said:

> I have long believed that . . . Christian doctrine and Christian worship must continue to have a close relation to the natural

processes of creation, (not merely to sex!), and the Roman Catholic liturgy and theology, including moral theology, in the United States have suffered as a consequence of having lost that relation.

One other apostolate drew a share of Ligutti's time in this period. He became a friend of the Ladies of the Grail from their arrival in the United States and remained their close friend and collaborator. In 1939 Dr. Lydwine van Kersbergen and Dr. Alberta Lucker attended an international Pax Romana Congress in Washington, D.C. Bishop Bernard J. Sheil, the auxiliary of Chicago, invited them to establish a Grail foundation in that archdiocese. In November, 1939, Bishop Sheil cabled the group about the availability of Doddridge Farm in suburban Chicago. At this time Cardinal George Mundelein officially invited the Ladies of the Grail to come to the archdiocese. The group came to Doddridge Farm, Libertyville, and worked closely with liturgical and social-action groups in the Chicago area. Shortly after their arrival Dr. van Kersbergen became a vice-president of the NCRLC.

From the beginning Ligutti advised the Ladies of the Grail to leave Doddridge Farm, calling it "a place where a carrot could not grow." He urged them to see Archbishop John McNicholas of Cincinnati who immediately took them under his wing. The Grail bought a "gentleman's farm" in Loveland, Ohio, twenty miles from Cincinnati. With the assistance of Ligutti and other friends, "Grailville" developed into one of the important liturgical rural centers in the United States, attracting many friends and families to the area. One such family was Mr. and Mrs. Daniel Kane who remained life-long friends of the Grail.

In later years Dr. van Kersbergen wrote:

> Monsignor Ligutti was instrumental in getting for us a large farm in Cornwall on the Hudson, in New York State, (two hours drive outside New York City, a magnificent place). His interest, his sound advice, his vision, his lectures, etc., have helped us greatly in the U.S.A., especially to make Grailville (with forty acres of good farm land) a dynamic center of the lay apostolate.

Rural life, liturgy, ecumenism, and the lay apostolate did not exhaust the monsignor's concerns. He was also watching with close attention developments at the newly-organized United Nations. Little did he then realize how these developments would shape the course of his future life. In these closing years of the

1940's, his was one of the few Catholic voices that sounded in behalf of the organization founded in San Francisco in 1945. The recent Vatican observer to the United Nations, Msgr. Alberto Giovannetti, rightly stated in 1973: "It would be safe to say that there would be no presence of the Catholic Church in any aspect of the work of the United Nations were it not for the important and decisive role played by Monsignor Ligutti."

Ligutti's interest in the Food and Agriculture Organization of the United Nations will be the subject of a subsequent chapter. At an age when most men are looking to retirement — Ligutti was fifty-three in 1948, the executive director of NCRLC was about to embark on what might be called his most important contribution to the Church and "the little people of the world." Within the coming decade he would experience the most crushing blow of his life.

CHAPTER FIVE

TIME OF TROUBLE

No decade in his life caused Monsignor Ligutti as many headaches and heartaches as the 1950's. It has been mentioned that one of Ligutti's problems was his inability to manage a national office and at the same time carry out his international commitments. This problem he was forced to face in this decade. It was, perhaps, the greatest cross he carried throughout his life. He was a one-man team, which had both its virtues and shortcomings, and this he was now forced to reckon with in many dramatic and heart-rending events.

The troubles began in 1954 concerning the future directions of the NCRLC. Financial difficulties were one aspect, personalities and principles were another. Closely involved in the issues were Fr. Michael Dineen of the archdiocese of Milwaukee; Fr. Edward Ramacher of the diocese of St. Cloud, and Fr. James Vizzard, S.J., of the California province of the Jesuits.

On April 29, 1954 Ligutti called Dineen concerning the office of executive secretary of the NCRLC. On May 10 Father Dineen and Ligutti discussed the operation of the office and the specific duties of the task. The following day Ligutti called Archbishop Albert Meyer, then archbishop of Milwaukee, and asked him about the possibility of Father Dineen coming to work for the Conference. Archbishop Meyer said, "Dineen is not the man suited as executive secretary of the Conference." Nevertheless, both Bishop Ralph Hayes of Davenport, then president of the Conference, and Bishop William Mulloy pressed for Father Dineen's nomination. Both prelates admonished Ligutti, "Don't go off traveling too often and don't stay away too long." Subsequently Ligutti said, "I think they were right, but I did not follow their advice."

During these months Ligutti was receiving substantial gifts and bequests from friends and foundations. These amounted to over $80,000 and this money Ligutti placed in what was called at NCRLC headquarters as the "Santa Claus Fund."

The following October, during the annual rural life convention, Bishop Hayes was in favor of Dineen becoming executive secretary of the Conference. On the other hand, Ligutti did not follow the bishops' advice, but continued to travel hither and yon throughout the world. Dineen was very much in evidence at the Davenport convention and made a good reputation for himself. In spite of Archbishop Meyer and Ligutti, the board of directors of the Conference then appointed Father Dineen executive secretary.

Father Dineen arrived as executive secretary of the Conference on November 1, 1954. The previous August, Ligutti advised Dineen, "Do not spend money unless you have it; spend only what you have on hand." On October 23 Ligutti and Dineen met in Chicago and planned the future of the NCRLC. When Ligutti returned from the Panama Rural Life Congress on November 17, Dineen had already taken charge of the NCRLC office and had established his own *modus operandi*. It was not to Ligutti's liking, but he said nothing. Already Dineen was "on the road," traveling throughout the country, contacting rural life leaders, and striving to make friends for the Conference. Ligutti wrote:

> On December 9 I find that Fr. Dineen had installed a private telephone for his private quarters. This I never did, of course, I just used the telephone of the house. And I was considerably distressed and worried about Fr. Dineen's expenses. Because it cost money to travel, and it cost money to run this organization, and to install telephones, and so forth....

In spite of accounting for all the sums and how they were spent, the principal difference was a matter of how the Conference should be directed. Ligutti firmly believed in small beginnings and build from there. On the other hand, Dineen believed in starting with major concepts and building from them. This was to be a continual point of friction.

Two other factors enter into the conflict of this period. Monsignor Ligutti was becoming more and more an international churchman, being appointed Vatican observer to the Food and Agriculture Organization, a consultant to the Point IV Technical Assistance Program of the United States government, and director of the International Catholic Migration Commission. More and more of his time was consumed by involvement in these and similar international projects.

On the other hand, Father Dineen was striving to build up the NCRLC. His ideas and plans, to be sure, were different from Ligutti's. The latter lived through the years of the Great Depression; the former was accustomed to the years of wealth following the Great War. Their economic sense of values, each so different from the other, were bound to clash. More than that, Ligutti felt that the NCRLC would be built on the shoulders of the poor and struggling farmers. Dineen felt it would be more practical to reach the leaders of agriculture-business in helping the small farmer. Such ideologies were bound to lead to a conflict.

Apart from philosophy, but closely joined to it, was the problem of finances at the NCRLC national headquarters. It was Ligutti's conviction that Dineen was spending too much money; it was Dineen's resolve to make the Conference better known to the general public through a massive public relations program. This conflict lasted from 1954 to 1958, coming to a resolution only at the Fort Wayne board of directors meeting in the latter year.

Throughout these four years, problems mounted. Unknown to himself, the fund established at the national headquarters, entitled the "Santa Claus Fund," was depleted. Ligutti drew upon this fund from time to time. Little did he realize at the time that Father Dineen was also drawing from other funds. By this time Ligutti had empowered Dineen to sign checks and withdraw from savings accounts. Subsequently Ligutti noted that Dineen never accounted for expenditures either to him or the board of directors. He later defended Dineen from several accusations, maintaining only that the latter spent the money on "wild schemes." By 1957 Ligutti discovered that the office was virtually bankrupt, with all money expended from the Santa Claus Fund and no new sources of revenue. He was alarmed.

Ligutti's philosophy of the NCRLC was built on the principle that it should be self-sufficient. Other leaders of the Conference felt that money should be secured anywhere, anyplace, as long as it promoted the Conference. In 1956 the Homeland Foundation, through the generosity of Mr. Chauncey Stillman, and the Catholic Relief Services, through the insistence of the then Msgr. Edward Swanstrom, contributed considerably toward the establishment of a fund to loan money to poor farmers for building homes and purchasing land. This was part of the York County, North Carolina, project.

In 1957 Dineen was busy with another project; namely, the publication of a monthly magazine called *Country Beautiful*, which was to be patterned after *Arizona Highways*. From the very beginning, Ligutti was wary of the project. On August 22, 1957 he wrote Dineen:

> I still believe that a real study of the market for *"Country Beautiful"* is a necessity. I am not convinced with present evidence that the magazine can get a worthwhile subscription list, particularly to draw good advertising income. The more I talk with various people in the game, the more they warn me of the limitations of the market. A real scientific opinion on the subject is an absolute necessity.

Country Beautiful, an attractive rural publication, however, was launched. In August, 1958, Dineen was no longer associated with the NCRLC and devoted full time to the magazine. The handsome publication was inaugurated at the beginning of the sixties and survived about three years. By this time the official treasurer's report for *Country Beautiful* revealed a deficit of approximately $750,000 according to Ligutti's records.

During 1958 Fr. James Vizzard, S.J., and Fr. Edward Ramacher were brought into the operations of the national office in order to stabilize economic problems. Fund-raising efforts were speeded up and at the same time personality problems heightened. Ligutti held no odium toward either priest. Even against the wishes of Father Vizzard's superiors, Ligutti secured the papal medal *Pro Pontifice et Ecclesiae* for this Jesuit.

With the Conference in dire financial straights, Ligutti again appealed to his friend Mr. Chauncey Stillman. The latter agreed to provide a grant of $50,000 to the Conference provided that its members and friends could match the amount dollar for dollar. Many bishops of the Conference were most generous. Diocesan directors bent efforts to secure financial assistance in their areas, and Ramacher traveled the nation raising funds during the six months that Bishop Peter Bartholome had loaned him to the Conference. Through such efforts the debt was gradually erased. Through the good offices of Bishop Leo A. Pursley of Fort Wayne, a generous gift was also received from *Our Sunday Visitor*. In the autumn, 1958, Ligutti entered a period of recuperation in Columbia Hospital, Chicago, where he previously underwent an operation which forced him to miss the Fort Wayne meeting of the board.

In Columbia Hospital Ligutti spent a month, with visits and calls from friends and associates. He was distressed spiritually and physically depressed, but not beaten. He tells his feelings:

After being flat on my back for several weeks, I was allowed to get up and walk around. I used to go for walks throughout the neighborhood. There I would recite my prayers. Over and over again I would say words such as these: "Lord, grant me the love to be friends to my enemies; grant me courage, to stand by my convictions; grant me strength, to do your will."

The course of Ligutti's life was gradually taking shape. As early as the executive board meeting on January 14, 1957 more than one member questioned his work in the international field. A month later Bishop Stephen Wosnicki of Saginaw, Michigan, then president of the Conference, expressed that Ligutti should take more interest in the needs of the Conference than in matters overseas. Wosnicki also revived the old question about the NCRLC becoming a department within the National Catholic Welfare Conference.

At this time Ligutti was juggling balls. He had received the promise of a matching grant from Mr. Stillman; he was trying to direct a national office and carry out his international work; he briefed Mr. Joseph Meisner, public relations director of the NCRLC, in April on the need of better public relations for the Conference. Ligutti was still a sickly man, recuperating from his gall bladder operation. He spent the closing months of 1958 with Fr. Caesare Donanzan in Chicago, with Mr. Stillman in New York, and Christmas with Fr. Leonard Miconi in Reading, Pennsylvania. During these months the financial problems of the Conference were working out, even though Ligutti continued to worry.

He was, knowingly or unknowingly, coming to a crossroads. The previous September he conferred with Montini and others in Rome concerning the permanency of the Vatican observership to FAO. He continued to mull over the fact that the previous November his superior, Bishop Edward Daly, had refused to make him a prothonotary apostolic, an honor requested by the Vatican Secretariat of State. A week later, in November, 1957, he was seriously thinking of residing permanently in Rome, and now, a year following, he was thinking of the same plan.

The events of 1958, as we have seen, were traumatic for both the executive director and the NCRLC. In January Ligutti met with the executive committee in Milwaukee. In March, 1958, he learned that Dineen was considering moving the national headquarters to Fort Wayne, Indiana. Ligutti was opposed to the idea. He saw no major advantage in the move and felt that as a priest of the diocese of Des Moines his roots were sunk so deeply in the soil of southwestern Iowa that there would be no particular advantage in moving the headquarters. On June 18 at the airport in Dallas, Texas, he received a call from Dineen telling him that Bishop Daly had ordered Dineen out of the diocese. This always remained a mystery to Ligutti because Daly never officially informed him of the decision. On July 1, Bishop Bartholome, at the time a supporter of Dineen, told Ligutti to "ride it out." The same day Ligutti sent a memorandum to the people in the national office telling them to do nothing except under orders of Bishop Wosnicki. Such events and surrounding circumstances, might well have wrecked the NCRLC if the charity and prudence of rural life leaders such as Bishops Mulloy, Wosnicki, Bartholome, and Joseph Marling of Jefferson City did not intervene.

The problem came to a head, as mentioned, during the 1958 meeting of the executive committee in the home of Bishop Leo Pursley in Fort Wayne. It was obvious to one and all that the situation in Des Moines could not continue. Dineen had returned to Milwaukee. Ligutti was in Columbia Hospital, Chicago. Vizzard proposed that the position of "director of international affairs" be created for Ligutti. Wosnicki favored that proposal. Bishop Wosnicki accused him of, first, showing partisanship to Italian immigrants and, second, spending more time as an international representative than as a national executive director. By the end of the year Ligutti was thinking more and more of moving to Rome. His dreams had exploded. Shortly after the Fort Wayne meeting, Ligutti wrote in his diary, "Must look upon this as a blessing for me personally and a forward step in the development of the Conference." Although attacked, he was not beaten. A week later, for the first time in his life, he drew up a will, naming his first assistant, Fr. John Gorman, the executor.

In the coming month, the Conference was turning the corner financially. Ligutti, also, was turning a corner personally. He marked his forty-first year as a priest on September 22 and recorded in his diary, "How many graces in one month!"

October, 1958, was autumnal for most Americans, but for Ligutti and the NCRLC it was a second spring. Through Ligutti's intercession with Stillman, the Conference was raising money and coming out of debt. Generous contributions from bishops, organizations, members, and friends of the Conference restored new life and vitality to its operations. Ligutti was recovering his health. *Country Beautiful* was a distinct operation. New personnel were being sought; new directions were being given. Few better expressed the sentiments of the leaders and members of the Conference than that indomitable friend, Bishop Mulloy, who wrote Ligutti as follows on October 14, 1958: "You know very well that I shall do everything in my power for the N.C.R.L.C., and its philosophy, and I am sure that under God's Providence, with plenty of prayer, that it will be blessed with success, both on the National and Inter-national level."

Ligutti, however, had by now turned the corner. On November 27 he had decided, "I want the title of Director for International Affairs." Later, on December 31, he closed his diary for 1958, "I hope there will never be a year like this again in my life — but I am thankful it was thus." As events turned out, the year proved "a blessing for me personally."

In March, 1959, he confided to his diary, "The more I get to know the more I distrust some people." His spirits rose on March 5 when he heard that one of his former assistants, Fr. Paul Marasco, had been named a monsignor. But he was restless. He knew that his days at 3801 Grand Avenue were numbered. On March 19 he left again for Europe and his native Italy. In Rome he talked again with Msgr. Giovanni D'Ascenzi, director of Italian Catholic Rural Life, and Msgr. Pietro Pavan of the Roman curia concerning a proposed encyclical on rural life. Again he had an audience with Pope John XXIII and discussed the proposed encyclical. He dined with Cardinal Montini, who was now the archbishop of Milan, and together they wondered whether or not Shell Oil Company was financing the campaign in *Il Borghese*, discrediting Montini. On June 1 he recorded the death of Bishop Mulloy.

In spite of travels and companions, he continued to worry about the NCRLC. He suffered much and did little. He was becoming weary. On September 1 he noted in his diary, "What a waste of time . . . fighting and doing nothing." By the end of the same month Stillman counseled him to resign and offered him a good retirement policy to continue his international work. A few days later he was in Rome, inspecting his apartment on Via S. Damaso, 15.

During September, 1959, Ligutti had another audience with Pope John during which he again talked about the encyclical on rural life and the Latin American survey being conducted by FERES, the center for sociological studies at Louvain University, Belgium. Canon François Houtart was a former director of FERES.

Ligutti participated in the FAO meetings and went his usual round of calls and appointments. On December 2 he was delighted to note that Msgr. Ernest Primeau had been appointed the bishop of Manchester. The following day he hosted a dinner at Zi Gaetana in honor of his friend Fr. Frederick McGuire, C.M. Two days later he was thinking of Msgr. George Weber of Salina, Kansas, as a possible replacement in the Des Moines office, the first reference to such a thought. A few days later he was visiting Monsignor Pavan and again talking about the rural life encyclical. In mid-December he was greeted by the good news that Bishop John Franz of Peoria would be willing to release Msgr. Edward O'Rourke to serve as full time executive director of the NCRLC. The last day of the year he was in Milan, dining with Cardinal Montini and introducing his young friend Joseph Gremillion to the new archbishop.

There are turning-points in every man's life, and for Ligutti 1959 was one such point. He was planning his permanent residency in Rome. He knew that the years of the NCRLC were behind him. He was assured that O'Rourke and Weber would be worthy successors. He had new and old friends, such as Walter Persegati in Rome and Gremillion in the United States. He returned home in early January, 1960, and visited his former assistant, Father Gorman. He recorded in his diary, "Back in Des Moines — no longer home. Too many heart-breaking experiences." In February he welcomed Father Weber to the national office. He briefed the new executive secretary during the next few days and visited old friends and neighbors. He called upon Bishop Daly who was pleased to know that he had taken up permanent residence in Rome. He recorded his loneliness in packing and leaving, recognizing that he had come to the end of a stage in his life. He traveled to Omaha for a final luncheon with Archbishop Bergan on February 24.

The following day he attended the episcopal ordination of Bishop Primeau in Chicago and had a lengthy conversation with Bishop Joseph Marling of Jefferson City, the new president of the NCRLC. He left the see city of his native diocese on February 25, 1960 and went on to Rome. He immediately moved into the Roman scene and was welcomed by many Vatican officials. He revealed himself still something of a country boy, even though living in a Roman apartment, for on April 25 he wrote in his diary, "Still can't see myself changing to urban life."

He became more international than ever in his apostolate, flying to Madrid for one meeting, to Paris for another, to Geneva for a seminar. He was at home away from home. Whenever he could, he would escape the duties of the Eternal City to return to the provincial area of Udine. He was still the country boy who loved the land and its people, one who had left a slice of his life and love in southwestern Iowa. He was continually in demand as a speaker, recognized as the rural life leader that he was. He promoted the 3-P's in Italy, as he promoted the 4-H groups in the United States. He introduced hybrid corn in Italy; more than one American seminarian recalls Ligutti in the field showing Italian farmers how to plant this special corn.

His home became a mecca for American visitors. His door was always open and he welcomed both the high and the mighty, the lowly and the powerful. Above the door of the home he finally built, he placed a ceramic that read: *Venit hospes — Venit Christus* — "When a guest comes, Christ comes." Ligutti was always faithful to that motto.

In the succeeding years he kept in close contact with the NCRLC, for he was its director of international affairs, a title he used well in Rome. During this period Bishop Marling exerted a strong and influential leadership upon the Conference. He secured the home for Ligutti in Rome and carefully guided O'Rourke and Weber during their early and trying days of leadership in the Conference. Ligutti was always grateful to Marling for his kindly, persuasive, and firm leadership of the Conference. He was, in so many ways, the embodiment of the virtues that Bishop Ryan had displayed in the early days of the NCRLC.

In October, 1960, Ligutti was in Rome, happy and contented. He had found himself after so many years of trial and travel. On December 9 he wrote in his diary, "Last year I was so concerned about Des Moines — now forget it!"

He had guided the NCRLC for almost twenty years. He had left his mark on the nation and on the world of rural affairs. He was opening new avenues and adventures. His coming to Rome was yet another chapter in his life, even though he himself little realized it at the time. His life for sixty-five years had prepared him for the great work that was before him. When most men were about to retire, Ligutti was only about to exert his influence on the international scene. As much as he made the NCRLC, the organization made him. Both were indebted to one another, in good days and bad days. Ligutti remains "Mr. Rural Life" in the Church of the United States.

CHAPTER SIX

TRAVELING WITH A PURPOSE

When Monsignor Ligutti paid a tribute to the memory of his friend Archbishop Joseph Schlarman, he wrote, "he traveled extensively and always with a purpose." Little did he realize that these words applied even more accurately to himself. Another friend, Bishop John P. Treacy of LaCrosse, Wisconsin, frequently and humorously referred to these travels with the remark, "Luigi's up in the air again." One would need a computer to estimate the number of air miles he traveled within the United States and on international trips that carried him to every continent except the Antarctic and almost every nation except Russia.

In the earlier years his apostolate was spreading the philosophy of Catholic rural life. He himself frequently admitted that from these journeys he derived invaluable information. In later years he realized that the problem of displaced persons and emigration after World War II was both alarming and acute. He then winged over Europe as a messenger of hope, an advocate of Christian charity, a promoter of resettlement, and a member of the International Catholic Migration Commission. For over thirty years he was hopscotching around the world, studying farming methods, examining soil, promoting human development, and being a friend and bridge between the local missionary and the director of agriculture and a field representative of the Food and Agriculture Organization. At all times he traveled "with a purpose," which always opened new avenues to explore, adventures to experience, and friends to meet.

At times, too, he went as an invited speaker to international Eucharistic Congresses being, it is believed, the only American priest ever invited to address four of them. He attended the congresses in Rio de Janeiro in 1952, in Barcelona in 1954, in Munich in 1960, and in Bombay in 1964. Other times he was asked by the Holy See to study conditions of the Church in various areas. From such requests came two of his most interesting travel letters, "Sunrise and Sunset," concerning Asia, and "African Safari," concerning what once was called the Dark Continent.

Ligutti's travel letters offer an insight into the personality and thinking of the man who surely must have been, in his generation, the most traveled priest of the United States. The letters portray the Catholic Church throughout the world during the middle decades of the twentieth century.

In the huddled heaps of humanity on a doorstep in New Delhi, as well as in the palaces of presidents, he was always raising questions. In these and other places he found many answers to add to his wisdom. He invariably sought out the wisdom of the peasant, and from a chance visit or twist of a phrase he found at times an answer to an economic, social, or religious problem that lay in the area of rural life. Most of the time he was suspicious, and sometimes less than a little satisfied, with the "elite" schools founded by many religious communities in missionary countries. He continually bemoaned the lack of preparation of missionaries in dealing with the obvious and essential human problems of nutrition, geography, soil conservation, and technical knowledge in rural areas. He was often amazed by the great work performed by zealous and self-sacrificing missionaries whom he looked upon as the spiritual heroes of the twentieth century. More than once Ligutti exclaimed, "If only someone would write the lives of these great men and women of God!"

Two themes recur time after time in all his travel letters. First, he gained an inner strength from these sources and, knowing what he wanted, no human or geographical obstacle prevented him from achieving his purpose. This purpose he expressed in a letter from Amman, Jordan, on January 16, 1952:

> I have gone through country after country and have urged Catholic authorities and institutions to take a greater interest in the economic and social life of the nation. I am making a special plea to Catholic educational and charitable centers for a more practical effort in their work. I am suggesting to hospitals the setting up of training schools for midwives; to high schools the extending of their courses to prepare real practical rural teachers for the villages . . . . If I had my say-so, I would go into the seminaries, both Christian and Moslem, and begin to sell the ideas and the techniques to

the future leaders in the rural districts . . . . If the religious leaders don't want to do it or judge it extraneous to their task, then they can hardly complain if the secular state takes over everything.

Second, he was constantly aware of the presence of God through his heavenly traveling companion, one of St. Isidore's angels. (Once when the patron saint of farmers was attending Mass and his employer was irked because the saint was not plowing, two angels took charge of the plowing and did the work of two men in the time of one man's labor.) He knew he always needed "an angelic companion ready and willing to go into parts unknown," and for this reason before each journey he beseeched St. Isidore to loan him one of his angels. He talked with his Isidorian angel all along the way; he mentioned the escapades of his angelic companion and recounted the angel's reaction to persons and places. Upon returning to the NCRLC headquarters at the end of each journey, Ligutti would first visit the shrine of St. Isidore and his wife St. Maria and give thanks for the loan of the angel and their safe return. In spite of a multitude of distractions, weighty discussions, and strenuous side trips to out-of-the-way places, Ligutti kept his interior calm and peace, realizing through his angelic companion the presence of God in all circumstances. A more skeptical and sophisticated generation will of course write off such devotion as child's play. With Ligutti, however, it was as real and as intimate as the rice paddies he waded through, the dust that blinded his eyes, and the putrid smells of an eastern bazaar that pierced his nostrils.

He revealed the same simplicity of soul in his love and longing for his family and the native soil of Udine. No journey to Italy would be complete without at least a hurried reunion with family, friends, and native surroundings. His writings revealed that his spirit was renewed, his strength restored, and his weary body rejuvenated after a few days among the beloved mountains and rivers of his native land. On July 11, 1952 he wrote:

> When in Rome there is always something else to do, someone else to see — no matter how lingering the stay. I cut off on Wednesday afternoon, July 2, and I hopped over the Appenines to Venice and the Udine-Trieste airfield. Between friends, relatives and brevity of time, it's as bad as elsewhere — or should I say as good as elsewhere, because the hearty welcome and hospitality at the Toffolini villa, the kindliness of dear old Archbishop Nogara and the evoked

memories render all efforts pleasant. A visit to the temple of Our Lady of Graces where my dear mother was wont to lead my youthful steps — in each old lady dressed in black, wearing velvet slippers and a kerchief tightly fitted around the head, I could see my own mother. And I prayed the old prayers while my heart beat as of old . . . with joy and excitement. How marvelous it is that this body of ours can duplicate sensations lost and forgotten for almost one-half a century! So as with the hills, mountain peaks and streams, the laughter or sad countenances of descendants remind one of grandsires and maiden aunts.

This, then, was the background to the travels of a man who after 1940 would spend a great deal of his life "up in the air" and "always with a purpose." Needless to say, he was a good traveler and always enjoyed his journeys, which form the substance of what follows. Although not necessarily chronological, they may fittingly be called "Travels with Luigi."

Ligutti's first trip to Europe since his coming to the United States in 1911 began on July 1, 1939 at the request of the Cooperative League of America. He was commissioned to study the credit unions and cooperatives in the Scandinavian countries and to touch bases with Catholic rural life leaders throughout Europe. He looked forward to the journey both to escape the pressures of the NCRLC presidency as well as to visit his native village and see again the members of his family.

He traveled through Denmark, Norway, Sweden, and Finland, visiting agricultural and cooperative leaders and cooperative farms. He played the role of the typical American tourist at Hamlet's castle in Elsinore and at the tomb of Gustavus Adolphus in St. Eric's Cathedral in Upsala; he visited the late Bishop James Mangers of Oslo and called upon a group of American sisters from St. Louis stationed in Helsinki. He was deeply impressed by the cooperative movement in Scandinavia and he felt that the movement in the United States had much to learn from it.

By boat he went to England, visited the great cathedrals of Durham, York, Coventry, and then boarded a train for Edinburgh. The intrigue of the sixteenth century Scot nobility came to life as he walked the Royal Mile and admired the fortress-castle on the hill overlooking the city.

The grime of Scotland's industrial capital, Glasgow, was excelled only by the poverty he viewed in the shanties of the workers. He did not tarry there, but after only one day took a boat to Belfast. With the natural affinity of the Italian and the Irish (and recollections of his friends Flanagan, Kerrigan, and Morrison) he felt at home in the Emerald Isle. He spent six happy days traveling throughout the cities and villages, again meeting with directors of cooperatives and credit unions, chatting with farmers in their peat bogs, and calling upon officials of Church and State. He came to Galway where he had been invited to speak before the national meeting of the Irish Catholic rural life movement called *Munitir da Tire,* and there for the first time he met Canon John Hayes. The two became instant friends and remained friends throughout their lives. After the convention he delievered addresses in Tralee, Tipperary, Wexford, Dublin, and all those hallowed spots that make Ireland so beloved to both the Irish and visitors.

On July 11, 1939 he crossed the Irish Sea and reentered England which he described as "urban, industrial and ugly." Here he visited Don Luigi Sturzo, then in exile because of the Fascist government of Italy; called on writers like Vincent McNabb, O.P., and Maisie Ward; was thrilled by a visit with the editor of *The Tablet,* Douglas Woodruff, and the historian and essayist, Hilaire Belloc. On July 15 he encountered together with millions of British people a frightening new experience — the first blackout.

He crossed the English Channel to Holland, visiting biodynamic farms and meeting with agricultural leaders. Neither the temper of the people nor the rumblings of war, however, were conducive for much serious discussion and study. He made a hurried visit to Aachen to visit the tomb of Charlemagne and view the statue of Fr. Leopold Kolping. In Belgium he listened with deep foreboding as King Albert pleaded for peace, even though he was hoping against hope that the Nazi fury would listen. At Louvain he attended a meeting of the Belgian National Catholic Rural Life. Here he heard a group of Belgian girls — the equivalent of an American 4-H group — sing psalms concerning rural life. He picked up the music and later it was translated into English and sung at national rural life conventions in the United States. Here, too, he met the future Cardinal Joseph Cardijn for the first time.

From August 24-31 he was traveling with the speed of lightning to escape the already foreseen storm building up over Europe. He made a hurried visit to the French cooperative headquarters near Paris, paid his respects at the office of the Young Christian Workers, witnessed the frenetic and fanatic pandemonium around the American Express office in Paris, and purchased three tickets — by plane, train, and car — to get out of Europe as quickly as he could.

The train brought him to Turin. Here he visited the Salesian Institute, called on friends and agricultural leaders, and then hurried on again to the peace and serenity of his native village of Romans. On September 1, 1939 he entered a personal and world-shattering event in his diary: "It still has the same smell," he said about his native village, and about the world he added, "War declared by the Germans."

He spent a week visiting the old places, the cemeteries (he always had an Italian's special attachment to the graves of family and friends), called upon old acquaintances, and visited places he knew and loved in the surrounding villages and countryside. In Udine he called upon brother priests who were his classmates in the minor seminary and paid his respects to the seminary faculty and the aging archbishop. He put down in his diary a conviction he held throughout his life and found to be true in every part of the world: "Religion rests on its priesthood." Without shame, he noted as he departed his native village and countryside, "I cried."

By train he traveled through Venice, Modena, Florence, and other cities during the following week. He visited families of his Italian families in Granger, bringing photographs of loved ones to those who had not seen them in many years. There were, needless to say, tears of joy and gratitude.

Then with his heart beating with joy, Ligutti arrived for the first time in the Eternal City. He took lodgings at the Minerva Hotel across the piazza from the Dominican church of Santa Maria sopra Minerva. He met Msgr. Giovanni Battista Montini of the Vatican Secretariat of State for the first time. Little did either realize how their lives and work would be so closely intertwined in the coming decades! He held discussions on rural life with officials of the Institute of Agriculture — the forerunner of the Food and Agriculture Organization — and, as he would continue to do throughout his life, paid courtesy calls to Church and State leaders concerned with the problems of rural and human development. Without a doubt, the highlight of this trip (as well as all subsequent visits) was his audience with the Holy Father on September 23. He called it "the day of days" and noted Pope Pius XII's concern about population trends. That night he matter-of-factly wrote in his diary, "Italy and the faith meet each other here."

On October 3 he noted in his diary that Cardinal Mundelein of Chicago had died and that war jitters hung heavily over the Rock of Gibraltar. He asked himself, "Why wars?" For the rest of his ilfe he would ask himself that question privately and in conversation with Dorothy Day of the *Catholic Worker,* Edward Skillin of *Commonweal,* and Eugene McCarthy, later senator from Minnesota, and Harold Hughes, later governor of Iowa. In 1939 he was, however, on the high waters of the Atlantic with time for recollection and reflection. He knew that the war had cancelled his study of the cooperative movement in Europe. From his travels he sensed, too, that a new world was being born. He was a happy man, nonetheless, in the prime of his life at age forty-four.

He landed in New York on October 11, visited his cousins Mr. and Mrs. John Tramontin (both natives of Manazzons), and took the train west to the Spokane NCRLC convention. Bishop Aloisius Muench boarded the train at Fargo and the two talked at length about a papal encyclical on rural life. On October 22 his diary succinctly revealed his sentiments: "Glad to be home in Granger — Good welcome — Resume school and parish duties."

A grateful exhausted world heaved a global sigh of relief when it joyfully received the news of an allied victory in Europe on May 8, 1945. Before the month was out Ligutti was in Washington to confer with the apostolic delegate, Archbishop Amleto Cicognani, concerning the status of cooperatives and credit unions in Italy. He feared they would be either left in shambles following the Fascist defeat or, even worse, fall under the control of Fascist elements in Italian politics. The apostolic delegate advised him to go to Italy himself and study the situation. Ligutti took the train to New York and conferred with Don Luigi Sturzo and Msgr. Patrick O'Boyle, then director of the Catholic War Relief Services. Both agreed that he should go to Italy and pursue this study. Monsignor O'Boyle said that Catholic War Relief Services would help finance the trip.

Throughout the summer and autumn months Ligutti was busy planning the journey, contacting Italo-American societies for relief aid to Italian farmers, and gathering as much information as he could from the Cooperative League of the United States. On New Year's Day, 1946, he arrived in New York, visited Don

Sturzo, and sought his advice. Four days later he noted in his diary that the air fare, one way, was $833.25.

Upon arrival in Rome Ligutti immediately contacted old friends and made new acquaintances, one of whom was Msgr. Andrew Landi of the Catholic War Relief Services. The two were to collaborate on many projects over the coming years. Once again he called upon his friend, the then Msgr. Ernest Primeau, rector of the house of studies of the Chicago Archdiocese, which for Ligutti for many years would be his home away from home.

Ligutti was a busy man in Rome during these weeks. He had a private audience with Pope Pius XII on January 21; held conferences with Church leaders, including Monsignors Montini and Tardini; met with members of the Italian cabinet; delivered personal documents from Don Sturzo to Premier Alcidé de Gasperi; met with relief officials and embassy officials in both the Italian and American governments. He explained his mission to Pope Pius XII and also mentioned his desire for an encyclical letter on Catholic rural life. He noted in his diary that the Pope was afraid of the Communist menace in Italian national life and also that he was enthusiastic about the work being carried out for the displaced persons in Germany (Some historians say that Pius XII was a Germanophile.).

At this time Ligutti called together a joint meeting of representatives of various cooperative Italian groups at Monteccitori on February 27 and acted as chairman of the one-day meeting. He summarized the results of this meeting:

1. It is not opportune to form a union of the cooperative movement in Italy, although some sort of federation is deemed necessary and useful.
2. An Inter-Cooperative Committee was formed to foster the cooperative movement in legislation and mould public opinion, at the same time establishing liaison with other international cooperative movements.
3. The wholesale cooperative of Milan was named the official representative for contacts with cooperatives in other countries.

With this background Ligutti set out on his mission to northern Italy, visiting cooperative headquarters and conferring with their leaders. In Florence he noted that the Socialists controlled the cooperatives while the Christian Democrats did not sponsor any groups. Later in Udine leaders of the Democrats informed him that they did not want him to visit the Socialist cooperatives.

He travelled through Fano, Rimini, Padua, Rivignano, Spilimbergo, Perdernone (the home of his friend Don Lozer), Milan, Turin, and Genoa. He was constantly asking questions.

Ligutti was dismayed by the extent of the ravages of war in his native Italy. Well he realized the work that must be done to restore a healthy economy to Italy. His report to the Vatican Secretariat of State stressed the need of choosing a few young Italians "to spend approximately three months in the United States and/or Canada to study cooperatives." He further recommended the establishment of institutes in about ten regional centers of Italy with "groups of men who know cooperatives and are above partisan politics to explain the philosophy, history, and techniques of cooperatives."

Ligutti returned to Rome for more meetings and interviews. Here he discussed the situation with Msgr. Romolo Carboni, then an official in the Vatican Secretariat of State, and suggested an encyclical letter on the problems of migration. He was present for the creation of the new cardinals by Pius XII on February 16, 1946, including the four Americans, Mooney, Spellman, Stritch, and Glennon. He was happy to meet again with Bishop Muench. He conferred with Bishop Antonio Caggiano of Rosario, Argentina, who promised to speak to the Pope concerning property, land reform, and immigration.

Before returning to the United States he presented a memorandum of his study of Italian cooperatives and credit unions to Monsignor Carboni and made definite proposals to officials of the Italian government. On February 27 he noted in his diary that Bishop Muench was commissioned by the Pope to prepare a draft for an encyclical on rural life. On March 2 he attended a farewell dinner at the Grand Hotel and in his diary thanked God for all that he saw and the people he met. The following day he departed from Ciampino Airport for the United States.

The following two weeks he spent in New York and Washington, reporting on his studies and observations, promoting more Church and Government aid for the dispossessed and displaced persons. He met for the first time a young monsignor in the apostolic delegation named Luigi Raimondi. He also discussed with officials in the United States Department of Agriculture how closer cooperation and collaboration between the Churches and its offices would benefit the victims of post-war Europe. He flew to New York and called again on Don Sturzo, still in exile; the

Italian priest said he would try to assist in drafting some suggestions for an encyclical on rural life. Unfortunately, he never did.

Ligutti left the East on March 15, noting that "so much can be done with the proper Washington contacts" and arrived home two days later. With satisfaction he noted that Bishop Bergan was pleased with his interest in immigration and colonization. He continued to pursue his work on a papal encyclical on rural life and migration and before the end of the month was writing letters to Bishop Muench and others urging their support on this project.

His next long journey began December 22, 1946 and ended on March 9, 1947. Monsignor Ligutti went "down under" to study problems of rural life and meet with agricultural leaders in the island continent of Australia and its neighbor New Zealand. In his letters of this trip entitled "Kookaburra Message," he noted that in 77 days he traveled over 27,000 miles and spent 144 hours "up in the air." "Down on earth" he was interviewed by 23 newspaper representatives, held private conferences with from 10 to 50 people 51 times, delivered 46 addresses to more than 50 people, visited 18 schools, conferred with 19 out of 29 bishops and archbishops, and gave 6 radio broadcasts. All of these experiences he recorded in this series of letters addressed to Mary, his niece, with whose parents he stayed before departing from Los Angeles.

His interest in immigration was sparked in the Australian bush country while sitting in a group of fifty people under the shade of a poinciana tree with the sweet scent of Australia's national flower, the frangipani, hanging heavy in the air. He wrote:

> Last night, a Mr. O'Shaunessy told us all about central Queensland — a veritable mine of natural resources — and yet only half a person per square mile. Until midnight we sat up discussing migrations of people and care of displaced persons. While Australians are quite insular, the present war has taught them that they are a part of the world. What an empire this country could be if enough human beings were here to develop its resources!

Here, too, he revealed his intimacy with nature: "I have made friends with a group of gum trees. I go out and talk to them four or five times a day. They are so responsive." His conviction concerning the relationship between land and civilization was supported by what he had seen in Queensland:

> I am convinced more than ever, that the soil is the only source and support of a permanent civilization. I have seen ghost towns in the mining districts of the United States; now

I see them here at every crossroad. I have watched the rivers of Queensland rush to the sea after the monsoon rains. Millions of tons of soil gone and the big cities growing bigger. I am repeating Monsignor Hildner's expression over and over again: "Keep the bucket of mud out of the bottom of the rivers to prevent floods. And keep that same bucket of mud on top of the hills to keep their fertility."

Ligutti also noted the prejudice practiced by the Australians during World War II against Italian immigrants, about 60 per cent of whom were interned in concentration camps. The result of such excessive nationalism literally wrecked the businesses, the savings, and the lives of thousands of Italo-Australians during this war-time hysteria. Ligutti compared it to the treatment the American government dealt the Japanese-Americans during the same war. "I am becoming convinced more and more," he wrote, "that economic causes are back of anti-racial prejudices and feelings. What United States anti-Semites say about the Jews is just exactly what some northern Australians say about the Italians — same stories, same accusations — only the names changed!"

In Newcastle, the Pittsburgh of Australia, he spoke to a group of high school boys. There he received one of the best answers he ever heard from youth. "I want to live on a farm," said one boy, "because you can have a good life there." In Sydney, the nation's largest city, he was the guest of Cardinal Norman Gilroy at the cathedral rectory. He was deeply impressed by the cardinal who was the son of poor parents and came up the hard way. "Just think," Ligutti exclaimed, "he used to deliver telegrams to Archbishop Kelly whom he succeeded in the see of Sydney!" He registered one dislike of the countryside: "The Australian landscape is [filled] with dead trees standing up everywhere. It's a monument to laziness and an ugly thing — a macabre assembly of corpses with withered arms lifted up to heaven." In general his impressions of the continent reflected his usual optimistic view: "I believe there is plenty of good land for all Australians and many, many more, provided they are willing to work. The world is not too small — it's we men who are too small!"

One of the greatest personal delights of the trip came as a total surprise on one of his last days "down under." He recounted this experience:

Exactly 45 years ago, about the middle of June, two seven-year-old, barefoot boys were sent by the village school teacher to ring the church bell for the 1:00 o'clock assembly.

A clear water stream was too inviting, so the little boys waded into the cool, refreshing waters. Soon they were hidden by friendly bushes. The school teacher waited in vain. It was great fun while it lasted. The end was tragic — some miscreant had stolen most of the skimpy array of clothing. (A teacher's perverted sense of humor!) Covered only by bare necessities the two little boys had to wend their devious way back to the school. Laughter, jeering, giggles — and a tanning without the protective coverage of a geography book. Some of its impressions have disappeared, but the memory lingers on. On last Sunday evening the Melbourne Italian community gave a reception in honor of a visiting "dignitary." One certain man came with his wife and lovely family. He smiled at the dignitary and said, "Do you remember?" Quoth the dignitary, "Do I!" The two little boys met again and talked over old times. There was music by an Italian orchestra — Neapolitan songs — speeches — a splendid group of people loyal to Australia, but very proud of their native land and its culture.

The following year the "dignitary" was traveling again on what he called "the dippy trail." It was not a vacation, nor was it a study of agricultural methods and developments. It was "a mission of mercy" designed "for acquiring greater knowledge of a very grave problem."

Monsignor Ligutti was one of six American priests appointed by the War Relief Services of the National Catholic Welfare Conference to study postwar conditions in Europe with emphasis on the problems and possible solutions the Church in the United States might undertake in solving the plight of displaced persons. Other members of the study-group were Msgr. John Mulroy of Denver, Msgr. Eugene Loftus of Buffalo, New York, Fr. Joseph Gremillion of Alexandria, Louisiana, and Fr. Russell Scheidler of Helena, Montana. They were briefed in Washington, D.C., by Msgr. Edward Swanstrom and Mr. Edward O'Connor of the War Relief Services and given further briefing and last minute instructions at the New York office from Mr. James Norris. The group departed from New York on June 16, 1948.

The choice of Ligutti for this assignment was no accident. He was already nationally known for his interest on behalf of the immigrants through his speeches and writings. The National Catholic Rural Life Conference, under his direction, was an ardent advocate of a just and reasonable immigration policy for the

United States. His own background and personal experiences made him a most suitable choice for this "mission of mercy."

The study group arrived in Frankfurt on June 22 and for the following twenty days traveled throughout Germany and Austria. They were deeply impressed by the sights of the devastating and debilitating effects of the war. Ligutti wrote:

> There is something that just grips my heart every time I walk around a station any place in Europe. On bulletin boards pictures with accompanying notices to trace missing persons. Back of the touching words, the variety of photographs. There are broken hearts, restless nights, prayers and tears. Oh, why should there be any need for wars! Or is there? God would not have given us human hearts if they have to be crushed by needless, purposeless suffering.

From Frankfurt they traveled to Kronberg to visit the apostolic visitor, their friend of many years, Bishop Muench. He spent the afternoon with the group and gave his first-hand impression of post-war Germany: "Materially it is almost wiped out in the large cities; spiritually it is stronger than ever."

"City people," Ligutti wrote, "like the displaced persons, look pretty well worn out. Low food rations, ruins everywhere, have very depressive effects. The eyes are the mirror of the soul, and eyes don't sparkle among these poor people." In spite of the poverty, misery, and grief, they were impressed by the high caliber of the displaced persons as a group. They conferred with the American Generals Huebner and Horrold in Heidelberg, both of whom praised the reliability, intelligence, obedience, and willingness to work of most displaced persons. "We Americans are lucky to get them," the generals said. The group stopped in Fulda to confer with American military personnel and to visit the tomb of St. Boniface. Ligutti prayed, "May the great missionary of Germany guide and protect his people to peace and happiness." Here the group met with the leaders of about six hundred Catholic priests who were living and suffering in the camps. Ligutti penned these words after the meeting:

> The priests among the D.P.'s have done a noble piece of work. They share the meager camp diet. They sleep in crowded quarters. They fight the people's battles. They comfort the sick and dying. They give up their thread-bare clothes to shivering children. Some are young and vigorous, some quite old with fire in their eyes. We American priests must offer a haven to these twentieth century martyrs.

Throughout the journey they visited camps, conferred with relief workers and army officers, and felt the situation in Austria was even worse than in Germany. Ligutti praised the work of Caritas, the German-Austrian equivalent to War Relief Services. He marveled at the Austrians' ability to mobilize resources to aid the native population as well as the millions of refugees who fled eastern Europe. He saw this work as "a saga of courage, determination and Christian love." In contacting so many scattered and broken families the group came to an over-riding conviction: the immigration policy of the War Relief Services must preserve the family. On his last night in Austria Ligutti gave vent to his emotions:

> The Catholics of America have only begun to give charity and help in the reconstruction of Europe. The big job is still to be done. The problems are not diminishing. We saw a group of two hundred Hungarians being processed as new arrivals. What a pitiful sight! One is really in the presence of one of the greatest tragedies in history. It grips your heart. It makes you wonder what is civilization; what is Christianity; what is progress. There must have been more pity among the wolves of the prairies, the lion in the forests. Man is little less than the angels but how low he can sink!

The group arrived in Villachi, a small Austrian town, on July 13 and stayed at a hotel in the British zone. At breakfast they were served lukewarm smoked herring, navy beans, and, Ligutti snorted, "infernal tea." They hurried across the Italian border and arriving in Tarvisio rushed to the nearest restaurant. Although it was only nine o'clock in the morning, the group ordered a hearty lunch and then, wrote Ligutti, "I bashfully asked the waiter, 'Is it a sin to drink white wine at this hour?' He arched his brows and glanced at the watch. I awaited the sentence and in typical Italian fashion he said, 'Just the right time.'"

Ligutti was thrilled to be back in his native province of Udine where he had a grand reunion with cousins and friends. Italy was in the midst of a turbulent election campaign, DeGasperi and the Christian Democrats waging a life-or-death struggle with Togliatti and the Communists. In one village Ligutti approached an old lady, who sat knitting, and asked, "Why aren't you on strike as Togliatti asked?" The old lady replied, "I'll stop working for a week if he dies in the state of grace!"

The American team made its way down the Italian boot, stopping in Venice, Padua, Bologna, Florence, Modena, and finally arriving in the Eternal City on July 21 for six days. The group conferred with Admiral George Mentz, chief of the International Relief Organization; with Msgr. Giovanni Badelli, president of the Pontifical Relief Commission; with Msgr. Walter Carroll, head of the Vatican Migration Bureau; and, of course, the highlight of the visit was a private audience with Pope Pius XII on July 25.

The stay afforded Ligutti the opportunity to call on Don Luigi Sturzo, who by this time had returned to his native land, and to partake in a delightful dinner at Santa Maria del Largo. In this residence for student-priests of the archdiocese of Chicago founded by Cardinal Mundelein and better known as the Chicago House, Ligutti stayed many times in the coming years. He found rest and relaxation, charm and cordiality, among the student-priests and the gracious rector who was in later years Bishop Ernest J. Primeau. During this trip Fr. John S. Quinn was living in the house. A former assistant at Holy Name Cathedral, Chicago, and later for many years the *officialis* of Chicago, Quinn had become a close friend of the then Msgr. Alfredo Ottaviani. Ligutti was introduced to the latter at a dinner one evening and observed, "I was really scared to meet him but he is a most common, everyday man, a wonderful priest possessing a delightful personality." The American group was also received by Monsignor Montini, who once again revealed not only his interest in rural life but also his deep concern for the pitiful plight of displaced persons.

On departing from Rome the Americans journeyed to Naples where they were joined by James Norris, associate director of War Relief Services. Before the group embarked for the United States on the S.S. *Saturnia,* Norris helped them draw up a three-page report on their observations and conclusions to be submitted to the Vatican. The drafting of the fuller, factual report was turned over to Gremillion and Scheidler to work on during their trans-Atlantic crossing.

Ligutti remained on his native soil, visiting more leisurely with friends and family. "The world is terribly small," he philosophized, "but the biggest places are the ones that are registered in our childhood memory corner." On August 18, with his friend Fr. Nino Toffolini, he was on his way to Milan and from there by train along the shores of beautiful Lake Como to Geneva.

Later, in England, Mr. Jack McCloskey and Dr. Kelly of the Paris office met James Norris and Ligutti and they visited families of displaced persons to see how well they had adjusted to their new environment. The group learned that the displaced persons were desperately needed for the work force in post-war England and through their efforts and talents were helping to stabilize the economy. Ligutti also reflected on a side of London that the average tourist does not see:

> Cities are wonderful but the grime and dirt of back streets makes one shiver. Children from London's slums look different, and how pitiful! I kept going through Southwark across the Thames picking out mews [alleys] and narrow streets. I walked into passageways to find a world of the real poor, living in misery.

On August 23 he left London and made a hurried stop in Washington, D.C., before seeing his garden and returning his angelic companion to St. Isidore. On August 28, at the Washington Hotel, he wrote five conclusions from this journey:

1. We must have families migrate together.
2. We must not concentrate the immigrants into camps or islands.
3. We must indoctrinate them while they are waiting for shipment. Pictures, books, movies must give these people a realistic picture of the country they are to become part of. Religious orientation will be needed for our Catholic people.
4. People here who are to receive them as fellow workers and citizens of a community must also be taught a few things — an understanding of other people's traditions and mentalities is *not* an American quality.
5. The various national groups in the D.P. camps must be given the opportunity of presenting the list of candidates and whilst we Americans should have the final say-so, we must not forget that especially for the Catholics, their own priests are the best judges of reliability, character, and especially Catholicity.

Ligutti was widely recognized for his interest in displaced persons and their dire needs. The United States Act for International Development sought to alleviate some of the pitiful conditions around the world through its Point Four Program under the direction of Dr. Henry G. Bennett. Ligutti was one of seven consultants from the United States to advise Dr. Bennett in planning future and evaluating present projects. On June 2, 1953 Ligutti testified before a committee of the House of Representatives. His concluding words were reminiscent of "The Song of the Plow":

Today is American Day. It is the United States Day. One hundred years from now, or 150 years from now, undoubtedly we will not be the leaders of the world. No one nation has ever endured in the leadership all these years. Other nations come up and develop some way or other. This is our day. Let us use our opportunity and let us fulfill our duty.

Before the committee Ligutti emphasized the need of "helping people to help themselves," as well as the need of engaging in many smaller projects more in keeping with the needs of the area than one or two larger projects over a larger area. At the conclusion of his remarks, Representative Bolton said that Ligutti had "certainly emphasized the notes that this committee is particularly interested in." Another committee member, Congressman Merrow, told Ligutti, "I think the principles which you have set forth and discussed are the principles that we should follow."

The Catholic world observed a Holy Year in 1950 with millions of pilgrims from the four corners of the earth coming to pray at the tomb of the apostles. Ligutti was one such pilgrim and entitled his series of nineteen letters "Pilgrim's Progress." In his mind it was chiefly a pilgrimage, although he sandwiched some business in between his prayers. He adhered to his intention as closely as possible, however, and these letters give an insight into his own soul. He stopped briefly in Paris for a meeting with Fr. Joseph Servé, S.J., and other leaders in the rural life apostolate. He spent a hurried day in Geneva with Father LeRoy of the French Secours Catholique and Fr. Edward Killion, C.SS.R., of the Vatican Migration Bureau. He arrived in Rome on February 26, 1950 and took residence at the Albergo Victoria, not far from the Chicago House. Again he brought along one of St. Isidore's angels, knowing that the latter had no need of the angel "until late in April for plowing purposes." In a few brief sentences he sketched post-war Paris:

> Orly Field as ill kempt as ever — the airport a little shabbier, and the bus as rattly as in the days of the Battle of the Marne! Berets, uniformed gendarmes, auto-graveyards, gardeners working in their small plots, the poplar trees trimmed to skin and bones. I have always pitied European trees along the streets and right of ways. What's the use of growing branches when you're going to get cut off so ruthlessly! I guess where resources are limited one must save. It's bicycle-prosperity and smoking a cigarette until it singes your mustache.

In Paris, Geneva, and Rome the meetings centered around plans and preparations for the First International Congress on Rural Life. On March 7 he had a private audience with Pius XII and afterwards wrote, "I was really touched by the Pope's interest in our hybrid corn gift, by his knowledge of CROP and his intense interest in the scientific field related to genetics." The same evening he boarded a train for a week's visit to his native countryside. He compared the surroundings and the people with his last visit in 1946 and noted that things were more normal and even showed "signs of some prosperity." He returned to Rome, spent some time in meetings with officers of CROP, but for the most part he concentrated on being one among the millions of Holy Year pilgrims. He spent a pleasant Sunday visiting Villa Barbarini, the papal farm at Castel Gandolfo, in the company of Dr. and Mrs. Emilio Bonomelli. He attended canonization and beatification ceremonies in St. Peter's Basilica and spent a great deal of time in reflection and meditation on the Church, the land, and civilization. On a two-day trip to northern Italy he inspected the results of the hybrid corn given through CROP with the cooperation of the War Relief Services. As he passed through the countryside he observed:

> Village after village, mile after mile — historic spots from the days of the Caesars to the rebuilt stations of today. We just hesitated within the walled city of Marostica, a wealth of civilization in a tiny spot. Our small towns could well learn a lesson in community development from medieval cities with their arts and crafts, their agriculture, and democratic self-government. Democracy and progress are not new.

He returned to Rome and noted, "Passion Sunday ushered in the traditional rites and ceremonies. Now two weeks of prayer and penance awaiting the glorious Easter sunrise." He reflected on the necessity of land ownership and grew in his conviction that the rural life apostolate should strive to secure as much possible contact with God's natural resources for as many people as possible. He believed this to be a right of every person simply because he was a human being. For Ligutti ownership implied security of tenure and this meant an economic unit of such a size as to guarantee "possibilities, work and production to a family unit." He smiled one day at a slice of Italian life:

> On the Sorrento peninsula — Palm Sunday — a cart and a donkey — an irritable young chap at the driver's seat beating

the donkey with an olive branch — on the wall in large white letters *"pace e libertá."* I wondered what the donkey thought!

The great days of Holy Week he spent visiting shrines and churches, starting his visits, as he remarked, "where I really should — at St. Isidore's Irish church." On Good Friday he visited the four major basilicas, not by walking but by horse and buggy, feeling that a car on that day would be out of place. He still felt that St. Paul's outside the walls was the most beautiful church in the world. He was happy as a pilgrim in Rome if, he added, "it were only to admire the devotion of fellow pilgrims." On Holy Saturday he thrilled to the sound of the ringing of the bells at the *Gloria* during the papal Mass, whose sounds reverberated throughout the city as all the churches rang out the joyous message of Easter. He felt extremely honored to be one of the eight monsignors who carried the canopy over the Pope's *sedia gestatoria* as he entered the thronged Basilica of St. Peter for Easter Sunday Mass. "The sacredness of the Mass," he wrote, "is so evident when 50,000 people can remain hushed and devout while standing amidst a sea of humanity for hours." Before departing for the Holy Land he visited Don Sturzo and wrote this tribute in his diary:

> He is a source of great strength to me, and the greatest of inspirations. He was preparing a message for the convention of Christian Democrats — the world-over meeting at Sorrento in a few days. His only recreation is a daily walk in the garden. He never goes out anywhere, yet he knows more about the world than 99% of the best informed.

Fr. Patrick Coyle, O.F.M., "a Baltimorean, former Army chaplain, with Franciscan habit, twinkling Irish eyes, a most delightful host and travel companion," met Ligutti at the airport in Tel Aviv. Thousands of pilgrims to the Holy Land would so describe Father Patrick and bless his name for his great hospitality throughout the coming decades. Ligutti sadly reflected on the ravages of the Arab-Jewish war, the misery of the displaced Arabs, the desolate countryside, and asked again, "Why wars?" He praised the works of mercy performed by the Catholic Near East Welfare Association through its field director, Msgr. T. J. ("Trans-Jordan") McMahon, even though he realized such efforts were but a drop in the proverbial bucket in a land so ravished by hatred and conflict. Then he recalled the purpose of his pilgrimage: "I am a pilgrim and not an economic and social observer. How I wish

I could shut my eyes and ears to all that surrounds the holy places. Christ certainly did not, so why should I expect a privileged status?"

He visited the holy places in Jerusalem, Nazareth, Ain Karim, Mount Tabor, Naim, Tiberias, Capernaum, Magdala, Cana, and, what he loved the most, the Mount of the Beatitudes. He also visited the Mount of Olives, the Dormitian Abbey, Bethany, Jericho, and the Dead Sea. Like every Catholic pilgrim he made the Way of the Cross through the narrow, winding, and bustling streets of the ancient city. "I hope," he wrote from the hospice next to the Mount of the Beatitudes, "that some day I'll be able to return and really stay awhile — a pilgrim to make progress. I have left a bit of my heart by the Sea of Galilee."

He also visited a kibbutz near the sea and observed:

> Zionism is essentially a back to the land movement. In its results it is giving the lie to anyone who says that Jews are not farmers, that they are merely traders and exploiters. The historical fact is that we Christians have not made it possible for Jews to own and operate land. Historically we have been afraid of their ability to work, save and sacrifice as we have placed every obstacle in the way of their land yearnings. The Zionist movement has given them a chance, and in land use they are making good.

Ligutti returned to Rome for an overnight stop and flew back to the United States on April 18. St. Isidore's angel was home in time for spring plowing. He ended these travel letters with two sentences every pilgrim to the Holy Land feels: "How can one regret being prayerful in the midst of such reminders? I am very happy I came to the Holy Land to complete my pilgrimage."

On May 13, 1951 he began a journey which, in the light of future developments, was surely one of the most important he ever undertook. In 1947, while in Australia he met Bob Santamaria, rural life director of the Catholic Church in Australia. Born in 1915 of parents who operated a wine shop on Sydney Road, Melbourne, he has been described by a close friend as one who "has stood out as one of the great and controversial figures in the social and political world of Australia." Santamaria has been praised by many and damned by others. A keen observer of the Australian scene remarked that "it is strongly rumored that Bob wrote many of the early social-justice statements issued by the Australian Bishops; there would be many who would not sign them these days." When Ligutti met Santamaria the latter said, "We should have an international meeting on Catholic rural life and it should be held in the United States." Ligutti replied, "Yes, we should, but it should be held in Rome."

Between 1947 and 1951 Ligutti talked about the congress, made plans for it and discussed it with countless Church and agricultural leaders. In February, 1950, he met with Father Servé and other rural life leaders in Paris concerning the congress. "We discussed dates, methods of procedure, topics, secretariat and language details," he wrote. "It is comforting to meet fellow workers in the fertile, rural life field, and we must work with them to shape up a world-wide mentality." On this occasion he also met with M. Quenette, general secretary of the French General Confederation of Agriculture, and M. Legendre of the French Department of Agriculture. He traveled to Rome and met with Vittorino Veronese, head of the Italian Catholic Action, and Monsignors Carboni, Montini, and Pavan in several planning meetings for the congress. He evaluated Pavan as follows: "After a treatise on original sin, he doesn't know Adam from Eve. But give him a starting point, and the whole of philosophy goes into motion, together with his hands. He is as clear and thorough in his thinking as anyone I ever heard." On March 6 Ligutti wrote, "I am making considerable progress with the arrangements for the 1951 International Rural Life Congress to be held in Rome." The stage had been well designed by a master technician. He was now ready to undertake a project that would far exceed his most optimistic expectations.

Ligutti tells the story of the congress in his series of letters dated from May 13 to July 25, 1951 and entitled "Rome Non-Confidential." He wryly commented in his first letter: "I wish I could write a set of letters entitled 'Rome Confidential.' I'll leave that to George Weller." Mr. Weller, a close friend of Ligutti's and a Harvard classmate of Mr. Chauncey Stillman, was a Pulitzer Prize reporter of the Chicago *Daily News* and one of Rome's longest-standing and respected American journalists.

The NCRLC executive director departed from New York on May 14 after a "little argument" with St. Isidore:

> He said that he and his angels were very busy — spring was so late, ground too wet, oats not in. Dear Saint Isidore, he is certainly a typical farmer, always complaining. Well, we compromised. He assigned me one of his angels from Australia. It is winter there and work is slacking off.

On May 18 Ligutti departed for Madrid because "my Isidorian angel is itching to fold his wings at the tomb of his and our saint protector." The following day he offered Mass at the main altar of the old cathedral in Madrid with great joy in his heart. High above the altar, he wrote, "is the casket containing the mortal remains of Saint Isidore. In front of it, but in a smaller box, the bones of his saintly wife, Maria; joined in their glory as they were together in life, work and trials." Again he made his usual calls at the embassy, the nunciature, and the department of agriculture. He spent several days in the countryside, visiting agriculture schools, rural pastors, and conservation projects. He reflected on a barefoot farmhand carrying a sick child, "Most people don't want too much — some work, a little bread, a prayer and a smile. Why should not society arrange to satisfy such humble requests?"

On May 24 he arrived in Rome and "found a perfect hideout for living quarters: ten-minute walk from St. Peter's, a big corner room with two windows overlooking a garden, fully equipped, no telephone, private chapel." After moving into the apartment he immediately drove to Castel Gandolfo to inspect Villa Montecucco, the site of the congress, and gave it his approval. He visited Villa Barbarini and paid his respects to the two bulls that the NCRLC presented the Holy Father. His report: "The Wisconsin (Chilton) boy is fiery and impetuous — the Missouri kid is phlegmatic and gentle. Both are reliable and within a few months will be proud papas." On the weekend he spent many pleasant hours with Monsignor Carboni and Mr. M. L. Wilson, at the time director of extension of the United States Department of Agriculture. On Monday he had an audience with Monsignor Montini concerning the congress. He described the occasion:

> One of the most interesting spots in Rome or the world is Monsignor Montini's *anticamera* (reception room). The world comes there and the world waits there. I stand in quite well with his two priest secretaries, so I got a very fine appointment. As I was ready to go in, a Cardinal from France shows up, so the world waited a bit longer. There was seated next to me a bearded Jesuit bishop from Ranchi, India. We had corresponded about FAO, and we met while waiting where the world waits.... A Mother General from Germany, the head of Catholic Action from Italy, Mr. Vittorino Veronese, and a priest who spoke perfect everything, were the remaining waiters! How Montini, a slight, thin, sharp-eyed, clean-cut, young ecclesiastic can turn from one language to

another, from one problem to another report; how he can remember names, events, decisions is a matter of wonderment, but *that* he does!

Activity for Ligutti is what air is to most human beings. After seeing that all arrangements for the congress were finalized, he dropped out of Rome a few days to return to his native soil, family, and friends. He admitted that "something comes into my throat" when he offered Mass at the altar where he served Mass as a little boy in Romans. He admitted, too, that his mind flooded with memories again at the graveside of his ancestors and friends, as he walked the corridors of the seminary in Udine, as he made his usual visit to the shrine of Our Lady of Graces. He indulged in a bit of history when he wrote from the rectory of his native village:

> I walk along pathways centuries old, the rugged landscape that nestled humble tillers of the soil when Vandals were passing across the valley below, when crusaders marched to Illiricum, when traders fanned out with spices from the Indies, when bearded missionaries trudged toward the north and martyrdom, when lords battled for crested castles, now in ruins, when Venice's doges summered nearby, when the new Italy arose, when wars, defeats and brotherly struggles reddened the green slopes. *Oh tempora, oh mores!*

He returned renewed in spirit and refreshed in body for the second purpose of this Roman sojourn, the formation of the International Catholic Migration Commission (ICMC), his chief preoccupation from May 25 to June 7, 1951. Next came meetings of the council of the Food and Agriculture Organization. Ligutti was caught up in the usual round of meetings, receptions, conferences, and dinners. He was pleased with the long discussions he had with Dr. John Reisner, director of agricultural missions of the National Council of Churches, who was recently appointed observer for the Protestant Churches to the FAO. Ligutti was responsible for the latter's presence, for he lobbied on behalf of his appointment and helped secure the necessary finances for his task. For many years the two had been friends and collaborators in the same apostolate. Ligutti wrote:

> The Christian churches of the world can do much and perhaps furnish the very spark that will make the difference between success and failure in the work of the United Nations' specialized agencies. We have set our minds and

hearts on that, and it will be done. If things go awry it won't be the church's fault.

The time of the rural life congress was approaching and Ligutti faced it with mixed feelings: "I hate to face the prospect of days full of events, hectic and full of surprises. But perhaps I don't fear them so much, for Lake Albano in all its placidity will be on one side and the wide expanse of the Campagna Romana will allow us to see the sunsets in all their glory." On the eve of the congress he was with the thirty delegates from the United States at a welcoming party hosted by Bishop Albert Zuroweste of Belleville, Illinois, and the NCRLC president. As he sat through the dinner Ligutti again reflected upon his personal feelings: "I must admit that to organize, plan and at least get all set for an international congress is no easy task. It means endless details and an infinity of painstaking activities that would make a saint swear." Of course, he was delighted to be with his friends from the United States. He spent three days with them sightseeing in the Naples area. At a cooperative headquarters near Naples he introduced Msgr. George Hildner as "Alfalfa George" to the puzzlement of the officials. Later Ligutti said, "I should have introduced him as '*Herba Medica Giogio.*'"

The First International Congress on Rural Life, which he called "the fulfillment of a dream," opened on June 25 with over two hundred participants registered (The committee had hoped for seventy-five). Bishop O'Hara was elected president and Pavan and Ligutti the secretaries. There were representatives from twenty nations, including a honeymooning couple from Holland, a fiery orator from Mexico, a Spanish bishop from Cordoba, a meticulous Frenchman who would rather argue than be right, an Irish delegation led by Canon John Hayes of Banshan, a young couple from Caracas, Father Hayden from Howlong, Australia, a young bearded priest from India, the zealous Joao de Souza from Brazil, the Italian minister of agriculture, who later became President Segni of Italy; Father Scharl and six hefty Bavarian leaders from Munich, and thirty ardent rural-lifers from the United States. Ten commissions were established, each with an elected recording secretary and a principal speaker who also acted as a moderator. Ligutti described the scene:

> The various units met in circles under the shade of the Villa's friendly lindens, oaks and scented oleanders. Seriousness and earnestness were dominant; plenty of heat, ample

disagreement, three hours of honest labor, then lunch, a siesta or a field trip — 4 to 7:30 p.m. more work, either listening to accounts of practical work or decide on specific expressions by subcommittees who had charge of drafting the final conclusions.

Without exception, the participants considered the congress a success. Among the speakers were Dr. Raymond Miller, Dr. Norris Dodd, director-general of the Food and Agriculture Organization, and Mr. Grove Hambridge, a special observer of the United States Department of Agriculture. Throughout the speeches and discussions all viewpoints were freely expressed. There were, as Ligutti said:

> Some pretty leftist exponents as well as rightists who don't have much right in these days of revolution. Yes, they too were there in force and with the persistency of the National Association of Manufacturers and of the American Medical Association. By the unreasoned stupidity of their claims in favor of large land holdings they are actually paving the way for their own complete destruction.

Each of the ten commissions drew up a set of resolutions that were subsequently edited and published by Fr. William Gibbons, S.J., and Msgr. Pietro Pavan. Ligutti noted that these "will serve as a sort of Magna Carta for the Catholic Rural Life Movement throughout the world." After the final session Ligutti and Bishop O'Hara were driving down the mountainside to the Appian Way. He said to the bishop, "It's easy going down — it was harder coming up." Then he recalled his own closing remark at the final session, "Some of my dreams have had a habit of taking life, walking and talking. Thank God, this is one."

The highlight of the congress was the audience with Pius XII on July 2, where the Holy Father delivered a major address in French concerning rural life. Because of the poor acoustics of the Clementine Hall of the Vatican palace, a good part of it was unintelligible. Ligutti noted that "only from a careful study of the text can its full import be appreciated."

The congress provided three happy surprises for the American delegation. The first was the special audience with the Pope on July 4. In the name of the group Bishop Zuroweste presented the Holy Father with a Ferguson tractor with all its accessories for the papal farm. The Pope blessed the tractor, gave the kiss of peace to Zuroweste, and talked individually to the delegation.

He took special notice of Mr. Alba Groves of Viroqua, Wisconsin, a long-time NCRLC supporter and a recently appointed Knight of St. Gregory. Second, at a farewell dinner the Americans held in Rome on the eve of their departure, Bishop O'Hara presented the double relic of SS. Isidore and Maria he had brought from Spain to Ligutti to be venerated in the shrine of the NCRLC offices. The third surprise was greeted with enthusiastic applause. The Pope honored the long-time supporter and promoter of the NCRLC, Bishop Joseph Schlarman of Peoria, with the personal title of archbishop. One and all recognized it both as a singular honor for a beloved friend and a recognition of the NCRLC.

By July 21 Ligutti was back home on Grand Avenue in Des Moines. He came down with a fever and was put to bed "with hot packs on my toe and penicillin elsewhere." He was happy and proud, pleased with the accomplishments, the memories, and events of the past two months.

In coming years he returned to Europe and the Eternal City many times. In May, 1952, for example, he returned to Italy for more meetings concerning rural life. On this journey he came to six conclusions about Italy:

1. Italy possesses limited resources.
2. These resources are being developed to a high degree.
3. The human resources of Italy cannot be utilized effectively in Italy. Expansion is needed.
4. The birth rate is decreasing but the working force is increasing, because of the peak in the birth rate twenty years ago.
5. The poverty and unemployment can swing Italy into Communism at the next election if not sooner.
6. Perhaps some of our great anti-Communist battlers in the U.S. might be credited by history for the establishment of Communism in Italy. What then?

In 1957 he conducted a NCRLC pilgrimage to Spain and the shrine of St. Isidore. On May 12 the pilgrims participated in the novena in honor of the patron of farmers, and Ligutti had the honor of carrying the Blessed Sacrament during the procession within the cathedral of Seville. In Madrid on the saint's feast day, May 15, the group had a place of honor in the procession between the bishop of Madrid and the civil and military leaders. "Throughout the celebration and all day," Ligutti wrote, "I thought of the humble farmers all over the world honored vicariously in the humble figures of a humble couple — tillers of the soil, saints of God, lovers of men."

From Madrid he returned to Italy, spending seven days in Assisi with the International Catholic Migration Commission and then on to Rome for the biennial conference of the Food and Agriculture Organization. He marked the fortieth anniversary of his ordination in the Basilica of St. Francis in Assisi on September 22, 1957. On November 26 he flew from Rome to Paris, traveled through Belgium and Holland, and returned to New York on December 7. He wrote:

> It has been my very great fortune to be in very close touch with personalities of considerable import. The ones that count are very humble, they are truthful, they are charitable, they are not stuffed shirts. Rome could furnish a wonderful research field in human communications, i.e., gossiping. A four-page weekly sheet called "Rome Confidential" might easily be filled with interesting forecasts or whisperings. But as they say here, "The ones who talk don't know and the ones who know don't talk."

The immigrant boy from Romans, the rural pastor from Iowa, the executive director from the United States, was also a world traveler.

In 1950 Monsignor Ligutti and Fr. E. Cazzanigna of the Pontifical Committee showed Pope Pius XII a sample of the hybrid corn distributed to Italian farmers through CROP, with NCRLC participation.

Monsignor Ligutti jokes with Br. Constant Brouillard, C.S.C., and a Filipino lady in Manila on December 6, 1955.

Visiting children in a displaced persons' camp near Naples following World War II.

Visiting a shrine in Turkey with the local archbishop of the Coptic rite and civil officials.

With some priests in Khartoum, Sudan.

Helping a youngster from Salerno, Italy, learn his alphabet.

With Cardinal Sebastiano Baggio and a young girl on Ligutti's visit to Brazil in July, 1969.

Monsignor Ligutti introduces Bishop Joseph Marling of Jefferson City to Pope John XXIII.

Listening to a speaker at the Eucharistic Congress in India in 1965.

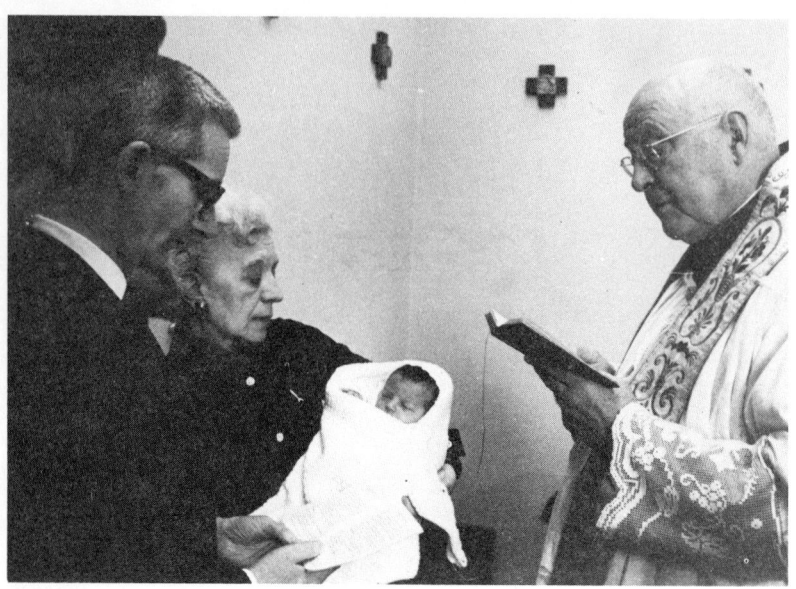

Monsignor Ligutti baptizes the child of Mr. and Mrs. Walter Persegati.

A quiet moment while boating on Lake Geneva in May, 1967.

CHAPTER SEVEN

SHARING WITH THE POOR

Seldom has the adage "The boy is father of the man" been more applicable than in the life of Luigi Ligutti. From his youth his experiences were preparing him for a work that was not as well known as his NCRLC directorship or his office as permanent Vatican observer to the UN Food and Agriculture Organization. The social demands of the Christian gospel forced him to become a vocal and effective advocate of the rights of the immigrant and dispossessed.

This conviction brought him into circles where he was at home with sympathetic people. It also drew him into contact with enemies he least expected in both Church and State. Ultimately it led him into a controversy that he tried to avoid but could not; it became one of the most shattering experiences of his life. In Cleveland on September 12, 1948, he said:

> In the process of formulating immigration policies we, as Americans, should be fully conscious of our heritage, not as of one but as of many . . . I, am an immigrant from Italy. I am a citizen of this United States — not by accident of birth but by choice. I am but one of the millions who sought opportunity, work, living space, in this land of ours — yes, and the privilege of sharing in the development, growth, and progress of our American democracy.

Ligutti, as we have seen, was dismayed by the havoc which World War II wrought on his native Italy. While grateful to many he was overwhelmed by the work to be done in restoring Italy to a healthy economy. He observed how the Fascists were using the cooperative movement as a tool to pursue totalitarian goals. In his report he stressed the need of choosing a few young Italians "to spend approximately three months in the United States and/or Canada for the study of cooperatives." He also recommended the establishment of institutes in about ten regional centers in Italy with a "group of men who know cooperatives, who are above partisan politics to explain the philosophy, history, techniques of cooperatives."

Ligutti became a member of the National Catholic Resettlement Council, which the American bishops established in 1947 under the auspices of the NCWC War Relief Services. As we have seen, he was one of six American priests selected to make a study-tour of Europe from June 10 to July 27, 1948. The seven points the group submitted to Monsignor Montini reflected Ligutti's thoughts concerning immigration.

In summary, Ligutti and his colleagues recommended that the Holy See direct a letter to the American hierarchy urging their support and assistance in establishing a sound, realistic program for displaced persons. The group also advocated that special consideration be given to displaced priests and that they be supplied the necessary vestments and utensils to celebrate Mass. It likewise urged the establishment of centers where displaced people might be orientated for life in the United States and that competent people be employed to direct such centers. Finally, the committee recognized that in spite of all the best efforts there would remain "a hard core of displaced persons who are sick, aged, and infirm for whom some provision must be made." Accordingly, it recommended that greater efforts be made throughout the Church in the United States to care for such people.

These conclusions impressed Ligutti. Ever since that year he kept an eye open and was quick to note in the countries he visited the opportunities for immigrants. This concern led him in the coming three years to devote considerable time in forming the International Catholic Migration Commission (ICMC). The apathy toward the plight of the refugee among many American Government and Church leaders psychologically forced Ligutti to become an outspoken defender of the dispossessed. Again he did his homework. He knew that World War II had taken its toll in the death of 14,735,000 soldiers. Each death represented for both victor and vanquished an expenditure of $104,000. He also learned that in postwar Europe there were 12,000,000 displaced persons. Their survival cost each year $400 per person. With other religious and government leaders he realized "the formidable time-bomb" of this situation and recognized that the migration of people from the dispossession of their native lands to the opportunities of new lands was both a Christian and human response demanded by the pitiful conditions of the time. Ligutti was firmly convinced, as he said, that "migrations, which favor and promote mutual understanding and cooperation on the part of all, give witness to and promote the unity of the human family."

Given this Christian ideal and humane necessity, all that was needed was the right man in the right place at the right time. Ligutti was the right man in one place. Dr. Johannes Schauff was the right man in another place. The International Catholic Migration Commission was formed out of this fusion.

The story has almost a casual beginning, the ICMC being conceived in Room 706 of the Gloria Hotel, Rio de Janeiro, at 5:30 p.m. on July 16, 1949. At that hour Schauff and his son called on Ligutti. A simple entry in the latter's diary states the origins: "Propose international Catholic migration group."

Schauff, a leader of Catholic Action in pre-war Germany, was deeply concerned about the conditions of the 12,000,000 expellees living in West Germany, cast out from their homes behind the iron curtain. Schauff had two close German friends in the Vatican, Msgr. Ludwig Kaas, director of research for St. Peter's Basilica, and Fr. Robert Leiber, S.J., personal secretary to Pius XII. With the assistance of these influential friends, Schauff presented a memorandum to Pius XII concerning the political and social problems in Europe; namely, "the question of her twelve million refugees." In this memorandum, a copy of which Schauff sent Ligutti, he observed:

1. Organization of migration work cannot be simply the concern of the donor-countries, but also the specifications and conditions of the countries of destination.
2. Germany, because of lack of diplomatic channels and an innate distrust and resistance on the part of some countries, cannot handle this problem by itself. At the same time, however, Germany is bearing the heaviest burden of the refugees.
3. Exaggerated "charitable" assistance prevents the migration of the refugees based upon economic considerations and the principles of the self-esteem and self-respectability of the refugee himself.
4. So enormous a problem demands the consideration and action of international agreements and organizations, such as the International Relief Organization, the International Labor Organization, and the European Recovery Program (Marshall Plan). In such organizations it is chiefly North

America which contributes the funds, South America which gives the land, and Europe which sends the people.

5. A Catholic Office for Refugees, Emigration and Settlement is desperately needed to coordinate all Catholic efforts, to exert influence on international organizations, to create healthy public opinion and to serve as a liaison with religious orders engaged in missionary work in the countries of destination.

6. The immediate need is the creation of an International Office with a few staff members, but permanent and first rate experts from Europe, North and South America. This office should have liaison with the Holy See in order to implement the latter's directives and coordinate efforts through the various nunciatures and apostolic delegations in the receiving countries.

7. The Holy See should appoint one European and one American to initiate discussion and action in accord with the above principles.

On September 29, 1949 Schauff wrote Ligutti that the apostolic nuncio in Rio de Janeiro had informed him that the Pope was willing to act immediately upon the memorandum:

> One main point is to find an able American layman who will take part as one of three acting directors of the preparation committee in Geneva. My friend, Mr. Eugenio Bonardelli of the Italian Embassy, mentioned the name of the brother of the Papal Nuncio in Belgrade, Mr. Patrick Hurley. What do you think of it? I don't know him and I would like to have your opinion.

On October 27 Ligutti replied:

> I don't know what type of an American layman you would want. I should think that the first requisite would be a knowledge of colonization and agriculture. If you want a man like that the best man on the Northern continent is Mr. John Lanctot, 422 Rue Notre Dame Est, Montreal, Canada....

Events dovetailed and action followed swiftly. In a letter to Ligutti on February 27, 1950 two names were mentioned for the first time, both of which had a decisive influence on future developments. Schauff wrote:

> I'm now in Europe. Last week I was in Rome. It was a good coincidence, that just a week before Cardinal Frings from Cologne was there and had handed over to Father Leiber a

memo for His Holiness about our subject, which was kept in the same way as my own proposals. As I was present and just about to go to central Europe and as Monsignor Montini was ill, Father Leiber brought the questions directly before the Holy Father, who agreed with the suggestion to make use of our, your and my, presence in Rome in March/April and to join some committee and organization. The written authorization for inviting other people I shall find at Bishop Muench's office in Kronberg. I'm thinking of certain individuals from Germany and Austria out of the circle of the refugees themselves, of course, after having gotten in touch with the episcopate. Cardinal Frings mentioned in Rome the name of Mr. Norris, who — if I'm correct — is working in Frankfurt a.m. for W.R. (War Relief Services) and who has visited the Cardinal together with Monsignor Swanstrom, to discuss questions of the refugees of German origin.

One of the most interesting documents concerning the formation of the ICMC was a letter Leiber sent to Schauff on March 15, 1950. The letter reveals not only the major influence Leiber had with Pius XII but also sets down for the first time a program of action. The idea of ICMC had moved from proposal to reality. Leiber wrote:

As regards the International Catholic Commission, I can inform you of the following: In the meantime, the official letters have been written, which I suppose, have already reached their destinations. One of them went to Cardinal Frings, for he, as head of the Fulda Bishops' Conference, on occasion of his last visit to Rome, submitted a note proposing the formation of an International Catholic Commission (i.e. Conference which requires the prior formation of a Commission): the official letter is the answer to the note. The other letter went to Father Killian (sic) in Geneva. The contents of the two letters are: The Holy See has prepared the foundation of an International Catholic Commission for emigration from Europe, especially of those expelled from East Europe, and nominated 3 persons who should form the nucleus of the Commission: Msgr. Ligutti, Dr. Johannes Schauff, Mr. Norris. — Because Cardinal Frings, when he was in Rome, gave the above mentioned note through me to the Holy Father, I saw myself obliged to inform the Cardinal in detail of that which took place at the time of his stay in Rome, and that the 3 persons of the nucleus intended to meet in Rome between the 1st and 5th of April.

Msgr. Ligutti is in Europe, Dr. Schauff would be in Rome in the beginning of April, and it would not be difficult to have Mr. Norris present also. I have also informed the Cardinal of the definite points which would prevail in the Commission: (strongly international; with exclusion of all German societies or groups tainted with nationalism; the St. Raffaelsverein also cannot represent the Commission; the building of the Commission from men with the necessary experience and consideration in the field of Emigration, but especially of Immigration and Colonization; Immigration and Colonization must be carried out economically-socially and not charitably; as seat of the Commission Geneva is proposed.)

It is not to be forgotten: That Geneva as seat of the Commission is mentioned in the two official letters written by Msgr. Montini. In my letter of the 11th of March, I stressed that the Commission was not a Commission of the Holy See, should not be a Papal Commission, but one which was recognized by, and in connection with, the Holy See. My letter to Cardinal Frings was written on the 9th of March.

So much have matters progressed. Msgr. Ligutti I have not yet seen; however he has discussed the questions in detail with Prelate Kaas. All questions will have to be deliberated at the meeting in Rome, especially — at least, so I imagine — the expansion of the Commission. I think also that the completion of the Commission will be the task of the persons who form the nucleus and who are already recognized by the Holy See.

At this point James Norris entered actively into all future plans of the ICMC and he continued to serve for the next twenty-five years as president and the principal force behind its work. Writing Ligutti again on July 3, Schauff said about Norris: "I introduced him to our friends, Father Leiber and Msgr. Kaas. They were very impressed with his reports about the practical work of NCWC in the field of D.P. immigration to the United States and with the personality of Mr. Norris himself." At this time Montini also became actively involved in forming the commission. Both Schauff and Norris agreed with Montini that the committee should be a coordinating rather than an operating one.

There was, quite understandably, during this formative period no little resistance among those in Rome who felt that the Vatican Migration Bureau was sufficient. Under the direction of Pius XII,

Montini wrote Norris and asked him to join Schauff and Ligutti in establishing the organization. He lent his advice and support to the drafting committee, consisting of Ligutti, Schauff, Vincentini, and Norris, and he also asked apostolic nuncios and delegates to secure representatives from the various nations to serve as members of the council. Montini attended the organizational meeting and assured the committee of his full support of the ICMC.

On May 8, 1950 Montini wrote to Archbishop Francis P. Keough, vice-chairman of the administrative board of the NCWC. He pointed out the serious problem of emigration from Europe, "especially from the Central European countries," and noted that "it would indeed seem more than strange, if the Catholic Church were to show no active interest in the question of emigration." He mentioned the formation of the ICMC and then came to the heart of the matter:

> The work of the Committee now being formed is warmly recommended by the Supreme Pontiff to the Most Reverend Bishops of the United States. The exemplary, self-sacrificing and bounteous spirit with which they and the faithful entrusted to their pastoral charge contributed so mightily to alleviate the sufferings caused during and after the war, encourages the Holy See to count with confidence on their full comprehension of the task presented to the Church today by the emigrants from Europe and on their effective interest in its accomplishment.

In a letter dated May 22 Montini sent Ligutti a copy of his letter to Archbishop Keough. Once again he pointed out "the personal interest of His Holiness in this Committee and its work to relieve the unfortunate lot of so many millions of refugees and other persons in over-populated areas."

By mid-September, 1950, Norris received the approval of his superior, Msgr. Edward Swanstrom, to serve on this steering committee. Ligutti had interceded with the latter on Norris' behalf in New York. On September 14 representatives of Catholic voluntary agencies gathered at the Ristorante Raineri in Rome to form what was then titled the "International Catholic Committee of Immigration." Those present were Msgr. Joseph McGeough, representing the Vatican Secretariat of State; Monsignors Swanstrom and Andrew Landi, NCWC War Relief Services; Monsignor Crivelli, Caritas Internationalis; Father Froehling, the St. Raphaelsverein; Mr. Vincentini, Italian agencies; Msgr. John O'Grady of the National Conference of Catholic Charities, representing Monsignor Ligutti who was unable to be present; Fr. Edward J. Killion, C.SS.R., representing the Vatican Migration Bureau; and Norris and Schauff.

The three pages of minutes, recorded by Killion, reflected the consensus of all present on the need and importance of this organization; the necessity of locating its office in Geneva; the need of representing all migrants, including part-time workers serving in countries other than their own; the inclusion of consultants from the United States, Canada, Australia, Brazil, Italy, Argentina, Germany, Austria, France, Switzerland, and Great Britain. The committee also delegated Norris, Schauff, and Vincentini to draft a proposed constitution. In the name of Ligutti, O'Grady stated that the success of the committee's work would depend upon NCWC War Relief Services. Swanstrom expressed the willingness of the WRS to lend financial assistance for the first year. Swanstrom also voiced his desire to see the constitution drawn up as soon as possible and asked that the scope of the committee be broadened.

Norris, Schauff, and Vincentini wasted little time. By October 4 Ligutti received a copy of the proposed constitution from Schauff with the request to return "as soon as possible any comments you may wish to make about the sketch." Ligutti found no need to make any emendations or corrections. Three days later Schauff again wrote Ligutti, telling of his audience with Pope Pius XII:

> Immediately he asked if you were present, how the things with the Migration Commission stand, that for a long time he had heard nothing about it, that he hoped, as it is so urgent, that in the next few months great forward steps will be taken. Fortunately I could give him the news of the results of the conference the day before and the positive answer of the U.S. bishops. He said that it is his wish, especially to you and to me, that the practical work starts soon and that he hears about it. I think that the initiative of the "Segreterio di Stato" was a consequence of his admonishment. So we have a special responsibility — that no more time may be lost.

In the same letter Schauff said that contacts with national hierarchies should be made at once, with Norris contacting Great Britain and France and Schauff, South America, Germany, Austria, and Switzerland. He asked Ligutti to negotiate with Canada and recommend a member from Argentina. He also mentioned that the proposed budget for the first year amounted to $55,300. Again he mentioned the need of a capable layman as general secretary of the new organization and proposed either John Lanctot or Dr. Eugenio Bonardelli.

The planning that had been so carefully carried out during the past two years came to fulfillment on April 12, 1951 in a personal letter to Norris from Montini. The letter informed Norris that the Holy Father had approved the provisional constitution and that the organization would be named the "International Catholic Migration Commission." Three conditions were added: (1) The commission should work closely with the Holy See and local hierarchies; (2) Constitutional changes and appointments of the chairman, members of the council, and the general secretary should be approved by the Holy See; (3) The acts of the commission's meetings should be submitted to the Holy See prior to publication. The opening paragraphs of this letter also reveal how well Pius XII and Montini understood the importance of the commission. The letter stated Montini's feelings:

> You are well aware of the urgent reasons which motivated the Holy Father in nominating a Committee, over which you preside as Chairman, for the immediate establishment of an international Catholic organ of information, coordination and representation, that would concern itself with the grave problem of surplus populations and migration.
>
> This problem, so intimately linked with the spiritual welfare of multitudes of immortal souls, has taken on a particular urgency at this time owing to the industrial and social conditions resultant from the war. While reasons, chiefly of a political nature, did not allow in the immediate post-war years the movement of large groups from one country to another, the time has now come for a great number of emigrants, not workers alone but together with their families, to find new homes and a new field of labor. It is only too clear that this pressing need for migration, particularly in view of the very considerable proportion of Catholics involved among the refugees, displaced persons and surplus populations, calls for a more intensive effort of broadened scope on the part of the Church.

Less than two months passed and the International Catholic Migration Commission held its first meeting in the Eternal City. Norris, Schauff, Vincentini, and Ligutti spent a day planning the agenda of the meeting of the full commission. Ligutti wrote his friends:

The International Catholic Migration Commission has officially come into being. It's a dream come true. I hope it will walk and talk. To marshall the Catholic forces all over the world in behalf of freedom of movement; to help the people in their search for work and peace; to remove, at least partially, some of the causes of unrest; to help in the establishment of humble but happy homes; to fill the countryside, now empty and useless, with the playful shouts of rosy-cheeked children! High high the hopes! What a task to face, but "God wills it!"

Ligutti maintained close contact with the ICMC throughout the succeeding decades. In 1953 he undertook a study-tour of South America to determine the direction that ICMC should take in these nations. In his memorandum to the ICMC council he insisted again that the work of ICMC lay in education on behalf of migration and the absolute necessity of having competent and sympathetic laymen and priests to carry out the ICMC's goals. In 1952 at the ICMC's general conference in Barcelona during the international Eucharistic Congress, Ligutti delivered a major address. He based his remarks chiefly upon papal utterances concerning migration and from these drew his practical conclusions. His speech revealed his philosophy on migration:

> The right of human beings to move in an orderly but free manner and to have access to natural resources is not even debatable. Society must devise ways and means to make its effectuation possible.
>
> Christian nations have an obligation in justice to which must be added the obligation of Christian love.
>
> Even though an injustice benefits a nation or group it is to be realized that on the long-term basis such benefit may and will resolve itself into a detriment. The fundamental principles of natural rights must be faced fearlessly and without quibbling, without excuses and disabling qualifications.
>
> The Church must educate its leaders and membership to the objective truth and importance of the above verities and must persuade its Christian-minded membership to apply cold logic in forming conclusions and courage in application. The greatest efforts are to be in the formation of public opinion, i.e. in creating proper mental attitudes.
>
> The country of origin cannot be considered as prepared to furnish manpower only because it stands in need of emigra-

tion. Too often emigrants are ill prepared; physically, morally and mentally unfit for adaptation into a vastly different environment. Receiving countries need to learn much on the subject: Immigrants are not mere bodies, or slaves, or objects of charity.

Capital investment is needed. Large scale international loans at low rates of interest and long amortization plans must be encouraged. Such investments will be most secure and profitable. The Church must lend freely, willingly, intelligently and zealously all possible assistance. Only the best fitted priests should be employed in work among migrants. Educational institutions should furnish the scientific background for the selection and exploitation of natural resources.

Social worldwide peace must be based upon social justice and Christian charity. There is no other way.

Again, in 1957, Ligutti addressed the delegates to the Third International Catholic Migration Congress in Assisi, Italy. On September 23 he opened his remarks: "How can Catholic migration work be coordinated in the international field?" In preparation he had sent a questionnaire to sixty individuals and organizations acquainted with migration work and commented upon the replies he received. In his closing paragraphs he introduced a personal note that revealed his own sense of history:

> I have always been interested in migration of peoples. It's the story of the world's progress. It seems to have been conceived in the very fundamental plan of creation. Christianity, and specifically the Roman Catholic Church, from the day of Pentecost to this very day, has been the leader and the protagonist in worldwide migration and communication. The International Catholic Migration Commission is but the latest manifestation of this age-old tradition.

In a brief time ICMC "walked and talked." For twenty-five years it has fulfilled the dreams that Schauff and Ligutti envisaged for it in 1949. Throughout this time it has been both served and inspired by Norris, the president of the governing committee. From 1952 to 1970 the ICMC has assisted almost 114,000 people with loans enabling them to emigrate to a new land and a new life. Throughout these years more than $30,000,000 were made available to migrants and refugees who have repaid these loans and thus kept several revolving funds operating for future migrants and refugees. Ligutti's vision "to fill the countryside, now empty and useless, with the playful shouts of rosy-cheeked children" had become reality.

Although never actively associated with the NCWC War Relief Services, from its beginning in 1953 Ligutti was a staunch supporter of the American bishops' worldwide organization rightly called "America's Good Samaritan." He numbered among his collaborators such officials of the agency as Bishop Bryan McEntegart, the future Cardinal Patrick O'Boyle, Bishop Swanstrom, Monsgnor Landi, Norris, and Mr. Jack McCloskey, the Paris-based director. In his travels he touched base with many regional offices of War Relief Services (later changed to NCWC Catholic Relief Services). His thinking paralleled that which the then Bishop Swanstrom voiced on the floor of the Second Vatican Council. "Everyone," said Swanstrom, "must consider his every neighbor without exception as another self, taking into account first of all his life and the means necessary to living it with dignity, so as not to imitate the rich man who had no concern for the poor man Lazarus." Catholic Relief Services worked closely with the ICMC from its very beginning. A fact little known at the time, and unfortunately too quickly forgotten, was the emigration of 150,000 displaced persons to the United States within a few years after World War II. This massive migration program was organized, directed, and carried out by Catholic Relief Services with Bishop Swanstrom's generous support.

By working closely with the CRS officers, Ligutti stressed his social philosophy concerning migration and happily saw it fulfilled in CRS's programs. Of special concern to Ligutti was the establishment of self-help and development projects throughout the world. A CRS brochure spelled out the philosophy of these projects:

> Human development (self-help) has always been basic to the programs of CRS-USCC. These are directed toward the development of the whole man, materially and spiritually. CRS-USCC, through self-help schemes, encourages conscious efforts by individuals and groups to change for the better the conditions under which they find themselves.

In 1971 CRS sponsored 452 self-help programs, which amounted to an outlay of over $2,500,000. Such projects Ligutti constantly advocated from his years of association with the cooperative movement and throughout his worldwide travels. He expressed his thoughts on this matter in a memorandum to Swanstrom on July 9, 1957:

> If the receiver, although in evident need, is partially or totally made to feel or feels that such gifts are due him out of justice, or that such gifts tend to make him unwilling to work so as to earn his full living, or that such gifts tend in general to pauperize him (i.e. with dependence on public relief as an *established* condition or fact among a people), then the act of giving to such a person and/or group is not a proper expression of Christian love for neighbor. The results achieved tend to debase the noble and Christian character of the recipient, and thus the filling of his stomach or the clothing of his body are basically more harmful than good....
>
> There are illustrations and examples of giving, which require on the part of the recipient, some work for self or family or community improvement; e.g. why should the streets of a village be in a state of disrepair while most of the villagers are the recipients of free food? Why should children with dirty faces be given milk to drink without requiring them to wash their faces?

In 1952, however, immediately at hand was the issue that would cause Ligutti to spend many sleepless nights and involve him in a controversy that would affect the Catholic Church in the United States, including many members of the hierarchy, clergy, and laity. Ligutti could not escape involvement. As a founder of ICMC he was committed to raise the standard of the Christian social gospel against the McCarran-Walter Act of 1952. His stand was that of Archbishop Joseph E. Ritter of St. Louis, who said on October 23, 1952:

> The time has come for the American people to disavow discriminations against all races and all peoples. We can no longer merely countenance the flagrant discrimination against the peoples of southern and eastern Europe. The time has come now for the American people to think in terms of an immigration program that is consonant with our own domestic needs and our leadership of the free nations of the world.

Ligutti's opposition to the McCarran-Walter Act was but one facet of his life-long struggle on behalf of human dignity. Discrimination against the immigrant in the fifties was but the predecessor of discrimination of the blacks in the sixties and the oppressed in the seventies. Ligutti simply could not tolerate discrimination in any guise and thus found himself in the storm center of this controversy.

Stripped of legalistic jargon and lace-curtain sophistry, Public Law 414, the McCarran-Walter Act, expressed the deep-seated nativist prejudice practiced for over a century in the salons of wealthy Americans, in the private clubs of the WASP aristocracy, in the high-sounding phrases of political platforms, and even in the sacred precincts of legislative, judicial, and religious sanctuaries. The law was named after Senator Patrick McCarran of Nevada, a Catholic, who introduced the bill in the Senate, and another Catholic, Congressman Francis Walter of Pennsylvania, who introduced it in the House of Representatives. Well did the senator from Nevada understand the bill's controversial nature, for in introducing it, he said, "I do not present this bill to the Senate as legislation which in every particular is wholly satisfactory to every school of thought on the subject." The bill contained over three hundred sections whose purpose was "to harmonize, clarify, and unify in one single statute some 200 laws enacted throughout a century." The McCarran-Walter Act reaffirmed the two basic principles of the 1924 immigration law which adopted a highly restrictive immigration policy as a reflection of the nation's isolationist attitude following World War I. These two principles were, first, to place a ceiling on all permanent immigration and, second, to establish a quota system for the number of immigrants from each country.

Mr. Paul B. Rava, chairman of the International Law Committee of the Missouri Bar, stated the crux of the problem before an institute on immigration sponsored jointly by the National Conference of Catholic Charities and the St. Louis Committee on Immigration Policy. He said in October, 1953:

> Nobody questions the wisdom of setting some limit upon the flow of immigrants. On the other hand, there is serious disagreement as to (a) how many immigrants can usefully be absorbed into our community, both from an economic and social standpoint and (b) how the applicants should be chosen.

The act had other discriminatory items, such as violation of the constitutional principle of due process, the arbitrariness by which an immigrant of long-standing could be deported from the country, and the provisions that, in effect, made second-class Americans of naturalized citizens. Regarding this last matter, Senator Hubert Humphrey of Minnesota, one of the principal antagonists of the McCarran-Walter Act, made public this letter from five representatives of American Indian tribes:

> As America's only non-immigrants, we would like to go on record as being opposed to the major aspects of the McCarran immigration bill.... We are against this bill because of its basic philosophy... which accepts and provides for the continuance of racial discrimination. To this we are unalterably opposed....
>
> As American Indians we are not immediately threatened by laws to stop immigration and to deport men and women born abroad. Sometimes we wish we had established such a law in 1492....

As was expected, President Harry Truman vetoed the bill and called it "infamous." Nonetheless, Congress made the bill law by overwhelmingly passing it over the presidential veto. Later, President Dwight Eisenhower flatly stated that "it must be rewritten." The Anti-Defamation League of B'nai B'rith called the act unjust, pointing out that "it discriminates against the peoples and therefore in effect the religions dominant in the southern and eastern parts of Europe." B'nai B'rith also called the act "basically unsound" because "it affords the largest quotas to countries that need them least, and the smallest quotas to those that need them most." It also noted that the national origins quota system had been attacked as "undemocratic" and "feeds particularly the anti-American propaganda of totalitarians."

The feature of the act that aroused the apprehension of many religious leaders was the question of "how the applicants should be chosen," or the national origins quota system. They found that the act thereby continued the religious prejudice previously embodied in the 1924 immigration act. No one addressed himself more vehemently and rationally to this question than Dr. Constantine E. McGuire, a consultant to NCWC in the 1920's, a long-time public servant and distinguished Catholic layman. On September 13, 1924 he submitted a three-page analysis of the anti-Catholic elements in the 1924 legislation, which was carried by the NCWC news service. Largely as a result of McGuire's efforts, a memorandum was addressed to Bruce Mohler, then director of the NCWC Immigration Department, dated February

21, 1928. That memorandum, authored by the NCWC general secretary, quoted the minutes of the April 27 meeting of the NCWC administrative committee. That memorandum read in part:

> The subject of the "national origins policy" again received the attention of the Committee. If the finances permitted, the Committee recommended that a copy of Senator Shipstead's recent speech on "National Origins Clause" be sent to all pastors in the United States. The Director of the Bureau of Immigration had recommended that this be done.
>
> Note: From these items, it is evident that the Administrative Committee is opposed to the present Bill founded upon the National Origins Clause.
>
> The Administrative Committee, is therefore, definitely against the National Origins Clause as it now stands.

In 1928 the bishops of the United States in clear, unequivocal language went on record as opposed to the national origins clause. At a meeting with Dr. McGuire on December 9, 1952 Ligutti sought the background of this decision in order to make crystal clear the position of the American bishops in 1952 regarding the McCarran-Walter Act. Following that meeting, McGuire wrote to Ligutti on December 11 and recounted the events surrounding the 1924 immigration act and his efforts to mobilize the American bishops against it, even though McGuire admitted that by the time he had succeeded it was too late. He concluded his letter: "The full gravity of the momentous change in our policy was now quite apparent to all; but it was too late to change it. And I fear that the prospect is no better today."

Two incidents happened in May, 1952, that sparked the immigration controversy within the Catholic Church in the United States. On May 15 Senator Blair Moody of Michigan requested on the floor of the Senate that the list of organizations which supported the Humphrey-Lehman bill (which was opposed to the McCarran bill) be published in the *Congressional Record*:

> I ask unanimous consent to have this lengthy list, headed by the National Catholic Welfare Conference and the National Council of Catholic Women printed in the record at this point in my remarks. It lists groups which certainly are American and certainly should have the consideration of Congress.

After these two organizations, three other Catholic groups appeared at the top of the list; namely, the Catholic Committee for

Refugees, NCWC War Relief Services, and the National Council of Catholic Charities. Such action did not escape the notice of officials at 1312 Massachusetts Ave. N.W. in Washington. On May 19 Msgr. Paul F. Tanner, NCWC assistant general secretary, in the absence of his superior, wrote to Senator McCarran:

> I should like to take this opportunity to correct an error in column 2, page 5301 of the *Congressional Record* for the Senate of May 15, 1952. Neither the National Catholic Welfare Conference nor the National Council of Catholic Women have supported the Humphrey-Lehman bill.
>
> I do not know how our names got into Senator Moody's list and I am sure that there was no intention to mislead anyone. However, in fairness I think it is necessary to record the fact that we did not endorse the Humphrey-Lehman bill, but rather we favor the McCarran-Walter bills as amended.

This was the flint that struck the spark. Immediately such leaders as O'Grady, Swanstrom, and Ligutti interpreted this reply as not only a reversal of policy established by the American bishops in 1927 but also, in supporting the McCarran-Walter bills, a violation of Christian social principles. Ligutti did not hesitate to point out on many occasions during this period that the NCRLC was the only Catholic organization that publicly opposed the McCarran-Walter bill. O'Grady did not blush in the least when accused of "button-holing congressmen on the hill while lobbying against passage of the bills." Swanstrom rightly pointed with no little pride to the immense humanitarian work carried out by NCWC War Relief Services in resettling 150,000 displaced persons through the implementation of the Refugee Act of 1948.

Fortunately the Catholic press, with few exceptions, overwhelmingly opposed the bill on the basis of the discriminatory aspects of the national origin quotas. Fortunately, also, the majority of Catholic bishops, priests, and laymen opposed it. Instinctively they saw behind it the same type of bigotry as manifested by the American Legion in 1924 with its demand that Congress close the door to all aliens for a five-year period. Another positive aspect was that President Truman had vetoed the bill and that two leading archbishops, Ritter of St. Louis and Cushing of Boston, publicly and fearlessly opposed the act even by disagreeing with NCWC officials.

Tanner's statement that "we favor the McCarran-Walter bills as amended" puzzled O'Grady. He was one of the officials present at a meeting on March 3, 1953 in the NCWC headquarters which proposed recommendations for changes in the McCarran bill. In a letter to Archbishop Ritter on June 2, O'Grady directly stated that "by and large these recommendations have not been followed in the McCarran Bill as it passed the Senate." His lengthy letter to the archbishop of St. Louis pointed out many other discriminatory points in the bill, and, enclosing copies of Tanner's and Mohler's letters, he flatly stated that these letters "represented a reversal of the attitude that was expressed at your Committee's meeting and the attitude represented by the Administrative Board of Bishops." He then pointedly made his case:

> On inquiry we find that Monsignor Tanner says that they really cannot offend Senator McCarran; that they have to depend on him for favors and, of course, undoubtedly Senator McCarran controls the Immigration and Naturalization Service including all policies of immigration legislation. Every now and again Mr. Mohler is able to do a favor for the Apostolic Delegate and for some Bishops who want to get some people into the country or to prevent some people from being deported. Now Mr. Mohler has to be on good terms with those who depend on Senator McCarran, but over against this we have a basic question of policy. We have a type of legislation that relegates millions of our people, including Italians, Poles, Slovens, Croats, to the condition of second-class citizens. This is the basic issue in immigration legislation.... how far is our country justified in going along on the principle of Nordic superiority? Can we accept the principle that those who come from Northern Europe represent superior races and those who come from Southern Europe represent inferior races?

O'Grady also pointed out that other religious groups had attacked the discriminatory features of the McCarran bill and that they had asked the NCWC to join them in this struggle. "The general assumption around Washington today," he added, "is that if our group had stood by and used the instruments at its disposal for the promotion of a sound Christian policy of immigration we could have won the day." In a postscript O'Grady added that he discussed the situation with Archbishop Patrick O'Boyle of Washington, D.C., who was of the opinion that Ritter "ought to insist with Msgr. Howard Carroll on calling another meeting of the various groups interested . . . to discuss where are we going from here."

Ritter's reply of June 11 was cutting. He wrote Carroll, general secretary of the NCWC:

> Ever since the passage of the McCarran Bill, I have been wanting to write to inquire what has happened to the Immigration Department. It is difficult to understand how the N.C.W.C. representing the Catholic Bishops of the country could support such a Bill, continuing the discriminations of our previous Immigration legislation....
>
> I would therefore, request again that frequent meetings be held at which would be invited representatives of all the groups interested in this problem, not only War Relief and the German Refugee Committee, but also Monsignors O'Grady and Ligutti.
>
> I am sure you appreciate the fact that this is a very serious problem, and it would not surprise me at all if we were to receive a reprimand from our superiors for taking the stand that we have taken.
>
> That the Immigration Department of the N.C.W.C. did not represent the Catholic thinking of the country is evidenced by the editorials in our Catholic newspapers and periodicals, and I am confident it did not represent the thinking either of the Administrative Board of Bishops of the N.C.W.C.

By this time the pressure cooker was bubbling and Carroll responded in a devious manner that appears to be less than honorable. He sent a memorandum dated September 9 to only a few bishops, obviously seeking their support in defense of the NCWC, while ignoring the majority of the American bishops. His memorandum was a frontal attack chiefly against O'Grady, but also included both by name and implication Ligutti and Paul McCormack, executive assistant to Swanstrom. He listed eleven points concerning written or spoken statements made by O'Grady and attempted to refute them point by point. It was a pitiful refutation. When he wrote, "Through the new McCarran Bill, much that the Holy See and Bishops have been requesting for years has been written into the law," Carroll showed either an abysmal ignorance of papal pronouncements and the 1927 directive of the American bishops or an underestimation of the intelligence of the American bishops. His defense of Mohler, although admirable in any superior, was *ad hominem* and not *ad rem*. Perhaps the most damaging remark in his memorandum was the manifestation of a deep-seated prejudice not against immigrants but his fellow Americans of other religious persuasions. In regard to working with Protestant and Jewish groups for the defeat of the bill, Carroll wrote, "The N.C.W.C. based on its experience, regards such joint action as neither possible nor desirable."

At this point the archbishop of Boston entered the scene. It is not known whether he received Carroll's memorandum nor is it known who, if anyone, persuaded him to voice his protest against the McCarran bill. Nonetheless, in a letter dated September 30 to Phillip B. Perlman, chairman of the President's Commission on Immigration and Naturalization, Archbishop Cushing wrote, "It is my considered opinion that the Act should be amended to purge it of several un-Christian and un-American provisions." His opposition to the bill focused on three objections:

1. The lamentable *National Origins* theory of the Immigration Act of 1924 is continued and made more rigid by the McCarran-Walter Act....
2. The provisions of the McCarran-Walter Act will make it practically impossible to admit ordinary unskilled immigrants into our country....
3. The McCarran-Walter Act gives the American Consuls abroad virtually unlimited powers to exclude any immigrants who, in their judgement, are liable to become dependents or delinquents at any time during their natural lives."

He called these features "a grave potential threat to our domestic development and our international leadership."

Such an attack from a respected citizen and religious leader could not escape national attention. The following year the archbishop of Boston sponsored an immigration institute at Boston College similar to the institute sponsored the same year at St. Louis University. Congressman Walter submitted for publication in the *Congressional Record* an editorial that appeared in the March 22 Washington *Times-Herald.* Pushing the panic-button, the editorial declared that the Boston College institute "could wreck the United States and mean the end of its existence within a generation, if it were successful." In voicing the usual arguments in favor of the act, the editorial spelled out the vicious implications of it:

1. This country belongs first to the people already in it. We are not a garbage can. We are a nation of free citizens governing ourselves as a republic and we intend to stay that way.

2. Of all the nations in the world, this one always has been, is now, and will continue to be, most friendly and receptive to new faces. After all we are a nation of immigrants from everywhere.
3. But, immigration to the United States is not a right that belongs to the foreigner who wants to come here. On the contrary, it is a privilege and a gift extended from the people of the United States to special cases and it is not to be handed around lightly.
4. Nobody can come here unless he first passes reasonable tests that show whether he would make good company.

No doubt the five American Indians who wrote Senator Humphrey would interpret that statement radically differently than the editorialist intended! Emotion escaped reason when the editorialist concluded his patch of prejudice with the sentence, "The McCarran-Walter Act is a good law, well founded in American national interest. We firmly believe that if it falls, this country falls with it."

Opposition by some NCWC officials and inflammatory remarks by public speakers did not, however, prevent Ligutti from continuing to oppose the act. On October 1, 1952 Fr. William J. Gibbons, S.J., appeared before the President's Commission on Immigration and Naturalization. Father Gibbons, then a professor at Fordham University, was the Washington-based NCRLC liaison officer. On October 11 Ligutti himself appeared before the same commission when it met in St. Louis. Both spoke against Section 2-3 of the act, which stated: "The effect of our immigration laws and their administration, including the national origins quota system, on the conduct of the foreign policies of the United States." In his testimony Gibbons made these seven observations:

1. The movement of people over international boundaries... has a relationship to economic and social conditions within the country of emigration as well as the country of immigration. In a world in which our nation cannot escape from international cooperation, and in which conditions elsewhere must be taken into account, it is very important to remember this relation of immigration practice to foreign policy.
2. The countries with the largest quotas, especially Great Britain and Ireland, do not send immigrants in numbers comparable to the quotas, whereas many countries with smaller quotas fill theirs regularly, and in the case of

countries of origin of refugees there is an oversubscription for years to come.

3. I am not at all convinced that foreign policy of the United States would best be assisted in the immediate present by merely putting unused visas into a pool for redistribution on a "first-come, first-served basis." In normal times this would probably work out quite satisfactorily, and could therefore be considered in connection with finding a substitute formula for permanent immigration policy. But I for one sincerely hope that present conditions in Europe will not be permanent.

4. There are several ways in which the 150,000 — 250,000 visas a year could be distributed to Europeans. One would be to remove all restrictions based on nationality and recognize a "European man" which is actually coming into existence, in fact existed before but was obscured by national animosities and differences.

5. It needs to be emphasized that a sound policy regarding European immigrants could do much to minimize the antagonisms and resentments among the Europeans themselves. This is certainly in accord with U.S. foreign policy objectives.

6. U.S. foreign policy vis-a-vis Russian communist imperialism must be and remain flexible and prepared for temporary action at the same time long-term objectives are being pursued. Proper handling of the European emigration question is related closely to such a policy.

7. United States action in supporting resettlement of European problem categories would encourage other nations to act. It would also encourage various adjacent noncommunist states, which have refugee problems of their own, due to various conflicts, to solve these problems through active resettlement. Resolution of such refugee problems would greatly reduce the financial strain placed upon the limited budget of the nations in question and of the United Nations.

Ligutti's remarks before the same commission, although similar in intent to Gibbons', were much more succinct and reflected his inimitable manner of making a point:

I have had occasion to travel far and wide throughout the world.... I have heard the following statements made: "Hitler tore pages from the U.S. Congressional Record when he shouted forth his claims of Teutonic racial superiority."

"Is democracy, which you Americans present as the salvation of the world, based upon the unity and equality of the human race, or do you define it to suit your own convenience and prejudices at various times and places?...."

Of course, the U.S. alone cannot solve the problem of overpopulation in Europe or elsewhere. Neither can America open the floodgates of unregulated immigration, but we can do at least four things:

1. Adopt an immigration policy which is Democratic and Christian.
2. If a national-origins quota is to be kept, let it be based on the national origins of the boys who gave their lives in World War II and in Korea. That would represent an unbiased standard, (and very up to date).
3. Consider and favor in a special way the reunion of families.
4. Help solve the unbalances of population and resources in the world by our leadership, through capital investments and movement of people.

While deeply preoccupied with the principles involved in this controversy, Ligutti faced a major crisis of his life. It not only involved his activities and career but cut deeply into the core of his priestly ministry. It concerned not only his own but the future of the NCRLC. Nonetheless, he faced this, as other crises, guided by his philosophy:

> My understanding of obedience and reverence to my bishop is an obedience and reverence in keeping with man's fundamental natural rights, priestly dignity, and, above all, in keeping with truth. I do not consider it my duty to obey or revere my bishop if such an act would debase me as a man or as a priest.
>
> I do not consider myself bound to assent to a statement which in conscience I feel is not the truth.

This statement was found scribbled on a sheet of paper among his records, with no date and with no reference to a particular incident.

Indications that a storm was brewing came from a request by his friend Bishop Albert Zuroweste of Belleville, Illinois. In a letter dated October 23, Msgr. Howard Carroll wrote, "Some Catholic spokesmen in recent weeks have charged publicly that Bishops of the United States, and the NCWC, have through the years favored a policy of restrictive immigration to the United States." In replying to the bishop of Belleville, Ligutti drafted a four-page memorandum answering Carroll's charge since it seemed obviously directed against him. Carroll's statement was prompted by a letter Ligutti had send privately from Rome on June 29 to personal friends:

> For over 100 years the population pressure problem has been present. Most of the Italo-Americans are descendants of migrants from southern Italy. Sao Paolo, Brazil is filled with Calabrians. Where did the Omaha Italians come from? Sicily of course. Oro Crucoli near Crotone has fathered the Sarcone clan in Des Moines. After the first World War Australia took some in. Then came the famous exclusionist policy — first of all in the U.S. The speeches made in Congress at the time the quota laws were passed favoring Anglo-Saxons as against Latins were as Nazi in philosophy as anything Hitler ever said. Our labor unions were afraid of cheap labor. Our Catholic Hierarchy went on record as favoring the practical stoppage of Italian immigration. They were afraid our church couldn't handle them, and needless to say they were anxious to keep the German-Irish ascendancy in Catholic circles.

Ligutti conceded that he made a similar statement on August 12 in the board room of the NCWC in the presence of department heads and a few other invited guests of Carroll. "I would not," he wrote Zuroweste, "consider either the letter or the statement as *public utterances* or 'made in *recent weeks.*'" Perhaps the most telling part of this memorandum, however, is his source for making the above-quoted statement. He called upon Carroll to produce the report written by Dr. McGuire already mentioned.

> I was told by staff members of the NCWC that this report does exist in the NCWC files, and that it does support the first part of my statement.

> There is a difference between a statement and its implementation, between believing in something and not doing anything about it. The Quota Law has been on the books for 30 years. I ask, "What has the NCWC done to bring about remedial legislation?" Here are a few personal instances which confirmed me in my conviction and fortified the report I heard.

> On a certain occasion (I can produce the exact date and hour) I was in Mr. Mohler's office and I asked him, "What

are you doing about trying to get the National Origins Act changed?" Mr. Mohler replied angrily, "You're Monsignor O'Grady's spy — just leave immigration matters to us."

At another time I met Mr. Mohler in the Apostolic Delegation in Washington. There were present one of the members of the staff and an Apostolic Nuncio. Again Mr. Mohler warned me about leaving these legislative matters to him and the NCWC.

During the discussions before the enactment of the D.P. Act the record shows that Monsignor Carroll, whenever present, had only objections to offer. (Again I can produce date, time and place.)

I have watched very carefully for official or unofficial statements emanating from the NCWC within the last five years condemning the National Origins Quota system. I have asked members of the staff to produce such statements. Where are they?

In this memorandum Ligutti further pointed out that in June the NCWC officially endorsed the McCarran-Walter bill, and this endorsement was interpreted by Congress, the press, and the public at large as exhibiting a restrictionist attitude. He expressed his gratitude that Mohler presented "a complete reversal of trend and policy as expressed in the past" during his appearance before the President's Commission on Immigration on October 29, 1951. "For this," he added, "I certainly feel grateful to God and am most happy." His concluding paragraph reflected an aspect of the entire controversy that ran counter to Ligutti's innate respect for truth. He wrote, "The throwing up of a smoke screen by Monsignor Carroll is *per se* the greatest damaging evidence against the action of the NCWC in its approval of the McCarran-Walter bill. It is an attempt to avoid the real issue, and it is neither fair nor honest."

This was a warning of the storm that was about to envelop Ligutti. On November 11 he received the following letter from his superior, Bishop Edward Daly, O.P., of Des Moines:

Since I have reached Washington this week my attention has been drawn to a sort of newsletter posted at Des Moines and done over your name and under a Roman dateline. You are aware that there is in the letter that which unfavorably reflects upon the archbishops and bishops of this country, as touching their attitude toward the country's laws on immigration. That I wish you to know is in my opinion and in the opinion of responsible people unjustified.

On the statement as it concerns me I feel no need to comment. Since, however, the letter went out from your office in the city and diocese of Des Moines, and since the Bishop of Des Moines is considered to be the moderator of the NCRLC, I hereby sever all connection with the NCRLC and request that my name be taken from your letterhead and kept out of all publicity of the NCRLC. You will please have this request promptly honored so that no other means will be necessary to effect it.

Ligutti answered the letter, stating that in his opinion an injustice had been done him. He also asked Daly to reconsider his decision to sever relations with the NCRLC. On December 1 Daly again replied in tones revealing a greater lack of charity than understanding. He cast aspersions upon Ligutti's character and veracity and again reiterated his withdrawal from the NCRLC. Ligutti respectfully replied on December 6 and said he would call for an appointment after his return from the East on December 16. Even in so tense a situation, his priestly qualities showed through. He wrote:

> If I have in any way offended or shown disrespect or lack of proper obedience towards Your Excellency, personally or officially, if I have in any way shown disloyalty to the Catholic Church or the Catholic Hierarchy, I wish to humbly beg Your Excellency's and/or the Church's pardon, and I stand ready to make amends.

He sent both Daly's letter and his reply to Mulloy and Zuroweste with a covering note: "I don't want to carry this to Washington. I hope and pray that it can be solved right here, and perhaps even without your help. It has worried me considerably, and I have even lost some sleep, but I hope this will be the biggest worry or difficulty in my life."

Upon returning from Washington Ligutti again wrote Daly on December 17, enclosing copies of Tanner's, Ritter's, and McGuire's letters addressed to himself. Daly objected to Ligutti's travel letters entitled "Hop-Skip-Jump," which we have previously discussed, on the grounds that he used these letters as propaganda within the NCRLC. To this charge Ligutti replied that of the 189 letters distributed only 21 members of the Conference and only 25 diocesan directors and members of the board received them. He further pointed out that "practically every person receiving the letters did so receive them for reasons of personal friendship" and that "I have always stated that these letters were written from a friend to friends and for friends." There the conflict with Daly ceased but from then on relations between the two men were more strained than they had even previously been.

By the end of 1952 the attitude of NCWC had radically changed from Tanner's statement that "we favor the McCarran-Walter bills as amended." Many people and many internal and external factors brought about this change. Surely the archbishops of St. Louis and Boston exerted considerable influence. Although difficult to determine, the work of O'Grady, Swanstrom, and Ligutti was no small factor in bringing about this transformation. All three suffered but their suffering helped to bring about a change in official and public opinion concerning immigration within the Catholic Church. Great was their joy in reading President Eisenhower's State of the Union Message of February 2, 1953. Therein the President called for a new law "that will at one and the same time guard our legitimate national interests and be faithful to our basic ideas of freedom and fairness to all."

Although the tone of his February 5 letter to Swanstrom was more officious than cordial, Archbishop Karl J. Alter, chairman of the NCWC administrative board, did express an about-face in official policy from that which Monsignor Tanner enunciated eight months previously:

> It was greatly encouraging to read the paragraph which President Eisenhower included in his State of the Union message concerning the problem of immigration. The fact that the discrimination and injustices of the existing legislation were frankly recognized is a first step toward their correction. If the Congress will review the highly questionable criteria on which the immigration quotas were originally based, then the President's request may eventuate in a substantial modification of the present law and the correction of the thirty-year-old inequities.

That, in a word, was precisely the question that O'Grady, Swanstrom, and Ligutti had consistently fought to bring to the Catholic consciousness.

As we have seen, Ligutti both as a priest and a humanitarian was throughout his life concerned with the poor and the oppressed. As an Italian immigrant himself he quite naturally was concerned about his native countrymen who suffered severely the ravages of war. That the Italians were among the more neglected by American Church and State leaders and that he was an influential Catholic leader of Italian descent, thrust upon him the mantle of leadership in the area of relief and immigration for Italian people. He emerged as this leader as a result of an address he delivered before four hundred Italo-Americans who were attending the annual meeting of the National Civic League in Kansas City, Missouri, on July 8, 1945. In that speech he coined the phrase that served as his guiding light in activity the remainder of his life. He said, "For every war dollar — a dollar for peace."

He did not plead for support of the relief program for Italy because, he said, "That is a question of both justice and charity for all of us of Italian descent." He marshalled his facts and figures to depict the havoc wrought by the war upon the Italians. He quoted American government and military leaders to emphasize the urgency of immediate relief to a people standing on the brink of national disaster. He pointed out that Italy must be restored to a sound economy if there is to be any hope of restoring stability to the total European economy. His address was widely quoted in the general and Catholic press and in no small way turned the tide to provide immediate and massive aid to that prostrate nation.

For Luigi Ligutti, however, relief was only one facet of reconstruction. The other two were human development (self-help) and emigration. His experience with the ICMC and his involvement in the McCarran-Walter Act controversy convinced him that further efforts must be made for Italian immigrants. This conviction led him to become one of the organizers of the American Committee on Italian Migration (ACIM). The present executive secretary of the organization, Fr. Joseph A. Cogo, C.S., expressed Ligutti's role in ACIM: "We are particularly indebted to him because he spearheaded the movement that eventually was responsible for the coming into being of this Organization."

Ligutti spoke at an informal meeting at Our Lady of Pompei Church, New York, on March 29, 1951. Others present were Fr. Remigio Pigata, C.S., provincial superior of the Scalabrini Fathers, and several priests of that congregation; Msgr. Joseph M. Pernicone and other Italo-American priests of the archdiocese of New York; Fr. P. E. Ansaldi, C.S., rector of Scalabrini College, Staten Island; and Fr. Luigi Donanzan, P.S.S.C. Ligutti advocated the establishment of an Italo-American organization to exercise influence upon immigration legislation, care of the immigrant when he arrived in the United States, and the promotion of legislation that would protect the sacredness of the family unit in national immigration policies. "Immigration," he said, "occupies a central position in the Christian solution of the present international social and economic crisis."

As usual, the executive director of the NCRLC had done his homework. He had sent a memorandum to thirty Government, Church, and Immigration leaders detailing his thinking on forming such an organization. Among those whom he wrote were his associates in the ICMC, eight American bishops, leaders within the Italo-American community, and such government figures as Congressman Peter W. Rodino and Senator John O. Pastore. In his cover letter he wrote:

> In this business of promoting legislation, etc., "supermen" are not needed. I feel the Italo-American group can learn the ropes and act efficiently, wisely and prudently as well as any other group. Because of the fact that the Italians in the U.S. have not been organized and because of the variety of the fragmentary and geographic organizations that exist, I feel that the Catholic Church furnishes the strongest tie of unity.

In this memorandum he proposed two phases for "the solution of the international people-resources problem": (1) The U.S. share in the solution of the problem from an international viewpoint (international movement of people); (2) The U.S. share in the solution of the problem from the U.S. viewpoint (i.e., migration into the U.S.). His four proposals in this memorandum are significant as they ultimately became the cornerstone of the philosophy of the American Committee on Italian Migration:

1. It should be in the hands of Italo-Americans.
2. It should be under the leadership of the Scalabrini Fathers who are the official religious leaders of the Italian immigrants. They are in charge by the express wish of the Holy See and subject directly to the Consistorial Congregation which is in charge of migration matters.
3. This leadership does not exclude but rather necessitates an Italo-American lay leadership. But let us not forget that unless it is well-chosen, carefully screened and prudently directed, plenty of dangers will be present.
4. Sporadic and unrelated efforts will not bring about real effects. They will create confusion, give rise to cliques and endanger the final effort.

Ligutti's "spear" penetrated willing hearts. Within a year the American Committee on Italian Migration (ACIM) became a reality. Throughout its twenty-year history it has been directed by the Scalabrini Fathers and Italo-American lay people. At present it numbers many self-sustaining chapters throughout the country and maintains a national office in New York City. The chairman of the present board of directors, Bishop Swanstrom, is the son of an immigrant Swedish father. Through energetic and effective leadership the ACIM has assisted in promoting legislation enabling the entry of more than 140,000 immigrants from Italy and 250,000 from other low-quota nations. One of its solid accomplishments was the promotion of the Immigration Reform Act of 1965 which abolished the discriminatory national origin quota system. Referring to this law in the presence of an ACIM delegation at the White House on July 1, 1968, President Lyndon Johnson said, "No group has worked harder or with more dedication than the American Committee on Italian Migration."

It was a consolation for Ligutti to deliver the homily at the Mass opening the second ACIM symposium in the Basilica of St. John and Paul in Rome on May 7, 1961. He said:

> Both in pagan and Christian Rome, the lesson of "welcome stranger" was exemplified; and this is precisely the lesson I wish to convey to you today with the hope and prayer that the spirit and the tradition of Rome Imperial, Papal and Modern might become a pattern in this widening and shrinking world of ours.

He called Rome "the city par excellence of immigrants" and reminded the delegates that they are "particularly concerned with the religious care of the ones who leave their native land for foreign shores."

Little need was there for that reminder. At present the ACIM is committed to safeguarding the gains achieved with the Immigration Act of 1965 and ensuring that the humane principle of the law emphasizing family reunion be kept intact. This was the principal consideration throughout the sixth symposium held in Washington, D.C., on June 6-8, 1971. On that occasion President Richard Nixon addressed the delegates:

> ...I know that this organization was set up because of your concern that the laws of this land would become too restrictive and that people of Italian background and of other backgrounds, as well, would not be allowed to come here. Let

me say that will not be the case.... I hope America will always be the land of the open door, because as long as that door is open, it means that this land will continue to prosper and continue to have that drive which makes a great nation.

The delegates were also encouraged in their efforts by Senator Edward Kennedy's address during this same symposium. In discussing several bills then pending in Congress, he said:

A second item on the agenda involves the reunion of families. This traditional concern of immigration policy must continue to be a primary objective in any new legislation. In fact, new legislation must strengthen our goals. We should give preference status to parents of permanent resident aliens.

We should facilitate the admission of the mentally retarded child whose family has been cleared for immigration.

We should increase the number of visas available to refugees who frequently have relatives in the United States.

All of this seemed like a dream come true to Ligutti who quite understandably cherished in his heart the work of ACIM. He had spent long and arduous years in seeing such objectives become national policy. Of the numerous memoranda he had drafted, studied, and read, and of the countless letters he received, no letter perhaps brought him more personal satisfaction than an autographed letter from John Fitzgerald Kennedy, who wrote him as a senator from Massachusetts on July 22, 1957:

I am very grateful to you, for your interest in my efforts to obtain the passage of immigration legislation.... I certainly appreciate your comments and support and assure you that I shall continue my efforts to secure enactment of immigration legislation during the present session.

Kennedy was true to his word for years to come. As thirty-fifth President of the United States, he said, "Immigration policy should be generous; it should be fair; it should be flexible. With such a policy we can turn to the world, and to our own past, with clean hands and a clean conscience."

In his closing years Ligutti looked back upon his position concerning relief and immigration. Many of his collaborators had died and were not so fortunate to see the realization of their goals in this life. It was a consolation to Ligutti that God granted him this blessing. In this matter, as in others, he expressed his position better as a poet than a philosopher. He recalled the words he spoke before the President's Commission on Immigration and Naturalization in St. Louis on October 11, 1952:

> Our American heritage is not as of one, but as of many. America is a sturdy tree. Its branches and leaves enjoy God's sunshine, rain and breezes. Its vigor, health and beauty are drawn from Mother Earth — through myriads of roots. This type of America we beseech God to bless, maintain and prosper.

CHAPTER EIGHT

UNDER THE SOUTHERN CROSS

Monsignor Ligutti's interest in Latin America resulted from his interst in rural life and the welfare of the Church. As he watched the mahogany carvers of Port-au-Prince he observed what in coming decades became the hallmark of a compassion that kindled but never consumed him. "The lowest of the lowest," he wrote, "possess the highest of the highest of artistic abilities. So is man!"

His first two journeys "South of the Border" occurred during the winters of 1943 and 1944. They were fact-finding missions to discover rural problems and methods in the Land of the Virgin of Guadalupe. Bishop Joseph Schlarman invited Ligutti to join him and Fr. Frank Kaiser on the trip. The three met at the Gunter Hotel in San Antonio on January 28, 1943 and traveled the highways and byways of Old Mexico until March 2. Also, the following year, Ligutti, the bishop, and Abbot Lawrence Nohs, O.S.B., of St. Bede's Abbey, Peru, Illinois, visited Mexico for five weeks. Schlarman's travel notes eventually found their way into his book *Mexico, Land of Volcanoes.*

This first trip to Latin America left a deep mark on Ligutti when he came face to face with the bitter anti-Yankeeism of Latin American neighbors. Throughout the next two decades, he became a crusader in both Church and State circles, pointing out the folly of ecclesiastical and governmental policies that fostered rather than diminished this bitterness of United States neo-imperialism. On the other hand, he had nothing but praise for the Point IV Program of the United States Department of State, the Department of Agriculture, and private groups such as the Rockefeller and Ford Foundations, who generally worked wisely and efficiently among Latin Americans. Upon returning from his many trips to Latin America, he recounted the beneficial results of such technical and financial efforts.

He expressed in two statements his conviction concerning the lack of greater success among the Latin Americans with so many programs of the United States. In a letter from Mexico, written in January, 1951, he stated:

> No great social or material improvement can be achieved without a deep understanding of cultural anthropology, and that means local mores and particularly religious tenets and practices. Take the whole of Latin America. There is only one stable and continuing institution there. That's the Catholic Church. No matter what we try to do, if we don't take the Catholic Church into account, we are just wasting our time, our efforts and our money. The same can be said of most mission fields. *And for heaven's sake, don't think you can make them think the way you think they ought to think.*

Two and a half years later, in a memorandum addressed to Mr. Stanley Andrews, administrator of the United States Technical Cooperation Administration, of which he was a consultant, he returned to the same theme:

> No matter what we North Americans think or judge; no matter how other people may be wrong; the fact is, they are what they are. They think the way they think and we can't kid ourselves into believing they are going to accept us, our ways, our views, just because we have dollars. If we have failed in Latin America, it is chiefly because we have failed to interpret our aims, purposes, and even our U.S. existence to the Latin Americans.
>
> If Milton Eisenhower and Mr. Cabot Lodge do not pay their respects to the local ecclesiastical authorities on their visit through Latin America, they are missing the biggest bet for building up good will. Take it or leave it. That's the way it is.

On several occasions he pointed out how wise the British government was in appointing Catholics as ambassadors and embassy officials to Latin American countries. He was delighted when Mr. William O'Dwyer, former New York mayor, was appointed the first Catholic-American to serve as ambassador to Mexico. Frequently he quoted Ambassador O'Dwyer's comment: "There are more Catholics per square inch in Mexico than in any other place in the world — to the square inch in the Catholic churches on Sundays."

Ligutti was deeply impressed by the virility of Mexican Catholicism:
> Make religious practices less of a pious mummery and put the teachings of Christianity into practice in today's world, applying Christian remedies to today's evils, then there has to be a reviviscence of religion, pure and undefiled. The blood of martyrs is the seed of Christians.

The strengthening of religion, economic and cultural development, and technical education and assistance were, in Ligutti's thinking, the three great needs of Latin America. He saw all three fit together as hand in glove.

His first journey through South America began in Baraquilla, Colombia, on January 7, 1945 in the company of his congenial traveling companions Schlarman and Morrison.

The high point of their visit to Santiago, Chile, was the meeting with Bishop Manuel Larrain. Ligutti assessed him as "one of the most learned men I have ever met and has a charming personality, is very social-minded, knows languages and has learned the latest American slang from the Maryknoll priests."

In later years Ligutti and Larrain would be major forces in establishing closer ecclesiastical ties through the formation of the North and South American Bishops' Liaison Committee, the NCWC Latin American Bureau, and the annual CICOP meetings. The two also worked closely together during the Second Vatican Council in promoting and carrying through into the final text many Christian social principles embodied in the pastoral constitution on *The Church in the Modern World*. Both South and North America lost one of their greatest friends in Larrain's tragic and untimely death in an automobile accident in Chile.

The traveling trio arrived in Buenos Aires on February 6. Ligutti's great delight was to meet his cousins, the daughters of Pietro Ligutti from the province of Udine. He was wined and dined by his relatives whom he had never met before, and once again the strong ties of Italian families were manifest throughout the stay in Argentina's largest city. Near Porto Alegre, Brazil, he visited Caxias, a city of 25,000, mostly of Italian descent. He wrote:
> It has a bishop and it is the center of wine-making. Italians came there in 1875 or so. They were all from Veneto, Piemonte, and Lombardia. Their grandchildren are quite Brazilian, although they understand Italian. They kept their faith quite well. Not rich, but have fine families.

As they came to Sao Paolo he noted that over 50 per cent of the population was of Italian descent. One day the North Americans drove in the archbishop's car to Campinas, about eighty miles away. Ligutti recounted the experience:

> The bishop at Campinas received us and, of course, served coffee demitasse with sugar. That's all I do now. Sip demitasse! Great coffee and you get it everywhere. I was in a bank today, in the president's room, and we had coffee; we were at the Governor's palace and we had coffee! At Campinas we had lunch in a fine big mansion on a dairy farm. A perfect farm. A bath for every cow every day, and a face massage at both ends three times a day. For modesty's sake, they milk the cows in private rooms! That's Latin America for you!

As most visitors, he fell in love with Rio de Janeiro and recalled his first impression from the airplane in one sweeping sentence:

> The figure of Christ with outstretched arms is located on top of a peak and hovers protectively with loving kindness and gentleness above the inlets, the bays, the tall buildings, the chapels on the hills, the curves, the beaches, the distant mountain ranges, and the rippleless sea!

Again, the usual visits with dignitaries and government officials, the side trips to agricultural areas, the late dinners, and superb wines. And another reflection: "Wouldn't it be sensible to use some of the immense expanse of land in Brazil to settle many poor people from all over the world? Either that is done or we'll have more wars in years to come." On the night of their departure, February 24, he concluded his last letter with a statement which many visitors to the city by the Sugar Loaf have made: "It is very true that Rio is the prettiest capital in the world!"

Less than five years later, the executive secretary of NCRLC was again heading south, this time on a special mission and an apostolate dear to his heart. In 1949, at the invitation of the United States Department of State and the Catholic Action Movement of Brazil, he was invited to lecture at a month-long rural life institute near Rio de Janeiro. The event afforded him the opportunity to spend an extra month studying rural and social problems in many areas of Latin America On June 12 he left Des Moines, leaving behind his garden, flowers, shrubbery, trees, hedges, grass — and weeds. "I am thoroughly convinced," he wrote, "trees, vegetables and flowers know the man who cares for them." In Washington, D.C., he stayed at the Washington Hotel awaiting visas and briefings from officials of the State Department. There he indulged in a bit of rural philosophy:

> I love to sit on the roof garden of the Washington Hotel, especially after a rain. The tree tops must feel so refreshed. The *Asperges* from on high must please the lindens and the chestnut trees. Even the equestrian statues seem to wiggle their bronze coverage. What would happen to civilization if the rain would stop? Water and civilization are even more closely allied than soil and souls. A fine mist has been falling all day. It must be an apologetic rain because of its prolonged absence. Big city people rely on the daily press for news of the drought. Farmers look to the crops, to the flowers. I really prefer to look at the sun in order to find out which is north and which is south.

Once again he sensed the strong anti-American feeling among the people he met. He recalled a cynical remark attributed to President Theodore Roosevelt: "We can never conquer South America because they are Catholic." Ligutti added: "There is an iron curtain in South America. It's applied by the ordinary South American and especially by the Catholic South American toward and against the *yanqui-norte americano,* and most vehemently, *protestante.*" Frequently in his diaries and letters he regretted this feeling, and the more he met with it the more diligently he tried to overcome it in both Civil and Church circles.

In an article that appeared in the June 14, 1958 *America,* he returned to the necessity of accepting Latin America as a continent of the Catholic faith. "All the Madonnas and the shrines may be useless superstition in the eyes of others," he wrote, "but many Latin American army corps reckon our Lady as an honoray officer (with pay)." While waiting for an airplane one day in Colombia, he asked an ordinary citizen what he thought of the persecution of Protestants in his country. He replied, "The Protestants are terrible; they are persecuting us; they insult the Blessed Virgin, the saints. They speak disrespectfully of His Holiness, the Pope; they call us ignorant, etc. etc." Reflecting on Vice-President Nixon's visit to Colombia in 1958, Ligutti wrote:

> The recent attacks on Vice-President Nixon, deplorable as they were, might teach us a lesson. He was the victim of pent-up emotions. Yankee imperialism, dollar diplomacy, the Colossus of the North, are not as much resented as the

uncouth conduct of U.S. tourists, the display of riches, their ostentatious spending. I heard an American say in a luxury hotel in South America: "How ignorant these people are — they don't know any English!" "*Adios*" was all the Spanish *he* knew.

Realist that he is, Ligutti stated the matter directly: "They see the Protestantizing of Latin America as only a starting point. They take it as an incontrovertible fact that the U.S. Government furnishes all the money for Protestant missions." Through his writings, speeches, works, and deeds, Ligutti became the first effective roving ambassador of the Church in the United States among Church and Government leaders in Latin America.

He reported the 1949 trip in sixteen letters entitled "the Corcovado Letters." "Like a cork bobbing up and down and always on the go," Ligutti said, "describes my present trip most accurately." His first stop, on June 21, was Kingston, Jamaica, to visit his friend and collaborator Fr. "Co-op" John Sullivan, S.J. In a pregnant sentence Ligutti sketched the central problems of this West Indian island:

> Slavery and emancipation resulted in a seventy per cent rate of illegitimacy and poverty; a population of over one million, three hundred thousand with only four hundred thousand acres suitable for agriculture; the ever-present problem of land distribution and political ineptitude.

Sullivan had spearheaded a movement of credit unions and cooperatives which were having an impact, even though inperceptible, on the development of the country. Ligutti delivered two addresses to the Ninth Annual Credit Union Convention and participated in the lively, practical, and realistic discussions that followed. His observation: "Give small people a chance, and they'll show the world what they can do. Take care of the little people everywhere or the little people will take care of the big people in a very summary form."

Three days later he was in Caracas, Venezuela. As the plane winged over sea, forests, woodlands, winding rivers, deep valleys, high mountains, jungles, and oil wells, he raised a question that he would repeat time after time wherever he went in the following decades: "What right has the present generation to use up so much of the exhaustible natural resources — oil, coal, minerals? Do they belong to us today, or were they intended for all human beings? Have we a moral right to use them up?" Caracas also brought home to him the problem of immigration that he had personally been working on for the past five years. He noticed the large number of displaced persons throughout the city. "It's a long story and a sad one. I am prying into it from every possible angle." He continued:

> A good-intentioned do-gooder gets eloquent, a smoothy paints a rosy picture. It's a story of unpreparedness, of lacking of selection standards, of hatreds and loves, of amorality and immorality, of justice, charity and exploitations. We cannot expect for displaced persons and immigrants any more or any better than the country offers to her own.

Reflecting further on the same problem he observed the tremendous resources of Venezuela, which, unfortunately, was allowing its exhaustible natural wealth to be drained away by get-rich-quick investors:

> The various political leaders are either unwilling to fulfill an obligation toward future generations or unconscious of the dire results in the future. Drainage, reclamation, sanitation, conservation, irrigation, plus education to use the resources, are the needs.

He arrived in Rio de Janeiro on June 2 and to the place that he would call his "home away from home" for the next month. After touching base with Civil and Church officials in the then capital city, he attended the opening session of the Pan American Social Welfare Conference, where one of the speakers was his old friend John O'Grady. He participated in an intellectually stimulating session called the Pope's Day Program at the Colegio S. Ignacio. In the afternoon Ligutti, fellow-lecturers, technicians, and priest-students literally crawled into a rickety bus and drove to the agricultural school, which was so new that it had no name other than "School Kilo 47," as it was forty-seven kilometers from the city. One of its students was the future Archbishop Helder Camara. The month's study-institute in problems of rural life was the fulfillment of a dream, a bit of daring-do, and persistent work by a young man named Joao Consalves de Souza.

Joao Consalves was a student of Dr. J. H. Kolb in the rural sociology department of the University of Wisconsin. While there de Souza visited the NCRLC offices in Des Moines and was impressed by the work of the Conference, especially the rural life institutes conducted by the Conference at St. John's University in Minnesota. Upon returning to Brazil he was fired with the idea of conducting a similar institute for the priests of his native country. He recognized the problem: in a nation whose population was almost 70 per cent rural and nominally Catholic, there was not even one pamphlet or book concerning the problems of Catholics in rural areas. Compounding this problem was the abysmal ignorance of the priests stationed in rural areas concerning the socio-economic problems of their people, the methods that could be employed, and the agencies already existing that could help alleviate many problems. Consalves enlisted the aid of Dr. Hilgard O'Reilly Sternberg, Dr. Carneiro, Dr. Manuel Ferreira, Dr. Roberval Cardosa, and a handful of other apostolic laymen associated with the Catholic Action Movement. The group set to work by promoting the rural life institute among the bishops and priests of Brazil. Their efforts were rewarded by the opening of the summer session with an enrollment of thirty-four priests from twelve states, representing twenty-six dioceses from every corner of the country.

Ligutti built his series of lectures around the document "Man's Relation to the Land." All the while that Ligutti was sharing his experiences and knowledge with the priest-students, he was also gaining deeper insights into the rural problems of Brazil. He learned, for example, that of the priests present none had less than 10,000 parishioners, and some had parishes of 20,000, 30,000, and even 50,000 people. He came to understand more deeply the vastness of the country, and the variety of people made stock-in-trade answers impossible. He realized once again, as he did in the United States, how many subjects taught in the seminary were seldom related to the practical problems and situations of local surroundings. He was elated when a former student of the agricultural school of the University of Iowa lectured on hybrid corn and promised to send a kilogram of hybrid seed to each rural pastor. He summarized his feelings:

> I am learning Brazil through their good social priests. What a variety in this country — not one but at least five distinct regions with many sub-areas. A Fulda Franciscan tells about the impenetrable jungle of Matto Gross; The German, Italian and Polish priests (all natives) about the parishes of the south. And so day after day in the halls, on the campus, in the dormitory I listen and I ask questions.

From his room in the Gloria Hotel in Rio de Janeiro he reflected on the rapid change of pace that confronted the priest-students as well as the Brazilians. He noted how the nation was thrust from the Middle Ages into the Atomic Age without the intermediary step of the Industrial Revolution. "Here," he wrote, "planes roar into Rio near the public market where peasants deliver their products in chests balanced on their heads." The summer school, however, convinced him that there were favorable omens in the sky for the years ahead. He left Rio on July 24 and first stopped at Anapolis in Central Goyas, staying overnight with the American Franciscans. He wrote:

> In my opinion the easily habitable sections of Goyaz and Parana could take care of Europe's surplus in handsome fashion, and create a very superior civilization. But it will take capital besides land and men. That's where Point Four comes in. Invest productive dollars that will come back to us. For every war dollar, a dollar for peace, and not charitable dollars either! If the world uses good sense, it can be done. If it insists on a senseless pursuit of selfish interests there will be more destruction and more unhappiness.

The brief stop in Argentina's metropolis witnessed the usual rounds of calls at the American embassy, the apostolic nunciature, the archbishop's residence, the department of agriculture, and, of course, his cousins. He discussed the status of the Christian family with the nuncio, Archbishop Giuseppe Fietta, pointing out how its influence has been weakened during the past generation and yet still remains the only effective social unit for transmitting social and religious loyalties. Both agreed that parish and school are not as powerful as they had been and that the question today should be: Why not work directly with the family? Ligutti also noticed that Catholicism was stronger in Argentina than in other Latin American countries because of better living conditions and a larger, stronger middle class.

Then followed a brief stop in Montevideo on his homeward journey and a visit with Archbishop Rodolfo Barbieri, who showed him the Cathedral of La Plata, a combination of the architecture of Cologne, Chartres, and Notre Dame. The archbishop said, "I like it, but the cathedral is not so important." Ligutti understood very well what the archbishop meant.

He arrived in Washington on August 10, after a thirty-hour flight from Rio, and reported to the State Department. He then hurried to Des Moines where he was greeted by Fr. John Kelly from Australia, who had been holding the fort; Fr. Joseph Servé, S.J., a leader of the Catholic rural life movement in France; and a displaced Latvian couple with two boys who were housed in the Conference's headquarters. They clasped the monsignor's hands and said, "Thank you." With joy in his heart he replied, "This is your home as it is mine."

South America called again and like the mythical sailors on the Rhine who listened for the siren's song from the cliff overhead, Ligutti answered the call. This time his purpose was of greater magnitude and importance. For ten days, January 9-18, 1953, he was one of the leading figures at the Second International Congress on Rural Life (the first in Latin America), which convened in Manizales, Colombia, in the heart of the Andes. This time he called his travelog "Andean Notes," which consisted of twenty letters and forty-four pages. He left on Christmas Day, 1952, after celebrating midnight Mass in his chapel on Grand Avenue surrounded by nephews, nieces, and their children. He would return in three months after visiting twenty-nine cities in all the countries of South America except the three Guyanas. In twenty-seven hours he was transferred from the cold of Iowa to a humid ninety-degree temperature of Port-au-Prince, Haiti, where he stopped to visit his personal friend Archbishop Francesco Lardonne, the papal nuncio.

The immediate result of so many air miles logged, so many weary days and sleepless nights, so many meetings, dinners, side trips, and lectures blossomed forth in this and three other international congresses on rural life held in Latin America. Ligutti was not only the guiding light, the behind-the-scenes planner, the promoter among friends and acquaintances throughout Latin America and the world but also the person who raised over $100,000 to sponsor the three congresses. His genius in fund-raising showed itself in that the congresses received grants from government agencies, private sources such as the Ford, Rockefeller, and Homeland Foundations, and individual friends and associates who were convinced of the worthiness of the cause because of Ligutti's contagious zeal.

In planning the international congresses his aims were threefold. First, he insisted that local planning be carried out by local people, for by involving them in planning and administering the congresses he knew that they would also be determined to carry out some, if not all, of the resolutions and ideas which the congresses proposed. Second, he secured the best men possible, no matter where they were, what their religious beliefs, what the cost of transportation and lodging. He sought the men who knew the most on such subjects as rural hygiene, nutrition, transportation, crop improvement, housing, conservation, education, or parish life. Third, he always preferred practical addresses, seminars, study sessions, and resolutions. He stressed the technical above the speculative; he emphasized the need of action above theory; he wanted implementation rather than idealization. With moral, spiritual, and financial assistance from many quarters and with the approval and support of high officials in the Vatican, the local hierarchy, and government offices, he undertook these three congresses with a firm conviction of their results.

Ligutti had visited Manizales the previous August to assist in making final plans for the first congress. He had received a letter from Montini assuring him of the pleasure and support of Pius XII. Bishops throughout Latin America were promoting it and many promised to send representatives. Many of those involved in the final preparations he already knew, and for him it was, as always, like returning to his "home away from home."

His plane arrived in Manizales on January 6, 1953 for a last-minute checkup before the opening-welcoming day on January 9. He was pleased to meet many friends at the airport, including Archbishop Antonio Samore, the papal nuncio to Colombia; Bishop Albert Zuroweste, the NCRLC episcopal president; Msgr. Frank Kaiser of Germany, director of Caritas Internationalis; and Mr. George Dugan, religion writer for the New York *Times*. As the group deplaned they were welcomed by the governor of the province and the motorcade proceeded into the city. Over 10,000 people lined the narrow streets to welcome the papal nuncio and to shower the cars with a seemingly infinite variety of flowers. The next day Ligutti met his friends and associates, Monsignor Morrison, Fr. John Ireland Gallery, Fr. Caesare Donanzan, Fr. Frederick McGuire, C.M., and others. There were forty representatives from the United States registered for the congress, including Bishop Edwin Vincent O'Hara and Bishop Raymond Lane, M.M., superior general of the Maryknoll Fathers.

Archbishop Samore officially opened the congress in the cathedral by offering Mass and preaching a sermon entitled "The Popes and Agriculture" on Sunday, January 11. "Crowds everywhere," Ligutti wrote. "We walked, we marched, we stood at attention as the national hymn was played. Civil and military authorities, barefooted urchins, graceful mantillas, warming ruanas, and the canons of the cathedral trying to keep step, in spite of their stiff knees and paunchy setting." Over six hundred participants had registered, including twenty-four archbishops and bishops and representatives from twenty-three nations. That evening the civic opening was held in the Grand Olympia Theater with a formal address by Zuroweste and a scholarly lecture by Dr. William Hernandes de Alba entitled "The Contribution of the Catholic Church to Latin American Agriculture." That Thursday over four hundred delegates were guests of the governor at a dinner held in the Club Manizales' ballroom where Ligutti answered the toast of the governor. The bishop of Manizales hosted a formal reception in his home on Friday night. The outdoor Mass in the stadium attracted over 25,000 people, especially the poor, who walked all day or rode in wobbly trucks down the mountain trails. Bishop Luis Concha of Manizales (now the cardinal-archbishop of Bogota) offered the Mass and preached on "The Duty of the Catholic Church toward Rural People in Latin America." The gathering was called the *Concentracion Campesina*. Schlarman, who died the previous November 10, was memorialized at a Mass offered by Zuroweste and in a sermon preached by Bishop Manuel Larrain of Talca.

The real work of the congress, however, was performed in the two assembly sessions each morning and in the study and discussion groups in the afternoons and evenings. Over thirty speakers from ten nations presented addresses, among them Zuroweste, O'Hara, Morrison, and Mr. Raymond Miller, a director of the National Council of Churches; and Mr. Wheeler McMillen, editor of the *Farm Journal*. The ten planned discussion groups increased to thirteen, the three additional groups dealing with alcoholism, vocations, and the Indians.

On his first night in Manizales, Ligutti went for his customary walk. He wrote, "A young, imaginative, black-haired priest told me, as we walked in the silence of a moonless sky, 'The Southern Cross is a brooch our Blessed Lady lost when she was assumed into heaven.' It was something to meditate on and pray." When the delegates were departing, the speeches delivered, the conclusions drawn up and published, he sat down again and wrote, "There are days when one should feel both proud and grateful. This is one of them for me."

The satisfaction with the Manizales meeting had been distilled in many grateful hearts when already Ligutti was thinking of another international congress on rural life. Feelers were sent out to friends and associates and Ligutti received encouraging replies. Good propagandist that he always was, he knew well that once a project succeeded the best thing to do was to have a repeat performance. His diaries tell the story of the Third International Congress on Rural Life held in Panama City, Panama, from April 17-24, 1955. Neither his journey through Africa nor the routine work of the NCRLC and other concerns prevented him from planning this congress. His diaries for 1954 and 1955 reflect his many concerns. On April 15, 1954 Joseph H. Pernicone was consecrated auxiliary bishop of New York and Ligutti noted: "The first Italian-born bishop in the United States since 1870." On May 25: "When the phone rings I hate it; when it does not ring I wonder." On July 28: "I like to do humble physical work." On August 11: "Monsignor Montini wrote informing me that I have been appointed to the International Catholic Migration Council." On September 9: "I sent a personal check to Daly — $500 for education of seminarians." On November 26: "Wrote Dr. Bonomelli asking to see if Father James Byrnes can be made a monsignor." On January 22, 1955: "A priest's work is *not* exclusive to make people join the Church." On March 21: "Thank God for my sixtieth birthday." Nothing escaped his attention; events large and small were duly recorded. During the middle years of the twentieth century he stood with Fr. John LaFarge, S.J., as perhaps the two most vocal spokesmen of the Church's social gospel.

On March 31, 1954 he flew to Panama to initiate the preparations for the congress. He noted that the archbishop was less than enthusiastic about the congress and tried not to have it in his see city. After much persuasion, however, he did appoint a priest, Father Gleason, to study its plans and possibilities. Here Ligutti met Fr. Thomas Clavel, who immediately became a champion of the congress. Later, as the archbishop of Panama, Clavel would become one of the progressive voices among the Latin American hierarchy.

Preparations were set in motion, following the same guidelines that were established at Manizales. In February, 1955, Ligutti returned to Panama to discuss the financial needs of the congress. On February 1, Archbishop Paolo Bernier, the papal nuncio, wrote Ligutti that the congress had the archbishop's approval. In March Ligutti returned for more discussions concerning finances. He was disappointed to see the confused state of local preparations. He returned home to raise money for the congress. On March 26, 1955 he returned to Panama to assist in the press arrangements and to finalize immediate preparations. He was delighted to meet Fr. Marco McGrath, C.S.C., with whom he became a good friend. Neither at that time realized how their paths would intertwine in the coming years when McGrath became a leading figure and spokesman for Latin America at the Second Vatican Council and subsequently the archbishop of Panama.

The structure of the congress followed the pattern established at Manizales, with the usual round of dinners, receptions, outdoor Masses, informal gatherings, and excursions in and around the city. The delegates from twenty-three countries included archbishops and bishops from North and South America. Great stress was given the role of cooperatives and credit unions, with a layman from Santa Domingo presenting a paper on "The Effect of Credit Unions on Souls." The resolutions proposed an institute for the study of cooperatives and the formation of a federation of credit unions throughout Latin America.

Ligutti sent his usual letters to friends and associates, prepared his report to Msgr. Angelo Dell'Acqua, head of the Vatican Secretariat; was delighted that all the bills for the congress were paid, took his place at the farewell dinner, and left for Washington, D.C., on April 28. Two days later at a picnic supper with friends in the nation's capital he mentioned the need of another international congress and felt that it should be held in Chile. Already he was planning his first step for action. That action culminated in the Fourth International Congress on Rural Life, the third in Latin America, from March 31 — April 8, 1957, in Santiago, Chile.

Ligutti arrived in Santiago from Buenos Aires on March 11 and went about the usual rounds of last minute preparations for the congress. On March 16 in a conversation with a Chilean priest, well-educated and very social-minded, Ligutti discovered that 49 per cent of the farmers in Chile owned less than 2 per cent of the land and that figure did not include the property-less farm workers. "Our coming Congress," he wrote, "seeks to bring these facts into focus." He was happy to meet Fr. Roger Vekemans, the sociologist from Belgium; to have the support of the papal nuncio, Archbishop Sebastiano Baggio; and to see again his close friend and collaborator Bishop Manuel Larrain. He had nothing but praise for the assistance of Ambassador Lyon of the United States; his first secretary, Mr. Robert Corrigan; and the chief of mission, Mr. Albion Patterson. He was grateful for the presence of the press corps, knowing that only a few hundred hear a speech but through the media millions throughout the world get the message.

In spite of the impressive array of speakers, the registration of over seven hundred delegates, and the excellent facilities in the Hotel Carrera, the congress was beset by external problems. In Manizales the chivalry of the local bandits imposed a ban on thievery during that congress. In Santiago the delegates who had assembled to start a "peaceful revolution" found themselves in the midst of revolution, riots, and bloodshed. The spark that lit the fuse was a one cent increase in streetcar fares, preceded by a steady rise in the cost of living and the pitiful low wages paid the workers. Angry mobs, following the lead of the university students, first attacked the transportation system by overturning and stoning streetcars and moved on to frontal attacks upon the unpopular police force. The evening of March 31, when the congress convened, transportation ceased and on April 1 martial law was declared and the army moved in. This was the signal for further rioting, looting, and wrecking. Such chaos had its effect upon the rural life congress.

The theme of the congress, "Man and the Land in Latin America," was examined by over six hundred participants, including Cardinal Jose Caro, archbishop of Santiago; the papal nuncio, Archbishop Baggio; and eight archbishops and bishops. Speakers included such leaders as Mr. Stanislaw Mikolajczyk, president of the International Peasants Union; Mr. Harry Schwartz, analyst of Russian economic reports for the New York *Times;* Mr. Douglas Hyde, the ex-Communist editor of London's *Daily Worker;* and Mr. Alexander Magnet, a brilliant young Chilean writer. The newly elected Senator Edward Frei, later president of Chile and head of the Christian Democratic Party, attended many sessions. The threefold purpose of the congress was to establish that Communism comes into power through the dissatisfaction and despair of the poor, to examine the *real* situation in Latin America, and to demonstrate what could be accomplished in Latin America through the application of Christian social principles. The congress carried out its deliberations, formulated resolutions, and left an impact upon its participants who carried the gospel of rural renewal and land reform back to their native lands. Ligutti summarized the results:

> Personally, without vanity or pride, I believe they (the effects) are beyond all expectation and of tremendous historical significance. The shots were heard around Latin America, and these shots were the fundamental principles of Christian social justice. The world is moving at a terrific

rate. Christianity cannot lag behind. It must be dynamic, it cannot become fossilized. Bureaucracy must not be stabilized and consecrated. Christianity has the answer, but not the Christianity of word without deed, of form without substance.

Apart from other notable results, the Santiago congress was a high-water mark in the thinking and the career of Ligutti. At one session in a major address he expressed his thinking and reflections gained from a decade's experience in his travels and conversations throughout the two American continents. The address was entitled "Human Dignity and Economic Efficiency." After working several months in preparing it, Ligutti had the then Msgr. George H. Speltz of Winona react to it, and then Dr. S. Rottenberg and his associates at the Catholic University of Chile translated it into Spanish. The opening statement expressed the thesis of the address:

> Modern technology in industry, commerce, or agriculture functions more effectively and profitably in the production of goods and services when the human beings involved operate in keeping with their personal dignity, welfare of family, and when they can share in the ownership of the means of production, and in its results.

The clarity of his style is marked on every page as he stated his case objectively and forthrightly. "If some human beings seem hopeless," he said, "it is because some of us have neither the intelligence nor the love to extend a helping hand and make God's infinite and universal love visible. The battle for the dignity of man has not yet been won." In response to those who maintained that productive efficiency could only be guaranteed by large landholdings, either by corporations or governments, he countered:

> There is another way of assuring efficient land use and fuller production; i.e., private ownership and operation on an economic unit basis with the assistance of public and private authority and free cooperatives in management, production, credit and sale of goods. All this implies a change in traditional patterns of land tenure, inheritance laws, taxation, etc.

Finally, he answered those who hold that it is practically impossible to educate and change great masses of people who are steeped in age-long traditions:

The faith in God and man as found in the minds and hearts of the Latin races, their imaginative and loving character mingled with the tremendous abilities and endurance powers of the Indios makes the difficult task a challenge, but a very attainable goal. It can be done. On the entirely reasonable assumption, then, that religion and education will be fostered, most men will be found capable of ownership.

Ligutti also applied his own thinking on Church support to Latin America. Convinced from his own pastoral experience that self-help is the best help, he always considered "that a member of the Church has a duty in conscience, as part of his duty to worship God, to return to God (for God's works in this world) a share of what God gives to him." This conviction he applied also to Latin America and spelled it out further in a memorandum dated December 6, 1960 to Archbishop Romolo Carboni, then papal nuncio to Peru. Ligutti never believed that the Church should be dependent upon the State. "It would be interesting to point out," he wrote, "that where the Catholic Church has no financial support from the State and where it does not rely on income from ownership of properties, the Church is really and truly prosperous and flourishing." He insisted that Church support was not an act of generosity but of justice, a personal duty and not a State subsidy. "The weekly contributor," he observed, "is a better Catholic all around."

He stated the case bluntly: "To manage land properly requires much capital and ability. The Church usually possesses neither." He suggested that the Church rid itself of all property not needed for religious purposes. "What a magnificent public relations impression would be made in Latin America," he wrote, "if the Church would pull out from ownership of land at the present time. Some of it would be donated outright to settlers, the rest sold before confiscation and the receipts invested in anonymous stocks and bonds." In recent years he was happy to see that such actions were taking place in many places throughout Latin America, confirming his conviction: "We need not fear for support of God's works if our faithful are real Christians."

He did not abandon his interest in Latin America after the Santiago congress. He continued to visit the continent for addresses at national and continental meetings on cooperatives, credit unions, and land reform measures. He spoke several times before the board of governors of the Inter-American Bank and attended meetings sponsored by the United Nations' Food and Agriculture

Organization in various parts of Latin America. In the 1960's he inspired and inaugurated two projects of lasting significance, the one awakening the intellectual world to Latin America's potential and the other assisting Christian missionaries in a better understanding of the people they served. He also carried on his campaign for a better understanding of Latin America by Civic and Church leaders north of the Rio Grande.

"Yankee Go Home" was more than a slogan shouted at Vice-President Richard Nixon on his visit to Latin America in 1958. It was a bitterness and resentment ingrained in the thinking of the Latin American people, rich or poor, farmer or government official, cleric or housewife. Ligutti continued to call the attention of his fellow-Americans to this phenomenon.

Perhaps he expressed himself best in a letter-to-the-editor of the Washington *Post* of August 17, 1961. He admitted, as did many officials in the United States Department of State, the confusion in Washington about U.S. — Latin American relations, aggravated by the "deteriorating internal conditions in most Latin American countries." He also pointed out that this situation arises from a complicated pattern of social, historic, and religious patterns as well as economic possibilities and failures that are neither clearly understand nor easily defined by the North American. "Anti-Yankeeism," he wrote, "is very evident and rampant in Latin America. Why not make a real study of it?" Then he proposed:

> A clinical examination, thoroughly objective and completely scientific, is the first step toward discovering the cause of the malaise, its roots, and branches. Evidently the U.S. has never attacked the problem except onesided and haphazardly.... Modern sociological scientific research could be used to uncover, measure and evaluate the Latin American problem facing us now. It is not what we think that matters, what it is that counts.... Latin America, biologically and economically is too precious for centuries to come to be misunderstood or dealt with lightly during the last half of the 20th century.

Ligutti was never a man to pose a problem and merely suggest a solution. An idea meant action. Shortly after this letter he set to work on a "Project of Study on Anti-Yankeeism in Latin America." It became the germinal seed for the Homeland Foundation study carried out by the International Federation of Institutes for Social Research (FERES) with headquarters in Fribourg, Switzerland. He proposed a four-part scientific study of the Latin American press, a psycho-sociological research carried out through extensive interviews, an objective study of facts learned in order to determine the objectivity of anti-Yankee feelings and the external influences increasing anti-Yankeeism such as Communism, commercial exploitation, religious groups, and trade unions. In seeking facts, Ligutti proposed that they would help to establish the mutual portrait of the North and South American with regard to each other, what South Americans like and dislike about North Americans, the culture and way of life of South Americans that North Americans should understand, the reasons Latin Americans give for anti-Yankeeism, and the attitude Latin Americans have toward foreigners of other nations. He suggested that the study be carried out in a period of fourteen to twenty months and estimated that, including the printing of five hundred copies of the findings, the project would cost about $200,000.

The grant was allotted and the study was assigned to FERES under the direction of Canon François Houtart, professor of sociology at Louvain University. After intensive research and diligent study FERES produced forty-two paperback volumes containing the results of the study. These have proven over the years to be an invaluable aid for governments and religious groups in understanding the conditions in Latin American countries.

Ligutti also initiated a study of missionary activity in the Third World. He had secured the approval of the Vatican's Office for the Propagation of the Faith as well as the interest of the World Council of Churches for a joint study. In a memorandum of November 23, 1962 to Mr. Dean David of the Ford Foundation, he listed seven reasons why an inventory of institutions of religious bodies and their impact on social and national betterment in developing countries was worthy of consideration:

1. The survey-inventory is promoted by the two highest bodies of the Catholic and Protestant Churches. Their agreement to make a request in unison is very significant and marks a milestone in the road towards Christian unity.
2. The lack of organized information as to the work — past and present — of the Christian leaders in the emerging nation-countries has been a handicap in the formulation of plans and a cause of misunderstanding on the part of the local people.
3. The survey-inventory is being planned and will be carried out by two most qualified organizations, the International

Federation of Catholic Institutes for Social and Socio-Religious Research (FERES) and the Institute of Social Studies (ISS) with Protestant and Catholic background. Here again a step of scholars in the right direction.
4. Most enthusiastic reception has been given to the plan by all groups involved.
5. For future plans of work the Western Groups need to know — even among themselves — the results of their work in the past, their present resources, their possibilities and particularly the present needs of the developing peoples.
6. The announcement to the world that the Ford Foundation will sponsor a project would have a tremendous effect upon the Christian leaders and the world. I am a participant in the II Vatican Council and I can feel the desire, the hope for Unity on the part of the Council members. It may take centuries to bring it about but it will have to start in what we call "the mission field."
7. The survey-inventory is not to be a mere sterile effort but it will furnish the foundation stones for future plans and action. This is the determined will of the ones involved. It is not to be a mere geological-like prodding into the hidden facts of mother earth — but a discovery for practical use of atomic forces for peace and love among humans.

In this memorandum to the directors of the Ford Foundation, he listed the present situation of religious institutions and their contributions to the developing world. He also proposed pilot institutes for leadership training to advance human development. This proposal was made jointly by the National Catholic Rural Life Conference and the agricultural missions department of the National Council of Churches. When the directors of the Ford Foundation asked for the approval of the World Council of Churches and the Vatican Office for the Propagation of the Faith, Dr. Roswell P. Barnes readily secured the former and Ligutti obtained the latter. Ligutti had laid the groundwork in his usual style of attending to all details and touching all bases.

Msgr. Joseph Gremillion, at the time stationed in New York City and working with the Catholic Relief Services, acted as quarterback for the team. On May 28, 1962 Ligutti wrote Gremillion:

May I extend to you sincerest thanks and congratulations on the magnificent success of our proposal for the Ford Foundation. You certainly must be given the full credit for the preparation and for the presentation. All the credit I can take is the fact that I prayed very hard, and you know how effective my prayers generally are, when you are doing the preliminary work, with the Holy Ghost.

The missionary survey-inventory was undertaken, again under the direction of FERES and the National Council of Churches, with Canon Houtart as the coordinator. Ligutti's dream of a scientific sociological study had been realized. The Ford Foundation granted $403,300 for the project. Case studies were undertaken in Colombia, Brazil, Cameroun, Iinda, Indonesia, and Tanzania. The information which was gathered, correlated, and published is an invaluable help to Christian missionaries throughout the world in their work of elevating the human person, teaching agricultural methods, and collaborating with other private and governmental agencies for improving the quality of life in the developing world.

Ligutti, several years later, in 1967, revealed another aspect of his priestly soul when he wrote as "a loving father" two reprimands to his friend Houtart. He was saddened when Houtart and other professors at Louvain University, together with five hundred students, protested Pope Paul VI's pilgrimage to Fatima on the grounds that it seemed to approve the dictatorship of President Antonio Salazar. With a disturbed mind and a heavy heart, he wrote:

> Really and truly, François, I just did not expect any such action on your part. It is not only because it was an act of disrespect toward a Vicar of Christ but an act of unjust accusation against a good and honest man — a lover of peace and a man who detests tyranny and autocracy. To write an open letter to the Pope reveals a cheapness in action for the sake of publicity and notoriety.

The following year, on November 27, 1968, he wrote Houtart again as "a loving father." He objected to the canon's remarks in a speech he delivered in Washington, D.C., concerning the papal visit to the Eucharistic Congress in Bogota, Colombia, where the Pope resided at the papal nunciature. Ligutti reprimanded his young friend:

> The nunciature of Bogota is one of the lousiest in the world. The Holy See had nothing to do with cars used. Where would you house the Pope if he came to Belgium? Where did the "liturgists" stay in Washington? Why not resurrec-

tion city? .... If you had laid out the details of the Pope's itinerary just what would have been the details? Things are changing and have to change for we are living in a world which does exist and has to be faced as it is.

One of Ligutti's joys was to serve as a papal envoy in 1970. Paul VI established the *Populorum Progressio* Fund in honor of the encyclical by the same title. Six months after returning from the Eucharistic Congress of August, 1968, in Bogota, Pope Paul deposited $1,000,000 in the fund, income received from the sale of Vatican property in Paris. It was a gesture aimed at encouraging individuals and organizations to contribute to the fund which was designed for a fairer distribution of wealth throughout the world.

In December, 1970, Monsignor Ligutti journeyed to Punta del Este, Uruguay, to serve as a panelist at the eleventh annual meeting of the board of directors of the Inter-American Development Bank. Also on this journey he presented the $1,000,000 gift of the Pope to three *campesinos* in Colombia. The gift was to be administered by the Colombian Institute for Agrarian Reform and was to be distributed among three different groups of farmers living in the Cauca River Valley in southwestern Colombia. In presenting the gift, Ligutti said:

> Its programs are aimed at seeing that those so-called "poor devils" can become what they are truly called to be, and to have a better living — not as a handout but as the result of opportunity. Anything less is contrary to the dignity which belongs to every man because he is a human being. The first requirement in land reform is man reform.

The money was to educate the people for self-help through academic and technical courses as well as practical ventures, such as cooperatives, credit unions, and leadership-development institutes. Ligutti estimated that from ten to thirty thousand men, women, and children would benefit directly from the papal gift.

In a letter from South America, Monsignor Ligutti wrote his friends, "As I look at the Southern Cross each night I will be saying a little prayer for you — provided you look at the North Star and say a prayer for me." Without a doubt today there are thousands of Latin Americans looking at the Southern Cross and praying for this modern apostle of Latin America.

Cardinals Richard Cushing of Boston and Raimono Miranda of Mexico City shared a mutual interest with Monsignor Ligutti in the problems of Latin America.

At the White House President John Kennedy visits a group of Italo-Americans, including Monsignor Ligutti.

Monsignor Ligutti returned to his native province of Udine whenever possible.

A favorite spot was his cousin's home in Manazzons, about 70 miles from Venice.

Fr. Theodore Hesburgh, C.S.C., president of Notre Dame University, conferred an honorary doctor of letters degree on Monsignor Ligutti at the March, 1966, commencement.

In 1968 Monsignor Ligutti received an honorary doctor of letters from the Catholic University of America. Left to right: Fr. John Whalen, Fr. Edward Bunn, S.J., Senator Edward Brooke of Massachusetts, Cardinal Patrick O'Boyle, Ligutti, and Dr. S. Dillon Ripley.

Pope Paul VI in October, 1971, addressed the delegates of the Food and Agriculture Organization.

Monsignor Ligutti on September 17, 1967 delivered the sermon at the Mass in the parish church in Granger celebrating the golden jubilee of his ordination to the priesthood. At home "with the people I love."

The monsignor with his friends Fr. John Gorman (left) and Mr. Chauncey Stillman.

With his former students at the golden jubilee of Dowling High School, Des Moines, in 1972.

Monsignor Ligutti, canon of the Basilica of St. Mary Major in Rome, and his biographer, Msgr. Vincent Yzermans, on the steps of the basilica in January, 1974.

Villa Stillman near Rome.

CHAPTER NINE

LONELY GUARDS WHO WATCH

Latin America was one interest of this American priest who could literally make his own John Wesley's words, "The whole world is my parish." There were other lands calling, other peoples needing aid, other bridges to be built between the Church and the world, between Christians and pagans, between missionaries and technicians. This interest impelled Monsignor Ligutti to broaden his horizons, moving from Rome, a center of Christendom, to the sources of Christianity in the Near East, to island-hopping and continent-hopping in the land of Buddha and Confucius, to exploring the hope and promise of Africa. Few could write with more candor and honesty than Ligutti when he penned a somewhat critical commentary on the conciliar decree concerning the Church's missionary activity:

> My deep love for the missions of the Church has prompted me to make these observations. I make them in the light of first-hand observations gained through frequent visits to the missions. They also, I believe, reflect the thinking of most of the missionaries whom I have met in my travels throughout the past decade. These observations are made by one who has striven to be a servant of the Church which we now see in these post-conciliar days as, above all else, a Servant Church.

In November, 1951, Ligutti was preparing for a journey to regions that even so experienced a traveler had not visited. He said he wanted to see the land of the crescent, "to visit Mohammedan countries, the cradles of civilization, the land of the cedars and the Garden of Eden; where music, art and literature were in full bloom while our Nordic ancestors lived in caves." He was on these journeys the apostle of the Third World — a term just becoming popular in Catholic circles. No one could better describe his purpose than he did himself when he wrote from Amman, Jordan, on January 16, 1952:

> I have gone through country after country and have urged Catholic authorities and institutions to take a greater interest in the economic and social life of the nation. I am making a special plea to Catholic educational and charitable centers for a more practical effort in their work. I am suggesting to hospitals the setting up of training schools for mid-wives; to high schools the extending of their courses to prepare real practical rural teachers for the villages.... If I had my say-so, I would go into the seminaries, both Christian and Moslem, and begin to sell the ideas and the techniques to the future religious leaders in the rural districts. This is the easier approach. If the religious leaders don't want to do it or judge it extraneous to their task, then they can hardly complain if the secular state takes over everything.

This was his mission in the three journeys that form the subject of this chapter. The first, lasting from November 8, 1951 to February 10, 1952, he described to friends in a series of twenty-three letters called the "Cross and Crescent" letters. He discovered, however, throughout Turkey, Iran, Iraq, Syria, Lebanon, Israel, and Greece an abundance of crescents and very few crosses.

His abiding interest in the classics and history was given free rein and, as to be expected, he was thrilled at every turn he took in the Near East. As always, however, his journey was sandwiched between two important meetings. The first was the Food and Agriculture Organization Council meeting, followed by the full conference, lasting until December 15. On his return he attended a three-day meeting of the executive council of the International Catholic Migration Commission in Geneva. He returned to Des Moines on February 10, was greeted by the new executive secretary of the National Catholic Rural Life Conference, Fr. Daniel Dunn of Boston, climbed the stairs to St. Isidore's chapel, and mumbled the prayer, "Thank God I am home." His Isidorian angelic companion added, "It's comfy."

The trip was marred at the outset by news that cut into Ligutti's heart. He described the loss in a letter written from New York on November 11:

> On Friday noon Monsignor Morrison and I had lunch with Archbishop Schlarman. It was a most pleasant reunion of the three fellow travelers to South America back in 1945, and it was to discuss plans for a Catholic Rural Life Con-

gress in South America that we broke bread in fraternal fashion. The Archbishop stayed over purposely — one last effort for a friend and for a cause. Within a few hours he answered his final summons. His whole life was a preparation for his daily Mass, and he died preparing for Mass.

Misfortunes, losses, and blessings seem to pile up so quickly. Another of his former presidents had gone from his midst, Bishop Ryan of Bismarck. Ligutti wrote:

> It was he who was greatly responsible for the editorship of our NCRLC bible, "The Manifesto on Rural Life" published in 1939... Physically frail and small in stature, he revealed himself an intellectual giant in some of his writings, speeches and actions... The wound was sharp, stinging, cruel and it will be lasting. Prayer alleviates; prayer furnishes assurance springing from faith in eternity. Thank God! I know we shall meet again."

Rome was, as always, a constant whirl of activities, meetings, and receptions. Ligutti noted that the extreme heat had subsided and "the dear old monsignors and the dashing young diplomats feel better." He reflected on the traditionalism of Roman life and ways. "I would like to be around," he wrote, "when someone will attempt a few, not to say many, radical changes. What fun!" On November 26 he visited Don Luigi Sturzo to greet him on his eightieth birthday. "To kiss his hand, to kneel in blessing before him is really a sacramental for me," he noted.

The strenuous work of the official Vatican observer to the Food and Agriculture Organization was completed. On December 15 he boarded KLM Flight 289 and within four hours had traveled from the land of the cross to the world of the crescent. As the plane hummed over Greece this traveling Vatican diplomat (a term he never relished!) was far removed from the world of protocol and deep in recollecting the classics. "I kept thinking," he wrote, "of Ulysses and Aeneas — their wanderings. Penelope could not have done much weaving and unweaving if Ulysses had flown a KLM, and Aeneas might have saved Dido's life if he had taken off before sunrise and the love-smitten queen had not seen his ships making for the horizon." In Istanbul he stayed at the apostolic delegation as the guest of the eighty-three-year-old Archbishop Andrea Cassulo, successor to a previous delegate, Angelo Roncalli. He recalled the three names of the city, Byzantium, Constantinople, and Istanbul and a bit of history he had learned many years ago:

There is more diversified history on the Golden Horn than any place else in the world. What a kaleidoscopic review could be presented from prehistoric days to 1951! In the Museum of Antiquity, not far from S. Sofia this morning I saw the rich evidences of unsurpassed art and architecture, Greek and Roman; the sarcophagus of Alexander the Great; statues of Zeus and Apollo; the sarcophagus of the mourners, a great study of grieving faces of women.

On December 17 he departed for ancient Ancyra, now Ankara, which was the center of the Galatians. He recalled the sermon Archbishop Schlarman preached many years ago at Westphalia, Iowa, entitled "St. Paul to the Galatian Farmers." He was not, however, too impressed by the capital of Turkey built by Ataturk where he noted with a bit of lonesomeness "a lone little Christmas tree in the back of a truck." The weather was cold, snow was drifting, and his plans to visit old Cappadoce and its famous monasteries carved out of the rocks had to be cancelled. He visited the agricultural university and met many good scientists and agronomists. He was pleased to learn that Turkey was one country "where the problem of land tenure, large land holdings and a rural proletariat do not present a real problem." He was also pleased to hear that some good agricultural schools were scattered throughout the country and the experimental stations were being effectively developed. He visited a farmer's home, where he was cordially received and where he noted the cleanliness, neatness, and good taste of the adobe house with its red roof. He admired the women of the village who clung to ancient traditions, and he philosophically observed, "Rural folk the world over are the great preservers and the begetters of revolutions." He could not refrain from thinking of Paul, the first great missionary:

> Centuries ago Paul of Tarsus saw these hills and mountains. In his letter to the Galatians he said, "Bear ye one another's burdens." He thus stated the Christian principles underlying cooperatives. We in far off America have heard his inspired words. Perhaps our technical assistance program is our answer to his call.

He returned to Istanbul "on the shortest day of the year on the Bosporus." He stayed at the Park Hotel and spent the next few days visiting churches and shrines, listening to the echoes of history as he walked the streets of the Golden Horn. He visited the Church of the Savior, the most precious jewel of the city, and reflected on the early Christian devotion to the Mother of God: "The *dormitio* scene furnishes proof of the belief's extent in Byzantine days. We have nothing in the Latin Church that surpasses the love exhibited toward the Virgin Mary by the art of the early and late Greek Church." Sadly he continued:

> There are but few Crosses among the Crescents now. The Turks are tolerant, but once they conquer they put on the squeeze process. There never was any real prohibition of Christianity, but it's like Israel now and Germany before the war — no jobs, no business, no civil service, a massacre now and then (as the Armenians). A church is not used — well, let's make it a mosque.

As a result of such unofficial intolerance he noted that practically all Catholic churches were inconspicuously buried behind a courtyard in some out-of-the-way street. On December 22 he met his friend of the Catholic War Services stationed in Rome, the Brooklyn-born Msgr. Andrew Landi. They exchanged a hurried greeting and planned to spend Christmas Day together. He boarded the plan for Tehran, Iran. As he departed from Ataturk's nation, he observed:

> Turkey impressed me as a land of possibilities, perhaps not a land of probabilities. A religious philosophy of life has much to do with material development. I judge they are more deeply spiritual in out-look than we Christians, as the Latin is more than the Anglo-Saxon. I feel certain that Turkey could double its agricultural production and care for double its numbers at a higher standard of living than enjoyed at the present time. Over 30,000 Turkish-Bulars have been nicely resettled. Over 600,000 acres were parcelled out last year to landless villagers. I saw evidence of drunkenness and opium usage, but these vices are not prevalent, I am told.

Never before had Ligutti experienced so lonely and tragic a Christmas Eve as he did in the Park Hotel in Tehran, a city that reminded him so much of Denver. The "sadness that lowers my low spirits tonight" he recalled as he sat with pen in hand in the emptiness of his somber hotel room.

> My good friend Dr. Bennet, his wife and party were burned to death in a plane crash near the Tehran airport the night before last. My plane landed in a clear field only a few hours before. Dr. Bennett's plane of Egyptian Airlines was coming in at 7:30 p.m. The snow was falling thick and fast.

A poorly serviced airport, a careless pilot, and tragedy ensued.... His wife was at his side, not disturbed, quiet, unassuming, brave withal. They died together in a loving embrace as they had lived together for many years. Side by side they plunged to their deaths in a little dry river bed at the foothills that surround the valley of Tehran.... I was in my room and heard it. Many people saw it.... The big plane had skimmed the top of a small hill, hit lower at the next one, over the third knoll and came to rest in a narrow canyon — all burned to a crisp except toward the rear.... Dr. Bennett died in the line of duty. He was the chief of America's invisible weapons, the exponent of Christianity and democracy at work. He held the torch high against the gathering dark clouds.

In a rare expression of sentiment he also recalled this Christmas Eve the many happy gatherings of previous years when members of his family and friends gathered for midnight Mass in St. Isidore's shrine in Des Moines. He thought, too, of his happy years as pastor when the consolations of administering the sacraments to his people helped to ease the memory of happy family gatherings in childhood and youth. "To be so far from home in a Moslem country on Christmas eve" he wrote, "makes me realize how deep in my heart are the strings that bind me to America, to Des Moines, to my little chapel of St. Isidore."

His spirits were better when he began his letter of December 28 with "There are 1,200,000 asses in Iran. I am leaving on Monday. No use crowding the joint. I would not advise you to come." Monsignor Landi arrived on Christmas afternoon and the two Americans spent the evening together in fond memories and fraternal conversation. Ligutti described Tehran "like an adolescent boy whose feet are getting bigger, the shoes smaller, stumbles and is afraid of girls." He pictured Iran as a triborough bridge touching Europe through Turkey, the North through Russia, and the Far East through Afghanistan. He saw it as an underdeveloped country with only 50,000,000 acres under tillage and an additional 83,000,000 acres that could be used, but as he observed: "The world is not too small; it's we who don't know how to use God's gifts to advantage."

He admitted that he knew little about Iran but felt that "the preparation teachers for the country districts will accomplish more than all else." With his characteristic vision he almost foretold the present situation in the Near East when he warned, "Our inflexibility may play into the hands of the Russians, and if we lose Iran it won't be long before the Arab world will follow suit. If that happens, we are sunk." As usual, he visited as many missionary centers, parishes, and schools as he could. On the last day of 1951 he posed a question that would continually haunt him not only on this trip but later throughout his travels in Asia and Africa:

> I wonder if Catholics in the world at large and particularly in the U.S. and Rome realize the importance of the priests, bishops and people who live in the outposts of Catholicity. Much of the strength of our church comes from the outposts, the isolated pillboxes, the lonely guards who watch the Cross amidst the Crescents.

He bid farewell to Monsignor Landi and welcomed the new year in Baghdad, Iraq. On the Iraqian Airlines flight from Tehran he enjoyed a pleasant visit with Senator and Mrs. Owen Brewster of Maine as they shared views and impressions of the countries they had visited. As he gazed upon the flat endless valley of the Tigris-Euphrates Rivers, he noted the outlines of irrigation canals and laterals that thousands of years ago made the area one of the richest and most fertile in the world:

> Water and civilization are synonymous. If water is put to use, dams and artificial lakes up the river would prevent disastrous spring floods and electric power should be available at a small cost. Salty bottoms can be washed easily. A modern version of the earthly paradise would greet the eyes and the nostrils of the visitors from Mars.

Sadly he noted the extreme poverty in a country where with a little financial and technical aid no man should go to bed hungry. Instead, from Babylon to Ctesiphon he saw "the stark evidences of land ill used and humanity at the bottom of the scale." He recalled the countless hours of work and seemingly interminable struggles carried on against land tenancy in Iowa back in the thirties. On a two-hour journey by car from Baghdad to Babylon he indulged in a reverie mixing history and Scripture:

> Only ruins and piles of broken bricks greet you. It takes imagination and the warmth of the noonday sun to reconstruct banquet halls and besieging armies, Nabuchodonosor Rex, Queen Semiramis and the hanging gardens, Manetechel Phares, the great processions, the feasting and the sacrifices. I always wanted to visit Babylon. As a young chap I remem-

ber the impression made on me by the Psalm: "*Super flumina Babylonis illic sedimus et flevimus cum recordaremur Sion* — We sat down by the streams of Babylon and wept there, remembering Sion." (Psalm 136, v. 1) The Jews of the captivity, their work, their silent yearnings, and Sion. The prophecies of the Old Testament are indeed fulfilled. A gazelle ran off and disappeared among the ruins of the Greek theater. A grouse arose from the midst of Russian thistles near the Ishtar gate. *Sis transit gloria mundi!*

By January 8, 1952 Ligutti was in Syria, offering Mass at 5:00 a.m. He hurried on to Damascus, "a city of great Pauline memories, the gate, the street called straight (quite crooked), Ananias' house and the window from which Paul was lowered in a basket." Sadly he noted that throughout the Decapolis district they were passing through there were once twenty-four dioceses and now none.

He left Syria by car with the Syrian Archbishop Pietro Chami of Bosra and Horan as his host. They were on their way to Beirut, Lebanon, bringing the travelers back from the lands of the crescent to the country of the cross. The Maronites are the most numerous Catholic rite in the small nation and by constitutional law the president of the republic must be Maronite. Over half of the population is Christian and both the Melkite and Maronite patriarchs reside in Beirut. In 1952 Ligutti referred to the refugee situation that would in time become one of the most critical, if not the most critical, international powderkegs in the cold war of balancing power:

> Just now, a large number of Palestinian refugees are here — many of them Moslems. That may upset the delicate balance and even cause political upheavals, for the million or so refugees whom the Jews of Israel expropriated and caused to escape may well prove the undoing of western civilization. If the Arab world turns to Russia, this is exactly the reason why.

On January 14 he left by Arab Airways for Amman, Jordan. He was met by Father Antonio, O.F.M., principal of Terra Santa College, and escorted to his hotel. He climbed the steep seats of the ancient Roman theatre across the street from the hotel, as well as the ruins of a smaller theater, the Odeon. In both places he noted that poor people made their homes in the ancient dressing rooms of the gladiators or under the broken arches of the ancient walls. He punned: "If and when the communists come along these poor creatures will say, 'What have we to lose? Just our fallen arches...!'" He described Jordan as a kingdom of less than 40,000 square miles, mostly desert, stretching from Aqaba in the south to the Lake of Galilee in the north and including Bethlehem, Jericho, and old Jerusalem. He made one of his rare political observations while writing in his hotel room in Amman, the ancient Philadelphia:

> As I passed from Cross to Crescent and Crescent to Cross I can certainly detect more than considerable animosity against the U.S. on the part of the Arab world. They feel that the U.S.'s quick recognition of Israel, the continued official and private financial aid are the only props on which the very unstable economy of Israel stands. Remove them and down will Israel go. Thus the expatriated Arabs will regain possession of their ancestral homes!

Once again he was a pilgrim in the Holy Land. He had said he would come back to the land where Jesus walked. He had crossed the guarded armistice line between old Jerusalem and Israel. Again his genial companion was Fr. Patrick Coyle, O.F.M., and both were happy that all the red tape involved in crossing the line took *only* a half a day!

From January 19-22 he was lost in prayer and meditation. He mentioned the joy of offering Mass in the Church of the Dormition on Mount Sion, a stone's throw from the Cenacle; his "heart fluttered with joy infinite" as he stood silently and reverently (no external signs of veneration are permitted) in the Cenacle; he knelt in prayer at the altar of the Annunciation in Nazareth; visited the church in Cana and "stayed overnight in one of the loveliest spots on earth, the Mount of the Beatitudes."

He boarded the plane at Lydda for Athens. Two events stamped final impressions of Israel on his mind. As they were eating breakfast, a rabbi sitting next to him said, "Two eggs, what luxury! We were lucky to get three per week in Israel." Across the aisle a Jewish lady from Chicago added, "I have not had any meat since October." Ligutti added on January 22, "The planes out of Israel are always filled."

He spent three days in the land of Homer and Socrates, making his base the city that once erected an altar to the unknown god. He spent time in conversations with agriculture officials (noting that about 65 per cent of the country was agricultural) and inspecting agricultural schools. He talked with people about the Greek Orthodox Church and discovered it influenced the people little because it was too closely allied with the government. His classical bent was stirred as he climbed the steep ascent of the Acropolis. "What history on that rock!" he exclaimed.

Ligutti ended his journey with the rapidity of a Shakespearean tragedy. He hurried on to Rome where "it was really not hectic days, it was hectic hours." As always, he enjoyed "a few good Roman repasts" that were sandwiched in between visits with high and low. He flew to Geneva for the meeting of the International Catholic Migration Commission, then on to New York, Washington, Chicago, and home. He expressed much more by what he did not write than what he did in closing his final letter: "Old friends are the best friends after all, and America is best. I am seldom lonesome, but never satisfied until I reach home."

Ligutti's work as permanent Vatican observer to the Food and Agriculture Organization was involving him more and more each passing year in the work of international development and the Church's opportunities and challenges through the ministry of her missionaries. More and more clearly he was seeing not only the advantages but the absolute necessity of closer collaboration between missionary activity by the Church and technical assistance by the Food and Agriculture Organization. He was pleased by the $21,000 the Holy See made to the United Nations' Technical Assistance Fund.

On October 8, 1953 he departed from New York on what he called the "L.G.L. Safari" and did not return to Des Moines until April 10, 1954. He was fifty-eight years old and undertaking one of the most arduous journeys of his life. Its distance and inconvenience would be a challenge to most men half his age. In his typical fashion he paced himself so that he could combine leisure, meetings, study, and research in such a manner that what would be a burden to most was a joy to him. The immediate purpose of the trip was the meeting of the Food and Agriculture Organization in Rome and the meeting of the Inter-governmental Committee on European Migration in Venice. He was occupied with such meetings from October 16 until November 28.

He left New York in the company of Bishop Alan Babcock of Grand Rapids, Michigan. He stopped overnight in Paris for a traditional dinner of snails with Mr. Jack "Oui Oui" McCloskey, the Paris-based director of Catholic Relief Services; then a hurried stop in Geneva, and on to Ciampino Airport and Rome. He attended the centennial celebration of the North American College and proudly noted that five presidents of the National Catholic Rural Life Conference were present — Muench, Mulloy, Treacy, Hayes, and himself. He spent two busy days calling on people and visiting Vatican and FAO offices. Off again to Venice and the meeting of the Inter-governmental Committee on European Migration.

Happy was hardly the word for the feeling that swelled his heart as he arrived in Udine on October 17 and sat contentedly in Father Toffolini's flower garden as the moon smiled down upon the two classmates. "There is joy in friendly living," he thought, "in the absence of rush, in the quietness of an evening in a village after the *Ave Maria* has rung, when the only murmurs are the *Gloria*'s and *Pater*'s of the family Rosary." He was present in Udine for the golden jubilee of the old archbishop and thought of Ralph Adams Cram's remark as he took his place in the choir stalls, "The most beautiful thing in the world is a pontifical high mass in an old cathedral." The cathedral of Udine qualified; it was built 450 years before 1776. He spent a hurried day visiting friends and relatives, made his customary pilgrimage to the parish church in Romans and was off by train to visit the African Missioners in Verona.

On October 20 he passed through Milan and on to the Hybrid Corn Experimental Station near Bergamo. "I got a firsthand report of the results achieved," he wrote, "partially through our CROP and GROW contributions. The record — 205 bushels per acre! Again I repeat, 'The world is not doomed to starvation.'" In the company of his friend Count Sandro De Asarta, they drove to Pavia to visit the tomb of St. Augustine; on to Piacenza to visit the seminary of the Scalabrini Fathers; then to the tiny village of Piozzano. He met for the first time a cousin Don Cesare Ligutti, the pastor. He boarded the train in Milan and returned to Rome in time to witness the episcopal consecration of Archbishop Romolo Carboni, newly appointed apostolic delegate to Australia.

Carboni, the present papal nuncio to Italy, Ligutti called "a man of great vision with a boundless love for the Church." He modestly refused to refer to the assistance he gave the rural life apostolate throughout the years he worked in the Vatican Secretariat of State. He well knew the great good that was accomplished by the First International Congress on Rural Life and was an ardent supporter and promoter of all succeeding international rural life congresses. Ligutti called him "a great and good man."

In Rome, Ligutti was again a guest at the Chicago House, in the company of Msgr. Ernest Primeau, the rector, and Msgr. Andrew Landi. Of the latter Ligutti wrote, "He is beginning his tenth year in Rome, and what days he has gone through! What rich experiences have been his during the years of unselfish dedication to God's poor. He is forever guilty of the heresy of good work."

While in Rome on this trip, as all his sojourns, Ligutti was a blotter. He gathered together every scrap of information he could find. Then, as a squirrel buries nuts for the winter, Ligutti stored away every particle of news for future reference. The Trieste affair was in danger of becoming an international crisis. Israel and Lebanon were at daggers' points. The French cardinals were in Rome to plead the cause of the priest-workers. On this matter he voiced his opinion: "If a priest works like a priest, he does not have to go into a factory or labor union to sell religion. The best and most effective way is through the family and in the homes." These were strange words to many who looked upon Ligutti as the most energetic and active rural sociologist in fostering cooperation between the Church and governmental agencies, in promoting technical know-how with the preaching of the gospel.

One evening he dined in a Roman home and never forgot what the lady of the house said as she tended her cooking: "With three pans on our small gas stove, I feel like the conductor of a philharmonic." Ligutti's Roman stop was coming to an end. He wrote:

> I am off on Saturday night, November 28, headed for Cairo. On December 1, I'll join Monsignor Pavan and Dr. Veronese for the first leg of the journey, through Cairo, Luxor, Karthoum, and to Entebbe in Uganda where the African Lay Apostolate meeting is to be held from December 8 to December 13. I go to Africa to visit the work of the various mission groups along agricultural lines.

While waiting to board the airplane christened "Star of Iowa" at Ciampino Airport, he watched a comet blaze across the sky. He thought of his friends Dr. and Mrs. Ray Miller, who recently arrived in Rome after a two and a half hour flight from London. "And some stupid fellows," he thought, "still believe isolationism is possible or even advisable." He departed at 10:00 p.m., stopped in Athens at 1:30 a.m., and "by six a.m. I saw the sunrise over the minarets of Cairo, in the land of the Pharaohs, and the crescent of the prophet — thousands of years apart, only a few hours near." He stayed with the African Missioners from Verona, called on Archbishop Alberto Levame, the papal nuncio, and wasted no time in visiting historical spots and missionary schools in the area. He called at the FAO regional office and the Point IV headquarters and had a pleasant chat with Mr. Jefferson Caffrey, the United States ambassador. "We Catholics," he wrote, "can be very proud of him as one of America's chief diplomats. Egypt rules pretty well the Arab world. It's smart to have a top man at this post." He was deeply impressed, as every tourist is, by the grandeur of ancient Egypt.

He visited agriculture schools and spent many hours with agricultural officials. From Cairo he flew to Luxor on December 2 and reflected on the sunrise, "Always a symbol of hope, even over the parched sands and the thorny acacias." Again he sadly viewed "agriculture in its most primitive form — oxen and crooked stick plows; water carried in earthen jars on women's heads, mud huts, camels in humpy caravans." Before leaving Egypt he jotted down his observations concerning self-government:

> Some claim a portion of mankind is unable and/or unready to rule itself. Others would thrust complete and unchecked self-rule upon most primitive peoples. Certainly neither is right. I firmly believe that an opportunity for self-government is the right of any social group. Actually such opportunity helps to bring out the great hidden resources found in men. The fundamental requirement is really not what is called political maturity, but rather, honesty and sincerity. Naturally some book learning and, in a modern world, at least a modicum of technicians are necessary. Give a nation some honest public servants who will dedicate themselves to be the instruments of their fellow men, and any group is ready for self-rule.

On December 4 he left Egypt, flying over the Lybian desert, and arrived at Khartoum — "that thin strip of land jutting out where the white and blue Nile meet." He noted that natural resources were limited in Sudan, that many people suffered from malnutrition, and that the influx of black people from the South was creating a serious social problem.

On December 11 he was writing from the shores of Lake Victoria in Uganda. He treasured the relic of Blessed Charles Lwanga, one of the Ugandan martyrs canonized during the Second

Vatican Council. He was deeply moved during the Mass offered by a black bishop from Tanganyika and listened with interest as Bishop Giuseppe Kiwanuka of Uganda spoke of the martyrdom of Blessed Charles and his companions. He watched with no little emotion as "men, women and children marched to the Communion rail — women and girls with shaven heads; barefooted nuns; women with babies, dressed in their gaudy long and shapeless gowns."

He joined Pavan and Veronese from Rome and O'Grady from Washington to take part in the first congress on the Apostolate of the Laity ever held in Africa. The meeting, conducted from December 8-11 in Entebbe, Uganda, attracted about three hundred participants, including the apostolic delegate, Archbishop James Knox; the cardinal of Mozambique, eleven bishops, and three prefect apostolics.

Ligutti addressed the congress on "Man's Relation to the Land." His conclusion revealed his continuing crusading spirit as an apostle of rural Christian living:

> In a very small way, the National Catholic Rural Life Conference of the United States has been seeking to pioneer — through its national congresses it influences public opinion, Church and State. Its international congresses instruct and influence others far and wide. Our motto is, "Christ to the country, the country to Christ." What Christ preached, Africa must have.

He was happy when Archbishop Owen McCann of Capetown, a native of that city and son of Irish immigrants, opened his address with "Fellow Africans." Even the slightest detail, serious or humorous, did not escape Ligutti's notice. "How diligent Maryknoll Sisters are!" he exclaimed. "During a French speech one of them was saying her office. At the end of the speech she interrupted Compline to clap. How polite!"

The Congress was completed and Ligutti was off again. From December 14 he was traveling by car, jeep, boat, and on foot, visiting mission centers, inspecting farm schools, and offering suggestions, talking with people, and making notes. He visited the major seminary near Gulu, Sudan, conducted by the Mission Fathers of Verona for native clergy, and observed:

> The indigenous clergy are given a hard and long period of training. A few have already been ordained. Some are converts from paganism. They are just emerging from the bush and the spear stage. It's amazing how well they take the strict training they have to undergo. Of course, they are

needed. No one knows how long the whites can remain. It is at a place like this that one finds the various tribes represented. Each possesses peculiar characteristics of physical stature, mental ability, obedience, pride, carelessness, lack of foresight.

He advocated self-sufficiency for the mission schools and advised equipping each mission center with efficient production tools, such as machinery for plowing and harvesting. He learned that the plow was not even known in southern Sudan:

> A very rudimentary hoe is the only cultivation instrument. Cut the crutch of a branch, about eighteen inches long on either side, two inches thick; an iron hoe at one end, a bent-over girl or woman at the other end; and that's agricultural production in southern Sudan. There is a sickle for cutting tall grass, reeds, and dura. All else is gathered by hand, threshed and crushed by hand.

On December 30 he wrote from Juba, Sudan, while waiting seven days for a plane. He noted the absence of wagons and donkeys in southern Sudan, "indicating that the wheel has been unknown and that trade has not been practiced." He commented on the culinary arts, claiming that antelope was by far the best wild game he had tasted. Although there was no abstinence on Fridays, there was abstinence on the Vigil of Christmas. Father Giogetti, mission director, announced, "On the day before Christmas you must not eat rats." A big rat is the only meat that the natives eat. Before departing the Sudan at the end of 1953 he noted that the phenomenal success of the Catholic Church in the area can be attributed to the mission schools.

He reflected on the African woman and maintained that the Christian education of women was essential for the survival of Christianity. He described her plight in African society:

> By and large, the women are the farmers. They hoe. The man condescends to plant. Weeding is done by women, and the harvesting, such as it is, also is done by them. She shells and winnows. She kneels before a hollowed stone, and with another stone she crushes the dura into flour. She gathers the wood, she keeps the fire going, and tediously stirs the polenta. When ready, in many places, she kneels in a corner while the man eats, and the children wait with her.

Ligutti was also moved by the children. He mingled with them wherever he went and welcomed every opportunity to talk to them about life in the United States. In Usumbura, the capital of Urundi situated on Lake Tanganyika, he witnessed forty boys marching into the mission compound with drums tapping and voices singing. They had walked two days through the jungle, eating and drinking whatever they could find along the way, to see the bishop and ask him to establish an elementary school in their district. Ligutti reflected: When I shall hear of Catholics in the U.S. refusing to support a Catholic school, what I saw and heard on January 3, 1954, will forever come back to my mind.

Flying from Albertville to Tabora, Tanganyika, he thought of the great good cooperatives might do for Africans. "In my opinion," he wrote, "these territories are ripe for a real campaign in behalf of cooperatives — consumer, producer, credit and service. American and British coops could well sponsor an effective campaign with the cooperation of the missions." He came to the Nzega Mission near Tabora to visit Fr. Arthur Lacasse, a white priest from New Hampshire and head of the mission, who had already organized consumer and plowing cooperatives. He studied Father Lacasse's work, such as securing simple plows and arrows and a small sum of money to purchase oxen through CARE. These simple, even primitive, needs enabled twenty-five families to double their food production. Then with his customary vision, Ligutti observed what would later become reality in the shape of the Peace Corps and Papal Volunteers. "How much more could Father Lacasse accomplish," he wrote, "if he had one or two young laymen who could assist him in supervising and educating along all these lines. And what an experience for young Americans!"

Once again Ligutti enunciated his firm conviction:

> It is my contention that the steps taken in making Christians ought to be broader than mere religious instruction. I consider as basic: Food production, distribution and marketing, housing, sanitation, health, diet, etc. I believe that a bit too much effort is put on formal education, especially the preparation of white collar workers.... Certainly in these parts ninety-eight per cent of the people are farmers, so our missionaries are really rural missionaries. And yet our mission training institutes never prepare, even remotely, a missionary to deal with the bread-and-butter and starvation problems of his future flock. Of course, the missionaries have so many things to do, but I wonder why their view is not broadened in this day and age.

With a cordial Maryknoller as his guide and companion, he arrived in Nairobi, Kenya, on January 23, 1954. He described the city as "an armed camp" and observed the terror and slaughter caused by the secret society of the Mau-Maus:

> The British certainly have their hands full. Sudan is lost. Uganda boils. Kenya is murdering. To an unprejudiced observer and certainly to me, the British have done much more good than harm in their African colonies, and yet they may lose everything. And the ones who may think themselves the gainers will lose the most.

On January 28 he flew to "the harbor of peace," the city of Dar es Salaam, was welcomed by Archbishop Edgaro Maranta, and received as a guest in the rectory of St. Joseph's Cathedral. He accompanied the archbishop to a benefit dance for the cathedral and noted that racism was practiced socially as "in the seating within the sacred precincts of the churches." He noted that there were few conversions to Catholicism because of polygamy and other tribal customs that were against Christian morality.

In Nyasaland he noted that the land was poorly used with over-crowding in some areas and idle land in others. In the two Rhodesias he again observed that the time was fast approaching when the indigenous blacks would want to govern their own land. He recorded a conversation with a native white Rhodesian who said, "I was born here, and I certainly should have some rights as well as the black native born. It is well to say 'Africa for Africans,' but I, too, am an African."

On February 7 he drove with Bishop Giuseppe Fady along the western border of Nyasaland. He noticed that one of the favorite sports of the small boys was digging up fat crickets or catching rats to roast and eat. The following day he spoke at the major seminary. It came as a surprise to the seminarians when he told them that the soil could be worked over and over again without depleting it. He spoke also to a group of missionary sisters, pointing out that a contact person with agricultural officials was just as important as a secretary for education. A sister replied that it was easier to teach Shakespeare than agriculture. Ligutti answered quickly, "But you can't eat Shakespeare!"

American-born Archbishop Celestine Damiano, the apostolic delegate, and his secretary, Maine-born Msgr. Thomas Clancy, met Ligutti at the Capetown airport on February 17. He was saddened to receive two days previously in Pretoria the news of the death of his brother-in-law Joseph Romano and Fr. Michael O'Connor of Wiota, Iowa. "It's somewhat disconcerting," he confided in his letter, "to be so far away at a time when loved ones suffer, and to return home to find vacant chairs and familiar smiles no more." One day he traveled to Cape Point, where the Atlantic and Indian Oceans meet, and the sight prompted this reflection: "Perhaps here is a lesson for world unity and amity without the useless and wasteful clash of arms and human suffering."

Even in so hurried a trip he noticed the racial tensions of South Africa. Such tension was heightened by the political discord and regional rivalries existing among the various states of the Union of South Africa. On February 28, Ash Wednesday, he was in the air again, making a hurried stop in the Belgian Congo. In Leopoldville, the capital, he witnessed one of the major problems facing all the African nations; namely, the rapid urbanization creating almost insurmountable problems for both Church and State. "Young men come into the cities," he observed, "leaving their wives and babies back in the area. The family is broken, and wholesale evils are the result. Men with a wife back home and a concubine in town, or women prostitutes (abandoned wives) don't belong to the Holy Name or Ladies' aid."

He visited Angola, the Portuguese colony dating from 1575, as the guest of Count Marzano whom Ligutti met earlier in Rome. The count had served as private secretary and aide-de-camp to King Umberto of Italy. Ligutti wrote, "His recollections of political events, intrigues, back-stage happenings during the last fifty years in Italy are really worth listening to." Although he respected the count, Ligutti was not impressed by the policy of the Portuguese government towards Angola.

By March 10 he was back in Leopoldville. He visited the Lovanium in Kisantu, "a sort of extension of Louvain in Belgium, where civil administrative assistants, agricultural and medical assistants are prepared." Here, too, he discovered the *kintwadi* movement, an association of people doing things together. "For instance," Ligutti explained, "there is a *kintwadi* pig — a group of families feeds it, and when it is butchered, the meat is shared." He considered the movement one of the hopeful signs in Africa.

During 133 days in Africa he conferred with all the papal nuncios and apostolic delegates and over thirty local ordinaries in seventeen African nations. He visited countless mission centers and schools conducted by thirty-five different religious communities of men and women. He could not possibly keep a record of the number of government officials and agricultural leaders with whom he held conferences. He estimated that he covered 25,000 miles by air and 10,000 miles on foot or by oxen, horses, cars, buses, jeeps, or trains. He could not attempt to count the addresses he gave nor could he possibly remember all the priests, brothers, sisters, and lay leaders that he met.

On March 27, 1954 he left Lisbon for Caracas, Venezuela, to attend an FAO conference. Four days later he was in Panama, "not to see the sights or the Gatun locks" but to initiate the organization of another international congress of rural life for February 13-20, 1955. Ligutti was off to Washington, D.C., to make his usual round of calls on government officials and to experience the sheer joy of taking a hot shower. On April 10 he was home again and concluded his letters with two simple sentences: "It was good to be on a safari. It's good to be back."

He had not, however, completely finished his safari. There was homework to be done. He drew up a report of his African journey. In some cases, events of the past twenty years have sometimes sadly and sometimes fortunately fulfilled the valued judgments and predictions Ligutti made in this report. The safari made Ligutti more sensitive to the needs of the missionary Church. He concluded his report:

> If I had not believed in mission work before, I would not be a fervent and enthusiastic supporter of the foreign missions. If I had never believed in the possibility of human greatness, I can now say, I have seen it with my own eyes. If I never believed in the Divine Origin of the Catholic Church and its guidance by the Holy Spirit, I would now bow my head and say, "*Agnosco et credo.*"

He sent his report to the Vatican Secretariat of State. On July 14, 1954 the report was acknowledged by Montini, who wrote, among other things:

> The information which you have provided is interesting and will undoubtedly be useful in relation to the conditions and the activities of the missions. I have sent a copy of your report to the Congregation for the Propagation of the Faith under whose jurisdiction lies most of the territory that you covered.

That is Rome's way of saying, "Thank you."

"Seventy per cent of the world's people are tillers of the soil. They produce the food but do not eat as well as others. They raise the cotton and are poorly clothed." Thus, Ligutti addressed the Detroit First Friday Club on June 8, 1954, less than two months after his return from Africa. He had seen, perhaps, more than any other cleric of his time, a greater number of these tillers of the soil in Australia, Latin America, the Near East, and Africa.

The Orient also cast its spell on the Italian peasant boy who became an Iowa pastor. On October 13, 1955 he began a series of twenty-seven "Sunrise and Sunset" letters with the exclamation, "Here I go again!" He wanted to go "island hopping and mission visiting," and, of course, his motives were the same as those that induced his previous journeys. He may have already seen and studied a good share of that 70 per cent, but he knew that there was even a greater percentage of those beloved tillers of the soil in the mysterious, intriguing, and enchanting countries of the yellow and brown people.

There was work to be done, however, before Ligutti undertook his journey to the Far East. He left Des Moines on October 13 to make contacts in Washington, D.C., and New York City to prepare for the tenth celebration of the Food and Agriculture Organization in Montreal on October 15. Before leaving he drew up his will, the first he ever prepared, had a serious discussion with Father Dineen on the latter's use of NCRLC funds, and put the finishing touches on the annual NCRLC convention scheduled for Lexington, Kentucky, from October 22-26. He was pleased with this convention, rushed back to Des Moines for a quick glance at the work on his desk, packed his bags, and departed from New York, via Paris, and on to Rome for FAO's biennial conference.

Rome is traditional and Ligutti fell easily into a pattern of conferences, meetings, dinners, receptions, and attendance at the FAO sessions as permanent Vatican observer. He did not, however, succumb to Roman ways. He wrote:

> When in Rome I never do as the Romans do. I get up at five, awaken myself with an ice-cold shower, pray and work at the desk until seven-thirty, say Mass, take a cup of coffee. At eight-thirty off to the office of Monsignor Landi for a variety of needs. Then to our FAO observer office in the Vatican, calls from or to various officials, and out to the beautiful FAO headquarters for meetings and conferences. As a rule, a pleasant luncheon engagement, more meetings to six or seven p.m., a reception of some sort, 8:30 p.m. dinner and back home wearily for a good rest by 11:00. When that lengthens into four weeks, it may sound rather monotonous, but I find it challenging and exhilarating.

Within the week he wound up his work at FAO, with circular File 13 loaded down and overflowing. "Poor Gaetano!" he thought. "I presume he wondered why I would carry up so much paper just to have him carry it down a few days later! No one will know (neither will I), but it happens!" On November 29 he boarded the KLM Constellation at Ciampino Airport and after crossing 110 degrees on the world map and after thirty-three hours in flight he reached his destination, Manila. He moved into the Ateneo on Loyola Heights near Quezon City and was prepared to take his part in the All-Asia Congress on the Lay Apostolate from December 3-8.

At the congress Cardinal Valerian Gracias of Bombay presided and Archbishop Egidio Vagnozzi, apostolic nuncio, and Archbishop Rufino Santos of Manila occupied chairs of honor. Sixteen Asian nations were represented and 85 per cent of the delegates were lay people, with women taking a prominent part in the proceedings. Again Ligutti noted that the speeches were extremely long and at times triumphalistic, although he found the discussion groups that met from 3:00 until 6:00 p.m. both stimulating and refreshing.

Ligutti not only addressed the participants of the congress but also, at the request of Pius XII, undertook this 30,000 mile journey to promote the betterment of agriculture and farm life. He delivered his address on rural problems before a large and attentive audience on December 6, advocating that the Catholic Church in Asia take a more active interest in rural problems since 70 per cent of the Asian people are rural. Again he stressed land tenure, effective land use, agricultural know-how and do-how, credit unions, cooperatives, and closer identification of the Church in the daily problems of the people. He sounded a warning for Catholic leaders: "From Russia to China, Communism has ridden to power on the shoulders of a dissatisfied peasantry."

The congress closed on the feast of the Immaculate Conception "in a blaze of processional glory." Over 25,000 people packed Luneta Park and Ligutti fondly recalled the congresses at Manizales and Santiago. "I wasted no time in getting around" was his masterpiece of understatement for the activities of the coming weeks. He spent four more days in the Philippines visiting agricultural officials and missionaries. He addressed a student convocation and received a rousing applause when he stated that he was against large landholdings no matter who owned them. Here again he observed a universal problem: *latifundia* and *minifundia,* too large and too small landholdings. "The one creates a miserable proletariat," he wrote, "the other an inefficient land use."

He called the Philippine "Federation of Free Farmers" a bright spot in rather gloomy surroundings. He felt the organization must be right because it was opposed by the large landowners on the one side and by the Huks on the other. The organization promoted peace between landlords and tenants, defended tenants in court free of charge, and informed the unlearned and suspicious workers of their rights. Ligutti felt it was the only effective organization preventing Communism in rural areas. He also noted that the rural people were woefully neglected because of the shortage of priests and the difficulty of easy transportation. He also observed the scarcity of tractors and that women worked keep-deep in water planting rice. In one day six women planted 35,000 rice plants on one acre of land.

On December 12 he bid farewell to the only nominally Catholic country in Asia and departed via Pan Am to Hong Kong. He put down his immediate impression:

> We went through shack town after shack town, some fire-scarred, some under the porticos of business streets. The contraptions used for shelter exceed the queerness and ingenuity of "believe it or not." And yet there is a noticeable absence of dirt and unpleasant odors. The water supply is no-where near sufficient.

Ligutti visited the weaving school established by Father Dempsey, M.M., and once again saw the results of private enterprise. "Everywhere and by everyone who knows, you hear it said, 'Give a voluntary agency $1.00 and they'll give you $5.00 worth of work. Let the government do it alone and for $1.00 you'll get 50¢ worth'." In Hong Kong he noticed that the Southern Baptist missions willingly took government subsidies to operate their schools. He wondered about their incongruity; in favor of government aid here and opposed to it in the United States.

On December 15 he flew to Taipei, Taiwan, and on December 20 landed in Tokyo, one hour after Cardinal Francis Spellman deplaned to visit the American troops on his annual Christmas journey. He was again the guest of the Maryknollers and his mind, as always, was preoccupied with the land as he sat down on Christmas Day to write his seventh travel letter. Concerning Japan, he observed:

There are 13 million acres of cultivated land, and this part is as intensively used as one can imagine. There are over six million farming families. Figure for yourself what the average size farm has to be. Take into account farm house and sheds, bamboo lot and family cemetery. I have said very often that no human being has yet gotten out of one acre of soil all that God has put into it. The Japanese are coming closer to it than anyone I have seen.... Indeed, the great crime of our age and the blind spot in our civilization is to kill off human resources while we behold and bewail the existence of superabundant natural resources all around us.

From Tokyo, Ligutti on December 28 flew to Seoul, Korea, a country of ancient and recent martyrs. He noted, as most observers do, the striking similarities between the Catholics of Korea and Ireland, no doubt in some way occasioned by the work of the Irish Columban Fathers. He wrote:

> The two towering problems are credit and warehousing of rice and other perishable products. The incredible rate of interest, but very common, is 20 percent per *month* (not year but month!). Even the government loans a sack of rice and within six months the farmer must give back two sacks of rice. The rice producers are small farmers, and are forced to sell the rice in September (harvest time) at, let us say, eight. That same rice is sold in February at 14 (fourteen). Then a taxation system which is not only burdensome but a continued nuisance. A very inefficient array of civil servants and police officers are forever asking for donations; untrained public officials, very few technicians, poor teaching staff.

He returned to the Philippines, picked up his mail (always welcomed from home), and spent New Year's Eve at the Ateneo with the Jesuits from the New York province. "Again," he wrote, "memories of the past — two years ago in Sudan, four years ago in Bagdad, the future — only God knows, but that's always best." He spent the first eight days of 1956 visiting missions centers and talking with missionaries, always asking questions and making mental notes, such as, "Mindanao has good land and very few people on it" or, "Negros is one island where the large landowners hold sway." On January 9 he wrote from Dutch New Guinea: "The Philippines hold much promise. Much could be done effectively there by our own Catholic groups. I hope we can."

In New Guinea he was the guest of Bishop Leo Arkfeld, S.V.D., a native of Panama, Iowa. He is one of the few bishops in the world with a pilot's license and has his own plane to reach the far-flung areas of his diocese of many islands. The torrential rains afforded Ligutti the opportunity to remain longer than he planned in one place or another as he flew with Bishop Arkfeld. This leisure provided the opportunity for reflection on the life of the missionaries and the problem of colonialism. On the first he wrote:

> My old-time complaints on the diet of the missionaries can be repeated here. It's the same as elsewhere. The good men are so busy and occupied with so much work and thought of others, they forget themselves completely. Their superiors do not insist on regularity for meals or a balanced diet. The results are, too often, sickness and disability. All sorts of rationalizations can be worked out. There can be an excuse for almost everything. Virtue, however, does not consist in making oneself sick or unable to work.

During these years nations of the Third World were agitating for home rule and independence from the mother country. Imperialism was a vulgar word to most people. Here in Dutch New Guinea Ligutti wrote:

> When visiting such places as New Guinea, the age-old question of colonialism comes to the fore. Is political independence possible or advisable for any and all colonies? What are the economic and social prerequisites? To my way of judging some strong ties with a real "mother" country are necessary. Also a considerable amount of regional unity is a must. A place like New Guinea is completely unready for any sort of self-rule. If the West abandons such spots either internal exploiters take over or Communist imperialism sweeps in.
>
> Where the civil authorities lag in action or are short-sighted in vision, our missionaries could and should step forward. Even if no baptisms were registered for years to come, the process of Christianization would have been put on a solid natural basis.

Little by little, either subconsciously or unknowingly, he was formulating the policies that would direct Agrimissio in years ahead. Here, too, he met a person he called "a most remarkable man." In pidgin English a native called "Yauiga" said, "We want to be helped to help ourselves; show us what to do, how to do it; we can do it."

By January 21 he was back in Australia, visiting Queensland (where he noted that within fifty years over 75 per cent of the population will be descendants of Italian immigrants) and flying on to Sydney where he stayed with Carboni, the apostolic delegate. Here he remained only three days ("It would be strange if I stopped for three days without moving....") and was off by plane to the national capital of Canberra. He attended the Australian Citizenship Convention because of his interest in the problems of migration. On January 29 he was in Melbourne. He called again on Archbishop Mannix, whom he described at "ninety-two years old, as erect as an athlete at twenty, as alert-minded and keen-witted as any man alive, well-informed, not living in the past, with a vision of the future, with a directness that amazes." He had many long conferences with Bob Santamaria, the Australian leader who was the first to suggest an international congress on Catholic rural life. Ligutti had the greatest admiration for Santamaria:

> Soon after the war the Communists began infiltrating and capturing trade unions. Then a group of very alert and capable Catholic men organized the so-called "Movement." By using the same easy or rough tactics of the Communists they actually succeeded in clearing most of the Communist officers from the unions. In this effort Protestant and Jewish anti-Communists collaborated magnificently. Mr. Evatt, the Labor Party leader and considerably to the left, began to howl and raised the sectarian cry of Catholic domination. That split the party and the Labor Party lost at the polls. The whipping boy was Bob Santamaria, upon whom all the possible ignominy, blame and accusations were laid. He is one of the most intelligent and educated men I have ever met. He is Australian born of Aeolian descent (Lipari Islands). In his forties, he is the father of seven lovely children, humble but determined, logical and persistent. I believe that the technique developed by him and his group through "the Movement" is the most effective yet devised to uproot Communist infiltration in labor or other groups.

After an overnight delay in Darwin because of bad weather, Ligutti was winging his way over the Java Sea and deplaned in Djakarta on February 4. He described Djakarta as a crowded city with a few nice buildings, many modern homes, and a lot of markets and poor housing. He noted then what urban planners today are realizing more and more, "No one can cope with the problem of a rapidly growing capital city."

He traveled through the new nation of Indonesia, visiting missionaries on many of its major islands. On February 14 he wrote again from the island of Bali, where he met Fr. Norbert Shadeg, S.V.D., a native of Minnesota's St. Cloud Diocese and the rector of a minor seminary with thirty students. Ligutti wrote, "I met the priest who was the first one to come here, saw the first church, and shook hands with the first convert. All this was established less than ten years ago." Here, too, he noticed the new Catholic church built in pure Bali style over whose entrance was inscribed: *Allah - Adalah - Kasih* — God Is Love. "So, on Valentine's Day, what else could I say?" So he closed his letter from Bali.

> From Singapore he wrote:
>
> United States capitalism in the minds of most people in these parts is really and truly a veritable devil. We may sell our products abroad, but our reputation is as low as one can imagine. We are accused of everything under the sun. We are crooks, we are mistrusted, we want to subjugate people, to conquer them, make them pay through the nose. Modern decent capitalism, fair competitive service, lower prices for products, mass markets, higher wages and living standards, plus a fair justifiable profit have not been sold as part and parcel of capitalism.

Taking note of the different cultures throughout the world, he mentioned:

> Some years ago I celebrated three Christmas Masses — Roman, Greek, Armenian in the Near East; this year three New Years — January 1 in Manila, Chinese; February 12, in Makassar; February 15, Balinese — so by this time I know it's 1956!

Again, from Singapore, he noted:

> The thing to watch in this emerging country is the non-publicized struggle for leadership and/or supremacy between the Malayan-Moslems and the Chinese. From all appearances the Malayans have the upper hand, but the Chinese have the money, the businesses, the properties, and when the chips are counted, who will be the winner? Too many Chinese are pro-Communist, so it is said.

In eight days he traveled from Singapore to Saigon, from Cambodia to Thailand. His host in Vietnam was Msgr. Paul Harnett, Saigon representative of the Catholic Relief Services. Ligutti had nothing but praise for the tremendous charity performed by that organization and its field representatives. Almost as a prophet, he foretold the Vietnam tragedy of the 1960's:

> The North in the hands of Ho-chi-minh — Communist, the South under President Diem, who is putting things in order with great American aid. It's a long story of intrigues, considerable stupidity, and it is not finished yet. It would take a prophet to foretell the final outcome. However, the U.S. must be there. It's no mistake to spend money and effort on Vietnam, and to back Diem who is truly pro-American.

He made a hurried exit from Thailand to spend a day and a half in Rangoon, Burma, and from there, on to Dacca, East Pakistan (Bangladesh). Here he felt he was back at Notre Dame University in Indiana, staying with the Holy Cross Fathers at Notre Dame College. On March 12 he departed for Delhi, India, and was welcomed by the Salesians at the old cathedral compound called the "Portuguese church." He met there a missionary from Udine, Italy. In the afternoon he was on the road in a station wagon to Krishnagar, the diocese in charge of Bishop Luigi Morrow, a Texas-born American. He described Bishop Morrow as a writer of catechetical texts and a perpetual and effective beggar. Then he added:

> Bishop Morrow is a highly respected civic leader. He battles for water and sewage systems, better roads and bridges, health facilities. He is all things to all men. He has undertaken a housing project among the poor. Yes, he has built brick houses of simple construction, and with a bit of porch. And, people like them. This gives the lie to the ones whom I hear repeat constantly, "People don't *want* something different."

In Benares, the holy city on the west bank of the Ganges, he observed the piety of the pilgrims who came to bathe in the river. "But the burning of the corpses by the side of the river did strike me as terribly gruesome," he added. "The cracking of the skull to release the spirit, or the burial of the holy men without cremation in the middle of the river were sights I shall never forget."

He arrived in Colombo, Ceylon, on March 24 and was the guest of Fr. Peter Pillai, O.M.I., director of St. Joseph's College.

He liked the Ceylonese people, calling them "exceedingly capable and charming." By late March he was in Trivandum, on the Malabar coast, and assisted at the Mass of the Oils on Holy Thursday in the St. Thomas-Mylapore Cathedral. He noted that the area was densely populated, land ownership fragmentized to the terrible minimum of less than an acre to a family, and in spite of extreme poverty, the area held the highest percentage of literacy in all India. On Easter Sunday he participated in the Resurrection ritual and Mass in the Malankar rite. The following day he was in Quilon and visited Bishop Angelo Fernandes who the previous year had visited the NCRLC headquarters in Des Moines. On April 8 he departed for Karachi, Pakistan, after observing in his letters:

> A person need not be in India very long before he discovers and meets some very superior people — in the political field, in the social-economic field and among the religious leaders. Men, and even women, with tremendous natural abilities, possessing culture, keenness and drive! That explains the sudden and almost incredible giant steps taken since independence. The vastness of the country and its immense variety and backgrounds explain both the progress and retarded movements. I have met over one-fourth of the Hierarchy, and I have conferred with quite a few lay Catholic leaders. I was highly impressed.

The "awfullest sight" of his trip he witnessed in Karachi. Never anywhere before did he behold such extreme poverty as here. "As I walked through such human misery, my heart sank, I swallowed hard," he wrote. "I clenched my fists, and yet people and children smiled as they greeted me: 'Salaam Padre.'"

He found in west Pakistan a greater sense of appreciation for United States aid than in any other country he had ever visited. On April 12 he boarded a Qantas Super-Constellation in Karachi and after fourteen hours was in Rome and back at the friendly table of Santa Maria del Lago with American friends. He spent little time in the Eternal City, only remaining long enough to make the necessary visits to officials. On April 19 he was in the peace of Father Toffolini's flower garden in Udine. A hurried trip to his native surroundings, prayers at the cemeteries of his ancestors, visits with his cousins, and off again to Madrid. He offered a Mass of Thanksgiving at the altar in the old cathedral where the mortal remains of SS. Isidore and Maria de la Cabeza are enshrined. He made preliminary arrangements for the next year's NCRLC pilgrimage and hurried on to Paris, Washington, Chicago, and Des Moines. In Rangoon he had written down the purpose of this lengthy journey:

> I am making an all-around plea for better public relations in the rural field. Most of our missions are in rural districts, and I would like to see at least a few of our leaders know what services are available; what the credit evils really are; what simple cooperatives could accomplish. Too often I draw a blank, but I never give up. Facts, and facts, plus logical conclusions, are of the essence. Planned training of the missionaries that would make them effective in their tremendous task; that would keep them in good physical trim; healthy and thus better able to carry on.... Science is the progressive discovery of God, and God expects us to find out for ourselves the breadth and depth of His omnipotent love for His creatures. It's lack of real religion that makes us unmindful of what science has to offer to us here and now.

He was happy as a schoolboy on the first day of vacation as he knelt in his garden in Des Moines weeding the strawberry patch. That night, May 6, 1956, he wrote: "There is romance in travel, crossing of seas, and the sunset and sunrise over the oceans are thrilling and memorable — but the good earth on which I kneel and hold in my hands in my garden is forever the *Good Earth* for me."

CHAPTER TEN

COUNCIL CONSULTANT

By chance or Providence a thread woven into Ligutti's life constantly placed him in the center of important events. He arrived in Rome in 1959 on the eve of the most important event of the Catholic Church in the twentieth century, the Second Vatican Council. After the trying experiences of the previous year, he was content to direct the international affairs of the NCRLC. His superior, Bishop Edward Daly, and Roman officials permitted him to reside in the Eternal City.

He was not happy, however, in his apartment on Via S. Damaso. It was too confining for a man who had spent most of his life in the open spaces and fields of Iowa. He was determined, however, to remain in Rome, and on March 30, 1961 he wrote his decision to his friends Fr. Leo Gannon and Msgr. Newman Flanagan.

He discussed his plans with Walter Persegati of FAO for building a home on the property of the Consolata Fathers. However, legal difficulties prevented using that site. Persegati advised him not to build a home for the FAO observer or the NCRLC lest there someday be the danger of eviction. In June, 1961, he returned to the United States, told his decision to Msgrs. Francis Gilligan and James Byrnes in St. Paul, who both heartily endorsed his decision to remain in Rome. That same month he proposed to the NCRLC executive committee that he build a home in Rome and it met with their pleasure. At this meeting, also, it was determined that Bishop Joseph Marling, C.PP.S., of Jefferson City, then president of the NCRLC, would ask Mr. Stillman for a gift of $25,000 to $30,000 for building the house. Later Ligutti recalled, "If it were not for Bishop Marling and his asking Mr. Stillman for the finances, there never would have been this home in Rome."

In July Ligutti returned to Rome. The site of the Consolata Fathers' property was discarded. Mr. Zuppi, an associate editor of *L'Osservatore della Dominica* and a friend of Persegati, suggested a site on the property of the Sisters of the Poor of St. Catherine overlooking the Via Aurelia Antica. On July 27, Zuppi, Persegati, and Ligutti examined the site and found it ideal. Ten days later they met with the mother general and the procurator of the community and discussed the possibility of securing the site on the edge of a cliff overlooking the ancient Roman road. They agreed that Ligutti would use the house as long as he lived, and upon his death the house and property would revert to the religious community. On August 11 the architectural firm of Sciascia and Avetta examined the site, and seven days later Mr. Louis Warren, a board member of the Homeland Foundation, informed Ligutti that, acting upon Bishop Marling's request, Mr. Stillman would pay for building the house. The architects, following a general floor plan which Ligutti designed, drafted the blueprints for a two-story structure built into the side of the cliff. For these plans Ligutti paid $300. On September 9 he was in New York and during conversations with Mr. Stillman and Mr. Warren $40,000 was agreed upon for building the house.

He returned to Rome the following month. The architects presented the final plans on October 16 and two months later the architects and the sisters conferred about the house. On January 5, 1962 Dr. Emilio Bonomelli, director of the Vatican farms, informed Ligutti that government approval for the house had been secured. This was the first time that Ligutti referred to the house as "Villa Stillman," the name that it came to be called. On February 7 the sisters signed the contract for the house according to the above terms. On May 4 Ligutti was in Cornwall, New York, unpacking his possessions that were in storage. Some he sent to Rome but most he donated to the Ladies of the Grail and the Scalabrini Fathers. He was definitely to become an American among the Romans.

The summer months were devoted to many activities concerning the building of Villa Stillman. He was as happy as a child with a new toy. On June 19 he took his friend and fellow schoolmate Cardinal Ildebrando Antoniutti to examine the site and progress on the construction. The cardinal was the first of many friends to visit the site in coming months. During the first session of the Council, on November 15, 1962, Ligutti brought Bishop Daly there. The bishop said he was happy that Ligutti had decided to remain in Rome. The autumn was occupied with conciliar affairs. On the last day of the Council's first session,

Archbishop Gerald Bergan and Bishop Ralph Hayes attended the villa's formal opening. The former presided at the formal blessing.

On December 8 the Council Fathers and experts had returned home. For Ligutti the city seemed empty. On Christmas Eve he confided to his diary, "I always feel a little depressed at Christmas, not because of the memories of home and family, but because of parish work, the snow and the joy of seeing parishioners at Midnight Mass."

The new year dawned. Ligutti joyfully moved from the apartment into Villa Stillman. On February 12, 1963 Cardinal Carlo Confalonieri blessed the new home, left a picture of Pope John, and took part in the first of many receptions in Villa Stillman. In the afternoon Cardinal Antoniutti called, left water colors of saints of agriculture from the Madrid cathedral, and gave his whole-hearted approval to Villa Stillman. Ligutti was at home, with room to move, air to breathe, and land to cultivate. He was proud and pleased and at peace.

But a decade of intensive and arduous work lay before him. One of the major preoccupations of the pastor from Iowa was the Second Vatican Council. In January, 1962, he wrote the executive committee of the NCRLC:

> My presence in Rome during the past three years has indeed been a rewarding and useful experience; at least it has not been harmful to the standing and reputation of the NCRLC. Our past work in Latin America is indeed bearing abundant fruits and proper credit is being given to our pioneering endeavors. The hopes and the prayers of decades ago are now being fulfilled, thank God.
>
> Other work to the same end but in a different fashion is carried on right here in Rome. We must have vision, courage. That which is right will ever prevail. During the past two years and probably for at least another year Rome will be immersed in Ecumenical Church matters.

On November 21, 1960 Ligutti was appointed a consultant to the Council's preparatory commission on the Apostolate of the Laity. He then joined the ranks of the novices, for as Pope John remarked, "When it comes to an ecumenical council we are all novices." Ligutti was appointed to the sub-committee on social action and was pleased to work closely with his friends Msgr. George Higgins and Msgr. Pietro Pavan as consultants. He made new friends with two men he admired, Bishop Emilio Guano of

Livorno and Msgr. Achille Glorieux, secretary of the commission. Among the members of the commission were such true and loyal friends as Archbishop Paul Helder Camara of Olinda and Recife, Brazil; Archbishop Mario Castellano of Siena, Italy; Bishop Joseph Blomjous of Mwanza, Tanzania; and Bishop Manuel Larrain of Talca, Chile. President of the commission was Cardinal Fernando Cento.

It was no easy matter organizing the work of the commission. The saying, "The ones who don't know talk and the ones who know don't talk," stated the problem surrounding the work of all twelve preparatory commissions. There was, also, either ignorance or the lack of willingness to follow parliamentary procedure. At times the chair would rule exactly the opposite of what was almost unanimously approved by the members the preceding day. Bishops and superiors of religious orders and Catholic universities were invited to express their opinions on several subjects. Those working in the general secretariat of the Council, headed by Archbishop Pericle Felici, sifted through these opinions and parcelled them out among the commissions. "The ones living in Rome," Ligutti wrote, "meet every week or at least twice a month. I have gathered at least 500 type-written pages of material for study and as a basis for discussion — imagine what others must have!" These factors and others made the work of the preparatory commission on the Apostolate of the Laity extremely difficult and tiring.

After a year's experience in attending meetings of the commission, Ligutti observed in 1961:

> February 1 — Pavan, Higgins and myself objected to putting *bonum Ecclesiae* before *bonum commune*.
>
> February 2 — I objected to Quadri [auxiliary bishop of Pinerola, Italy] running down the Protestants.
>
> March 3 — I stressed the need of forming public opinion in training the laity.
>
> March 24 — I suggested that we need a translator in order to understand sociological jargon.
>
> April 14 — There is great need of meeting and understanding the Italian mentality.
>
> April 21 — Meeting of commission group quite instructive. Clear-cut mind of Pavan. Typical light men like Ferrari and Quadri. Scholarly Jarlot. Detailed Glorieux.
>
> July 3 — Two months' discussion on state presented by Germans under Bishop Hengsbach. Much discussion on women's work. Cento in very late.

July 6 — To third floor hall of Vatican palace for meeting of commission. Lots of formal talking. Pope in at eleven with Archbishop Felici. His Latin rather poor — Read talks by Castellano, Hengsbach and Gasperri — not much. Cardijn, long talk but old stuff. Pope went around to meet all of us.

Meetings continued in October and November, and resumed in January. During December Ligutti set to work promoting a statement on tithing to be presented to the Council. On December 19 he met with Fr. Christopher Berutti, O.P., secretary of the commission of the Discipline for People and Priests, to discuss drafting a statement on the duty of tithing and stewardship of property. Berutti told him to draft a memorandum and he would see to it that it reached the desk of the central commission. In the evening Knight Commander Bonomelli, associate director of the Vatican office of FAO, came to visit at Villa Stillman and mentioned that Ligutti was being considered a candidate for a canonicate of the St. Mary Major Basilica. On January 7, 1962 Ligutti drafted the memorandum on Church support and added to his diary, "I am convinced of the fundamental truth of the statement and have stressed the aspect of worship."

In January the preparatory commission on the Apostolate of the Laity held further meetings. Again Ligutti noted in his diary:

January 2 — Pavan presented a good analysis on the relationship of the natural and supernatural.

January 3 — Vagnozzi and Fenton criticised by all the Americans in Rome.

January 23 — Reading of finished chapters — a few changes suggested on families and migration — minor points — they did quite well with some of my suggestions.

January 24 — To *cancelleria* for Lay Apostolate commission — I made suggestions on "families" as education agency in technical work — To *cancelleria* for II sub-commission — a few new suggestions — Higgins on freedom of conscience — backed by Toniolo.

January 27 — Went to Morino for translation of my tithing statement. Good Latin. At 8 Higgins, Kelly, Lupi, Cappone and me. All about Council, then Delegation, then curia, then U.S. bishops.

March 13 — Meeting of sub-commission on non-Catholics and the family.

March 17 — Commission meeting — Discussion of women's work in the home.

April 4 — Commission meeting — Guano reading preamble, etc. Really a waste of time — Back to *cancelleria* — more useless discussions — Sheen wanted statement on tourism and sports removed — Cardijn and Garonne opposed it — Tomorrow there will be a vote — Terribly slow procedure.

April 5 — To *cancelleria* — Discussions and reading went on and on although more quickly and more regularly — Glorieux isn't afraid to express himself plainly and strongly — Hengsbach not feeling well — he wants me to go down to So. Am. to evaluate use of *Adveniat* gifts — Bus at 12 and to Domus Maria for dinner — Cento — host — I near Pavan, Quadri, Higgins, Kelly, Ferrari, Civardi — all afraid of state-church relations proposals by theological commission.

So the work of the commission continued. Ligutti served faithfully and expressed himself well on subjects that he felt needed discussion. With an obvious sigh of relief he wrote in his diary on April 8, "To *cancelleria* for final meeting — over by 12:30 — not much discussion — same remitted to Roman group — candy from Cardinal — a good experience to have served on this work." Then he added a personal note: "I am finding that I get tired too quickly, that my legs begin to ache. It's better not to eat much and sleep longer. Thank God for old age creeping in."

The summer passed swiftly. Bishops around the world received the drafts from the preparatory commissions. They were expected to do their homework. As usual, there was back-stairs politicing in Rome for positions and titles of honor during the Council. Little did Rome hear during these months the growing thunder on the horizon as bishops around the world gathered in groups to register their dissatisfaction, even disgust, not only with the drafts prepared for them but also with the structure members of the Vatican curia were building to seal off the *vox populi*.

Never was there to be such a day in the twentieth century of the Church as October 11, 1962. Seldom was there such an oration heard in any assembly throughout this century as the address of Pope John XXIII inaugurating the Second Vatican Council. That story has been told elsewhere, as has the unfolding of that Council. Ligutti was a part of that story.

In January, following the Council's first session, Ligutti wrote to the officers and executive committee of the NCRLC:

To be able to see day after day the *Patres Conciliari* at their daily task, to listen to speeches, to wait for the votes being announced, to mingle with the other *periti* from all over the world are indeed experiences of a lifetime.

There is also work not merely in the private discussions of the Commissions but in the informal off-the-record meetings in private studies or at informal dinners. As you know, there have been set up two coffee bars in small rooms off the main naves of the Basilica, Bar-jonas and Bar-abbas. I must admit that much of my useful work has been done in the "real background" of the Council. I have met with Bishops and priests from all over the world, renewed acquaintances, met new people, and yes, talked rural life on occasions in season and out of season.

Somewhat surprisingly, Ligutti was not at first named a *peritus* or consultant of the Council. Some have felt that his name was omitted because it was well known in Roman circles that Archbishop Pericle Fellici cared little for Americans. Be that as it may, it was more significant that the former under-secretary of the Vatican State, Montini, who was then the archbishop of Milan and living within the Vatican palace with Pope John, on the very first day of his arrival at the Council crossed over in the rain to the Palazzo San Carlo to greet his friend Ligutti. Later Montini wondered why Ligutti was not a *peritus*. He did more than wonder. On October 31, twenty days after the formal opening, Ligutti received his appointment as a *peritus* of the Council. On November 7 he wrote in his diary, "I'm glad that Montini took interest in my appointment."

Ligutti became a center around which American, Latin American, and missionary bishops gravitated. He became the elder statesman of the American *periti*. He was the diplomat without portfolio between the offices of FAO and hundreds of missionary bishops and priests who gathered in Rome during the Council. His apartment during the first session, and later at Villa Stillman during the remaining three sessions, became the center for educating foreign bishops and priests in Roman ways and the *stylus curiae*. His home, too, became a rendezvous for planning strategies, writing *modi*, and disseminating memoranda to key participants in the Council. He was, in many ways, the unofficial and untitled American ambassador to the Vatican, making appointments, opening doors, arranging luncheons and dinners for many American bishops and priests unfamiliar with Vatican protocol, curial traditions, and Italian obstructionists. As he served the American bishops who sought guidance and assistance, so he also served the hundreds of missionary bishops and priests who were equally lost in Vatican methodology.

For example, five days before Cardinal Leo Suenens delivered his "open to the world dialogue" address on December 4, 1962 before the Council Fathers, Archbishop Helder Camara approached Ligutti. Driving out to Via Aurelia Antica to view the progress on Villa Stillman, the archbishop told Ligutti that Pope John promised to come to Brasilia for the inauguration of the new Brazilian capital provided there would be no "big show." He also asked Ligutti to see Cardinal Carlo Confalonieri about establishing a conciliar commission to study modern problems and present such a draft for the next session.

All dinners and meetings, however, were not sheer hard work. Many an afternoon or evening Ligutti spent in the pleasant company of his friends from every corner of the world. In many ways his home became a haven of fellowship and friendship, a stop of rest and refreshment for the many pilgrims in Rome striving to restore the image of the Pilgrim Church to its pristine beauty. Thus, for example, he recorded in his diary on Sunday, September 27, 1964:

> At 12:30 Bishop Bartholome, Bishop Speltz and Godfrey Diekmann, O.S.B., in for dinner. Conversed on liturgy changes, U.S. politics and Goldwater, etc. A very profitable meeting, the kind I like with people who know and are open-minded. I said: Rome very sensitive to letters and protests.

The first session closed and the city once again emptied. Well did Ligutti sense, however, the obstructionist tactics taking place behind the scenes. He knew, as did most other participants, that the Council was hopelessly bogged down by clumsy rules of procedure. By the end of January, 1963, he was at work on the problem. He received a letter from Fr. Joseph Buckley, S.M., superior general of the Marist Fathers, containing a memorandum outlining possible means to expedite Council procedure. Previously he had discussed the matter with Cardinal Suenens, who was also terribly concerned, and later with Cardinals Fernando Cento and Confalonieri. Father Buckley's principal thrust was:

> Introduce substantial changes in the *Ordo*, not only in the procedures of the General Assembly, but also in the structure of the Presidency, in the functioning of the Commissions,

in the powers of the Commissions and their Presidents, in the rapport between the Commissions and the Council Fathers not members of the Commissions themselves.

Ligutti carefully read Buckley's suggestions, incorporated many of them in his own memorandum, and stressed how procedure operates in international organizations such as the FAO in order to expedite a conclusion to a discussion and a clear and definite vote on the issue. He concluded, "The purpose of customary international-conference organization is to ensure smooth functioning, with a minimum of disruption and maximum saving of time. It presupposes that the ordinary work is done in smaller sessions of committees and working parties." On January 30 he wrote Father Buckley:

> The former Italian deputy — now a priest of Bologna — Don Dossetti, has been assigned the job by Cardinals Urbani and Suenens to draw up a suggested *regolamento* — incorporating some of your proposals. He and I had long conferences. He is a clear-headed young man and knows what the story is all about. He will send me the outline of his proposals and I will study them. On Feb. 20th I will drop off in Bologna and discuss the matter further. — Cardinal Suenens is a very determined man — and he is honest. He does not know Rome as well as he should, but is picking up plenty. I am deeply convinced that the procedural structure will spell success or failure for Vatican II. I'll leave no stone unturned because I believe in the cause and I believe that "Things never happen — *they are done.*"

Success crowned these and similar efforts. On September 27 *L'Osservatore Romano* announced the new regulations governing the Council. The ship was out of dry dock and on water again.

Throughout 1963 Ligutti continued to study material and attend meetings of the conciliar commission on the Lay Apostolate. His diary continued to register praise for Monsignor Pavan as well as for another consultant to the commission, Fr. Robert Tucci, S.J., editor of *Civilta Catholica*. Ligutti spoke during these meetings on matters that he was experienced with and about which he felt most keenly. On one occasion he objected to the statement that blamed material nature for original sin. On another he said that the document should praise all families and not just Catholic families. He continually insisted that in the realm of practice the cardinal virtues were just as important as the theological virtues. He chuckled over the debates concerning the term "Catholic Action," feeling that those members of the commission who felt it was a sacrosanct phrase were too limited in their vision. He insisted that the commission seriously study the causes of poverty and express these causes in the document. No doubt he shocked more than a few venerable gray hairs when he said, "Private property a hundred years from now may well be only a memory."

On May 31, 1963 Cardinal Paul Marella notified him that he was appointed a *peritus* to the conciliar commission on Bishops and the Government of Dioceses. The first meeting of this commission that Ligutti attended, however, was not until March 3, 1964. Again, as in the commission on the laity, he noted how poorly organized the meeting was because of the lack of understanding of procedural rules. Once again he startled not a few members of this commission by asking, "Is a bishop an administrator or an apostle?" By September the commissions were diligently at work during the third session. Ligutti was immersed in meetings with the commissions on the Lay Apostolate, Bishops and the Government of Dioceses, and *Schema* 13. The third session settled down to serious work in spite of two observations that Ligutti noted. On September 15 he wrote, "Felici talks to the bishops as if they were fifth graders." Six days later he recorded that Archbishop Dino Staffa and Richard Cardinal Cushing had asked that the Council adjourn.

October was a more than busy month. Ligutti recorded time after time how tired he was at the end of the day. Little wonder. He was carrying on the work of the Vatican Observers' office of FAO, attending meetings and holding conferences at the FAO headquarters, attending morning meetings of the Council, meeting with the three commissions, entertaining guests in his home for dinner and supper, and continually lobbying for rural life, the poor people of the world, and stewardship.

That month Bishop Emilio Guano asked if he would become the assistant director of the lay auditors of the Council. Guano approached him because "the lay auditors are presently being deprived of all the technical and practical assistance such as is truly necessary for their active participation at the Council." On October 6 Ligutti received his letter of appointment to this position from Archbishop Pericle Felici. The task meant more than acting as host to the group. It entailed supplying them with conciliar documents, arranging conferences at least once a week, and assisting them in their material needs while in Rome. At his first meeting with the auditors on October 19 Ligutti met confusion in the ranks because of lack of preparation by conciliar officials.

While bishops in committee meetings were hammering out statements on religious liberty and the Jews and while journalists were acting more as lobbyists than reporters, Ligutti was quietly discovering the real facts behind closed doors. On October 13 he and Dr. Bonomelli had an hour's audience with Pope Paul. That day the Rome papers carried a rather alarming announcement that the central coordinating commission was going to override the statement on religious liberty and the Jews. Ligutti recorded this meeting in his diary that night:

> I thought it was not true. But at night Paul VI was very strong in his statement to me and Bonomelli after the Lebanese had presented his project. Frings was in and the Pope quoted his argument with the cardinal. He said concordats were out, there is too much freedom and hit strong against these council statements.

The following day Ligutti related the Pope's views to Bishop Ernest Primeau. He told the latter of Pope Paul's absolute intention of rejecting the statements on religious liberty and the Jews:

> The newspapers class him as a defender of the liberals. *Periti* and some bishops are accusing Felici of stalling the commission and ruling arbitrarily. If they had just heard what Frings, Lebret [Fr. Louis Lebret, O.P., consultant to the Secretariat for Non-Christians] and I had heard from his own lips.

It was a bad week. On Sunday Ligutti had learned of the death of his close friend Bishop John Treacy of LaCrosse. Ligutti scratched in his diary, "What hectic but historic days!"

November was the stormy month, both weather-wise and within the Council hall. Crepe hangers were plentiful and justifiable, for there was little cause for rejoicing. The meeting of November 19, 1964 marked the lowest morale of the American bishops. Ligutti recorded that electrifying morning:

> What a morning at the Council! Tisserant postponed the vote on religious liberty after announcing it for today. U.S. bishops up in arms. Cardinal Meyer, mad as Tisserant, tried to convince him. Meyer turned white. U.S. bishops' leader was Bishop Reh who secured signatures for a sharp petition. DeSmedt, the relator, was applauded for one minute. My

opinion: must never take for granted that a Roman curial member will not resort to all the tricks of the trade. It is sad that Paul VI is vacillating. He gives in to pressure and is undulating as a rocking chair. He fears to take personal responsibility for decisions; fears diplomatic consequences.

There was little joy in Rome as the Council Fathers departed after the closing of the third session on November 21, 1964. Before Christmas Ligutti entertained a group of laymen who felt that the changes would only be very small and informal. That night Ligutti wrote his opinion in his diary — an opinion undoubtedly shared by the majority of the participants of the Council and members of the Church: "Changes *have* to be big or world will not be satisfied." Away from Rome and the scene of the Council, two months later Ligutti was in Rio de Janeiro and asked himself, "Who will be right fifty years from now in interpreting the Council?"

The Council's fourth session opened September 14, 1965, and all keen observers could see from the opening ceremony that Pope Paul intended to take more direct control of the Council and meant to bring it to an end with that session. Ligutti continued his work as usual, attending commission meetings, helping the lay auditors, and lobbying as only he could at luncheons, dinners, receptions, and — of course — in the coffee bars. His attention during these hectic weeks was centered on three ideas: (1) the social teaching of the Church applied to the social needs of men everywhere, (2) the insertion of a clear-cut statement on stewardship in a conciliar document, and (3) the establishment of a secretariat for justice to fight poverty.

October, 1965, was a striking contrast to the same month the preceding year. He was chosen to be in the papal party that flew to the United Nations in New York on October 4 where the Pope uttered his plea for peace with his cry still echoing around the world: "War never again — never again war!"

Four days later victory crowned Ligutti's tireless efforts. On October 8 he noted in his diary:

> Vatican car picked me up at four for meeting of lay apostolate commission meeting in the Apostolic Palace. Many details discussed but all approved in sub-commission and text is passed by plenary commission.' First half is most important.... At 6 p.m. in Apostolic Palace stewardship passed. Castellano read the wording.

Two days later he was sworn in as a prothonotary apostolic, but that satisfaction was nothing compared to his joy with the passage of the text on stewardship. He breathed more than a sigh of relief and a prayer on October 20 when Cardinal Cento closed the last assembly of the commission on the Lay Apostolate.

He was, however, not finished. As a member of the subcommission, a month's work was before him in helping provide for a secretariat on justice and poverty. The final three days of the Council Ligutti expressed in two brief sentences the sentiments of the worn and weary bishops, priests, and lay people who participated in the never-to-be-forgotten event. On December 6 he wrote, "My system is in bad shape." For the closing session on December 8 he secured good seats for the lay auditors on the right side of the papal altar. With joy he noted the new crucifix and candlesticks designed by his friend the artist Graham Carey were on the papal altar. Regretfully, he noted that the farmer was absent from the group of philosophers, artists, industrialists, and workers saluted by the Pope. And he signed his own *finis* to the Council with the expression, "What a day of glory and of history!"

The three overriding interests of Ligutti throughout the years of the Council sprang from deep-seated convictions implanted and strengthened by his forty years' experience. His entire priesthood was dedicated to promoting social justice for people everywhere. He did not particularly like to be called a rural sociologist (which, in fact, he was); rather he preferred to be called a pastor.

His leadership and experience in social justice prompted officials of the Council to name him a *peritus* of the mixed commissions drawn from the lay apostolate and doctrinal commissions. The ultimate result of endless hours of meetings and discussions and informal conversations resulted in the second section of the third chapter of the pastoral constitution on *The Church in the Modern World*. The section is entitled "Certain Principles Governing Socio-Economic Life as a Whole." From the previous accounts of Ligutti's travels, writings, and speeches the reader can readily see the imprint he himself left on the entire section and, most notably, Paragraphs 71 and 72. Therein is stressed the causes so close to his heart: ownership of private property, development of human dignity, land reform, cooperatives, conservation of resources, worldwide prosperity, and the promotion of peace. Ligutti echoed these thoughts and at the same time summarized his own thinking on socio-economic problems of the past forty years in a brief introduction to a book authored by Fr. Boavida Coutinho on the history of the Antigonish Movement entitled *Community Development through Adult Education and Cooperatives*. Therein Ligutti wrote:

> The fundamental ideas expressed [in this book] are simple and to the point, vis. : man possesses a noble personality; man can and must develop the gifts with which God has endowed him; God has put at man's disposal an infinity of material and spiritual possibilities; by joining forces with his fellow human beings man enhances his powers and achieves heightened results for himself as a person, for his family and for society.
>
> Man-caused problems can be and should be solved by man with God's help. What a man can do by joining forces should be done by men themselves on a voluntary and independent basis. The marshalling of small group endeavors can be widened to the whole world's community thus bringing about peace and love among men.

We have already referred to Ligutti's work in promoting the concept of stewardship among the Council Fathers and his efforts at securing a statement on the same in the conciliar documents. Rightly was Ligutti considerd the pioneer of tithing within the Church in the United States. Already as a pastor in Woodbine and Granger he promoted the concept of stewardship among his parishioners. Throughout the years he kept his interest alive and drew about him a circle of priests, notably Fr. John Ireland Gallery of Chicago, who were interested in stewardship. He viewed the Council as the opportune time to present the idea of stewardship to the universal Church. He left no stone unturned in his path.

After the first session of the Council Ligutti was worried about the status of stewardship. In July, 1963, he wrote his friend Bishop Floyd Begin of Oakland, California, known for many years as a staunch supporter and promoter of stewardship. He asked whether or not there was any mention of stewardship in the revised drafts sent to the bishops after the first session. Bishop Begin replied:

> As far as I know there is no mention of tithing in any of the schemata of the Council, nor are all the bishops of the United States in favor of the tithing program. I believe it is a matter of education. It may take a long time. I brought the matter to the attention of Cardinal Cicognani and was not given too much encouragement. I am afraid he was a

bit too busy to give the matter his undivided attention. I shall make a new effort when I get to Rome.

And so Begin did. He actively promoted the idea among his fellow bishops, working closely with Zuroweste and Ligutti in the undertaking. Significantly, he was the only American bishop to address the Council Fathers on the specific subject of tithing. This he did during the third session on November 9, 1964.

Shortly after the fourth session opened Ligutti set to work. On September 22, 1965, the forty-eighth anniversary of his ordination, he drafted a *modus* on stewardship, which read: "It is the privilege of the Christian to return to God a share of the material goods which God gave him. This is to be treated as a sacred trust, strictly associated for and used for the establishment and development of God's work in this world." He asked Walter Persegati of FAO to translate the statement into Italian and gave it to Msgr. Claude Morino to translate into Latin.

The following day he gave a copy to Bishop Albert Zuroweste of Belleville, Illinois, who for many years had shown a keen interest in stewardship. Two days later he wrote Zuroweste reminding him that "it is most essential that Cardinal Cento's approval and sympathetic backing be assured." He suggested that Zuroweste make sure that the American bishops intervene in favor of the statement and that he and others should personally contact the bishops and consultants of the commission on the Lay Apostolate to secure their support. Ligutti also suggested that his own presentation entitled "Give Back to God the Things that Are God's" be sent with his personal letter supporting the statement. Both the proposed statement to be added to the text as well as Ligutti's paper were sent to the American bishops and to the bishops and consultants on the commission of the Lay Apostolate.

Ligutti's paper, written and delivered several years previously, both summarized his own thinking on stewardship and stated the principles which would underlie the National Committee for Diocesan Support Programs. He pointed out that from the earliest of times man was aware that he should return to God as *an act of worship* the gifts that God the Creator had bestowed upon him. He further stressed that such an offering was not merely man's obligation but rather "an opportunity and privilege of professing and showing gratitude, which each one ought to have, to God for his own creation." He sketched the abuses of past generations in the Church's financing and suggested possible ways in which contributions to the Church might more effectively become both an act of worship and service to mankind. "It is necessary," he concluded, "that we be convinced that where there is persuasion, there is will, and where there is will, there is a good and effective way."

On September 19 Ligutti wrote in his diary, "I am a bit nervous on tithing but it went across without a change. Camara was not satisfied and Yu Pin a bit skeptical." He wrote John Ireland Gallery on September 25:

> I waited until the news could be definite. The Bishops voted on chapter III, *De Apostolatu Laicorum*, no. 10. Bp. Zuroweste passed the *modus* to the U.S. bishops. 2023 voted — 1707 *placet*, 311 *juxta modum* — that means that a goodly group did insert the suggested *modus* statement. Now: subcommission II will discuss it. Archbishop Morris is the key man. If the subcommission approves it the text goes to the full commission on the Lay Apostolate.... If it goes to the aula, no question about approval. Then no need for speeches; The canon law will have to incorporate it in its general form. If it does go through we shall celebrate — and you may be here for it. At any rate, so far so good. Pray for continued success.

On October 8, as we have seen, the full commission on the Lay Apostolate approved this statement. Joyfully Ligutti wrote in his diary under November 9, "Gallery here. Stewardship-tithing article voted in at 11:45 a.m. Thank God." That evening Gallery, Zuroweste, and Ligutti went out to dinner to celebrate the passage of the statement — which read: "IT IS A DUTY AND HONOR FOR CHRISTIANS TO RETURN TO GOD A PART OF THE GOOD THINGS THEY RECEIVE FROM HIM." Therein was contained a lifetime of preaching and teaching that Ligutti carried to the four corners of the world. Never for a moment did he forget that his Christian consciousness on this matter had been stirred by his Protestant brothers. Readily he admitted that the concept of tithing practiced in the early Church had been lost for centuries within the Catholic communion. In recent times it was restored as a practical act of worship in several Protestant Churches, such as the United Methodists and the Seventh Day Adventists. From leaders in these Churches he had learned the basic principles of stewardship, one of which was, "I believe that I am a steward for a brief period of time — till the Lord shall say: 'Thou shalt be a steward no longer.'"

Ligutti was a promoter, an animator, and an expeditor. He much preferred to act as stage manager than the star of the performance. Through his countless contacts he invariably knew the right man for the right task. He knew the avenues to follow, whether it be the assembly halls of international organizations, the corridors of government bureaucracies, or the silent sanctuaries of the Church. At no time did he act more fully and perfectly as an *enabler* than he did in the establishment of the pontifical commission for Justice and Peace. His great contribution was putting the right men together and facilitating the means by which a paper directive of the Second Vatican Council would take on flesh and bones and breathe its spirit across the world.

By the dawn of the Council serious men and women throughout the world were becoming more and more alarmed by the devastating effects of war. The astronomical costs of war machinery, the hawkish stance of governments and peoples, the rattling of missiles, and the race to outer space were but a few of the major factors creating an ever widening gap between the rich and poor, resulting in the hardening of men's consciousness of the universal sins against justice. Anxious men and women heard the anguished cries among "a generation of rising expectations," the dire poverty of "the third world," the fettered chains of economic and human oppression binding "the under-developed countries." International organizations, such as FAO, UNESCO, WHO, and ILO, and governments were deeply disturbed, for they well knew that social injustice was the hotbed in which the seeds of war were planted. Religious leaders, too, were alarmed because they also shared the guilt of humanity in not fulfilling the gospel mandate, "Do unto others as you would have them do unto you." No one put the religious dimension so pointedly and poignantly as the British author Sir John Boyd-Orr when he said to Ligutti in the mid-1940's: "The Gospel says that man is a temple of the Spirit, but what kind of a temple is it if it has rickets and a nasty discharge from the left ear?"

Many sensitive Catholic leaders who had viewed these social injustices were deeply disturbed, and some resolved to take action. One such person was James Norris, a man with courage and vision. His superior in Catholic Relief Services, Bishop Edward E. Swanstrom, was another; Msgr. John Bayer of Caritas Internationalis, Msgr. Jean Rodhain of French Secours Catholique, and Barbara Ward (Lady Jackson), one of the world's leading economists, were others. Catholic leaders were also in the front ranks of the growing army of justice and peace. Conspicuous among them were such men as Archbishop Helder Camara of Brazil, Archbishop Angelo Fernandes of India, and Archbishop Patrick O'Boyle of Washington, D.C. The Spirit was stirring in the Catholic Church; no human instrument can adequately measure the impetus given the cause of social justice by the publication of Pope John's two great encyclicals *Mater et Magistra* and *Pacem in Terris*.

Although there was much talk about the problem in the Council's first two sessions, it was for the most part just talk. One of the first most direct and effective actions taken was by James Norris on October 7, 1964 in a memorandum entitled "World Poverty and the Christian Conscience," which was widely circulated among the Council Fathers. Norris stated the problem directly:

> The Christian conscience of the West is today confronted with the historical fact that 16% of the world's peoples, living around the North Atlantic, have unprecedented wealth — 70% of the entire world's wealth — and they live side by side with hundreds of millions of people living in poverty, hunger and degradation on a scale unknown in history.
>
> This wealth is in the hands of members of societies that are Christian by inheritance if not always today in practice. A profound moral obligation rests on the Christian conscience to take note of the situation for the following reasons:
> 1. The Divine Command to feed the hungry, clothe the naked and shelter the homeless is explicit, and is accompanied by promises of rewards and punishments. In the past, resources limited the scope of this command, but today this is no longer so. The West has both the wealth and the skill to permit action.
> 2. The problems and dilemmas of the poor countries are often the result of policies and actions of the Western nations. This makes the moral obligation to act all the greater.
> 3. The alternative offered to the developing countries by communism would cut them off, at least for a time, from the Gospel and millions of children would be trained systematically as atheists.

Norris urged the Council Fathers to show concern for the problem "in a dramatic and concrete way" and proposed that one day, "a part of a general congregation be devoted to a discussion of World Poverty." He also proposed that on a given day the Pope would celebrate Mass for the poor of the world, that a competent lay person address the Council Fathers on the dimensions of world poverty, and that bishops urge further study of the problem.

On February 8, 1965 Norris met Ligutti and Gremillion in New York. Their discussion centered on the necessity of fighting poverty and establishing a secretariat in Rome for that purpose. The following day they met again and determined that there should be an international group established to study the problem. Ligutti was assigned to write Cardinal Dell'Acqua, Archbishop Antonio Samore, and Knight Commander Bonomelli, enlisting their support. By February 17 Norris had drafted a proposal for a secretariat on poverty in Rome which he passed on to Ligutti. Three days later Norris and Ligutti lunched with Barbara Ward and again discussed the proposed secretariat. At that time Ligutti suggested that 1 per cent of the income of the Church, from the local parish to the central offices in Rome, be set aside for the development of the poor people of the world.

Ligutti returned to Rome in time for more meetings of the commissions in April and May. In July he heard that the Pope wanted the Council to close on December 8 and instinctively knew then that action must be taken quickly on the proposed secretariat. On July 23 he met Lady Jackson at Rome's Quirinale Hotel. The following day he wrote in his diary, "I hope this undertaking can be put across. I would approach it in a different fashion, small at the start and with no backing of authority, but all towards an end and I hope to achieve it." For the following week they both made many contacts concerning the proposed secretariat.

During the summer he used his considerable influence among friends and associates in securing grassroots support for the project. In a June 11 memorandum, he wrote:

> The proposed Secretariat for World Justice and Development is not intended to be an aid agency nor a coordinating agency for aid. It is to be a top-level advisory body — a sort of cabinet in the Church to state how best the moral force of the Church's international social doctrine can be focused and joined to the complex realities of economics, sociology, demography and politics related to the central problem of our age: World poverty and underdevelopment. It is intended to be an agency of the Holy Father consisting of experts appointed to advise him in this field. Its primary functions

would be to educate people about the dimensions and implications of world poverty and to stimulate to action.

He noted a statement in FIDES, the international news service published by the Congregation for the Evangelization of Peoples, which he circulated also. Speaking before an Institute for Social Action in Asia held in Hongkong, Fr. José M. Abad on August 10 said:

> The vicious spiral of poverty in underdeveloped countries must be broken and will be broken...within 15 years... half a generation. This will happen either with the Church or without the Church, that is, according to human principles or against them.... The present distribution of wealth in the world is certainly not a reflection of the will of God and it cannot continue. Christians must decide to be a part of the solution or be left behind.

On August 1, Ligutti worked on two continents. That morning in Paris he dictated the story and status of the secretariat for poverty and development to Mlle. Lemercier (Houtart's secretary), and in the evening in New York he visited with Monsignor Gremillion concerning the secretariat and the latter's coming to Rome. Three days later he visited Bishop Swanstrom and asked him to secure O'Boyle's support of the secretariat in Rome. At the same time he asked Swanstrom to intercede with Cardinal Francis Spellman to nominate Gremillion as its executive secretary. With the opening of the fourth session a foundation for the secretariat had been laid.

The yeast was in the dough. It was now only a matter of a few public speeches in the Council hall, the drafting of the precise wording by Subcommission 8 (of which Ligutti was a member), and the final voting, first by the full commission of the draft on *The Church in the Modern World,* and finally by all the Fathers of the Council. Over seventy speeches were delivered on the problem of world poverty. Words, however, were not enough; action was demanded. This Swanstrom pointed out in his speech, stating directly and emphatically:

> In order to call with persistence the attention of the People of God and in fact all men of the human family to the sad plight of a majority of God's children, and to teach the message of Christ's love for the poor and His justice in and out of season, this Sacred Synod proposes that a secretariat

of the Holy See for promoting world justice and development be established.

Archbishop Angelo Fernandes seconded the proposal in a dramatic speech delivered in the name of the bishops of India and over a hundred bishops of the Far East, Europe, Africa, Latin America, and Canada. He asked, first, that a paragraph be added to the document showing clearly the urgency and extension of the problem of world poverty, and then added:

> My second plea is that some definite step should be taken to solve this problem. It is clear that it is not for the Council to descend to concrete details in attempting a solution to suit a world-wide and many-sided problem. However, the Council can, and should propose the formation of a postconciliar structure through which concrete methods could be suggested from time to time, and an effort made to implement them. The fine spirit of the Church in Council should continue to manifest itself in the days ahead, and in fact should in some ways be incorporated into the organization of the Church.

Other bishops enthusiastically endorsed the proposed secretariat both on paper and in speech. Few spoke more eloquently than Very Rev. Gerald Mahon, superior general of the Mill Hill Missionaries:

> ...since we last discussed this *schema,* 35 million people have died of starvation; at this moment 400 million people are hungry; and 1,500 million are subject to the diseases that follow on malnutrition.
>
> A permanent, top-level structure would clearly demonstrate to the world that the Church appreciates the dimension of this problem, and is genuinely concerned....

The result of so much action and direct appeal by the Council Fathers was the insertion of the following sentences in the pastoral constitution on *The Church in the Modern World*:

> In view of the immense hardships which still afflict the majority of men today, the Council regards it as most opportune that some agency of the universal Church be set up for the world-wide promotion of justice for the poor and of Christ's kind love for them. The role of such an organization will be to stimulate the Catholic community to foster progress in needy regions, and social justice on the international scene.

The victory had been won after countless hours of meetings, discussions, and planning by Ligutti and all those who labored for just such a clear-cut sentence from the Council. The history of the establishment and development of the Pontifical Commission for Justice and Peace falls beyond the scope of this work. Undoubtedly it will be recounted by a more competent historian. Suffice it to say that in May, 1966, Pope Paul established a committee to advise him how such a secretariat could be established and how it would function.

The following July 7 the Pope appointed a provisional committee, with Cardinal Maurice Roy of Quebec as its chairman, to execute the conciliar proposal. On January 6, 1967 Pope Paul established the Pontifical Commission on Justice and Peace with the *motu proprio Catholicam Christi Ecclesiam,* which outlined the general purpose of the commission:

> Its aims shall be to arouse the People of God to full awareness of its mission at the present time, in order on the one hand, to promote the progress of needy nations and encourage international social justice, and on the other, to help underdeveloped nations to work for their own development.

In October, 1967, writing in the *American Ecclesiastical Review,* Fr. Arthur McCormack, M.H.M., a consultant to the commission, observed:

> The name Justice and Peace must be understood in the following way: Justice means social justice within and between nations so that every human being should have conditions of life in keeping with his human dignity which will enable him to progress towards a fully human development — to the fullness of a more abundant life — and enable him also to make his contribution to building a new and better world.
>
> Peace is to be understood, not so much in the sense of maintaining peace or working for peace in the political or diplomatic sense, but in the sense of building peace — "The new name for peace is development" — producing the conditions that are fundamental for peace, a more just, humane, better world....

Ligutti's interest in the Pontifical Commission for Justice and Peace, however, did not end with the passage in Paragraph 90 in the pastoral constitution *The Church in the Modern World.* He continued to see the recommendation of the Council Fathers through until the commission was established and then actively cooperated with it for five more years. This he did by carefully working to see that the commission would not become merely another ecclesiastical paper organization; second, by seeking the appointment of Gremillion as its executive secretary, and by actively participating for the next five years as a member of its central steering committee.

Perhaps Ligutti's greatest contribution to this commission was, however, not so much his own work as that of his long-time friend and protege Msgr. Joseph Gremillion. A priest of the diocese of Alexandria, Louisiana, Gremillion first came to Ligutti's attention in 1942 while the former was still a seminarian at the Catholic University of America. Following his ordination, Gremillion served as pastor of St. Joseph's parish, Shreveport, Louisiana. As a young priest he was an active member of the Liturgical Conference and the National Catholic Rural Life Conference. He was one of the priests that the Catholic Relief Services chose to study the conditions in displaced persons' camps in post-war Europe. He was, however, a restless soul. He was among the zealous priests of Arcadian descent who burned with a desire to serve the Church in a broader ambit than the bayous of Louisiana. From this group came some of the most dynamic leadership of the Church in the South during the post-war years. Some people mistook their zeal as ambition and maliciously called them "climbers." Nothing, however, could have been further from the truth with Gremillion.

Ligutti early recognized the exceptional ability of the soft-spoken, gentle, and ever-smiling priest. For several years Ligutti tried to secure Gremillion as assistant director of the Conference. The latter's ordinary, Bishop Charles Greco, however, refused to release him. After many discussions and negotiations, all of which failed, Gremillion told Ligutti that he was not interested in the offer but rather preferred to work in the international area. This was 1952. Three years later Ligutti proposed Gremillion for an office with Catholic Relief Services, a position he ultimately accepted. In 1957 Ligutti was delighted to hear that Gremillion was coming to Rome for graduate study at the Gregorian University. While visiting with Cardinal Montini in Milan, Ligutti mentioned the name of his protege and later sent a memo to the cardinal, who by then had become pope, praising the abilities of Gremillion. It came as no surprise to Ligutti in January, 1967, that Pope Paul had appointed Gremillion as secretary of the Pontifical Commission for Justice and Peace.

As Ligutti expected, Gremillion entered the Roman scene filled with enthusiasm and bristling with ideas. Although the future of the new commission would pose numerous problems, it was safely in hand as long as Gremillion was steering the ship. Ligutti was pleased. Years later, recalling the events that led to establishing the commission, Ligutti said, "I think one of the things that should be very inspiring . . . is how much determination it takes. This commission was not just cooked up in one month and implemented. It took years before the preliminary decree was finished, and this took very hard work by some of the best minds."

By the end of the Council Ligutti was exhausted. His stomach was giving him great pain and his blood pressure was over 170. He left Rome on December 9 for a rest and the mud baths on the island of Ischia where he stayed at the Reginella Hotel. The following day he received a call from James Norris who said he, his wife, and two boys were coming to Ischia. When the Norris family arrived the next day, Ligutti was feeling stronger already. Again both men discussed Gremillion's coming before Norris returned to Rome for an appointment with Archbishop Samore on December 19. The night before returning to Rome himself on December 22, Ligutti did a bit of soul-searching. In his diary he wrote:

> So many conclusions can be drawn from the cure: 1) I should not try to take the world on my shoulders; 2) A complete revision of my role in my office in time and work; 3) Plans for making FAO better known in the field where it operates; 4) Cut down on social life and entertainment, not so much at home or going out; 5) More regular medical care and periods of rest and little travel; 6) More light garden work and more walks under porches and bed at ten o'clock.

He closed the year with a final note in his diary: "This year has seen a lot of activity by me and work in FAO and the Council. Also some more physical pains for me, but all in all, quite satisfying. Thank God for all."

Whether the cause of social justice, the promotion of stewardship, or the establishment of the Pontifical Commission for Justice and Peace, Ligutti had one dominant spiritual motive that prompted him to work day and night. He said in 1974:

> I think that if I did not seek to influence others that I would be completely ungrateful to Almighty God for whatever gifts

He has given me. I use in some of my talks two little candles. I light one candle that produces light and heat. I hold my hand over it. Then the other candle, but it isn't lit. Then I take and light the second candle with the first candle and what happens? I don't take away anything from the first candle, only I add more heat and more light to the surroundings. So you don't lose anything by encouraging others and lighting someone else's lamp.

Ligutti was the lamplighter for hundreds of people during the Second Vatican Council.

CHAPTER ELEVEN

VATICAN OBSERVER TO FAO

A historic event that occurred in Quebec, Canada, on October 16, 1945 did not escape the attention of the executive director of the National Catholic Rural Life Conference. The creation of the Food and Agriculture Organization on that day — nine days before the establishment of the United Nations in San Francisco, was both a joy and a challenge to Monsignor Ligutti. Its potentialities for peace were a joy; its possibilities for love of mankind were a challenge.

The events leading up to that memorable October 18, 1945 and the decision accepted by the forty-two participating nations decisively altered the course of Ligutti's life. The move from Granger to Des Moines was but a trickle compared to the torrent of activity and achievement that would be his for the next twenty-five years as a result of the creation of the Food and Agriculture Organization of the United Nations.

Few, if any, members of the Church knew at that date — and, for that matter, even as late as this date — better than Ligutti, the energies and opportunities unleased in the world through the creation of the Food and Agriculture Organization (FAO). From its beginning Ligutti was guided by its fundamental ideals and labored for the next quarter century to make them operative within the Church. The first of these principles he voiced on January 19, 1947 to Frank Bruce, first president of the FAO: "What's good for people is good for the Church." The second he confided in his diary on March 21, 1949 — his fifty-fourth birthday: "No matter how long one lives, it's how fully we live that counts." The third he vigorously practiced throughout the next twenty-five years: to build a bridge between the Church and the world through international development. In this he anticipated Pope Paul's encyclical *Populorum Progressio,* where the Pontiff wrote, "Development is another word for peace."

Ligutti's esteem and support of FAO can only be understood by one who knows the aims and goals of the organization. This is not the place for recounting the history of FAO; it has already been written. A few highlights of its philosophy and activities, however, are necessary to better understand Ligutti's apostolate. The response of the popes during this period also reveals the impact that Ligutti had on ecclesiastical policy, as well as the direction and emphasis that he and his colleagues had on an overriding concern of the Second Vatican Council.

FAO was, in the final analysis, the dream-come-true of a quiet, persistent, and dedicated man. That man was Frank McDougall, advisor to Sir Stanley Bruce, the High Commissioner for Australia residing in London during the 1930's. Together they attended the 1933 London World Monetary and Economic Conference only to come away disappointed and disillusioned. The conference failed in proposing solutions to the world's economic ills, offered no new approaches, no daring programs to the somewhat complacent and frustrated delegates. McDougall and Bruce, however, found an attentive ear in Sir John Boyd-Orr, whose book *Food, Health and Income* was an overnight sensation in England, by pointing out that two-thirds of the British people were undernourished. Others, too, were concerned and their most powerful ally was the new science of nutrition. Research in England and the United States and the publication in 1936 of the League of Nations' report "Nutrition and Health" coalesced to show that "a large proportion of the world's population did not get enough of the right sort of food to eat and that hence food production should be expanded rather than restricted to meet nutritional requirements."

The result of these scientific stirrings produced the inevitable conclusion that a new approach to the problem of world health and hunger was overdue. McDougall set his pen to paper and drafted the famous "McDougall Memoranda" of 1935 and 1942. In the first memorandum, McDougall expressed his own and his associates' thinking on the relationship among agriculture, financial stability, and health. In this memorandum he sold the idea of the creation of FAO: "The deliberate association of the agricultural and health problems through the countries of western civilization is urgently necessary."

Time passed. World War II unleashed a new fury upon a world we came to call the Atomic Age. In the midst of war, McDougall and his collaborators were already planning for peace. While attending an international conference on the distribution of wheat in Washington, D.C., McDougall drafted a second memorandum dated October, 1942. He began by quoting Stanley Bruce (now Lord Bruce of Melbourne) in his famous speech before the 1935 meeting of the League of Nations. Said Lord Bruce: "Is it not possible to marry health and agriculture and, by so doing, make a great step in the improvement of national health and, at the same time, an appreciable contribution to the solution of the agricultural problem?"

Answering that question, McDougall proposed the overriding concern of the future FAO in two words: "Reconstruction and development":

> Freedom from want of food must be given high priority in the actions taken to fulfill the pledges of the United Nations. For not only is food the most essential of human needs but the production of food is the principal economic activity of man. We have determined to provide relief to the war-torn countries as soon as they are liberated. In this relief, food will be the most urgent need but we must carry straight on from relief and rehabilitation to reconstruction and development.

It was only a short step from the private circulation of that memorandum to the convocation of the Hot Springs Conference. McDougall won the ear of Mrs. Eleanor Roosevelt who, in turn, arranged a dinner meeting with the President for him. The Food and Agriculture Conference at Hot Springs, Virginia, in May, 1943, was the tangible result of that meeting. The delegates elected an interim commission to draft a constitution, whose work was carried on throughout the following two years. In October, 1945, it was proposed, amended, and finally ratified by the delegates of forty-two nations at the first assembly of FAO in Quebec.

Several basic ideas expressed that autumn in Quebec became the philosophical and humanitarian foundations of the newly-born FAO. One such conviction appeared and was ratified as a conclusion to the 1937 League of Nations' report on "The Relation of Nutrition to Health, Agriculture and Economic Policy." That report read: "The malnutrition which exists in all countries is at once a challenge and an opportunity; a challenge to men's consciences and an opportunity to eradicate a social evil by methods which will increase economic prosperity."

Another consideration that guided those pioneers of FAO was expressed by P. Lamartine Yates in his study of the first ten years of FAO entitled *So Bold an Aim*:

> Unquestionably agriculture constitutes the most cared-for and protected sector of the economy. Which does not mean to say that it is over-organized, over-cared for. That might be arguable if we saw incomes in agriculture higher than in other sectors and a rate of technical progress more rapid than in industry. In spite of all the representations, sometimes coniferous, of the farming community and of all the aid programs devised by governments, agriculture is still in almost all countries the least advantaged sector, the least well furnished with modern techniques and the least well paid.

These and similar principles were the seeds that eventually blossomed in the preamble of the FAO constitution drafted by an interim commission:

> The Nations accepting this Constitution, being determined to promote the common welfare by furthering separate and collective action on their part for the purposes of
> a) raising levels of nutrition and standards of living of the peoples under their respective jurisdictions,
> b) securing improvements in the efficiency of the production and distribution of all food and agricultural products,
> c) bettering the condition of rural populations,
> d) and this contributing toward an expanding world economy, hereby establish the Food and Agriculture Organization of the United Nations, hereinafter referred to as the "Organization" through which the members will report to one another on the measures taken and the progress achieved in the fields of action set forth above.

The growth of FAO throughout the years is marked with many crises but also a steady and successful advancement of "reconstruction and development" among the world's poor, oppressed, and disadvantaged. From an initial membership of 42 nations it has grown to 121 nations. From a rented house in Washington, D.C., the organization has moved its headquarters to a modern building in Rome. It has grown from a handful of staff members in 1945 to a staff of over 3,000 professionals, of which over 2,000 are in regional offices or engaged in field projects. Its success was significantly recognized by the member-nations who increased the biennial budget of $2,000,000 in 1945 to over $70,500,000 in 1970-71.

The work of FAO is a testament of what can be accomplished by people of goodwill. It also fulfills the mission Lester B. Pearson of Canada expressed in his introductory remarks of the Quebec *Conference Report*:

> The first of the new, permanent United Nations agencies is now launched. There are few precedents for it to follow; it is something new in international history. There have been functional international agencies with more circumscribed objects and tasks, but FAO is the first which sets out with so bold an aim as that of helping nations to achieve freedom from want. Never before have the nations got together for such a purpose.
>
> FAO will bring the discoveries of science to the workers in food and agriculture, forestry and fisheries everywhere and it will bring the practical problems of these workers everywhere to the attention of the scientists. It will assemble, digest and interpret information to serve as a basis for the formulation of policy, national and international. It can suggest action, but only through the activities of governments themselves can the objectives be finally won.

Ligutti's expertise in rural sociology, his travels throughout the world contacting agricultural leaders, his pastoral experiences in the diocese of Des Moines, and his firsthand observations among the displaced and dispossessed people of post-war Europe made him quick to grasp FAO's important mission. Two other considerations heightened his interest. First, Ligutti was always, and sometimes even passionately, the defender of "the little people of the world." Also, he firmly believed in the benefits mankind would reap by "the presence of the Church." This conviction, perhaps more spiritual than the first, but nonetheless compelling and constant, he frequently expressed in public addresses, correspondence with curial officials, and scribbled notations in his diaries.

For Ligutti "the presence of the Church" was the image of the Good Samaritan binding up the wounds of afflicted men, women, and children: "No matter if one is a king or a beggar, he can spread the cause of the Church." Again, on September 14, 1969, he asked himself, "What would the world be without the Cross of Christ?" In an address delivered in Milan on June 2, 1962, he remarked, "Nature is like a woman — to be loved, not raped." He was truly an ecological pioneer! He believed that through "the presence of the Church" Christ's ministry of healing and reconciliation responded to the world's constant need for "reconstruction and development."

Ligutti, however, was no mere idealist content to offer lip service to the lofty aims of FAO. These goals he accepted, made his own, and realistically set to work internationally to eliminate the economic roots of poverty. He looked upon this, again, as the "presence of the Church." He recognized and made his own philosophy what Carlo Giacehtti, S.J., wrote in his pamphlet entitled *Catholics and FAO*:

> Among the difficulties to be noted in one or the other of these types of country, or in both of them, are the following: inveterate customs and traditions, ignorance, sclerosis of economic and social institutions, acquired rights in which the social function of property imposes limits hardly tolerated, lack of financial resources, national egoism and above all international tension, with the consequent high level of investments in war material and space research which are no longer mere scientific enterprises but rather matters of indirect military prestige and first-class psychological coefficients in the cold war.

With courage Ligutti faced these obstacles at work within the minds of many of his colleagues and superiors within the Church. Were it not for the constant support and encouragement of two men within the Vatican Secretariat of State, he well might never have succeeded in overcoming these obfuscations within the ecclesiastical orbit. These two men were Archbishop Romolo Carboni, papal nuncio to Italy, and at this time, a secretary in the Vatican Secretariat of State, and Pope Paul VI, at that time, Msgr. Giovanni Battista Montini, the substitute Secretary of State. Largely through their support he achieved not only an effective "presence of the Church" at FAO but also the formal, even enthusiastic, approval of his work by the three pontiffs who governed the Church in the first quarter century of FAO's existence. Nor should it be overlooked that this papal approbation came at a time when many prominent leaders and members of the Church were all too quick to issue warnings and condemnations against what they called the "godless" and "Communist-controlled" United Nations.

Ligutti was quick to note this papal approbation in his diaries with no small pleasure each time a pope spoke favorably and encouragingly of FAO. Pope Pius XII spoke directly to the delegates of the biennial assemblies of FAO five times between 1948 and 1957. On the organization's tenth anniversary in 1955, the Pope offered this encouragement and praise:

> You know with what interest we have followed the various stages of your activity since the day FAO was founded.... This world-wide action is destined to affect not a privileged group, but the immense multitude of those who are often powerless and without defense. We are happy, above all, to see in it a genuine aspect of the charity which Christ showed forth in His life and His death and which He willed to make the distinctive mark of His disciples. This universal and selfless charity, demanding to the point of sacrifice, can find its root only in God's own love for men.

Less surprisingly, Pope John XXIII manifested not only a deep interest in the problems of world agriculture as well as the efforts of FAO. A son of the soil himself, he was rightly proud of his peasant origins. On four occasions he revealed his respect and appreciation of the work of FAO. Chiefly through his words and inspiration, he mobilized the moral and financial resources of the Catholic Church in support of FAO's Freedom from Hunger campaign. Pope John sent a message on July 1, 1960 supporting the campaign and work of FAO:

> We wish to renew our most paternal encouragement for this very generous initiative that corresponds so well to the true welfare of mankind and deserves so much to enlist the interest and collaboration of all men of good heart.
>
> The Church — as we have already had occasion to state — rejoices to see so many men of goodwill uniting for the successful accomplishment of this great undertaking. The Church is happy to note that the Campaign is strikingly designed to promote those "works of mercy" which It so warmly recommends that Its children practice.
>
> We, for Our part, would accompany with Our supplications and Our prayers the efforts of all those persons and institutions that will be taking part in the Freedom from Hunger Campaign, and with all Our heart We pray that Heaven will abundantly bless them.

Pope Paul VI was closely associated with FAO from its beginning. His friendship with Ligutti brought him frequently in contact with the leaders and staff of FAO. Five times between

1963 and 1965, he deliverd words of encouragement to the organization. Shortly after FAO extended the Freedom from Hunger campaign for another five years, to a crowd in St. Peter's Square on November 22, 1965 Pope Paul said:

> Among the voices in the world which we must hear in order to obey the council, and that means to obey the spirit of the Gospel, there is in these days the voice of FAO. This international organization, which studies the problems of nutrition, has its headquarters in Rome and is now holding its general assembly.
>
> What does this voice tell us? It tells us that half of the world's population does not have enough bread.
>
> This fact should stir in men of goodwill many new resolutions which the council is awakening: to learn about these problems and to rise from indifference about them in order to help those working to find remedies for them.

Twenty-five years, however, were spent in trials and tribulations, triumphs and tributes by Monsignor Ligutti in his dedicated service to the "presence of the Church" in FAO. This dedication placed him in the right place, at the right time, with the right collaborators. He could not write more honestly or candidly than he did on the twenty-fifth anniversary of FAO:

> Having been very closely associated with FAO since its very inception, I share its joy on the 25th anniversary.
>
> I extend sincerest congratulations and best wishes. I recall its earliest days, the trials and difficulties, I have watched its growth and development.
>
> It pleases me in a special way to see the FAO becoming one of the greatest leading influences in world history.

During this period he was the architect of a statement signed by eighty-eight leaders of the three major religions in the United States. The six-point program, which resulted from a meeting at the Grammercy Park Hotel in New York in August, 1955, may be summarized:

> 1. National economic policies designed to achieve and maintain full employment with full and efficient production both in industry and agriculture. With growing population, increasing labor force and mounting productivity this means not a level, but an annually rising gross national product.

2. Industrial wage and agricultural price policies which will produce a just and equitable distribution of consumer purchasing power throughout the economy.
3. Food and nutrition programs which will assure adequate and healthful diets for all Americans and for as many as can be reached and served abroad.
4. Expanded programs of technical assistance in the fundamental work of world economic and social development.
5. International trade and monetary policies designed to facilitate and expand the international flow of goods and services.
   Appropriate public aid should be provided to agricultural and industrial enterprises facing adjustments as trade barriers are progressively removed.
6. Foreign economic aid programs geared to meet situations of emergency and long-time human need. For this purpose both the offices of government and of the voluntary and religious agencies should be used.

These were the principles that guided Ligutti as the permanent Vatican observer to FAO, where he effected a union between the humanitarian aims of FAO and the spiritual goals of the Church. What follows is an evaluation of the first phase of this work.

On February 2, 1947 Ligutti called upon Dr. Tolley, an assistant secretary in the United States Department of Agriculture, to discuss the possibility of a Vatican representative to FAO. Four months later Ligutti and Tolley again discussed the subject. At this time, while attending a Washington reception marking the initiation of the Marshall Plan, Ligutti met Dr. Boyd-Orr and Frank McDougall, one of the leaders of FAO in its initial years, for the first time. On June 5 Bishop Swanstrom advised Ligutti not to bypass the National Catholic Welfare Conference, advice Ligutti did not follow. On the same day he lunched with McDougall who wanted to appoint Ligutti to the FAO board. Ligutti, however, declined but promised that he would secure a letter from Pope Pius XII in support of the aims of FAO. He followed up this promise with a letter to the apostolic delegate, Archbishop Amleto Cicognani, and enclosed documentation concerning FAO.

In later years Ligutti recalled his first contact with FAO:

Tolley was an economist in the U.S. Department of Agriculture and also a part-time consultant with FAO. He was the first contact I had because I didn't know Sir John Boyd-Orr or any other people. He made it possible for me to meet Sir Boyd-Orr. I had previously been in FAO's offices on

Massachusetts Avenue where there were about a dozen employees. In 1946 I had the famous meeting with Sir John and McDougall when we talked over the possibility of having the Holy See as an observer or member of FAO.

The summer months came and passed. While tending his garden at NCRLC headquarters, Ligutti reflected upon another offer he had received from Msgr. Edward Swanstrom. The latter offered him a position with Catholic Relief Services. The offer was, needless to say, attractive to Ligutti. However, summer came and went with Ligutti marking the thirtieth anniversary of his first Mass in Des Moines. More than a little bitterness was marked in his diary on September 30, 1947. Ho observed that, through his efforts, FAO asked the Holy See for a representative at the general assembly in Geneva and, he wrote, "Rome sent a Swiss."

Once again he visited McDougall in Washington in early November and returned again for lunch with him and Archbishop Aloisius Muench on November 23. He ended 1947 with a typical remark in his diary, "Only God can help one go at this pace." Although apprehensive he was not defeated. On January 4, 1948 he noted that the appointment of a permanent observer to FAO was not forthcoming. On January 12 he lunched again with McDougall in Washington and a week later complained to Frank Bruce of Milwaukee about the lack of the Vatican's recognition in FAO. Days passed into months and again, on March 7, Ligutti expressed his disappointment in his diary. He was not, however, content merely to express his resentment; he kept a steady hand on the helm. With no little delight he noted that Bishop William Mulloy wrote the apostolic delegate, recommending that Ligutti be appointed Vatican observer for FAO. On March 18 he noted that Edward Daly was appointed bishop of Des Moines and added, "I hope for FAO appointment no matter who gets it."

Summer came again. Ligutti was once more seeking an executive secretary for the NCRLC. Gremillion said he would be pleased to accept the task if his bishop would grant his permission. Ligutti talked with Archbishop Joseph Schlarman concerning Fr. Edward O'Rourke, but the archbishop would not let O'Rourke go. During these days Ligutti wrote the apostolic delegate and Msgr. Romolo Carboni in the Vatican Secretariat of State concerning the Vatican representative to FAO. At no period did any man play so important a role in Ligutti's life as did the future Archbishop Carboni. The turning point in Ligutti's life came on July 26, 1948, when he received a letter from Monsignor Montini appointing him Vatican observer to the FAO general assembly in Washington, D.C., the following November. At the same time Montini informed him that Dr. Emilio Bonomelli, director of the Vatican farms at Castel Gandolfo, was also appointed a co-observer of the Holy See to FAO.

Ligutti, of course, was thrilled with the appointment. It opened new vistas and visions for him, the NCRLC, and the Church. On August 1 he visited Dr. Bonomelli and the same afternoon walked with Montini at the papal villa in Castel Gandolfo. Two weeks later he lunched with McDougall in Geneva on his return trip to the United States. He visited FAO headquarters in Washington on August 27, met with Sir Herbert Broadley, and regretted that he could not see Dr. Norris Dodd, second president of FAO, who was sick. "But McDougall and his pipe were there," Ligutti noted in his diary, "There is plenty of joshing, but oh how terribly serious he can be when talking about food and nutrition." He returned to Des Moines and on August 22 received the letter of appointment as permanent observer of the Holy See to FAO through the apostolic delegation. Three days later he called on his ordinary, Bishop Daly, to inform him of the appointment. Daly was disappointed because the appointment bypassed him. Three months passed before the news of Ligutti's appointment appeared in the religious press. By this time, however, Ligutti was present at the fourth general assembly of FAO in Washington.

The beginnings of the Vatican observership to FAO cannot be told without mention of Fr. William Gibbons, S.J. He was as generous with his time and exceptional talents to this cause as he was previously to the National Catholic Rural Life Conference. Twenty years later, in a letter to Ligutti dated March 29, 1969, Gibbons recalled his association with FAO and other United Nations' agencies concerning the plight of displaced persons:

> In 1947, UN headquarters had already been in contact with me, as with Father John LaFarge, then editor of *America*, regarding the lot of displaced persons and refugees in postwar Europe. They needed cooperation from Catholic circles, as well as education of the public, and we helped to fill the gap. In fact, it was the Catholic Rural Life Conference and Catholic Charities, then presided over by Monsignor John O'Grady, who did much to stir up American Catholic interest. Fortunately, several articulate archbishops were interested

and Catholic Relief Services (then, War Relief Services) had some farseeing staff members who learned quickly what the problems were regarding refugees and DP's.

Gibbons, working in New York City at the time, also recalled the overtures by staff members of the United Nations and UNESCO toward securing greater cooperation and participation by the Catholic Church. During these early years, and continuing to the present, many leaders within the Church were opposed to the work of the United Nations. This arose, as Gibbons noted, "because of the positions taken by the UNESCO Director General on the subject of population and food supply." Nevertheless, in spite of ecclesiastical opposition, sometimes vocal and more often latent, Gibbons noted that "UN personnel saw greater opportunity for exchange of views with true representatives of the Church as desirable and a move in the right direction toward easing tensions and resolving problems."

In the same letter Gibbons recalled that the temporary headquarters of FAO were in Washington, D.C., during these years "and might have been there permanently had it not been for the determination of European delegates to have the specialized agencies based in Europe, since the United Nations' secretariat was in the United States. "Frankly," he added, "as regards to FAO, I have always regretted that development. Both FAO and the U.S. foreign-aid programs would have benefited by closer contacts in the United States, where considerable knowledge and effort about agricultural and economic science was largely based." Throughout this period of informal meetings, Gibbons stood beside Ligutti and assisted in every possible way in establishing the observership.

From the very beginning of these informal discussions the idea of full membership of the Vatican was excluded both by officials of FAO and Gibbons and Ligutti. Gibbons offered one reason for such exclusion: "The idea of straight membership seemed less appropriate, since that would have meant direct involvement in voting on issues that were being treated quite politically by FAO delegates." Another reason, adduced by Ligutti with his customary historical sense, was that the Holy See was excluded from the League of Nations due to Masonic influences among the French, British, and even American representatives. Thus, in order to avoid a showdown, it would be easier and wiser on all counts to have the Holy See present as an observer than a member. This principle, first established in regard to FAO, was later followed in all other United Nations' agencies and, indeed, in the organization's general assembly. "The concept of a permanent representative," wrote Gibbons, " with on-going consultative voice, was generally acceptable, however, and the 1948 Conference voted that for the Holy See."

A request for such an observership of the Holy See was formally presented in 1948 "to take part as a permanent observer in the Conferences, meetings, and activities of the Organization, both at the central seat of the Organization and in its regional offices, especially in those where the activity of the Holy See is likely to be most efficacious." On November 23 the general committee agreed with the view of the FAO council and, taking cognizance of "the unique status of the applicant," suggested to the delegates that "in the absence of any provision in the Constitution or in the Rules that would cover this special request, the Conference be requested to take a vote on the application, and unanimously recommends that it be accepted." The vote was taken during this conference, with one member-nation voting negative and another abstaining. The office of a permanent observer of the Holy See was a *fait accompli*.

Ligutti was waiting in the wings. With more than a little satisfaction he rose before the delegates on November 15 and delivered the first of many speeches:

> The Holy See feels deeply appreciative of the privilege conferred by the FAO Conference in being admitted to the special status of permanent observer. The Holy See renews its sentiments of admiration for the aims, purposes and work of the FAO.
>
> The Holy See pledges its full cooperation both directly and indirectly, in season and out of season. The Holy See feels that through its widespread and close contact with farmers and little people throughout the world she is in a position to assist in the fulfillment of the immediate and long-range aims of the FAO.
>
> The Holy See wishes to be of help in every possible way — as a link in a chain, that, with God's help, may bring the world out of misery, suffering, hunger, fear of war, not, perhaps to a perfect world but to a better world where the little people particularly may enjoy a fair share of Divine Providence's bountiful gifts.

Again, with no little pride, he addressed the FAO delegates on December 1, 1949:

> I report to you now that with purpose and determination the Holy See is fulfilling its pledge — through official and unofficial channels — both in working for immediate results and with the long tomorrow in mind. The outposts of the Church of Rome have been alerted to know of your work and to cooperate with you. The Church realizes the verity of the theological truth that body and soul form one integral unit — i.e. man — and that the natural is a necessary basis for the supernatural.

Another year passed. The council of FAO met in Washington, D.C., during November, 1950, for its eleventh session. On this occasion Father Gibbons served as a representative of the Holy See. With his precise and analytical mind, he addressed the delegates' attention to the problems of FAO as he saw them. The paragraph which follows aptly summarized the problems that faced FAO not only at that time but throughout its existence:

> In accomplishing the objectives of FAO there are a number of basic things which must be done. As we see them these are: (1) dissemination of necessary and accurate information about agricultural conditions throughout the world for the use of both governments and non-governmental groups and individuals; (2) careful study and analysis of situations within nations and regions wherein agricultural production and distribution and rural welfare are below satisfactory levels; (3) formulation of long and short-range programs, with the approval and cooperation of governments, whereby less satisfactory conditions may be improved; (4) provision of technical assistance, in the field of agricultural and rural welfare, to nations and territories requiring and requesting the same; (5) development of programs, with due regard for existing and projected international agencies, whereby commodities produced may be more satisfactorily distributed than is at present the case.

Ligutti's association with FAO is much more than a relationship between one man and one world organization. In more ways than one, it represents the union of the Church and the world in a series of events that forced individuals, organizations, and nations to come to grips with "the brave new world." Some of these events may be cataloged; others are only recalled by men and women accustomed to wisdom of age and grace. There was the bomb dropped on Nagasaki, the formation of the United Nations, the appalling evidence of displaced people, and the remarkable Marshall Plan. This same generation producd a cry heard around the world: Freedom! Colonialism was dying, new nations were being born. The youth revolution was upon us, signaled by the Beatles and echoed across the high school and college campuses of the world. New life-styles, fashions, and novels, the omnipresent television, and "the new morality" were upon us. Will it or not, we were creating a "new generation."

Few sensed this change in world thinking better than Ligutti. He sensed it among the college students he lectured to; he saw it in the eyes of a hungry Andean peasant child. He complained at times about "man's inhumanity to man," but wasted little time in moaning. He was a doer more than a thinker. He saw in this change an opportunity for the Church to "come alive" in this sometimes dangerous but always creative new world.

These, too, were the years of the encyclical *Humani Generis* that in ways was more incisive than *Humanae Vitae*. These were the years — as we shall see — when the curia was the Church and all the rest simply *belonged* to the Church. During this period, too, every member of that Church that Ligutti loved and served so well knew instinctively that the Holy Spirit was at work, renewing and reforming. Ligutti was no man to take the back seat. He knew what should be done, settled for what could be done, and hoped throughout this period that more would be accomplished than what he himself could foresee. In such a frame of mind he entered upon the international scene.

Ligutti, however, was not without opposition within the Church. First, there was the resistance of many officials of the Roman curia to the United Nations. Second, opposition came from the National Catholic Welfare Conference. Two of Ligutti's close friends, O'Grady and Higgins, interceded on his behalf with the apostolic delegate. Quite reasonably, Ligutti was bitter over this development. He had laid all the ground work, made all the official contacts, and persuaded Roman authorities of the importance of the "presence of the Church." When an appointment of a permanent observer was imminent, officials of the National Catholic Welfare Conference wanted the appointment given to an "organization man." At this point Msgr. Romolo Carboni of the Vatican Secretariat of State stepped in to advance Ligutti's nomination. Carboni was, in Ligutti's words, "the greatest help that I had because he taught me the means of getting in and out."

Ligutti completely understood his position as Vatican observer to FAO. "Rome," he recalled, "is always against everybody who is not in the career service. For that reason the FAO observer-ship was kept as an illegitimate child; it was not part of the structure."

The following years proved how accurate his estimation was. Eight years would pass before the Vatican observership would be recognized in the *Annuario Pontificio,* the official yearbook of Vatican offices, and before it would be allowed a Vatican office in the Palazzo San Carlo and the use of official Vatican stationery. There would be constant discussions concerning financing the office of the FAO observers, but to Ligutti's credit he paid his own way with the help of friends in the United States. There were nuisances, also, in the matter of using Vatican cars, Vatican passports, and receiving Vatican recognition. No one can count the hours Ligutti and Bonomelli spent in putting out the fires in Vatican offices, the reams of documents they sent to Vatican officials, and their appearances at dinners and receptions in the Eternal City to have the observership recognized by Vatican officials. The then Archbishop Angelo Dell'Acqua in the Secretariat of State, Archbishop Pietro Sigismondi in the Propagation of the Faith, and Archbishop Antonio Samore in the Latin America Commission were sympathetic but difficult to deal with because they knew little or nothing about the purpose of FAO. They were not alone, however. Bishops, priests, and religious throughout the world knew even less. Ligutti and his associates faced a monumental public relations task in "selling" FAO to the Roman Catholic constituency. Happily, Ligutti and Bonomelli were vindicated when in February, 1949, *L'Osservatore Romano* published the apostolic brief appointing them Vatican observers to FAO for three years.

On March 31, 1949 Ligutti wrote Monsignor Montini, expressing his appreciation for being appointed Vatican observer to FAO and asked what precisely would be the manner and extent of the relationship between FAO and the Holy See. He also sent Montini all the published documents concerning FAO as well as the documents concerning the observership.

Ligutti asked whether any other people could see the Vatican documents concerning FAO and recommended that Father Gibbons also receive them. He mentioned that he visited with McDougall in Washington and they discussed the problem of Neo-Malthusianism. He felt this should be a particular area of study by the Vatican observer. He also mentioned that officials of FAO were particularly interested in having a representative of the Catholic Church at its meetings and that he would always be happy to serve in the capacity of an "adviser." Practically speaking, he mentioned that it would not be necessary for the Holy See to contribute towards his support.

Ligutti's appointment was secured. His diary reflected his native enthusiasm for the new undertaking for the coming months:

> March 20 — Carboni says that Cicognani was opposed to his appointment as Vatican observer to FAO. March 21 — Ligutti advocated a letter from the Society for the Propagation of the Faith (and paid the postage for same) to missionaries throughout the world asking for their support of FAO. April 21 — Stopped in Washington, D.C., to pay respects to the officials of FAO.

The following month he sent Monsignor Montini a six-page statement summarizing Christian principles on rural life. In June he spent an hour visiting with Dr. Norris Dodd, the FAO director-general, in Washington, D.C.

His public addresses during this period also reflect the broadening vision of the world and the Church that he himself was endorsing. At the fourth annual meeting of FAO in Washington, D.C., on November 29, 1948, Ligutti raised his voice on behalf of the "farmers and little people throughout the world." The following year, again addressing the annual meeting, he said FAO is carrying out a long-standing policy of working towards the betterment of the world's food supplies. He cited as precedents of this interest the work of the Franciscan friars who brought wheat to Ecuador, Franciscan missionaries who introduced the grape to California, Jesuit priests who undertook the agricultural development of Paraguay, and Benedictine monks who reclaimed Europe at the end of the Dark Ages. In keeping with this rural sociology he was already advocating social security for farmers in 1949. In New Orleans on May 25, 1949 Ligutti raised the question and answered it. "Why should we have social security and unemployment compensation for the city worker and not for the farmers? Such benefits are for human beings, and you have human beings in the country as well as in the city."

Again in 1955, speaking in Rome before the delegates to FAO from seventy-one nations, Ligutti voiced his direct and matter-of-fact policy statement: "Land for people without land; people for land without people." He said:

> I believe that within this hall there are men and women of enough acumen and experience, capable and willing to work out an acceptable scheme whereby, without undue complication or interference with national sovereignties, citizenship, etc., people without land could be united to land without people on an agricultural concession basis. By artificially keeping separate the two elements we are not only going counter to God's evident purpose in creation, but we are causing human suffering. We are giving rise to senseless struggles and we are holding back the progress of mankind.

Ligutti further suggested that the nations of the world "might well lead in the attempt to exchange abundance, not only in agricultural products, but in the arts, the letters, music and song."

Attending the ninth general conference of FAO in Rome, Ligutti once again addressed the delegates, hailing "the spirit of unity, amity and cooperation within this one family of seventy-seven nations." Ligutti directed his remarks to the general theme of the conference, "the family":

> It is man and the family element that comes first. Quantity and quality production are not of much avail unless the man at the production end is really ennobled and his personality developed while he is producing. The improvement of his character, his physical, mental and spiritual make-up, are first on the priority list, and the worker's family should be the first to enjoy the fruits of such improvement. Then society almost automatically shares in the advancement.

He told a special session of delegates to FAO in November, 1950:

> I am here to pledge in behalf of the missionaries who work at the outposts of civilization their fullest and unqualified cooperation. If information is needed, if local facilities and technicians required, the FAO can rely on the missionaries. They are on the spot, ready to serve. They enjoy the confidence of the inhabitants and they know local physical conditions and culture. There is one plea that was evidenced in all their replies: "Give the Private agencies a chance to help."

The following year Ligutti addressed the delegates on the fundamental issue of human rights:

> Human beings possess certain fundamental rights that are God-given. One of these is the right to have access to natural resources, to use them, to husband them, to possess

with security. Such possession and such use are intended to help in the development of man's personality and in the welfare of the family.

On this occasion he also addressed his remarks to the problem of migration, a subject close to his heart for years:

> The right of human beings to move freely, not indiscriminately, but in an orderly, reasonable fashion, must be recognized and must come within the range of possible fulfillment here and now.
>
> The bringing-together of human beings, natural resources, technical knowledge and working capital will result in the increase of material wealth, cultural development and even biological improvement. The Holy See is most anxious to lend its assistance toward the solution of these most practical and urgent problems of surplus population in one locality and of unused resources elsewhere.

In 1951 Ligutti again addressed the delegates of FAO and promised them the support of the personnel and resources of the Catholic Church:

> You realize full well the need of a grass roots approach. You are conscious of native cultures, of deep seated persuasions. The village priest and the missionary in the most abandoned regions are close to the people who need your help above all others. It is through them and with them that you the scientists, the technicians, the humanitarians can reach the poor and forgotten and lighten their heavy burden with a ray of hope for better days.

Ligutti continued to stress over the years the beneficial results to mankind through the collaboration of the services of FAO and the Church's missionaries. Addressing the general assembly of FAO in 1955, he said:

> Quite often in the past the observers of the Holy See have given voice to their willingness and readiness to assist, particularly through the missionaries who are located in the most abandoned and forgotten corners of our globe. If through their influence with local inhabitants or because of their understanding of indigenous culture and habits they might lend a hand to the technicians sent by you, we can assure you that it will be done.

All during these years the concept of Agrimissio was taking root and growing in Ligutti's mind. Five years later he would develop the same theme in an address at the Angelicum University in Rome. "To develop the gifts of God," he said, "means to make use of material and human resources, collaborating with Divine Providence according to the intentions of the Creator."

Ligutti lived to see the results of the self-help programs he fostered. Speaking before the general assembly of FAO in 1962, he said:

> Having visited practically all the mission fields in developing countries during the past twenty-five years, I am very happy to report that a most pleasing change has occurred in the mental attitude and in the actions of both leaders and people. In place of the patient resignation to poverty, hunger, disease, and despair new hopes and firm assurance have become predominant.

That same year on July 2 he addressed the members of the rural life apostolate in Ireland:

> Were it not for the Irish people there would be very little Catholicism in the English-speaking world today. I would like to make the suggestion that in the field of education, health, and agriculture, Irish specialists in these matters should be sent to various parts of the world where they could be very effective and useful. The natural and Christian laws are among the essentials of farming. Also essential are love of work and soil as partners with God.

On this occasion Ligutti first publicly expressed a concept that would be close to his heart for the coming decade. He spoke of "micro-projects." He was never one given to large grants for immense projects. Rather, he believed in small grants of aid for small projects which enabled people to help themselves. This he learned many years previously with the homestead project in Granger. This same concept he sought to instill in the missionary projects of the Church and the self-help programs of FAO. He grasped the idea from the French Catholic Charities organization, Secours Catholique, which within two years had given almost $1,000,000 to more than 2,000 grass roots projects in Africa.

In the same interview Ligutti said, "I am sold on these micro-projects because they work. Missionaries know what is needed in small farm villages. Catholic groups can get in touch with them to find out what the people need. With the small projects all the money goes where it is needed." About this same time Ligutti was promoting his own interest in the Church's missionary work. Agrimissio was still a gleam in his eye, but it was there.

In an interview in LaCrosse, Wisconsin, in 1964 he was, wittingly or unwittingly planting the intellectual seeds for Agrimissio. At that time he called upon missionaries to collaborate with FAO leaders to promote a "grass roots" effort for the betterment of mankind. He called the number of United Nations' personnel available for assignment to developing countries "peanuts by comparison with the 250,000 Catholic priests, nuns and brothers in these countries. The same goes for the expenditures of our missionaries, to which in comparison United Nations' funds are small. So if the United Nations' agencies are to accomplish anything in these countries, they must work through the personnel in our schools and hospitals and other institutions."

In 1964, during the Freedom from Hunger campaign sponsored by FAO, he was on the trail again. Speaking at a study week in Assisi, Italy, during the same year, he said:

> Poverty, hunger, misery and squalor are brought about by man as a person or by the society of men. They are not caused by God. The greater evil is not hunger itself or even squalor, but the lack of the proper use of God's gifts. Charity must not be conceived of as an act of paternalistic generosity on the part of the giver, or of debasing pauperism on the part of the receiver. Charity is an act of brotherly love whose aim is to offer the opportunity to man to use some of God's gifts, and in so doing to foster his own personal development toward self-help and a better life.

Six years later he took the rostrum to enunciate his fundamental principle concerning food and hunger. Speaking at The Hague, Netherlands, during the World Food Congress in 1970, he directed his remarks to the central theme of the Congress which was "We are ALL Children of One Family." Here he took a positive approach and pointed out that Christian groups alone have almost 500,000 men and women working in education, health, and social service in the developing nations and this force should be reckoned with. He called upon "a balanced approach" between the resources of FAO and the missionary efforts of the Church:

> Man is fundamentally religious and religion in general terms is a force in the world. The possibility of using this power and leadership to aid in accomplishing the purposes of this congress is indeed very plain. The religious force would be mistaken if it thinks of going at it alone, and governments and international agencies would be just as mistaken if they think that they have the only right, the only superman power

of exclusive prerogative for such an endeavor. A cooperative mentality can accomplish wonders. Much less can be achieved even by honest and sincere efforts that are disjointed, separated and at times battling among themselves.

Throughout these years Ligutti himself raised the money to maintain the office of the Vatican observership. At no time did he receive any salary from the Holy See or the American bishops. On his own initiative he secured grants from both the Ford and the Homeland foundations to continue the work of the Vatican observership. Writing to the directors of the Ford Foundation on December 7, 1951, Ligutti summarized his activities:

> The observer participated in the FAO Council Meeting in May, 1951, and the Council and Conference Meetings held November-December 1951. He visited Newfoundland for conferences with the Premier and Cabinet Members. He also conferred with Adult Education and Co-operative Leaders. He spent some time in the western part of Canada and the United States for the purpose of informing Church leaders on the purposes and work of FAO. Within a few days he will depart from Rome and visit Turkey, Iran, Iraq, Syria, Lebanon, Transjordan, Israel, Egypt and Greece. While there, he will visit FAO projects, contact agricultural leaders and particularly Church officials, in order to acquaint them with the work of FAO. He will return to the United States towards the end of January 1952.

Raising money to finance the office was but one facet, and a minor one, of the office of the Vatican observers. Much more important were Ligutti's efforts in stimulating the interest of Church officials in the international work not only of FAO but also other United Nations' endeavors. Both Msgr. Alberto Giovannetti, Vatican observer to the United Nations in New York, and A. N. Das-Gupta, counselor to the United Nations' Educational, Scientific and Cultural Organization, were ready to acknowledge that the Church's presence in these organizations was due chiefly to Ligutti's influence. Ligutti made the first approaches for a Vatican representative with UNESCO. As early as 1950 Das-Gupta, writing from Paris and the headquarters of UNESCO, recognized this contribution. "I should like to inform you," he wrote Ligutti on April 21, 1950, "that in this memorandum I stated that the initial contact with the Vatican on this matter has been made by you entirely in a private and confidential capacity on my request."

Over the years as an observer Ligutti kept in close contact with the leaders of FAO. He was ever present in the early fifties, lending his support, advice, and counsel to Secretary General Dodd, Miss Reynolds, and other officials during the growing pains of the organization. During this same period he actively engaged in convincing the National Council of Churches of the necessity of a Protestant observer to FAO and noted with much satisfaction on November 11, 1950 that the Protestant observership was approved by the delegates of FAO. Throughout this period he kept Montini informed on the work and direction of FAO. By the same token, he received more than one request from Montini for reports of the progress of FAO, thus revealing the growing interest of the Holy See in the direction and goals of FAO.

Throughout these years Ligutti was busy hop-scotching from one continent to another, both as Vatican observer to FAO and executive director of the National Catholic Rural Life Conference. He was a troubled man, dividing his loyalties between a national organization and an international agency of the United Nations. No single man could possibly burn the candle at both ends such as he had been doing for almost ten years. His concern is reflected in his diary for 1957. Troubles were mounting at NCRLC headquarters in Des Moines, as well as in the office of the Vatican observer to FAO. Ligutti was caught in the cross fire.

Ligutti was as concerned as other FAO officials during these early years of the direction the organization should take. On November 24, 1950 Secretary General Dodd reported to the member nations and observers on the decisions taken at the tenth and eleventh sessions of the council and at the special sessions of the conference held during the same month in Washington, D.C. Monsignor Montini in the Vatican Secretariat of State received a copy of Dodd's letter, in which he wrote:

> ...the view of the Conference and Council was that with the lapse of five years since FAO was established it would be advisable to take stock of our policy and work in the light of past experience. FAO has a wide and diverse field of activity and has recently been increasingly faced with the problem, which confronts all new international organizations, of adapting its program to its possibilities. It is generally agreed that while FAO has made considerable progress in wide fields covered by the various branches of its work, it may now be desirable, not withstanding the many demands upon it from member countries, to concentrate on fewer

activities which are likely to produce practical results of value to as many members as possible.

On December 13 Montini sent Ligutti copies of Dodd's letter and documentation and asked him to draft some suggestions that he might make in his reply to Dodd. The suggestions that Ligutti drafted and that Montini subsequently submitted are important inasmuch as they reflect Ligutti's thinking concerning FAO during these formative years. He stressed the importance of good public relations, the formation of an educational-informational program before the establishment of a FAO project, the need of technical know-how, the collaboration with missionaries, and the pleasure of the Holy See to assist in any possible way with the aims and purposes of FAO.

Ligutti was constantly aware of the beneficial effects that would accrue to mankind by "the presence of the Church" in international organizations. On June 10, 1951 his travel letter entitled "Rome Non-Confidential" observed:

> This week the FAO Council is meeting. I held a long conference with Dr. John Reisner of Agricultural Missions. He is the Protestant churches' representative with FAO. The goodly man and I have been close friends for many years. Now we are working together again. The Christian churches of the world can do much and perhaps furnish the very spark that will make the difference between success and failure in the work of the United Nations' specialized agencies. We have set our minds and hearts on that, and it will be done.

In the same series of letters Ligutti wrote his friends at home his impressions and activities during the FAO Council meeting during the same month. Here he gave some insight into his own activities, the workings of the executive council, and his personal observations:

> And this past week I spent chiefly at the FAO Council meeting. The FAO headquarters has now been transferred from Washington to Rome. The Italian government has placed at FAO's disposal two of the finest buildings in Rome. New buildings in Europe are superior to anything we put up in America. Good materials and skilled labor at low prices combine to make this possible. The reorganization of FAO is proceeding splendidly under the capable leadership of Mr. Norris Dodd, its Director General. He has surrounded himself with a capable and hard working staff. They actually work harder here than they did in Washington.

The Council of the FAO is its Executive Committee. It is composed of 18 nations selected from the 64 member nations. The Council is presided over by an elected chairman, now Lord Bruce, a capable and charming elderly Englishman who wields the gavel graciously and firmly. A new chairman is to be elected next fall.

Each morning the plenary session convenes. Reports are presented that have been drawn up after months of study by specialists. Then the discussion takes place. Interesting as well as most boring remarks are made. Then they have to be translated. Just now the equipment for simultaneous translation is not set up. I certainly hope that by next November it will be available. It's very tiring to waste over one-third of the time in duplicating a speech in another language. Eventually, English, French, and Spanish will be the three official languages.

As the Official Permanent Observer for the Holy See I sit and listen. The Holy See is not a member but it has been granted the special status because of its unique position in the world. Therefore I do not have a vote (thank God) but I have a voice, and whenever I desire the floor it is readily granted. As a rule, I just ask for it once during each session. I spoke yesterday and that should be enough for this time. My remarks were directed particularly toward the problems of land tenure and migration. They were most cordially received and were reported in today's press. My appeal in behalf of India and the Near East evoked a beautiful tribute to the Holy See from India's ambassador who is representing his government at the meeting.

While I am quite faithful in my attendance at the meetings, I believe a good effective work can be done chiefly along the corridors, lobbies and at the numerous receptions — hours 18 to 20 (6 to 8 p.m.) — held almost every day in honor of the participants. The Catholic Church must cooperate with all men of good will in seeking and forming a better world. The Catholic Church can assist and, in some places, it is practically the only available agency.

The Protestant groups are also represented in the person of my dear friend, John Reisner of Agricultural Missions, New York, who is the observer for the Commission of Churches on International Affairs. He is here and we are having some very precious visits. Ray Miller will show up this week.

The problem of land tenure, or ownership of the land, was close to Ligutti's heart from the days he experienced the poverty of his people in Granger and served as a member of the Iowa governor's Land Tenancy Commission. Writing from Naples on April 2, 1950, he reflected on the past and stated his personal philosophy:

> When I was a little child — 50 years ago — 40% of the people employed in farming in Italy were hired hands. Today only 20%. Fifty years ago only 18% were owners — today 35%. Share croppers (rather desirable in Italian economy) are down by 2 or 3%....
>
> The fundamental aim must be to secure to as many people as possible contact with God's natural resources. It's a right human beings possess by the very fact they are human beings. Security of tenure is at the very heart of ownership and that is also essential. Free simple ownership is not necessary. It must be an economic unit geared for possibilities, work and production to a family unit. Therefore it is not merely acreage but arable and fertile land, rainfall, frost free days, housing, social needs, marketing facilities, only to mention a few musts that have to be considered.

Such statements recorded during these years reflect the atmosphere and the esprit de corps that animated Ligutti and his collaborators Dr. Bonomelli, Walter Persegati, and Miss Marie Grootheisen.

In his "Cross and Crescent" letters he recorded his activities during the 1951 FAO General Assembly which opened on November 14. Writing from Rome on November 18, he recorded these events:

> By ten o'clock on Wednesday I was in "medias res" and plenty deep. The FAO council met from Monday to Saturday, clearing the desks, approving or questioning, arguing or agreeing. Practically all the old timers are here — the staff first of all, and the delegates from the four corners of the world. To see and participate in the workings of an international organization is quite instructive and extremely interesting. From so many viewpoints and for so many reasons I feel highly privileged to be the Holy See's Official Permanent Observer with FAO. When I first covered the meetings in Washington I really felt that it was a gabfest, that but little was or could be accomplished. It just takes time to carry through from the survey to the planning stage, from the beginning to the desired end. The progress of the last two years is positively unbelievable. Inside politics, international complications, and petty personalities are all a

part and parcel of humanity and necessary stepping stones to progress, provided they don't rock the boat too much or wreck the structure. Tomorrow the new FAO building is being presented by the Italian government to the FAO. Then the full dress Conference opens....

On November 4 Ligutti was present for the unveiling of Bishop Giovanni Battista Scalabrini's bust at the Casa Generalizia, headquarters of the Scalabrini Fathers. Cardinal Adeodato Piazza and Monsignor Ferretto were there. The "Father of the Immigrants" is honored across the world, and rightly so. His apostolic zeal and work have been in evidence throughout the world, and his spiritual sons have heeded the Master's call and followed in the footsteps of Piacenza's bishop.

In 1955 Dr. Bonomelli had arranged a number of events in advance of the assembly. First, an opening Mass in the beautiful chapel of the North American College was offered by Archbishop Pietro Sigismondi, secretary of the Congregation of the Propagation of the Faith. The sermon, in French, was by Msgr. Jean Villot, presently the cardinal Secretary of State of Vatican City. In the absence of Bishop Martin O'Connor, the rector, Msgr. Francis Reh, was the host. The American seminarians escorted the visitors into the majestic halls and vista gardens overlooking St. Peter's cupola in a frame of ancient evergreens nearby. Present were Catholic representatives from almost thirty nations, as well as some from Moslem lands of the Near East, Buddhist countries, and black Africa. They mingled and knelt side by side with Latin Americans, Canadians, and bearded Frenchmen — all delegates of FAO.

Ligutti reserved November, 1957, for the FAO Biennial Conference. His schedule that autumn was hectic. September 6, Charlotte, North Carolina; September 8, island-hopping in the Caribbean; September 9-14, attending the constitutional assembly of the Caribbean Cooperative Confederation; September 15-19, Miami, Washington, New York, and two days at the Trade Winds Inn, Craigville, Massachusetts, for the fortieth anniversary reunion of his ordination class. (He exclaimed, "*Quadragesimo Anno* — Oh my!"); closing days of September at Assisi, participating in the congress of the International Catholic Migration Commission; more congresses and travel throughout October, and back in the Eternal City throughout November.

The cycles of nature had much meaning for Monsignor Ligutti. He said:

> ...frost will come — apples and pears will be picked, rose bushes laid away, bulbs dug and stored in a dry spot. Leaves will swirl in merry dances. I'll miss the beauty of God's trees in Iowa's Indian Summer. But, grapes, figs, pears, and wine making are awaiting me amidst Latium's hills, Tuscan valleys and the plains of the Po.

In October he attended the Second International Congress of the Catholic Laity in Rome, of which he wrote:

> If there is a *more* common failing in all these good people who come together it is this: Expecting to find a magical formula for the accomplishment of the impossible. I was enjoying a most pleasant dinner with a lovely group of Argentinians, and the same old question came up — "How can effective work be done to spread the Christian family movement?" Naively a goodly lady asked me to outline points 1-2-3. So I turned the question on her, begged her to tell us how she dealt 1-2-3 with all her five children. "Oh," she replied, "they are all different!" She realized that she had answered her own question.

Ligutti felt that among the nearly one hundred Americans present their influence was not felt and there was criticism in that no American was represented as an officer of the congress and no major speech was assigned to any American. Sadly he noted that Msgr. Howard Carroll of NCWC and Cardinal James McIntyre were in the city "but did not make themselves visible." Proudly he noted, "Monsignor George Higgins was present and active." No doubt Ligutti was pleased to be selected as chairman of the section on the rural apostolate in the English-speaking group. He recorded his own reflection on the week: "Perhaps more than ever during the past week I was conscious and grateful for the privilege which has been mine — to travel, to see the world, to meet people, to make friends, to love them."

Even though engaged in a seemingly ceaseless round of activities, he admitted to himself that "I could not help but introverting." As a priest of forty years, he was in a reflective mood. "I have never yearned to be an ascetic — not even the shadow or faint imitation of one," he confided, "Most of them are not real and God has made me out of a different mold. With so many visitors in the countryside of *Il Poverello* there are only a few hours a day when one can enjoy a peaceful walk and a quiet meditation."

During Thanksgiving week, 1957, he recorded his reflections on the recently adjourned FAO General Assembly. He wrote as follows in his "Ante and Post" letters to his friends: "A friend of mine said lately, 'A soft job you've got — just sit and observe.' It's not hard on the eyes — it's the sitting that hurts!"

FAO international headquarters in Rome is housed in two magnificent palaces on Terme di Caracalla. Each of the seventy-seven member-nations pay a portion of the total budget according to an agreed scale of contributions. The chief work of FAO is assisting governments at their request in agricultural and technical development and/or in meeting crises of production (such as locust plagues). There are four main regional offices — Washington, Bangkok, Cairo, and Santiago. Most underdeveloped countries have national FAO offices that plan and supervise work within each country. The project plans are forwarded to the central office in Rome where they are examined, studied, reshaped, and, if approved, the wheels are set in motion for their implementation.

Besides the United Nations' allotment to FAO of $8,000,000 per year, FAO receives almost as much from the Extended Technical Assistance Program of the United States. This money is also used for agricultural technical assistance. The FAO constitution requires that the general assembly meet every two years. In the interim FAO is guided by a council or executive committee of twenty-four nations, which meets once or twice a year. The director general, really the major power of the organization, is elected by the assembly for a two-year term and chairs the council.

Fundamentally, according to Ligutti, the observership of the Holy See is intended to accomplish two things:

1. Inform the Catholic Church, its officials, missionaries, etc. about the work of FAO, urge them to cooperate, and since our pastors and missionaries are really at the grass roots, to help the governments and the FAO in carrying out their work.
2. Serve as liaison between the FAO technicians at the headquarters and in the field and the Catholic officials no matter where. On the long term, the Catholic Church is the most stable institution in existence. It goes on and on, over-ground or underground.

Throughout the meetings the personality and the ability of the Indian Dr. B. R. Sen, director general, loomed into greater evidence. He was a smooth, diplomatic, and tireless worker who was present for all the meetings and yet found time to write well-conceived and expressed statements.

As an official permanent observer to FAO, the Holy See was expected to entertain the delegates. On November 3, 1955, for example, over 150 Catholic and non-Catholic FAO delegates attended a special Mass at St. Isidore's in Rome and then visited the Vatican museums and the Sistine Chapel. Then, a week later at the Grand Hotel, the Holy See hosted a dinner to honor the chief Catholic delegates. Among the ambassadors, ministers of agriculture, and high ranking ecclesiastics, Ligutti served as the master of ceremonies. Ligutti wrote:

> Not too many speeches, but good ones, and plenty of good laughs.... Besides the official goings-on there is a social side consisting of receptions and dinner parties. It's all nice and good, but it does weary one in spite of the enjoyable elements involved. There is no way of skipping an invitation, particularly when wearing a Roman collar. Small nations especially would be offended if the Holy See were not present. For South Americans it would become a *"casus belli."* That's exactly what it becomes when one eats too much! My dear beloved deceased friend Monsignor Morrison used to address me as "My dear Billy Goat," and verily, I must be that!

Such were Ligutti's activities with FAO during the fifties. The closing year of the decade marked a radical change in his life-style. It involved the "population problem," his moving to Rome, the continued and intensified activities of the office of the Vatican observership, and the opening of the Second Vatican Council. In many ways it was a milestone in the life of the Church and the world as well as in Ligutti's life. "The presence of the Church" was being felt; "the open window" of Pope John was readily noticed; the stirrings of the Holy Spirit were witnessed throughout the world. Few, however, would deny that Msgr. Luigi Ligutti did more than his share as one priest in the office of permanent observer of the Holy See to FAO to collaborate with the Church, the papacy, the world, and the Holy Spirit in promoting "the new Pentecost."

After serving twenty-five years as a Vatican observer to FAO, Monsignor Ligutti resigned from that position to inaugurate Agrimissio. Here he consults with the present director of Agrimissio, Fr. Boavida Coutinho.

On January 5, 1971 Cardinal Carlo Confalonieri, archpriest of the St. Mary Major Basilica in Rome, invested Monsignor Ligutti as a canon of the basilica.

As co-observers of the Vatican to FAO, Monsignor Ligutti and Dr. Emilio Bonomelli worked closely together. Here they are pictured at the papal farm with a tractor which the NCRLC of the United States donated.

In October, 1971, Pope Paul VI congratulated Monsignor Ligutti for his efforts in establishing the Pontifical Commission for Justice and Peace.

Welcoming FAO General Secretary Caldera Bresma to the opening of the FAO South American regional conference in October, 1970.

Fr. Giulius Tessarolo, C.S., superior general of the Scalabrini Fathers, and Monsignor Ligutti next to a bust of Bishop Scalabrini, May 18, 1968 at the order's generalate in Rome.

When Monsignor Ligutti learned on November 15, 1948 that he was recognized as the first permanent observer of the Vatican City State to FAO, he quickly penned this acceptance speech which he delivered that same day to the general assembly (see p. 243).

The monsignor's secretary, Miss Marie Grootheisen, gives him the schedule of the day.

At a general assembly of FAO, Monsignor Ligutti listens to a speech.

With the inaugural members of the Pontifical Commission for Justice and Peace. Monsignor Ligutti for five years was a consultant to the commission.

Monsignor Ligutti greets Pope Paul VI who came to address FAO on its twenty-fifth anniversary in 1971. Dr. Boromea, executive secretary of FAO, is between the Holy Father and Ligutti.

CHAPTER TWELVE

STILL GOING

Ligutti was always on the go, a human dynamo. His was a drive, a determination, a resolve to carry each task through to its completion to the best of his ability. At times, those who did not know him interpreted his determination as obstinacy. Nothing was further from the mark. He was neither careless nor hasty in his decisions, but once he resolved on a course of action no human power could deter him from accomplishing what he firmly believed was God's will.

This drive was both physical and spiritual. When asked how he could be engaged in so many activities at one time and accomplish what seemed in the beginning to be an impossible dream, he shrugged his shoulders, smiled softly, and replied, "God always blessed me with good health. He must have had a reason for doing so." Simplicity was, of course, the key word. Few men better exemplified the scriptural admonition of being wise as serpents and simple as doves. His simplicity, however, was never to be confused with duplicity or ignorance. It was more closely related to the wisdom of the simple peasant who could grasp the most profound problems and reduce them in a few words to basic principles. This gift, inherited from his peasant ancestry, was polished by his keen mind in the halls of academe and practiced throughout his life as a pastor and rural sociologist. His was the gift of expressing profound religious and social principles in pithy, homey expressions that were easily grasped by learned and unlettered men and women.

His spiritual life was marked by the same simplicity that is closely related to profundity. He wrote about St. Isidore's angels accompanying him on his journeys. This was not a figure of speech. He believed it. He viewed the liturgy of the Church not merely as an historical remembrance or a religious ceremony but as life, and he lived it. He promoted stewardship, for example, not as a means of merely raising money; rather, he continually insisted that it was an act of worship carried out in man's daily life. His prayers were neither eloquent nor elegant; rather, they were practical and to the point. For this reason he recited the novena in honor of St. Isidore every day of his life after it was published. He was constantly in touch with men throughout the world; more importantly, he was always in touch with the God he adored through the men he served.

For this reason Monsignor Ligutti was always seeking and striving for a better world willed by God for all mankind in this world and the next. He marked the golden jubilee of his priesthood in his beloved parish at Granger in September, 1967. Congratulations and best wishes poured in from every corner of the globe. He was thrilled most of all, however, to be home again with the people he loved. Such a milestone for most men would be the signal for retirement. His friend Mr. James Patton, former president of the Farmers' Union, sent his congratulations and urged Ligutti not to retire to green pastures. Patton had no reason to fear. Anyone who knew Ligutti well knew that "retirement" was not a word in his vocabulary.

Two other characteristics dominated Ligutti's life. He was consistent and loyal. His exceptional gift in putting the most profound principles in the simplest terms enabled both him and his audience to grasp basic truths in an ordinary manner. Thus, for example, his stand on social and religious issues was the same during his pastorate in Granger as it was before the delegates to FAO in his farewell address. Conditions might change, people might come and go, but the basic underlying principles always remained the same. This fact Ligutti grasped. He changed his approach as the circumstances demanded; he never changed his Christian social principles. Closely related to his consistency was his loyalty. He made friends quickly and kept them throughout his life. He supported, encouraged, and stood by them. To be sure, some abandoned him, some ignored him, or forgot him — and these were always painful for a man of such sensitivity — but Ligutti stood by in good times and in bad, ever ready to help if he could.

Latin America was not only an apostolate with Ligutti; it was an obsession. He never lost interest in its problems; he never ceased to be a Yankee friend. Manizales, Santiago, and Panama were not enough, even though any careful observer was quick to point out the influence of these congresses on rural life. But it was not enough for Ligutti. He must give it one more try, to assess results and plan strategies for the future. Thus was born the Fifth International Congress on Rural Life, held in Caracas, Venezuela, from September 14-19, 1961. Again Ligutti was in his element, drafting proposals, making plans, checking out details, and, of course, securing the necessary financial backing from his friends in the United States.

The congress was not intended to be a mass demonstration. Rather, it sought to gather together key representatives of Church, State, and agriculture from Latin America and the world in order to give serious attention to the problems of "the land and the people on the land." The congress drew over one hundred rural life leaders from throughout the world. Cardinal José Quintero, archbishop of Caracas, and Archbishop Luigi Dadaglio, nuncio to Venezuela, co-sponsored the congress. One of its highlights was the address entitled "If I Were Still a Communist Organizer, What Would I Want to Find in Venezuela?" by Mr. Douglas Hyde, former editor of the *Daily Worker*.

By this time Ligutti was universally recognized as one of the leading churchmen concerned with the socio-economic problems of Latin America. He was frequently interviewed and quoted in the secular and Catholic press in Latin America and the United States during the congress. His friend George Dugan, religion writer of the New York *Times,* who faithfully covered the annual conventions of the NCRLC, took notice of the congress in his columns. Few expressed the scope and aims of the congress better than Dugan:

> The congress will range over a broad field, including material resources and their use, historical development of land tenure, efficient use of the land, human and material factors in agricultural production, and distribution and marketing problems.
>
> These will be discussed in relation to Roman Catholic doctrine, rapidly changing technology, impending social changes and the world-wide advance of communism.

The Venezuela congress breathed the air of Pope John's encyclical *Mater et Magistra*. Its discussions centered around the teachings of the encyclical and its thirty doctrinal conclusions were drawn up and approved "in the light of the recent encyclical of Pope John XXIII." This statement is significant inasmuch as it reveals a progression in social thought throughout Latin America since the Manizales congress in 1953. Further, the resolutions, based upon the great Johannine encyclical, reveal a willingness — in fact, an eagerness — of both Church and State officials to follow directions and suggestions of the bishop of Rome — quite contrary to the situation of a previous generation when Pius XI's *Quadragesimo Anno* was not only scorned but even forbidden to be published in Mexico and Chile. The conclusions of this congress represented in many ways a laurel wreath for Ligutti. They expressed in forthright statements the philosophy and theology of social justice that he had labored for in countries South of the Border since his first trip there with his friends Schlarman and Morrison in 1945.

Latin America, however, was but one segment of the worldwide apostolate of Christian rural life. As Ligutti wrote:

> In the history of the world we can trace the rise and fall of leadership: Babylon, Egypt, Greece, Rome, Spain, England and, today, the U.S.A. Without fear I can state my belief: Latin America will be tomorrow's leader either for Christ or against Christ. We, as Catholics of the world today, can tip the balance. *Misereor* and *adveniat* — help and hope.

By 1961, at least to Ligutti, the scale had been tipped. His experiences at FAO headquarters led him to hear another drum and his conscience impelled him to follow the beat of the distant drummer. This time the martial sounds came from the Third World, and again he listened to the sordid tale of man's inhumanity to man. Africa was rioting; Asia was starving; the island people of the Pacific had no room, no food, no technology. Yet, the comfortable world centered around the North Atlantic was as far removed from this developing world as cottage cheese was from the moon before man landed upon it. Obviously, the first demand was to arouse the conscience of the Christian people of the West. One way was to resort to the press; another way was to convene a congress and invite key representatives of Church and State. There remained a third alternative and this was to hold a congress in the very heart of the problem area. Once again Ligutti was the sparkplug, stimulating editors, convoking leaders, and securing financial support from friends.

The Sixth International Congress on Rural Life convened in Rome from September 3-9, 1962. Again it was not a splashy spectacle; rather, it was a meeting of serious minds to make practical recommendations. Delegates from over thirty countries participated in the customary papers, discussions, and seminars. Seeds were planted and the gospel of Christian social principles was disseminated. The delegates were divided into four working groups and discussed five problem areas: (1) Agriculture and agricultural efforts within the framework of the general economic development, (2) Professional and economic organization in the agricultural field, (3) State organizations and interventions in agriculture, (4) The farmer, his family, and the rural community, and (5) Problems and forms of the apostolate in agricultural areas.

Msgr. Giovanni D'Ascenzi, director of the Italian rural life movement, served as general director of this congress that attracted almost five hundred delegates. Once again the deliberations centered around the teachings of Pope John's encyclical *Mater et Magistra*. Not surprisingly, the results of the congress were similar to those of the Venezuela congress the preceding year. That, however, was not the point. The meeting was significant inasmuch as it brought these basic Christian principles to a wider audience composed largely of delegates from the Third World.

Finally, Ligutti assisted in planning the First National Congress for Rural Development sponsored by the Philippine hierarchy from February 5-11, 1967. He welcomed the opportunity, for it would bring the gospel of Christian social principles as applied to agriculture to the most Catholic nation in the Far East. He spared no effort in assisting Bishop Mariano G. Gaviola, secretary-general of the Catholic Welfare Organization, in suggesting programs, speakers, and public relations techniques for the historic meeting. As with the previous congresses in Latin America, he saw this as an occasion of making the presence of Christ better known among the poor of the world. He was pleased with the theme of the congress: "The Church Goes to the Barrio." Especially gratifying to Ligutti was the presence of laymen and women from throughout the islands who actively participated in the deliberations and formulated resolutions at the three sites of the congress in Manila, Los Banos, and Cagayan de Oro.

At Ligutti's suggestion, Dr. A. M. Weisblat, a director of the Rockefeller Foundation, offered "A Challenge to the Catholic Church" in the opening paper of the congress. He traced the official teaching of the Church concerning problems of social justice in conciliar and papal documents. He then enunciated this challenge:

The brief and simple facts that I have presented concerning the Philippines should not be viewed with pessimism. They reflect the consequences of the rapid development and change that have occurred in Asia over the last 15 years. They are the result of a rapid evolution, extraordinary demographic growth, problems in modern economic development, inadequate social structures to deal with these problems and the need for social change. In other words, the Philippines, like Latin America and the rest of Asia, free of political colonialism, are setting out in a period of economic and social development. What we now need are ways and means of bringing about the social and economic development in a fruitful way — a way in which they will be able to benefit men and women of our society, from the positive effects of economic development. The challenge to the Church is clearly stated by the leaders of the Church both past and present. It is in ways and means through which it can help develop this process of social change, in a willingness to modify its own structures and outlook, if necessary, to bring about the modernization of society.

Ligutti responded to this challenge in the name of the universal Church. Speaking on the same platform, Ligutti said, "The Church Universal thanks you for the challenge and willingly, unhesitatingly, and with alacrity accepts it."

Ligutti always felt that the Philippine Islands were the showcase of Christianity in the Far East. For this reason he felt there was a responsibility of the Church before the people of the Orient. In August, 1970, he was asked by the Vatican Secretary of State to draft a memorandum for Pope Paul VI as to what the Holy Father might say on his Far Eastern tour. Accordingly Ligutti submitted "an examination of conscience" to answer the challenge of Doctor Weisblat's address before the Philippines' rural life convention in 1967. Ligutti submitted these questions to the Holy Father:

1. Are the great material and human resources of the Philippines being used for the development of man and society?
2. Do we perhaps expect the situation will change without our effective collaboration? (Man is the subject and object of development.)
3. Do we work together for the betterment of man and society or rather waste our time in battling among ourselves?

4. In the field of the family do we make parents conscious of the responsibilities of parenthood? (*Humanae Vitae* 10.)
5. If we are poor and afflicted, do we employ our abilities and possibilities rather than think that we are the victim of the fatalistic fortune, good or bad?
6. Do we respond to the Pauline counsel of Paul to the Galatians? ("Bear ye one another's burdens.")
7. Do we realize that to uplift the situation of the poor it is not sufficient to hand out gifts in a paternalistic fashion?
8. Are we conscious of the obligation that all must share in the good and not merely a few?
9. Do we realize that the general good will never be reached by class struggle but rather by "Love one toward another?"
10. Are we fully conscious that religion does not consist merely of a repetition of prayer or formal acts of worship?
11. If we have had the advantage of education, what are we doing so that those not so fortunate might soon share in the same benefit?
12. The same question concerning the artisan and farmer — Do we make our know-how available to the less fortunate?
13. If we hold positions of civic leadership, are we really the servants of the people and not the exploiters?
14. If we are the dispensers and arbiters of justice and law, are we just and impartial in our judgements?
15. With our laws and socio-economic planning do we offer all our citizens the possibility of employment and living wages and decent working conditions?
16. Do we pay wages commensurate with needs of a family — especially to the workers in agriculture?
17. What is our attitude and conduct on the employment of women — field, factory or domestic workers?
18. If I am a priest, a bishop or even the Pope, have I made my own the cause of the poor?

The population problem continued to haunt Ligutti, as it did the world and the Church. A year before his resignation as Vatican observer to the FAO, he received a form letter from the Vatican Secretariat of State, Cardinal Jean Villot, addressed to pontifical representatives and permanent observers concerning the population problems. Dutiful son of the Church that he was, Ligutti replied that he found the document "interesting" and, "on the whole, balanced." He assured the cardinal that he would do his best to carry out the instructions. Ligutti then revealed his direct style, avoiding curial niceties, and replied in ideas that he had spent most of his life promoting:

1. The whole document repeats arguments that are not at all new. There is no doubt that they are true, though ineffective. It is certain, in fact, that they are less and less accepted both by non-Catholics and Catholics and even by the clergy and hierarchy.

2. The suggestions regarding Pontifical Representatives and Delegates to International Organizations, as in Nos. 33-34, are certainly appreciable; it does not seem, however, that the procedures envisaged meet the purpose completely; they suggest rather a delaying action. The difficulties remain, therefore, since the inherent problems are not centered.

3. What is right — but is only just mentioned — is in Nos. 12 and 27: that is, an appeal to increase agricultural production; to improve housing, infrastructures, health care; to extend the literacy campaigns; to strengthen the purchasing power of the currency and improve the terms of trade; to plan the various elements of contemporary technical progress; to bring about a fairer distribution of the means of production; and greater justice in remuneration.

It is obvious, in fact, that every individual ought to be considered not only as a subject of consumption, but also of production, on the basis of a human-Christian civilization.

In the light of these principles the whole question of surpluses ought to be revised.

4. The fact should also be stressed that poverty is due to ignorance, social injustice, under-development, mental inertia and not to inadequacies of Providence or to the insufficiency of the natural resources necessary. Man himself is the greatest of these resources, provided he is given the opportunity to develop and is put to good use.

It is known today that a large percentage of the earth is fertile and accessible, but not exploited and used as it should be. On the contrary, some governments subsidize farmers to limit their production. Oranges are burnt in California (U.S.A.) and apples in Emilia (Italy) while children die in developing countries for lack of vitamins. The same idea can be said of other products. Over 50 percent of mankind have no incentive to occupy their physical and intellectual capacities.

These incongruities, these injustices must be brought to judgement in the various nations, international organizations, the whole world. *Praedicate super tecta* is our duty.

What kind of progress, and what advantage is there for humanity if a cosmonaut sets foot on the moon, or if the Pope can be seen at Pago Pago from every continent by means of a telestar, when so many millions of men lead lives that are inhuman.

Ligutti used other meetings and platforms to extend the social gospel of the Church. Two of these are noteworthy, for seldom, if ever, was one priest so privileged to address five international Eucharistic Congresses in a lifetime, much less than within fifteen years. He was invited to address the "Farmers' Meeting" of the international Eucharistic Congress in Munich, Germany, on August 6, 1960. His address was not so much a sociological study as an inspirational exhortation:

You farmers of the world are not only the partners with God in the ever continuing work of creation but you are the special partners with the priest, with Christ, in Mass and Communion. The offertory procession is in your hands! How noble your work! How elevated your position! How privileged your task!

Earlier at the same congress, he addressed the conference on international Catholic organizations on the Freedom from Hunger campaign currently being sponsored by the FAO. Here again he became the apostle of FAO in enunciating the following principles:

1. Help nations raise the standard of living.
2. Improve the nutrition of the peoples of all countries.
3. Increase the efficiency of farming, forestry, and fisheries.
4. Better the conditions of rural people, and, through all these means, widen the opportunity of all people for productive work.

Some of his listeners looked upon his proposals as too idealistic. Others felt that he was living in a utopia, precisely because they did not realize or comprehend the idealism and the immense goodwill exercised by the officers and members of the FAO. Opposition, however, melted away when he quoted in his closing remarks the words that Paul VI added to the motto of FAO.

The latter was, *"Fiat panis"* — "Let there be bread." Paul VI added: *"Fiat pax"* — "Let there be peace."

Munich was but one instance. Another occured in 1964 when Ligutti was invited to address the seminar on food and health during the Thirty-eighth International Eucharistic Congress in Bombay, India. Once again he found himself among friends and colleagues who were deeply concerned with the problem of universal hunger. Among them were Dr. Sen of FAO, Archbishop Angelo Fernandes, Cardinal Valerian Gracias of Bombay, and, of course, Pope Paul VI. Ligutti had throughout the years come to know the poor of the world — but never so well as he did during these days in Bombay. Behind the facade of the enthusiastic reception of the Pope — the first to visit India — Ligutti saw the trials and tribulations of the suffering poor. He could not remain silent. He raised his voice in his address on November 26, 1964. He briefly summarized the history of the Church in regard to agriculture, citing, as he had frequently done previously, the papal teaching on agriculture. From these references he concluded:

1. The Church universal through the official action of the popes and bishops is interested, as it should be, in increasing food production.
2. The Church has encouraged and is encouraging international and national organizations that seek to aid in the increase of food production. It also urges Church units to cooperate actively in such endeavors.
3. Within regional or national or diocesan or religious order units it would be appropriate to have someone especially interested in this field. The man need not be an agronomist, fishery, or forestry expert. He should possess a sympathetic understanding of the problems involved.
4. This may imply and require a certain amount of organization, educational campaigns, assistance, etc. However, the less complicated the better.
5. Personally and after much reflection and observation, travel and experience, I do not believe in setting up Catholic schools of agriculture. The so-called extension technique is by far more effective because it deals directly with the ones actually at work on farms.

He never wavered from this position. On the contrary, as we have seen, he lobbied for it in season and out of season throughout the coming three sessions of the Council. For Ligutti, international Eucharistic Congresses were but one of many means of spreading the gospel of social justice among the poor and downtrodden of the world. There was also another means he employed during these years; namely, the Inter-American Development Bank.

When asked how it was that he was invited to attend so many international meetings and congresses, Ligutti would smile and say it was just a matter that he knew one man who knew another man, and somehow or another he was invited. Dr. Karl Olson, an official of FAO from its earliest days, however, put it quite differently: "Ligutti was a man of such great human warmth and had such obvious concern for the needs of the suffering of mankind that people just wanted to be near him, listen to him, and profit from his immense experience."

One such person Ligutti met on his first trip to Mexico was a young agricultural technician named Filipe Herrera. In time Dr. Herrera became the president of the Inter-American Development Bank. This bank was established among those countries of the Organization of American States which accepted membership in the bank on March 31, 1960. Its purpose was to help accelerate economic and social development among its member countries. Through this bank the *Populorum Progressio* Fund was administered in Colombia. Between 1961 and 1966 the bank approved 368 loans amounting to over $1,700,000,000.

In April, 1967, the seventh annual meeting of the board of governors of the Inter-American Development Bank was held in Washington, D.C. At that time Dr. Herrera asked Ligutti to serve on a panel and speak on the general theme of the meeting, "Agricultural Development in Latin America During the Next Decade." Ligutti gladly accepted. His address reflected his continuing interest in the problems of social justice in Latin America. He emphasized the sociological, or spiritual, aspect of development. He enunciated what he called "very fundamental postulates":

> Man, as a person, and man, as a member of organized society, is the cause of success or failure, the beneficiary or the loser in all development. Man is the subject, i.e., the author and he is also the object, i.e., the recipient, of development.
>
> From these simple notions it is evident that real development cannot be superimposed or brought about by others. In the process of being the author (even though assisted) man thus involved does not only bring about an improvement in his external status but by his own action he improves and develops himself internally, i.e., shows forth the hidden powers he has always possessed in a dormant state.

The tragedy of hunger is not the tragedy of an empty stomach but the tragedy of a human intelligence not used. A farmer whose per hectare and per hour productivity is satisfactory or even superior is not merely enjoying a greater income but, by the very process of high productivity, his own total personality is improved, consciously or unconsciously, his abilities have been brought out and, he has prepared himself for more effective future actions. By his example he has also enhanced the social group to which he belongs.

In November, 1969, Dr. Herrera again invited him to be a panelist at the eleventh meeting of the board of governors the following April in Punta del Este, Uruguay. "Because of your deep and extensive knowledge of development matters," Herrera wrote, "I should be greatly pleased to have you attend our Round Table discussions as one of the panel members. I am certain that your participation would make a very substantial contribution to the success of the meeting." Ligutti accepted and prepared a speech, as was always his custom. He centered his speech on the theme of the meeting, "The First Decade of the IDB: Prospects for the Future." Throughout the session he listened to other speakers and began to realize that his prepared remarks were no more than expressions of his philosophy of development voiced many times previously. He then began jotting down questions, which almost unknowingly took the form of an examination of conscience. Thereupon he set aside his address, took the microphone, and delivered a public examination of conscience. The effect was overwhelming. The hundreds of assembled delegates were obviously moved. It was one of Ligutti's most dramatic speeches.

While *Time* magazine was reporting the strident call of "Freedom" rising from the depths of the anguish of a people oppressed and exploited, the Kingston Trio was singing a frivolous ditty to a packed house in many cities throughout the United States that began with the all-too-true words, "They're rioting in Africa...." Ligutti, however, wrote about his dream. "Ten years ago I spent six months in Africa. I certainly did not vizualize the complete change that would be a *fait accompli* ten years later. I thought it would come more gradually. Now it is here." He then pointed out two fundamental facts about Africa:

> 1. Africa possesses an almost infinite quantity and variety of material resources. The words "desert" and "jungle" will be changed into "cities" and "gardens."

2. Africa's human resources are capable of development and of becoming active working partners within the family of nations. Actually the jump from primitiveness to the atomic age is being made in an incredibly shorter space of time then we can imagine. To put it in plainer terms, how many centuries did it take us Westerners to learn the use of a knife and fork?

Also, his 1964 article entitled "Africa — Land of Promise" that appeared in *Jesuit Missions* revealed his abiding interest in what once was called the "dark continent" and reported his efforts at the FAO headquarters to improve the social conditions of the poor throughout the continent.

In 1968 the editor of the Long Island *Catholic* asked Ligutti, as well as other Church leaders, to give their impressions of the first five years of the reign of Pope Paul VI. Ligutti replied:

I. Greatest contributions to Church and world.

Ex aequo:
1. Encyclical *Populorum Progressio* and setting up of Pontifical Commission of Justice and Peace.
2. Rapprochement to Eastern Church and Protestant groups.
3. Ability to be considerate, patient and long suffering with the ones who have a tendency to reject even the fundamentals of the faith.

II. Possible criticism:
1. Failure to issue a pronouncement on the birth control issue as was apparently promised and expected from the world. Actually, statements were made but an *ex professo* one had been expected. That has caused considerable confusion in the Church.
2. Rather unsatisfactory and disappointing reform of the curia. His career background and gentle personal disposition have probably kept him from more radical changes.

His third literary contribution during these years revealed how deeply his own roots were sunk in the heart of the Midwest. In January, 1958, the diocese of New Ulm, Minnesota (possibly the most rural of all rural dioceses in the United States), marked its tenth anniversary. The editor of the diocesan paper, *The Catholic Bulletin*, asked Ligutti to contribute an article for the anniversary edition. The article Ligutti wrote took the form of a letter to young men. He advised them to marry early, raise a big family, and settle on a farm. It revealed the heart of a country pastor concerned with the welfare of his people. In part Ligutti wrote:

> What is life? What is man? What is happiness? And what is your vocation in life? These are the questions to be answered by each of us while we plan for our brief stay on earth.
>
> Where can I better serve God and my fellow human beings, where can I better develop the God-given gifts I am endowed with?
>
> I recall interviewing many years ago a splendid Catholic gentleman on his 100th birthday. I give you his reply to the query: "What would you advise a young man to do?" In a clear, smiling voice he said: "Get married early in life, raise a big family, and settle on a farm." It is still true today for anyone having a vocation to farm, for any intelligent young man, for a lover of real life on earth, for a girl wanting to be a queen in a home.
>
> The sentiments of Cicero are still true today also: "Of all the occupations by which a living is made, none is better than agriculture, none more delightful, none more becoming to the dignity of a free man."
>
> Or in the words of an unknown poet: "My farm is not where I must soil — My hands in endless dreary toil. But where through seed and swelling pod — I have learned to walk and talk with God."

One of Ligutti's offbeat interests during the sixties was the promotion of a commodity called "Cana Wine." In 1963, with his friend Ross J. DiLorenzo of Brooklyn, Ligutti discussed the idea of bottling wine produced near Cana in Galilee to be served at wedding dinners. A memorandum to DiLorenzo in December, 1964, expressed that the wine would be (1) processed near Cana, (2) sold in small containers as souvenirs for wedding parties, (3) marketed by an American firm, and (4) the NCRLC would derive a small royalty from the venture for charitable and religious works. On February 16, 1970, he wrote:

> There were two motivations which promoted and inspired my suggestion: one, the spiritual recollection of the Cana wedding feast of the Gospel to be recalled on the occasion of a modern wedding; the other, my desire to help the people of Israel in selling one of their products. They deserve more than well to be patronized considering the tremendous accomplishments during years of trials, struggles and sacrifices.

For six years Ligutti intermittently carried on this project. His friends in New York City invested money, established a company, and even took a market survey. His friends in Israel designed a special packaging for the wine and did, in fact, process and distribute it. By 1970, however, it was obvious that the product was not economically feasible, as high tariffs and import duties made the cost prohibitive.

One of the most difficult and time-consuming of Ligutti's responsibilities during the post-conciliar years was his appointment by the Holy See as apostolic visitator to Malta on May 7, 1969. His appointment to the sensitive post was both a recognition and an outgrowth of his interest in stewardship and expertise in Church finances. In an interview given Rome's *Daily American* Ligutti formulated four principles which he applied to the Maltese situation and which could be applied to every religious organization:

1. Any Church unit has a right to own property.
2. This type of ownership, however, does not have rights on a par with individual property ownership. The Church unit must act as the steward of its properties for the benefit of the "people of God" — that is, the people of whatever religion — that the Church should serve.
3. The "people of God" have a right to know how the money is earned and how it is spent.
4. Assets should be managed efficiently and honestly.

Financial difficulties in Malta had been brewing for years, brought to a climax by a thirteen-year struggle between the Church and the governing Labor Party and aggravated by the fluctuating devaluation of the British pound sterling. On November 8, 1968 Ligutti discussed the political and ecclesiastical situation in Malta with Cardinal Carlo Confalonieri and advised the latter to keep the subject secret, but it did not remain secret for long. On April 22 the following year Archbishop Michele Gonzi of Malta and Fr. Benjamin Tonna, a Maltese priest stationed in Rome, discussed the situation with Ligutti and mentioned the establishment of a finance commission for the Church in Malta. Events moved swiftly. On May 7 Ligutti was appointed apostolic visitator for financial matters to the Church in Malta. The next day Archbishop Martin O'Connor resigned as papal nuncio to Malta. On May 10 Ligutti discussed the affairs of Malta again with Father Tonna who said he would arrange Ligutti's trip to the island. The same day Ligutti met with Archbishop Giovanni Benelli and offered to go to Malta under the guise of the Vatican observer to FAO with powers of an apostolic visitator. Three days later Archbishop O'Connor said he was glad that Archbishop Gonzi asked for Ligutti's services. The same day Ligutti discussed with Father Tonna the possibility of securing accountants and wisely recorded in his diary, "We won't cross bridges till we come to them."

Ligutti crossed the first bridge via Alitalia Airlines from Rome to Valetta, Malta, on May 16. Coadjutor Archbishop Emanuele Gerada and three priests met him at the airport and there and then wanted a conference. Ligutti cut them short and went to his room at the Palms Hotel. Later at the archbishop's house he met with the archbishop, the coadjutor archbishop, the suffragan bishop of Malta, and two priests. Three unanimous decisions resulted from this meeting; first, to secure every bit of information available; second, to employ a British firm of accountants to investigate the finances; third, to establish a commission to study the situation thoroughly. The following day Ligutti returned to the archbishop's house.

In the meantime, Archbishop Gonzi, who at age eighty-five was as bright and keen as a man half his years, had drawn up a two-page statement embodying the points discussed the previous day. Ligutti insisted that Archbishop Gerada oversee preparing the reports and thereupon all three signed Archbishop Gonzi's statement. On May 18 Ligutti made notes and observations for the report he would later submit to Archbishop Benelli. That afternoon he returned to Rome. The following day he wrote his friend Mr. Latham-Koenig in London and asked him to suggest three firms, "British, preferably non-Catholic, to whom I may direct myself for possible advice." In this letter he outlined the preliminary decisions reached during his trip:

1. A complete listing of all assets must be made.
2. An independent accounting firm must be hired to check on this listing and financial transactions.
3. A Maltese Commission to be named representing the totality of the people of Malta — Church members or not, clerical or anti-clerical, etc. This Commission will be given the results of the research and the advice of the accountants, legal advisers, etc.
4. The end result should be an equitable adjusting of financial obligations doing away with medieval customs, traditions, etc., and handing over income properties of the Church to a corporation (non-governmental) or some such unit.

In one sentence Ligutti summarized the situation: "The Catholic Church in Malta must change its present status, must render an account of its stewardship."

The services of the London based firm of McKinsey & Company, Inc. were secured in February, 1970. The firm made an intensive three-month study of the financial condition of the Church on the three islands comprising Malta. The study was extremely difficult because it necessitated examining legacies of which half antedated the twentieth century (some even dating from the Middle Ages) and having a command of six languages, for documents were written in English, Italian, French, Maltese, Greek, and Arabic. The extensive report was not only a penetrating scrutiny of the financial condition in Malta but could well serve as a blueprint for a study of Church finances in any other country. The report directed its attention specifically to an overriding central issue; namely, the problems caused by over-complex administrative structure. As one example, the McKinsey accountants discovered there were 1,500 separate administrations under 250 administrators in a jurisdiction of a little over 300,000 Catholic people who were served by approximately 1,000 priests. McKinsey & Company summarized in three steps the action the Church in Malta should take:

1. Experienced professional management at the centre should manage the sources of revenue as a total income generating fund. This centralization should include all existing diocesan sources, including legacies, chapters, benefices, Mensa and diocesan institutions.
2. The Curia should allocate the revenues generated from Church assets to parishes, institutions and diocesan projects according to diocesan objectives, needs and obligations.
3. Decentralized, but simplified, parish and diocesan administrations should administer Church expenditures according to agreed policies, plans and budgets.

Such was the background to the tempest that would rock the island fortress. Ligutti was satisfied with the report, for it concretely expressed not only his own native concepts of efficiency but even more especially his religious conviction of the principles of stewardship.

Not a month passed throughout 1969 when Ligutti did not devote considerable time, energy, and talent to the Malta issue. Ligutti continued holding conferences with Vatican officials, such as Cardinals Confalonieri and Antoniutti, Archbishops Palazzini and Sebastiani, and O'Connor and Benelli. By July 12 he was informed that Benelli said Confalonieri had the authority in the Malta affair; yet previously the latter said it was not within his jurisdiction. The same day O'Connor told Ligutti that there was malicious gossip about him in Malta. Somewhat exasperated, Ligutti wrote in his diary, "Who is who and what?" In August he was back in Malta, meeting with Archbishop Gonzi, the provincial superiors of religious communities, government officials, and Archbishop Gerada. By this time Ligutti was beginning to see that the problem was not only financial but also personal. He admired the old archbishop greatly but suspected the sincerity of the coadjutor archbishop. He felt that the ordinary of the archdiocese would be more than happy to have his coadjutor transferred, even though the latter had neither the desire nor the intention of being transferred. In time, also, Ligutti realized the important connections that Archbishop Gerada had in the Vatican because of his former experience in the diplomatic service.

This is neither the time nor the place to recount the problems of the Church in Malta. It was one of many significant developments within the Church universal following the great expectations that the world hoped for from the Second Vatican Council. Ligutti had done his work well. McKinsey & Company had drawn up a comprehensive report and, if it would have been enacted, would have spared subsequent animosity and division within the Church in Malta. Ligutti, however, was learning that not everyone was in favor of *aggiornamento* and this cupidity to preserve vested interests and traditional ways made his task impossible.

Ligutti expressed his feelings only in his diary:

Malta is a cabal of intrigues (September 27, 1969).

What a mess! (October 27)

What a day of struggles! (November 24)

Malta work is getting my goat. (February 13, 1970)

I am nervous but determined. I saw plenty and the record is clear. (February 23)

Someday I should write "Maltese Fever." (February 24, 1971)

Hope I can deliver myself of Malta job. (March 1)

Under a large *Deo Gratias* Ligutti recorded his March 6 entry:

Phone call from the Secretariat of State telling me of "urgent" letter from Villot, dated March 5. Wonderful news! Villot says end of my job in Malta. So I will write him a note of thanks for relieving me of responsibility and worry and stupid accusations.... The work, the worry and the trial of the job has been a miserable experience.

Although Ligutti had been formally relieved of his position as apostolic visitor, the crisis in Malta did not cease. It only began. Divisions in the ranks of the clergy ultimately brought about the removal of Archbishop Gerada as coadjutor and returned him to service in the diplomatic corps. Archbishop Gonzi, through his own personal intervention and audience with Pope Paul VI, helped to still at least for a time the troubled waters lashing against the rocks of Malta. In many ways Ligutti became the symbol of the forces of renewal and both his work and person was widely praised among a large segment of the clergy and by the press.

A final footnote. On April 15, 1970 Ligutti had a private audience with Pope Paul. Ligutti wrote:

> Usual praise by the Pope. Then I gave him the story and found out that he knows practically nothing about the whole Malta work, or its purpose, details, etc. To the question: "What do you suggest?" I said, "Throw both of them out and put in a strong administrator and a good *nunzio*." He said that was impossible and he would leave Gonzi there to die. I was not too well pleased. He gave me a Council bell.

The "Malta affair" received considerable space in the world's press. That was so, Ligutti opined, because men today are deeply interested in the government of the Church and are beginning to realize their duty and right to be informed. If there were obstructionists in both Malta and the Vatican, it might best be explained by the current division of opinion within the Church on the subject of disclosing its finances.

Ligutti was never a man to rest on his laurels. No sooner had the statement on stewardship been approved by the Council than he set to work organizing an international seminar on stewardship. For the next eight years Father Gallery constantly prodded him to hold the seminar in Rome. Ligutti, however, felt the first consideration must be to organize a stewardship council in the United States. For several years he worked for that end not only by letters but also by personal contacts in Kansas City with Fr. Robert N. Deming, chairman of the Committee for Diocesan Support Programs in Kansas City, Father Gallery and his associates in Chicago, and Bishop Zuroweste in Belleville.

Then, on September 22, 1969 Ligutti proposed that the Council of the Laity support and promote a seminar on the sentence in the conciliar decree: "It is a duty and honor for Christians to return to God a part of the good things they receive from Him." At their sixth plenary session on October 4, the Council discussed the proposal. Apart from some misunderstanding of it, chiefly by Miss Bellosillo of Spain and Mr. J. Montemayor of the Philippines, the members generally felt as did Miss Rosemary Goldie of Australia, who said:

> The document needs perhaps a fuller presentation. To call the project "paternalistic" is to miss the point completely. All members of the Church, rich and poor, have responsibilities of "stewardship," both towards the Church and towards the world. Understanding of this is an important aspect of Christian formation.

Six days later the motion made by Mr. Ruiz-Cimenez was adopted; namely, "The Council on the Laity asks the Secretariat, assisted by the Planning Group, to follow up the examination of Msgr. Ligutti's proposal to hold a Seminar on 'Stewardship' and to report on it during the next Plenary Session."

The principal misunderstanding of Ligutti's proposal on stewardship was that it was no more than a subtle device to entice the wealthy to dole out more money to the poor, thus ignoring the obligations of all Christians to promote social justice. Ligutti answered this objection in a letter to Mr. Montemayor on January 14, 1970:

> It is my contention that the poor of the world built the glorious Cathedrals of which the poor are so proud. St. Patrick's in New York was paid for by the dimes and nickels of the Irish servant girls in Manhattan. There is a lovely country church near Vicenza, Italy, built by the parishioners themselves with material paid for by eggs (and only eggs) produced in the local farmyards. We don't need the rich to support our Christian institutions — we need loving people who share their poverty with a Church of the poor.

Ligutti continued to work behind the scenes in promoting the international seminar on stewardship. More immediately he secured funds from the Homeland Foundation to help meet expenses and housing and meeting rooms from the College of the Divine Word. Fr. Othmar Rink, O.M.I., agreed to coordinate the seminar and Msgr. Karl Bayer, director of Caritas Internationalis, gladly offered the secretarial services of the offices. The date was set, finally, for October 1-5, 1973.

Approximately one hundred specially chosen delegates from some thirty countries were invited. Most of the delegates were lay people, with a scattering of bishops, priests, and observers from other Christian Churches. Archbishop Simon Lourdusamy, secretary of the Congregation for the Evangelization of Peoples, set the tenor of the meeting in his opening remarks:

> The Hebrews believed that man not only has dominion over his environment; he is also responsible for what he does with it. Man has the task of harnessing the world's resources; he also has the responsibility of using these resources for the common good. The author of Genesis communicates to us the belief that man's responsibility is to give meaning, significance and direction to the world. The story of Adam who is commissioned to name the animals and till the soil conveys this idea. It is sinful, therefore, to abnegate this responsibility, for to disregard it is to place oneself at the centre of the world and to build up one's own image of self-sufficiency and egoism, fear and greed; such a man is like Adam, no longer free, but imprisoned within the walls of the kingdom he builds and in which he is hardly alive, nursing his illusions....
>
> Stewardship is indeed one of the fundamental roles of every man here on earth, particularly of every Christian — one of the essential ways he, as a member of the community, bears creditable witness to Christ, the perfect Steward — and, as it is well said by the organizers of the Seminar, his grateful response to God's redeeming love, and his sincere and concrete act of worship most acceptable to God and beneficial to his neighbors, particularly in our mission lands where there is much scope in this direction.

The five-day seminar sent sparks flying throughout the world, with delegates bringing the gospel of stewardship home with them to share with others. Few international seminars produced so many speeches and discussions of the high caliber that was reached during these days. A classic piece of historical research on stewardship from pre-Christian days through both Testaments, the early Church, the Councils of the Church, papal statements in canonical legislation, and the "contamination" of the Church through donations and civil legislation was presented by Msgr. Terzo Natalini, archivist of the Vatican Secretariat of State. Other major and significant addresses were presented by Cardinal Humberto Medeiros of Boston, Bishop Edward Swanstrom of the United States Catholic Relief Services, and Dr. Helge Brattgard, bishop of Skara, Sweden. A highlight of the seminar was an audience with Pope Paul on October 3. During his weekly general audience the Pontiff went out of his way to salute the participants in the seminar:

> We offer you our cordial greeting and thank you for wishing to pay us this visit. We know that one of the aims of your deliberations is to promote a spirit of sharing spiritual and material goods. You are striving to draw from the concept of stewardship all the richness of meaning which the term implies in the Gospel, and to show the value of offering to God, as an act of worship, part of the gifts received from His bounty.
>
> We are particularly glad to note that your studies are being directed towards the Mission countries, that the people of those lands may be helped to attain self-sufficiency through the gift of their time, talents, and resources.
>
> As well as promoting meetings of Catholics, you also make it your task to share your views and experiences with the members of other Christian communions. In so doing you are working to bring closer the day when there shall be achieved that unity for which Christ prayed.

Thus, under the shadow of St. Peter's dome, was fulfilled another dream envisioned fifty years before by a country pastor in Woodbine, Iowa, who then, and always, served the poor and little people of the world. Stewardship, however, was in Ligutti's mind but one of many means of promoting social justice in the world. It was intimately associated with the act of worship of the Christian individual and community. Ligutti felt, however, that another means could and must be employed. Some would call this an educational approach; others a public relations technique. For Ligutti it was a matter of stirring up the Christian conscience to bring the full import of the gospels to bear on the world's oppressing and oppressive social problems.

When Ligutti met in private audience with Pope Paul on April 15, 1971, three months after his resignation as Vatican observer to FAO had been accepted, the Holy Father asked if there was anything he could do for him. "*Niente* - nothing," Ligutti graciously replied. He needed nothing, nothing he desired. He had already been appointed a canon of the Basilica of St. Mary Major. "I have always had a great devotion to the Mother of God," he recalled, "and this appointment enabled me to give public expression to that devotion by honoring Mary in the mother church of all churches dedicated in her honor."

It was a long time since Ligutti first heard from Dr. Bonomelli on December 19, 1961 that he was being considered for a canonicate of the basilica. Nine years later on December 28, 1970 his friend Msgr. Terzo Natalini confided to him that he would be appointed a canon. On January 5, 1971 he was sworn in as a canon of the basilica following evening Vespers, and the following day he took his place among the canons in the chanting of Matins and Lauds in Latin. On January 14 he wrote in his diary, "It's great to be present for a chapter meeting of the canons."

For the next two years he faithfully fulfilled his duties as a canon, never missing the recitation of the Divine Office and the chapter meetings whenever he was in Rome. He came to realize that the basilica badly needed repairs and, even worse, no funds were available for that purpose. He set his mind to work on the project. In March, 1972, he suggested various ways of raising money for that purpose, including establishing a library, a museum, and a confraternity for the basilica. "If St. Peter's has a confraternity," he asked, "why can't St. Mary's?" Archbishop Benelli and Cardinal Confalonieri, then the archpriest of the basilica, endorsed his suggestions. In June, 1972 he drafted a memorandum for raising the money and on July 2 the chapter allotted the funds to restore the basilica's priceless interior. Ligutti was filled with hopes for the project. In time, two victories were registered: "The Confraternity of Mother of God and the Church" was established and restoration work was begun on the basilica's interior in 1973. He continued to push for an American promoter for the Confraternity and as late as January 14, 1974 he wrote, "I have not changed my mentality."

Ligutti's love for the missions of the Church was as world-embracing as world-renowned. Although his influence in changing the traditional approach of missionary evangelism and charitable distributions cannot be scientifically measured, all who knew his work were convinced he was one of a handful of churchmen who changed the Church's stance from "preaching" to development, from "handouts" to self-help. As we have seen, the Vatican observers' office of FAO was a haven for missionaries throughout the world, and a major part of its work was the practical implementation of Pope Paul's statement, "Development is another word for peace."

Ligutti's resignation as Vatican observer opened the door to a project called "Agrimissio" that holds great promise for the missionary work of the Church. The project was but a natural outgrowth of the many extracurricular activities that the Vatican observers' office carried on for twenty years. In 1957 Ligutti discussed the matter with the then Msgr. Ernest Primeau at the Chicago House in Rome, asking what the latter thought of the possibilities of Ligutti working with missionaries in Rome. In 1968 he secured the finances for a Miss Joan Overboss and her missionary group to conduct an extensive research project on the diet and health of missionaries around the world. After studying her report Ligutti made a practical and innovative suggestion that there should be a traveling team of medical people checking the health of missionaries around the world.

The concept of Agrimissio was becoming more clearly defined. On May 16, 1968 he discussed with Persegati the possibility of establishing an independent office to help missionaries in the area of social action and thus fulfill a function that the Congregation for the Evangelization of Peoples did not provide. In December, 1969, Ligutti discussed the possibilities of Agrimissio with Fr. Johannes Schutte, superior general of the Society of the Divine Word, who wholeheartedly endorsed the idea. Early in 1970 a task force examined more precisely the purpose and nature of the proposed organization. Throughout 1971 Ligutti continued to make plans for Agrimissio. He secured the services of Fr. J. G. Brossard, O.M.I., to work closely with him during these planning stages. On June 22 he secured a resolution of approval for Agrimissio from the NCRLC board of directors.

In accord with Ligutti's convictions, Agrimissio had a small, almost imperceptible beginning in January, 1972. Father Brossard served as its executive secretary and Miss Marie Grootheisen as the liaison officer for women's work. The board of directors was Sr. Therese M. Barnett, superior general of the Sisters of Charity, M.M., representing the International Union of Superiors General of Women's Religious Institutes; Dr. E. H. Hartmans, director of FAO Area Service Division, representing FAO; Msgr. J. Kempeneers, secretary general of the Pontifical Missionary Work for the Propagation of the Faith, representing the Congregation of the Propagation of the Faith; Msgr. Luigi Ligutti, chairman of Agrimissio, representing the International Affairs Department of the

NCRLC; and Br. Thomas More, superior general of the Xaverian Brothers, representing the Union of Superiors General of Men's Religious Institutes; he also served as treasurer of Agrimissio.

From its beginning Agrimissio was a "service of all involved in the missionary effort." It strives to fulfill this purpose by announcing the good news of Christ, by helping people share more fully in the benefits and efforts of development, by fostering collaboration between religious leaders and development agencies, by motivating and collaborating in on-going programs of group study and group action for education, and by encouraging and promoting a partnership in development among the poorer and richer regions of the world, as well as among the poorer regions themselves.

After Agrimissio's first two years an evaluation committee appointed in 1973 reported to the board of directors. Although the report, submitted by Br. Vincent Gottwald, F.C.C., on January 17, 1974, dealt extensively with such internal matters as finances, personnel, and amendments to the statutes, it also most significantly reexamined the goals of the organization. At that meeting Fr. Boavida Coutinho was introduced as the new executive secretary of Agrimissio. Although still a new service office, often feeling its way, Agrimissio may well become one of the most significant and dynamic institutions within the Church at the service of the missions.

From the earliest days with the NCRLC, as permanent observer to FAO, through the many congresses and seminars he helped organize, down to the founding of Agrimissio, Ligutti like St. Isidore also had two "strong angels" beside him. He came to meet Mr. Chauncey Stillman through their mutual interest in Georgian economics, Jeffersonian democracy, and the movement of *Land and Home*. Stillman became interested in the Granger Homesteads project and the two kindred souls then met in New York City. A deep and lasting friendship continued for the next forty years.

Chauncey Stillman dated his family back to the earliest colonial times. His family acquired considerable wealth through oil wells in Texas and banks in New York. He entered the Catholic Church, being received by Fr. Coleman A. Daily, S.J., for many years associated with the Mission Secretariat of the Society of Jesus. Stillman was a generous benefactor to the archdiocese of New York, the Scalabrini Fathers, the Ladies of the Grail, the diocese of Brownsville, Texas, the National Catholic Rural Life

Conference, the Office of the Vatican Observers to FAO, and other religious, educational, and charitable works. He also established the chair of Roman Catholic Studies at Harvard University and left it endowed with $1,500,000. On November 9, 1967 he was invested as a privy chamberlain, "a gentleman of the Pope," by Cardinal Francis Spellman. On October 11, 1967 he wrote to Mr. Persegati:

> Cardinal Spellman, whom I saw again yesterday, volunteered to invest me as Privy Chamberlain on my birthday, November 9th, and to have my family and any intimates I wish to lunch. He seemed highly pleased, and beamed at the mention of Monsignor Ligutti. Please tell the Monsignor, and thank him — in addition to everything else — for his advice in presenting the matter of the investiture to Cardinal Spellman in the proper way.

Needless to say, all in the office of the Vatican observers were extremely pleased. They cabled Stillman on November 8: "To the *Gentiluomo del Papa* greetings best wishes prayers on birthday. Sincerely: Ligutti Bonomelli Persegati Grootheisen."

Stillman distributed his extensive contributions to worthy causes through the Homeland Foundation he established. Ligutti, a member of its board of directors, through this association became a friend of Mr. Louis Warren, the treasurer of the foundation. A prominent New Yorker, Mr. Warren was associated with the law firm of Kelley Drye Warren Clark Carr & Ellis. He was also the legal counsel for Mr. Stillman as well as his close friend. Mr. Warren was delighted with the knighthood of St. Gregory which Pope Pius XII had bestowed on him. He suspected, as did all his associates, that Ligutti had petitioned the honor. Throughout the years Warren continually sought Ligutti's advice concerning the numerous requests he received for grants and financial assistance from religious communities, missionaries, and students from every corner of the globe.

In 1965 Ligutti wrote his last travel letter to friends. It was entitled "Still Going" and recounted his journey to Latin America. He began: "It's the third Sunday of Lent. It's the feast of St. Benedict — and my 70th birthday. Thank God for everything, and so much of it, and for so long."

This chapter has largely recounted the events he shaped and help shape. This was the septuageniarian who on his sixty-first birthday wondered what he would do after he became sixty-five. His many letters, speeches, and conversations of the last ten years bore the hallmark of his life—"Things are moving along well and rapidly...."

As the 1970's began counting off years, Ligutti indulged in a bit of recollection and reflection. On October 21, 1972 he looked over the notes in his diary for 1952 and wrote, "This is a slow process but a safe and interesting one for me. Only a few facts or names I don't recall." In reviewing 1953 he noted that he never took "No" for a reply and added, "I hope I can keep the resolution to the end of my days." In November he was looking back at 1954 and was thinking of his service to the NCRLC. He wrote:

> Saw the exact wording of the Pope in my regard—very pleasantly complimentary. And I proudly admit I have not done harm but much good during the 25 years of service. Actually it has given me an opportunity to exercise the gifts God has given me and for which I am grateful. In looking over 1954 I wonder now how I covered the ground and how I stood the gaff. I was all alone and doing my own cooking and some fancy stuff at that. I took care of the yard and flowers and even reduced 20 pounds.

EPILOGUE

In October, 1957, Monsignor Ligutti was home again in Romans, Italy, to dedicate the new rectory he had helped finance. He had celebrated the fortieth anniversary of his ordination in Assisi a few weeks previously. He was in a reminiscent mood. Little did he realize at the time the trials and tribulations, the joys and successes, that would be his during the coming twenty-five years when he indulged in this review of his life. Even now, only God and the angel of the Resurrection would know when he would be called, when his body would be returned to the hallowed ground in Granger, and over his grave a monument would bear the words, "At Peace With The People I Love." On that October day in 1957 he wrote his own eulogy:

> Fifty some years have gone by since I was a little boy, splashing in the river, playing hide-and-go-seek among the willows, rousing the ire of the miller, or causing the scampering of ducks and geese, single file as they were led by some sweet, rosy-cheeked girl to pond or swampy pasture. Were they the best days? Yes, but what followed was best too. The other day I drove by the old building where I spent a year in most glorious discomfort. I was not quite nine, and since my village school only went up to the third grade inclusive, I had to go to a boarding school for the fourth and fifth. Being naturally bright and a most diligent and obedient student, I made two years in one (so did the other 80 who were my classmates). Years of discipline followed one another — some weeping but ever so much laughter.
>
> Two weeks ago I drove up to see an old cousin of mine, a dear little lady, over 80 and practically blind. She was so good to me when I spent part of my vacation with her.

She taught me how to climb mountains, how to pick mushrooms. She read lovely stories for me, and now she smiles and hugs me closely as she did so many years ago. Then I reached up, now I have to bend way low. If I should ever be efficient in kissing — and *that* I am not — that's where I learned it.

Were those the best years? Yes, but my adolescent years were filled to the brim with so many changes and new experiences. Yesterday I stopped by the railroad station where I boarded the train that started me on my way to America. I could still hear the train in the distance. I could see it approach me. Part of my heart seemed to have wished to stay there while tears were streaming down my cheeks. The hectic changes of language, way of life rushed onto me at beloved St. Ambrose College, where I quickly learned American ways.

Best days, indeed, with new friends, new views, a completely new world — But St. Mary's, Baltimore, came next. Only three years, but how precious those days were. At Trade Winds Inn, Cape Cod, on September 17-19, almost a dozen of us classmates met, to recall best days, to laugh at old jokes, to recognize old smiles on wrinkled faces 'midst grey or balding heads.

The anniversary I celebrated in Assisi brought back the days of my early priestly life — student, teacher, and now my pupils are celebrating their 25th anniversary of wedding or first Mass. Days of youthful worries about classes and vacations, degrees and scholarships. How could I ever rank those days as second when I recall that I won a shirt off Father Powers' back while playing Rummy?

The five years in Woodbine, Logan and Magnolia as a young pastor, plowing through the mud, digging myself out of snow drifts, where I learned to hunt and fish and love dogs, when I had once more the loving care of my mother, so solicitous and so stern, where I read the classics, where I attended and shared in community meetings and enterprises, where I learned the value of little people, of their power and goodness.

Those were only preludes to 15 years in Granger where so many activities almost swamped me, and yet opened new vistas, new horizons. There is never a degree in best days. If we were ever to sink to "better days," we should, with

Epilogue

the 4-H'ers, make the better best, the best better — and enjoy it. Over 20 years of work in the national and international field of rural life with ups and downs, ins and outs, *ante* and *post,* can certainly rank as highlights in anyone's life.

Better days coming? How could that be when the best has always been with me? How sad it must be to be in a fog and not to be able to enjoy it and the sunshine above it!

APPENDIX

At the Fourth International Congress on Rural Life in Santiago, Chile, from April 1-6, 1957, Monsignor Ligutti presented this paper:

Human Dignity and Economic Efficiency

Thesis:

Modern technology in industry, commerce, or agriculture functions more effectively and profitably in the production of goods and services when the human beings involved operate in keeping with their personal dignity, welfare of family, and when they can share in the ownership of the means of production and in its results.

This thesis will be dealt with in a somewhat Thomistic style:
Part 1. Objections, analysis and reply.
Part 2. Positive proofs.

It must be noted that the emphasis will be on the industrial side, but it is clearly understood that these principles apply to all human endeavors including agricultural production.

PART I
Objections — Analysis — Reply

First Objection

Videtur Quod: (It seems that)

The majority of human beings are not capable of planning for themselves or of using God's gifts to the greateset advantage. The great advances in the technological fields have taken place either under a system of slavery (e.g., building of pyramids) or quasi-servitude as at the beginning of the Industrial Revolution, (e.g., England and other countries).

Therefore it is necessary for a few to plan for greater material developments and the common good.

E Contra: Quoad Primum:

This objection contains a measure of truth and a measure of falsity. Giving it a semblance of truth is the fact that pronounced accidental differences are to be found among men — differences in knowledge, justice and strength.

> We must needs admit that in the primitive state there would have been some inequality . . . as regards the soul, there would have been inequality as to righteousness and knowledge (St. T., Ia, q. 96, a. 3).

To deny this would be to fall into the false equalitarianism of Atheistic Communism. These differences, far from representing defects in the plan of God or in the order of nature, are necessary that the beauty of order might shine forth from creation.

> The cause of inequality could be on the part of God . . . so that the beauty of order would the more shine forth among men." (*Ibid.*)

The gifts of the superior man should be used for the benefit of others.

> If one man surpassed another in knowledge and virtue, this would not have been fitting unless these gifts conduced to the benefit of others (S.T., Ia, q. 96, a. 4).

The legitimate inference from the fact of individual differences is the one made by the Angelic Doctor, namely, that men will have diverse responsibilities in society. To men of talent and genius will fall the responsibility of envisioning new industries, new possibilities in agricultural production, new uses for agricultural products. It will be the responsibility of men of magnanimity and courage to risk capital and to carry new projects through initial difficulties. It will be their duty to organize, if need be, their weaker brothers into such groups as the Cooperatives. From the fact of differences it follows also that land and the instruments of production will be distributed proportionately, and not according to strict arithmetic equality. Land will better serve the common good when the more enterprising have more, the less enterprising, less.

This in no way admits the contention of the objection that the majority of human beings are not capable of planning for themselves. Such a contention is not borne out by the facts, and it is, moreover, unsound philosophically. In virtue of his very rationality man participates in the Divine government of things. Even as God sees things in terms of the Good, man also by the light of reason has a participated insight into the purposes behind things. By his reason he can ordain things to an end. In a word, he is radically capable of planning; and we cannot question this capability without questioning his very nature . . . .

Too often we do not see all that God has put in a human being, and because we lack vision and love we abandon much of humanity to fire and ashes, to worms and rottenness. I repeat, there are no hopeless human beings.

I care not for the Pyramids, the Arch of Ctesiphon, the hanging gardens of Babylon, the Acropolis of Athens, the Roman Forum erected by slaves, driven by inhuman masters. I prefer the artistic simplicity of a wayside shrine built by free men and women in fulfillment of a vow — where little children bring primroses and violets as offerings from pure hearts. No matter what material progress is made at the expense of human personality, it counts for nought. Man is the image and likeness of God here on earth; to debase man is to debase God.

If some human beings seem hopeless it is because some of us have neither the intelligence nor the love to extend a helping hand and make God's infinite and universal love visible.

The battle for the dignity of man has not yet been won. Particularly as regards industry, the present danger is that man will be exploited in a more subtle way by the economic system. Today the problem might be phrased in the following terms: May the good of the individual be subordinated to economic organization for the sake of high production? May we allow man's spirit to be tyrannized by the "demon of organization," or by the economic will of a single entrepreneur. In answer we say that the moral good cannot be subordinated to the economic good. Moreover the essential good of the individual (*finis operis*) cannot be subordinated to the purposes (*finis operantis*) of the head of the State or of an economic enterprise whether his objective be a monument, an empire, or an economic utopia. Pope Pius XII has made this problem the subject of his 1952 and 1953 Christmas addresses. In the earlier addresses he writes:

> In some countries, the modern state is becoming a gigantic administrative machine. It extends its influences over almost every phase of life. It would bring under its administration the entire gamut of political, economic, social and intellectual life from birth to death.

And again:

> Here may be recognized the origin and source of that phenomenon which is submerging modern man under its tide of anguish: his depersonalization. In large measure his identity and name have been taken from him; in many of the more important activities of life he has been reduced to a mere material object of society, while society itself has been transformed into an impersonal system and into a cold organization of force.

Years earlier Pope Pius XI saw the problem in an earlier stage: "dead matter leaves the factory ennobled and transformed, where men are corrupted and degraded."

Since men differ accidentally, a difference existing in the state of original justice and intensified by Sin, it is necessary that they be brought into organization for the common good. However, the head of the State or of any economic enterprise, must procure the common good without violence to the good of the individual. Any excess in this respect, in which the spirit of technocracy consists, involves the danger of violating the essential rights of man. Material gain may not be gotten at such a price.

Second Objection

Videtur Quod: (It seems that)

In the field of agricultural production some of the most deplorable examples of under-production and poor land use are to be found where many people own small parcels of land and each family produces for its own needs on an independent basis. Therefore, in order to make better use of the land and secure better production, large, efficient land holdings operated either by private citizens or by the government are a necessity.

E Contra: Quoad Secundum:

The above statement as to inefficiency of production is somewhat true with due exceptions (e.g. Japan). The general conclusions however are not true, because other remedies can be applied for the achievement of better land use and greater production.

It is to be noticed that both the collectivistic and hyper-capitalistic solutions are based upon the same assumption; i.e., only an oligarchy, private or public, can perform well and efficiently. This has been dealt with *ad primum*.

As to the conclusions of the second part: *Minifundia* are even more harmful than *latifundia* or the collectivization of land use. These are two extremes: It's Scylla and Charybdis. However, in *medio stat virtus*.

There is another way of assuring efficient land use and fuller production; i.e., private ownership and operation on an economic unit basis with the assistance of public and private authority and free co-operatives in management, production, credit and sale of goods. All this implies a change in traditional patterns of land tenure, inheritance laws, taxation, etc.

It requires real scientific studies of land and water availability and productivity. Land use specialists like Dr. Bandini and Dr. Wolf Ladejinsky will explain in detail these scientific and democratic processes as carried out in some countries. *Ab esse ad posse valet illatio*. If it has been done, it is possible.

To achieve ownership of property and proper management is no easy task. As social relations become more and more complicated, the problem of adequate arrangements, of checks and balances demand intelligent and conscientious actions.

It is for men of goodwill to find a satisfactory and a practical solution and where there is a will, there is a way.

Third Objection

Videtur Quod: (It seems that)

Much time is needed for the education of great masses of people steeped in age-long traditions, unaware of their own powers and possibilities. Too fast a change brings about revolutions and injustices. Furthermore, to have such social and economic changes occur, there is a need for technicians, sociologists, economists, financial experts and financing on a large scale, plus honest political leaders and the cooperation of all men and organizations of goodwill. All of this at the present time is a practical impossibility. Therefore, this is not the opportune time.

E Contra: Quoad Tertium:

The premise concludes to the difficulty of the task but not to its impossibility. The magnitude of the task is admitted. The moral or physical impossibility of working it out is denied. As someone has said: "The difficult can be accomplished; for the impossible, give me time."

If we compare this grave difficulty to a mountain over which we must pass to reach a certain position, this is my advice: Let us try to go through the mountain directly. If we cannot go through it, let us go over it. If we cannot go through or over it, let us go around it. If we cannot go around it, through it, or over it, then let us start walking in the opposite direction all the way around the earth and come up on the other side of the mountain.

Where there is a will, there is a way. Where there is no will, a thousand and one excuses can be adduced. One of the commonest objections ever heard is from a worn-out disk of a record player: "It takes money; it takes dollars, and we have none."

A very influential labor leader, Mr. Serafino Romualdi, writes: "It takes will to do it; if money is needed, it always comes."

I repeat, "Where there is a will, there is a way."

The faith in God and man as found in the minds and hearts of the Latin races, their imaginative and loving character mingled with the tremendous abilities and endurance powers of the Indios makes the difficult task a challenge, but a very attainable goal. It can be done. Shall this great unit of the human race, these children of the Roman Catholic Apostolic Church sit idly by while a determined group of atheistic materialists moved not by a godly ideology set about for the conquest and enslavement of tomorrow's world leader — Latin America?

In a given historical situation, however, it must be admitted that man has not always lived up to his capabilities for self-direction, since, de facto, he has failed in many instances to plan properly. This is not due, we repeat, to any natural incapacity. Rather it results from lack of any adequately organic organization of society on the one hand and, on the other, from failure to educate members of society in economic matters, failure to provide them with the means of economic advancement and failure to encourage and reward.

On the entirely reasonable assumption, then, that religion and education will be fostered, most men will be found capable of ownership. In the United States there is not wanting the manpower needed to supply the family-sized farms, small trades and crafts and industrial establishments that the nation's resources can provide. Moreover, the widespread hunger for land and productive property throughout the world is evidence that most men have not lost the spirit of initiative. God has implanted in the heart of man a desire for creative work and for security through productive property in order that he may work in a manner consonant with his rational nature and provide for himself and family. Again and again, the popes have called for a wider — far wider .. distribution of productive property (Leo XIII, R.N.). If in God's providence property is necessary for man that he may live in security and honest independence, then may we not expect that the average man will be endowed by God with sufficient knowledge and virtue to manage at least a small plot of land or business? How can the popes, who have always in mind the common good, advocate a wide distribution of property in land and in the arts and crafts, unless they are convinced that men, generally, are capable of effectively using this for the common good? The Pope's plea for property for the masses is a vote of confidence in them.

I do not desire to be facetious in such serious discussion, but I cannot refrain from relating a story of an African chief who came to one of our missionaries and asked to be received into the Church. After brief questioning the padre discovered that the chief, 50 years of age, was surrounded by 10 wives in his domain. He was told, of course that he must choose one and dismiss the other nine. The goodly chief reflected a bit and came up with the following compromise: "Give me a little time. This is not the opportune time to dismiss the nine faithful wives. I shall gladly give up one wife every five years. By the time I am 100 years old, the problem will be settled."

Russia waited too long, China was not in a hurry, the Slavic countries discussed with leisure and . . . what were the results?

What will Latin America do to solve its agrarian questions? We know the answer: God wills it! And God wills it *quam primum*.

PART II

Thesis:

"Modern technology in industry, commerce, or agriculture functions more effectively and profitably in the production of goods and services when the human beings involved operate in keeping with their personal dignity, welfare of family, and the common good, and when they can share in the ownership of the means of production and in its results."

We come now to the positive side of proving the thesis, from:
 I. Theological arguments and papal pronouncements.
 II. Testimony of Catholic authorities.
 III. Testimony of non-Catholic sociologists and economists.
 IV. Testimony of industrialists.

I. Theological Arguments and Papal Pronouncements

The earth and the whole world were created by God for the benefit of man, poor and rich, ignorant and wise, Jew and Gentile, white and otherwise. All the material goods of creation in their almost infinite possibilities were intended by God to be used by all men as a means of developing human personality to lead and enjoy a good life on earth, and thereby reach an eternal good life.

Pius XII, *La Solennita della Pentecoste* (Cronin, p. 469).

> Every man, as a living being gifted with reason, has in fact from nature the fundamental right to make use of the material goods of the earth, while it is left to the will of man and to the juridical statutes of nations to regulate in greater detail the actuation of this right. This individual right cannot in any way be suppressed, even by other clear and undisputed rights over material goods.

It is therefore incumbent upon persons and nations gifted with a true Christian culture to develop a satisfactory standard of material living, so as to fulfill God's will. This is desirable in a special way for the tillers of the soil.

Leo XIII, *Rerum Novarum* (Cronin, *Catholic Social Principles*, pp. 465-66):

> We have seen, in fact, that the whole question under consideration cannot be settled effectually unless it is assumed and established as a principle, that the right of private property must be regarded as sacred. Wherefore, the law ought to favor this right and, so far as it can, see that the largest possible number among the masses of the population prefer to own property.
>
> But if the productive activity of the multitude can be stimulated by the hope of acquiring some property in land, it will gradually come to pass that, with the difference between extreme wealth and extreme penury removed, one class will become neighbor to the other. Moreover, there will surely be a greater abundance of the things which the earth produced. For when men know they are working on what belongs to them, they work with far greater eagerness and diligence.
>
> Nay, in a word, they learn to love the land cultivated by their own hands, whence they look not only for food but for some measure of abundance for themselves and their dependents. All can see how much this willing eagerenss contributes to an abundance of produce and the wealth of a nation.

Pope Pius XII:

> There can be no incompatibility between a realism, healthfully nourished by facts, statistics and economic laws, and a social order quite legitimately involved with the aspiration for more justice and humanity.

II. Testimony of Catholic Authorities

Most Rev. Robert E. Lucey, S.T.D., archbishop of San Antonio, Texas:

> It seems to me that when a man's work is not in harmony with his personal dignity, the welfare of his family and the common good, a conflict is automatically and perhaps unconsciously set up. Man cannot be efficient in his labor unless his heart is in it.

Most Rev. Peter W. Bartholome, D.D., bishop of St. Cloud, Minnesota:

> To me it seems that more effective and profitable production of goods would ultimately result by taking into consideration the dignity of the human person and the welfare of the family and the common good.

Mr. Edward Skillin, editor of *Commonweal* Magazine:

> Apparently the thinking in the minds of the big executives of such companies as General Electric, Dupont, International Business Machines and, presumably, Eastman Kodak, stems from the experiment of several years ago at Hawthorne. The productivity of the group went up and stayed up from the very fact that they were the objects of special attention.

Rev. Theodore V. Purcell, S.J., assistant professor of psychology and industrial relations, Loyola University, Chicago:

> Because even business and labor leaders are coming gradually to see that greater productivity, worker satisfaction, cooperation, and so forth, are increased by better "Human Relations."

Rev. Leo C. Brown, S.J., Institute of Social Order, St. Louis, Missouri:

> People cooperate freely only when they are treated as persons, when their personal needs and aspirations are recognized. As a person, man needs self-respect. As a social being he needs the respect of others.
>
> The success of the profit-sharing plan at Quality Castings Company, which I studied and reported in *Social Order* some years ago, resulted not merely from the increased earnings which the plan made possible, but from the thoroughly democratic atmosphere which prevailed throughout the plant.

Dr. A. H. Clemens, associate professor of sociology, director of marriage counseling, Catholic University of America, Washington, D.C.:

> We have mistakenly thought that money is THE great incentive; this has been proved an error by a number of studies in industrial sociology.

Br. Gerald Schnepp, S.M., St. Mary's University, San Antonio, Texas:

> Persons who have a share in the enterprise will take more interest in it as a personal project rather than merely as a means of making money by working for someone else.

Dr. C. J. Nuesse, dean of social studies, Catholic University of America, Washington, D.C.:

> This would seem to be the implication of the growing literature of industrial sociology and the explanation of the changing practices of industry, probably farther advanced at home than abroad but under way everywhere.

Dr. Elmer Sauer, Soil Conservation Service, University of Illinois, Champaign, Illinois:
> I feel the high production per man in American agriculture is largely the result of free enterprise and our system of family farming, with the farmer as an owner (or a cooperator with the landlord) sharing in the products of his labor and being able to push ahead in accordance with his abilities, ambition and efforts.

Rev. Thomas Harte, C.SS.R., Ph.D., instructor, Catholic University of America:
> There is from the nature of things a direct correlation between effective recognition of the basic demands of human nature and man's capacity to produce efficiently and profitably.

III. Testimony of Non-Catholic Sociologists and Economists

At times we are given the impression that material efficiency is only possible when production is done on a mass scale with bigger and bigger machines, with more and more men on the production line acting as automatons. The United States certainly has acted on the supposition and is still largely relying on the colossal for efficiency in material production.

Nature seems to abhor the mastodonic. The large, prehistoric creatures did not survive. They are known now only through their fossilized bones and footprints.

The failure in the collectivization of agriculture will be explained by other speakers. It has proven to be the Achilles' heel of Communism. Large capitalistic private enterprise in agriculture, as wheat or corn or fruit ranches, sooner or later come to an inglorious end. It may take two or three generations but, somehow or other, at the end, history repeats itself.

On the day he inaugurated the River Rouge assembly plant for automobiles, the great modern industrialist, Henry Ford, is quoted as saying: "There is my biggest mistake."

There is a measure in all things. St. Peter's Basilica is a great monument to human ability and deep faith, but let us not forget that the same century which saw its erection saw also the rise of Protestantism.

One of the most prominent agricultural economists in the world is Dr. T. W. Schultz of Chicago University. He has been very helpful to me in the preparation of this paper. I shall quote from a lecture delivered by him at Cornell University, Ithaca, New York, August of 1956, contained in Bulletin 35, New York State School of Industrial and Labor Relations. The general title of the lecture was "The Economic Test in Latin America":
> We are, therefore, compelled to introduce a "working rule" based on a belief about the unknown facts. Our proposed rule presupposes that in poor countries, over the range of available observations, the rate of returns on effort and capital allocated (1)

to develop the quality of its people who engage in economic activity, and (2) to raise the level of the productive arts, has been and is greater than it has been and is on such allocations to increase the quantity of reproducible capital goods. . . . .

In a personal letter written to me December 19, 1956, he has this to say:

The deeper issues may be put into focus by:

1. The findings that ½ or more of the growth in production is not explained by additional land, labor and capital of the conventional types.

2. The unexplained part is coming in large part from what is happening to people favorable to production and from additions to our stock of useful knowledge.

3. In "what is happening to people" one must take account not only of such obvious things as better food, health, housing but also, the "values" which people live by.

4. Among the "values" which a people (have to) live by which bear upon your "materialistic thesis of more production!" I would put (1) being "free" and having the "right" to move about, change jobs, migrate, (2) having social mobility and (3) getting off to a more equal start as children and as young adults in health and education and increasingly in travel (equality of opportunity takes in much more than our good old progressive income and inheritance taxes).

On the negative side much can be said. Where people are "tied" to the land, or held there by "debts" or "obligations" to landowners, or by lack of education, or information about other opportunities, "output" is impaired to say nothing about more important aspects of human welfare. Where people are "pushed" about, denied an opportunity to improve their lot, treated as 2nd class citizens as are so many Indians in South America, of what is best in man in determining output is lost. Where wealth and power are mainly in the hands of a few families, an effective system of production is precluded because the many talents and skills of a people cannot be developed and brought into play.

It has taken Dr. Schultz not a few years of deep and searching study to come to these conclusions. We reached them by deduction; he, by induction. Both are valid and logical processes. Please note all the points he makes. It's an economist, a social scientist who is writing. I should place his brief remarks and words in one column and on a parallel a few sentences from the pronouncements of our popes and Catholic social scientists. You would see at a glance the perfect unanimity of thought. Well has His Holiness Pius XII defined science as "the progressive knowledge of God."

May I place an emphasis on some of Dr. Schultz's observations:

The hope and possibility of rising above conditions of birth is a great force in world progress. Let us not forget the phrase, "nothing good can come out of Nazareth." But God chose a humble maiden from that hilly and stony village to be the Mother of the Savior.

To be tied to the land or held there by debts, obligations or lack of education is not good for the person and not good for the nation. To be propertyless land workers does not bring about efficiency in agricultural production.

I have traveled over the greater portion of the earth. The highest agricultural production is to be found in free countries. It is to be found where the family owns an economic unit of land; where the tillers of the soil have a measure of know-how; where they have joined producing, buying and selling forces with their neighbors; where good wages and working conditions are present for the day laborers. There is a world-wide adage: "The oxen fatten by the sight of the master."

Harold D. Lasswell, professor of law and political science, Yale University, New Haven, Connecticut:

> The economic failure of slave labor camps and of slave labor plantations affords a classic example. Another major example is afforded by the difficulties in managing a modern labor force without full recognition of collective bargaining.

Mr. William H. Whyte, *Fortune* Magazine, New York:

> Technology is an extension of man's effort, not something in itself; and the more the individual is able to *fulfill himself* through the vehicle of technology that much more dynamic it will be.

Mr. Theodore Kreps, head of the business school, Stanford University:

> Your thesis, I feel certain, is valid. In our TNEC Hearings on Technology (Vol. XXX), I documented the proposition that technology was a blessing only if guided and developed by moral forces higher and wider than personal or material gain.

Dr. Raymond Miller, public relations consultant, lecturer, Graduate School of Business Administration, Harvard University:

> Because man is not a mere animal.

John H. Davis, lecturer, Graduate School of Business Administration, Harvard University, Boston Massachusetts:

> The recent report by the National Planning Association on the operations of Firestone Rubber Company in Liberia presents a case study of this type.

Dr. Elton Mayo, professor of industrial research, Graduate School of Business Administration, Harvard University, has written many books and directed many a research study in the industrial field. Two of his books worth studying are:

The Human Problems of an Industrial Civilization, Boston, Massachusetts, Division of Research, Graduate School of Business Administration, Harvard University, Second Edition, 1946. 194 pp.

The Social Problems of an Industrial Civilization, Boston, Massachusetts, Division of Research, Graduate School of Business Administration, Harvard University, 1945. 150 pp.

The former describes in detail the Hawthorne experiments. The latter is more analytical from an historical and philosophical viewpoint. He points out that certain actions, tendencies and ideological proposals stem from long discarded concepts, vid. of Hobbes and Ricardo: (p. 40 ff.)

In Ricardo's time, the influence of Hobbes, and beyond Hobbes that of Rousseau and the theory of a social contract, were still very strong. This theory, which still finds expression in unexpected places, regarded the life of natural man as "solitary, poor, nasty, brutish and short."

Clearly then the presupposition of scarcity lends support to the conception of competition for limited means of subsistence — especially perhaps in markets that are impersonal and in foreign trade and exchanges.

For many centuries the rabble hypothesis, in one or other form, has bedeviled all our thinking on matters involving law, government, or economics. From this theory is evolved the conviction of need for a Leviathan, a powerful State, which by the exercise of a unique authority shall impose order on the rabble. So that in these days many of our liberals and our lawyers have come to enunciating doctrines that are only with difficulty distinguished from the pronouncements of a Hitler or a Mussolini.

The question we should ask ourselves today is this: Must the gospels and the popes or Hobbes and Ricardo furnish a Christian civilization with the basic philosophy of action in matters economic and social?

IV. Testimony of Industrialists

One could multiply the testimony of highly productive, efficient and successful business enterprises on the subject. I must confine myself to but a few.

Dr. C. T. Carney, Des Moines, Iowa, who was the coal mine operator in my own rural parish, says:

> Another reason for this country's success is that human beings are allowed to operate industry in "keeping with their personal dignity, family welfare and the common good." Modern technology, capital, just labor relations, all are a part of the plan, which is proving so fruitful.

Francis A. Kutish, department of economics, Iowa State College, Ames, Iowa:

> In the Del-Mar, Virginia broiler area, the Armour-Chesapeake Broiler Farm (a corporation) found that to get the best results

they needed to organize their set-up approximating the family farm. When they had help on a straight hired basis they didn't get near the results as when they set up a house for a family beside each 40,000 capacity broiler house. The family has the job of raising the broilers in that house, and the responsibility that goes with that house. In the first few weeks broiler raising takes much closer supervision than in the last few weeks of the growing period. The family (husband and wife) can devote full attention to those birds then — something they wouldn't do if they punched a time clock. Then when the broilers are sold the family is given a week's vacation while a gang cleans up the house in preparation for another brood.

T. K. Krug, president, Bell Bakeries, Inc., Jamaica, New York:

As mechanization and the era of complex mass production developed management ignored the question of individual attitude, or was oblivious of its importance, and sought efficiency through operational devices and patterns; it was the day of Bidaut, Taylor, and the other time-and-motion engineers. Today, there is still a tendency in management groups to rationalize the problem of human attitude in the pleasant dream of the completely automatic factory, with "people problems" completely eliminated.

Today, management stands humbly before the towering fact of the human personality. Here is the problem — and the opportunity.

Man does not live by bread alone. He has a right to expect that he will be accepted and respected as an individual, that such individual talents and abilities as he may possess will be recognized, and that his natural desire to express his individuality will not be deliberately thwarted or denied.

Ben Sklar, agronomist, farm equipment division, tractor group, Allis-Chalmers Manufacturing Company, Milwaukee, Wisconsin:

Progress can only proceed from personal dignity. This concept is of greatest importance. Personal dignity is a God-given human right. It produces within the individual a sense of responsibility, initiative, thrift and courage.

Justice on the part of the employer requires justice on the part of the employee.

Ernest Dale, "Labor-Management Cooperation to Increase Productivity," American Management Association Production Series, Number 175, 1948, pp. 25-26:

Unions must go beyond collective bargaining and do all in their power to make their employer a successful businessman. Our free enterprise system cannot continue with unsuccessful and profitless business. It is the obligation of unions at all times to promote greater productivity and efficiency in production.

"The Improvement of Human Relations in the Undertaking," *International Labour Review*, LXX, 304, September-October, 1954, pp. 299-300:

> From the Belgian National Committee to the Tenth International Management Congress: "An undertaking is intended to be the servant of humanity and should never make humanity its slave."

Silverstein, Saul M. "Management as a Universal Language," in *The Office: Its Changing Functions and Structure*, American Management Association Office Management Series, Number 139, 1955, pp. 37-44:

> The responsibility of managers throughout the world is to recognize the fact that people are the key to all progress and that people are dynamic, not static, forces. As such, they can be counted upon to change constantly and, at times, become difficult. But we must never lose our faith in them. This requires humility, tolerance, and, most important of all, understanding.

Saul M. Silverstein, a graduate of the Massachusetts Institute of Technology, has been president of the Rogers Corporation since 1946.

C. G. Frantz, president, Apex Electrical Manufacturing Co., Cleveland, Ohio, "The Joint Development of Production Standards," *Labor-Management Cooperation for Increased Productivity*, American Management Association Production Series, Number 175, 1948, pp. 11-13.

Mr. Frantz explains the relations between the rise of Communism and the cultivation of its fertile field through social injustices:

> We believe that Communistic effectiveness would be greatly lessened by constructive work to harmonize present conflicting practices. It lies within our power to accomplish this, and to do so would be to destroy the fertile fields in which the Communists sow their seeds.

In a pamphlet issued by Standard Oil Company "*A Generation of Industrial Peace*," Standard Oil Company, Room 1626, 30 Rockefeller Plaza, New York 20, New York, 63 pp., I find the following statement on p. 45:

> What is appreciated by the employee:
> 1. Economic security
> 2. A chance to better oneself
> 3. To be treated like a person
> 4. To feel one's job is important to the community

E. I. du Pont de Nemours & Company, Wilmington, Delaware:

> We will say that the degree of opportunity for personal development available in America is in itself largely responsible for our unprecedented technological development.

General Electric Company, New York, New York:

> We have long recognized both the material and spiritual benefits employees expect from their association with the Company — good

wages, good health and welfare benefits, good working conditions, good supervisors, steady work, a chance to get ahead, full information, being treated with dignity and respect, recognition for their accomplishments, and general job satisfaction. We strive diligently to "do right voluntarily" in all of these matters in all ways and at all times.

Eastman Kodak Company, Rochester, New York:

I am sure that all members of our Company's management would agree with your thesis and the effectiveness of the industrial operation depends in great part on a proper consideration for the interests of the individual.

Without having actual facts at hand, I think it is safe to say that labor turnover is less, employee dissatisfaction is less, and individual effectiveness greater where a concern for individual rights and interests characterizes the management of a company's affairs. I believe our experience at Kodak tends to confirm this.

The September-October 1956 issue of *Operare* edited in Genoa, Italy, by Signor Vittorio Vaccari, published by UCID (Unione Cristiana Imprenditori Dirigenti), contains a contribution by His Eminence, Cardinal Siri and a very enlightening article by Professor Vaccari. It is interesting to note that he quoted the example of North American industries to prove his point. If Europe wants economic efficiency and success, it must adopt a policy of human relations efficiency, in all the sectors of production, and in all the orders of sale down to the consumer.

Rensis Likert, director, University of Michigan Institute for Social Research, "Motivation and Increased Productivity," *Management Record*, p. 1):

The critical weaknesses in the scientific management approach, of course, are the resentments, hostilities, and adverse motivational and attitudinal reactions which it tends to evoke. In my judgment these hostilities and unfavorable attitudes stem from powerful motives which scientific management has ignored in its theoretical basis as well as in the day-to-day operating procedures it has developed.

Harold J. Ruttenberg, president, Stardrill-Keystone Company, "Humanation," *Management Record*, XVIII, No. 11, November, 1956, p. 2:

Humanation results not only in higher living standards and greater profits, but — more important — in new dimensions for the lives of the participants that (1) give a greater meaning to their personalities as human beings and (2) add to the dignity of the individual.

The underlying philosophy of humanation is summed up in this slogan: "People are Our Most Important Concern."

Jervis J. Babb, chairman of the board, Lever Brothers Company, "Business Responsibility for Public Policy," *Iowa Business Digest*, XXVII, No. 12, December, 1956, p. 3:

Perhaps the strangest thing about the professional manager, as we know him today, is that he is not working primarily to get rich.

One of the most interesting organizations in the United States is the Council of Profit-Sharing Industries. Mr. Joseph Meier, its executive secretary, has furnished me personally with a number of testimonials and statements as to the effectiveness of the profit sharing practice in the efficient production process:

Gwylim Price, chairman of the board, Westinghouse Manufacturing Company, Springfield, Mass., March 3, 1950:

> The job of creating capitalists is one of the most important jobs American business management faces today. There simply are not enough Americans who believe in the system. One way to give employees a stake in the business is through profit sharing. I believe wholeheartedly in this method.

Thomas C. Cochran, *Harvard Business Review,* 1956, quoting Clarence Francis, chairman of the board, General Foods, *Time,* 1952:

> It is ironic that Americans, the most advanced people technically, mechanically and industrially, should have waited until a comparatively recent period to inquire into the most promising single source of productivity: namely the human will to work!

James F. Lincoln, chairman of the board, The Lincoln Electric Company, and trustee of the Council:

> We (as a nation) are sitting in the driver's seat at the present time for one reason only: We can produce more economically than any other nation in the world. If that disappears, we disappear with it. There is only one way that I know of that this advance in cooperation and increase in productivity is going to be possible, and that is by some system wherein all desire and want to work together for a common end.

Franklin J. Lunding, chairman of the board, Jewel Tea Co., Inc., *Sharing a Business*:

> What business needs today is not a return to anything, but a bold new approach toward a broader, more intelligent sharing of all the rewards and satisfactions of our competitive enterprise systems.

Henry L. Nunn, *The Whole Man Goes to Work,* Harpers, New York, 1953, p. 197:

> Workers who are treated as partners, who in fact are partners in production, develop a new sense of responsibility and dignity that benefits our democratic concept of the inherent rights of man.

Walter H. Wheeler, president, Pitney-Bowes, Inc.:

> Profit sharing is one of the best ways I know to bridge the gap between labor and management. Here are some of the results that profit sharing companies have experienced:

Notable increase in efficiency and productivity.
Labor turnover sharply reduced.
Reduction in tardiness and absenteeism.
Better care of equipment.
Increase in number and quality of suggestions from employees.
Decrease in grievances.
Reductions in reject and salvage material.
A waiting list of high caliber applicants.
Increased earnings for stockholders.
Reduction in prices of goods manufactured.
Employee zeal for the success of the company.

CONCLUSION

It is undoubtedly the desire of all right thinking men to produce efficiently both for self service and as a contribution to the common good. It is also evident that material efficiency is not achieved very often and that in certain places and at certain times the results are pitiful.

May I suggest the three chief points for observation and study in the analysis of material inefficiency. Examine:

1. The raw material — minerals deficient in basic qualities — soil that is not fertile, lack of water, etc., etc.
2. Production technique; i.e. the machine itself, tilling practices, poor seeds and fertilizer, ignorance of disease prevention, etc., etc.
3. The men who work — the leaders and the common workers. Unless know-how, interest, dignity, participation, coordination, cooperation and mutual respect exist, it is useless to look for material efficiency. There are no shortcuts, no slight of hand tricks in bringing about efficient production.

I repeat the thesis:

Modern technology in industry, commerce, or agriculture functions more effectively and profitably in the production of goods and services when the human beings involved are allowed to operate in keeping with their personal dignity, welfare of family, and the common good, and when they can share in the ownership of the means of production and in its results.

This thesis is true because it fulfills God's intention in man's creation, because it exhibits Christ's love for mankind, and because it furnishes all of us with the assurance of a good life here on earth and a good life for eternity.

INDEX

Abad, Fr. José M., 225
Agar, Herbert, 31
Agrimissio, 200, 249-251, 262, 290-291
Alexander, Rep. John, 36-37
Alter, Archbishop Karl, 143
America, 21, 39
American Catholic Sociological Society, 65
American Committee on Italian Migration, 144-147
American Ecclesiastical Review, 227
Andrews, Stanley, 150
Ansaldi, C.S., Fr. P., 144
Antigonish Movement, 219
Anti-Yankeeism, Latin America, 150, 153-154, 166-167
Antoniutti, Cardinal Ildebrando, 207, 208, 284
Arand, S.S., Fr. Louis, 9, 12
Arizona Highways, 79
Arkfeld, S.V.D., Bishop Leo, 200

Babb, Jervis J., 311-312
Babcock, Bishop Alan, 186
Badelli, Msgr. Giovanni, 99
Baer, George, 31
Baggio, Archbishop Sebastiano, 114, 162, 163
Baker, Msgr. Karl, 286-287
"Ballad of Sir Andrew Barton," 7
Barbieri, Archbishop Rodolfo, 157
Barnes, Dr. Roswell, 168
Barry, O.S.B., Fr. Colman, 68

Bartholome, Bishop Peter, 55, 56, 61, 79, 81, 213, 304
Bayer, Msgr. John, 222
Begin, Bishop Floyd, 219-220
Belknap, Fr. Arthur, 9
Benelli, Archbishop Giovanni, 281-282, 284, 289
Bennett, Dr. and Mrs. Henry, 100, 181-182
Bergan, Archbishop Gerald, 43-44, 56, 58, 63, 83, 94, 208
Bernier, Archbishop Paolo, 161
Berutti, O.P., Fr. Christopher, 210
Biondi, Joseph, 24, 36
Biondi, Virgil, 36
Blomjous, Bishop Joseph, 209
Bonardelli, Eugenio, 120, 125
Bonomelli, Dr. Emilio, 102, 161, 207, 210, 216, 224, 241, 246, 256, 257, 262, 289, 292
Borsoldi, Ralph, 31
Boyd-Orr, Sir John, 222, 232, 239-240
Boylan, Bishop John, 15
Brattgard, Dr. Helge, 288
Bresma, Caldera, 263
Brewster, Sen. and Mrs. Owen, 183
Broadley, Sir Herbert, 241
Brooke, Sen. Edward, 173
Brouillard, C.S.C., Br. Constant, 113
Brown, S.J., Fr. Leo, 304
Bruce, Frank, 231, 240
Bruce, Sir Stanley, 232-233, 255
Bryan, Rep. William Jennings, 7
Buckley, S.M., Fr. Joseph, 213-214

Bunn, S.J., Fr. Edward, 173
Burke, Ambrose, 5
Byrnes, Msgr. James, 54, 56-57, 58, 161, 206

Caffrey, Jefferson, 189
Caggiano, Bishop Antonio, 93
Callegari, Cardinal Giuseppe, 1
Camara, Archbishop Helder, 155, 209, 213, 221, 223
Cana wine project, 281
Carboni, Archbishop Romolo, 52, 93, 105, 106, 165, 187, 201, 236, 240-241, 245, 247
Cardijn, Cardinal Joseph, 89, 210, 211
Cardosa, Dr. Roberval, 156
CARE, 192
Carey, Graham, 218
Caritas Internationalis, 98, 123, 159, 222, 286-287
Carney, Dr. C., 308
Caro, Cardinal José, 163
Carroll, Msgr. Howard, 134-136, 139-141, 258
Carroll, Msgr. Walter, 99
Cash, John, 5
Cassulo, Archbishop Andrea, 179
Castellano, Bishop Mario, 209, 210, 217
Cather, Willa, 40
Catholic Bulletin, The, 279-280
Catholic Relief Services, *See* National Catholic Welfare Conference
Catholic Social Principles, 303
Catholic Worker, 91
Catholics and FAO, 236
Cazzanigna, Fr. E., 112
Cento, Cardinal Fernando, 209, 211, 213, 214, 220
Central Verein, 52
Chamri, Archbishop Pietro, 184
Chicago *Daily News*, 105
Christian Farmer, 61
Church in the Modern World, The, 151, 218, 225, 226, 227
Cicognani, Cardinal Amleto, 91, 219-220, 239, 247
Ciriani, Msgr. Cio-Batta, 1
Civilta Catholica, 214

Clancey, Msgr. Thomas, 193
Clavel, Archbishop Thomas, 161, 193
Clemens, Dr. A., 304
Cleveland, President Grover, 1
Cochran, Thomas 312
Cogo, C.S., Fr. Joseph, 144
Commonweal, 21, 39, 91, 304
Community Development through Adult Education and Cooperatives, 219
Concha, Cardinal Luis, 160
Confalonieri, Cardinal Carlo, 208, 213, 261, 281, 282, 284, 289
Congressional Record, 36, 136
Cooperative League of America, 88
Corrigan, Robert, 162
Country Beautiful, 78-79, 81
Coutinho, Fr. Boavida, 219, 261, 291
Coyle, O.F.M., Fr. Patrick, 103, 185
Cram, Ralph, 187
CROP, 70, 102, 112, 187
Cummings, Fr. James, 27
Cushing, Cardinal Richard, 133, 136, 143, 171, 215

Dachauer, S.J., Fr. Alban, 61
Dadaglio, Archbishop Luigi, 269
Daily, S.J., Fr. Coleman, 291
Dale, Ernest, 309
Daly, O.P., Bishop Edward, 63, 80, 81, 83, 141-143, 161, 206, 207, 240, 241
Damiano, Archbishop Celestine, 193
D'Ascenzi, Msgr. Giovanni, 82, 271
Das-Gupta, A., 252
David, Dean, 167
Davis, John, 307
Day, Dorothy, 91
Day, Msgr. Victor, 20
de Alba, Dr. William, 160
De Asarta, Count Sandro, 187
Death Comes for the Archbishop, 40
de Gasperi, Premier Alcidé, 92
Dell'Acqua, Cardinal Angelo, 162, 224, 246
Deming, Fr. Robert, 285
Des Moines *Register*, 21-22, 33
Tribune, 21, 33, 40, 44, 49
de Souza, Joao, 108, 155-156
Dickens, Charles, 4

di Clauzetto, Tonolino, 1
Diekmann, O.S.B., Fr. Godfrey, 73, 213
Di Lorenzo, Ross, 280
Dineen, Fr. Michael, 76-81, 196
di Tonolino, Giacomo, 1
Dodd, Dr. Norris, 109, 241, 247, 253-254
Doddridge Farm, 74
Donanzan, Fr. Caesare, 80, 159
Donanzan, P.S.S.C., Fr. Luigi, 144
Dower, Fr. Declan, 18
Dowling, Bishop Austin, 6-7, 8, 10, 11, 15-16, 69
Dowling High School, 11, 14-15
Drumm, Bishop Thomas, 16, 18-19
Dugan, George, 159, 269
Dunn, Fr. Daniel, 178

Eisenhower, President Dwight, 131, 143
Eisenhower, Dr. Milton, 150
Ellis, Msgr. John Tracy, 9
Elwood, P., 37-38
Extension, 40

Fady, Bishop Giuseppe, 193
family farm, defined, 66, 69
"Fargo trio," 53-54
Farm Journal, 21, 160
Felici, Archbishop Pericle, 209, 210, 212, 215, 216
Fernandes, Archbishop Angelo, 204, 223, 226, 276
Ferrari, Bishop Carlo, 209, 211
Ferreira, Dr. Manuel, 156
Fietta, Archbishop Giuseppe, 157
Fifth International Congress on Rural Life, 269-270
First International Congress on Rural Life, 71, 102, 105-106, 108-110, 187
Flanagan, Msgr. Newman, 44, 89, 206
Food and Agriculture Organization, *See* United Nations, FAO
Food, Health and Income, 232
Ford Foundation, 158, 167-169, 252
Ford, Henry, 38, 305
Fortune, 307

Fourth International Congress on Rural Life, 162-165, 297-313
Francis, Clarence, 312
Frantz, C., 310
Franz, Bishop John, 83
Free America, 31, 36
Frei, President Edward, 163
Frings, Cardinal Joseph, 120, 121, 122, 216

Gallery, Fr. John Ireland, 159, 219, 221, 285
Gannon, Fr. Leo, 206
Gaule, Fr. Edward, 25
Gaviola, Bishop Mariano, 271
Generation of Industrial Peace, A, 310
Geneser, Francis, 24
Gerada, Archbishop Emanuele, 282-285
Giachetti, S.J., Fr. Carlo, 236
Gibbons, Cardinal James, 8-9
Gibbons, S.J., Fr. William, 59, 109, 137-138, 241-244, 246
Gilligan, Msgr. Francis, 57-58, 206
Gilroy, Cardinal Norman, 95
Giovannetti, Msgr. Alberto, 75, 252
Glennon, Cardinal John, 93
Glorieux, Msgr. Achille, 209, 211
Goldie, Rosemary, 286
Gonzi, Archbishop Michele, 281-285
Gorman, Fr. John, 30, 39, 81, 83, 175
Gorman, Bishop Thomas, 9, 13, 23
Gottwald, F.C.C., Br. Vincent, 291
Gracias, Cardinal Valerian, 197, 276
Granger, Ben, 24
Granger, Iowa,
  Assumption High School, 27-30, 38, 39, 45
    Catholic School Journal, The, 28
  Assumption Parish established, 25
  economy, Great Depression, 25
  history, 24-25
  Homesteads
    national and international praise, 36-37
    petitioning Congress, 33-35
    photos, 47
    plan of, 33-35, 38
    planning committee, 33, 37-38

Index 317

Granger, Iowa (cont.)
  reason for, 34, 38, 39
  reminiscence by homesteaders, 36, 39
  selection of families, 38-39
  twentieth anniversary, 39
Greco, Bishop Charles, 228
Gremillion, Msgr. Joseph, 83, 96, 99, 168-169, 224, 225, 228-229, 240
Grootheisen, Marie, 256, 265, 290, 292
Groves, Alba, 110
GROW, 187
Grugiono, Michael, 24
Guano, Bishop Emilio, 208-209, 211, 215

Hambridge, Grove, 109
Hamilton, Dr. Stanley, 70-71
Harnett, Msgr. Paul, 203
Harte, C.SS.R., Fr. Thomas, 305
Harter, Will, 38
Hartmans, Dr. E., 290
Harvard Business Review, 312
Havey, S.S., Fr. Francis, 7
Hayes, Canon John, 89, 108, 187
Hayes, Bishop Ralph, 76-77, 208
Hengsbach, Bishop Franz, 209, 210, 211
Herrera, Dr. Filipe, 277-278
Hesburgh, C.S.C., Fr. Theodore, 173
Higgins, Msgr. George, 68, 208, 209, 210, 211, 245, 258
Hildner, Msgr. George, 108
Hill, James, 55
Home of the Free, 31
Homeland Foundation, 78, 158, 166, 207, 252, 286, 292
Homestead Cooperative Association, 39
Houtart, Canon François, 82, 167, 169-170, 225
Hughes, Gov. Harold, 91
Human Problems of an Industrial Civilization, The, 308
Humanae Generis, 245
Humanae Vitae, 245, 273
Humphery-Lehman Bill, 132, 133
Humphery, Sen. Hubert, 131, 137
Hurley, Patrick, 120

Hyde, Douglas, 163, 269
Hynes, Emerson, 28, 73
Hynes, William, 5

Ickes, Harold, 35
Inter-American Development Bank, 165, 170, 277-278
International Catholic Migration Commission, 77, 85, 107, 111, 118-129, 144, 145, 161, 178, 186, 257
International Federation of Institutes for Social Research, 82, 166-167, 169
International Labour Review, 310
Iowa Business Digest, 311
Iowa Land Tenancy Commission, 40, 42
Iowa Nurserymen's Association, 64
Ireland, Archbishop John, 15

Jesuit Missions, 279
John XXIII, Pope, 2, 53, 82, 115, 179, 208, 210, 211, 212, 213, 223, 237, 260, 269-270, 271
Johnson, Dr. George, 12, 27
Johnson, President Lyndon, 146
Johnson, Sidney, 34

Kaas, Msgr. Ludwig, 119, 122
Kaiser, Msgr. Frank, 149, 159
Kane, Mr. and Mrs. Daniel, 74
Kelly, Fr. John, 157
Kempeneers, Msgr. J., 290
Kenkel, Frederick, 52
Kennedy, Sen. Edward, 147
Kennedy, President John, 147, 171
Keough, Archbishop Francis, 123
Kerrigan, Leo, 5, 89
Killion, C.SS.R., Fr. Edward, 101, 121, 124
Kirk, Arthur and father, 6, 69
Kiwanuka, Bishop Giuseppe, 190
Knox, Archbishop James, 190
Kolping, Fr. Leopold, 89
Kreps, Theodore, 307
Krug, T., 309
Kutish, Francis, 308-309

Lacasse, Fr. Arthur, 192
Ladejinsky, Dr. Wolf, 300
Ladies of the Grail, 74, 207, 291
LaFarge, S.J., Fr. John, 161, 241
Lanctot, John, 120, 125
Land and Home, 291
Landi, Msgr. Andrew, 92, 123, 128, 181, 182, 183, 188, 196
Lane, M.M., Bishop Raymond, 159
Lardonne, Archbishop Francesco, 158
Larrain, Bishop Manuel, 151, 160, 162, 209
Lasswell, Harold, 307
LaValle, C.P., Fr. Malcolm, 24
Lebret, O.P., Fr. Louis, 216
Leiber, S.J., Fr. Robert, 119, 120, 122
Leo XIII, Pope, 1, 31, 42, 44, 302, 303
Levame, Archbishop Alberto, 189
Lewis, Sinclair, 24
Ligutti, Antonio, 1, 3, 16
Ligutti, Don Cesare, 187
Ligutti, Francesca, 1, 3-4
Ligutti, Msgr. Luigi G.,
  Agrimissio, 200, 249-251, 262, 290-291
  Aloysius Domenico, 1
  American Committee on Italian Migration, 144-147
  Anti-Yankeeism, Latin America, 151, 153-154, 166-167
  apostolic visitator, Malta, 281-285
  Assumption High School, 27-30, 38-39, 45
  Cana wine project, 280-281
  canon, Basilica of St. Mary Major, 210, 289
  Catholic University of America, 11-12, 34
  Church in the Modern World, The, 218, 225, 227
  classics and history, 6-7, 8, 12, 13, 18, 23, 50, 186, 295
  Columbia University, 14
  Congressional committees, 61-62, 65, 69, 100-101
  Daly, O.P., Bishop Edward, 63, 80, 81, 83, 141-143, 161, 206, 207, 240, 241

Ligutti, Msgr. Luigi G., (cont.)
  domestic prelate, 43-44, 56
  Dowling High School, 11, 14, 175
  early education, 3
  ecology, 63-64, 67, 236
  ecumenism, 17, 67, 69-71, 74
  emigration to United States, 4
  encyclical on rural life, 82, 83, 91, 92
  epitaph and eulogy, 45, 294-295
  Eucharistic Congresses, 275-276
  family and relatives, 1-5, 7, 10, 16, 17, 18, 23, 24, 26, 44, 56, 87-88, 151, 187, 295
  "Gino," 2
  golden jubilee of ordination, 44-45, 268
  Granger Homesteads, 33-39, 43-44, 45, 70, 291
  honorary doctorates, 13, 173
  hunting and fishing, 17-19, 23, 49, 295
  Inter-American Development Bank, 277-278
  International Catholic Migration Commission, 77, 85, 107, 111, 118-129, 144, 145, 161, 178, 186, 257
  International Congresses on Rural Life,
    First, 71, 102, 105, 106, 108-110
    Second, 158-160
    Third, 161-162
    Fourth, 162-165, 297-313
    Fifth, 269
    Sixth, 270-271
  Iowa state commissions, 40, 42
  land tenancy, 40-43, 164, 197-198, 218, 255-256
  McCarran-Walter Act, 129-144
  master's degree, 13
  minor seminarian, 3
  National Catholic Rural Life Conference,
    executive director, 52, 57, 58, 60, 63, 71-72, 76-81, 105, 117, 152
    international affairs director, 81, 82, 84

Index 319

Ligutti, Msgr. Luigi G., (cont.)
president, 51, 56
ordination and first Mass, 8-11
pastor,
    Granger, 23-45, 50, 56, 57, 58, 59, 174, 219, 256, 268, 295
    Logan, Magnolia, and Woodbine, 3, 16-22, 23, 219, 288, 295
photos, 48, 112-116, 124, 171-176, 261-266
Pontifical Commissions,
    Bishops and Government of Dioceses, 215
    Justice and Peace, 217, 218, 222, 224-228, 229, 265, 279
    Lay Apostolate, 208-211, 214, 217, 218, 220, 221, 286
    Schema 13, 215
prothonotary apostolic, 80, 218
radio addresses, 40-41, 42-43, 61, 68-69
rural life philosophy, 32, 41, 49-51, 58-59, 62-66, 67, 68-69, 85, 94-95, 190, 218, 255-256, 279-280, 297-313
Rural Roads to Security, 57
St. Ambrose College, 4-5, 7, 44, 295
St. Isidore's angels, 87, 100, 101, 104, 105-106, 110, 178, 182, 267, 268, 291
St. Mary's Seminary, 7-10, 69, 295
tithing and stewardship, 20, 26-27, 210, 219-221, 286-288
travel letter themes, 86-87, 94, 101, 105, 178, 196, 254, 256, 259, 292
travels,
    Africa (1953-1954), 188-195
    Australia and Indonesia (1956), 201-202
    and New Zealand (1946-1947), 94-96
    Europe (1939), 88-91
    (1945), 91-93
    (1948), 96-100
    (1951), 104-110
    (1952), 110
    (1953), 186-188
    (1957), 110-111

Ligutti, Msgr. Luigi G., (cont.)
and Near East (1950), 101-104
Far East (1955-1956), 196-200, 202-205
Greece, Turkey, and Near East (1952), 178-186
Latin America (1943, 1944), 149-166, 170, 178-179
Udine visits, 84, 87-88, 90, 92, 98, 102, 107, 187, 204, 294
United States citizen, 11-12
University of Chicago, 14, 18
vacation schools, 19-20, 28, 39, 45
Vatican observer to FAO, 75, 77, 80, 83, 85, 106, 107, 111, 117, 178, 179, 186, 187, 188, 195, 196-197, 206, 212, 214, 215, 229, 231, 232, 235-236, 238-260, 262-265, 268, 270, 273, 275-276, 279, 282, 288, 289-290, 291, 292
Vatican II
    lay auditors, assistant director, 215-216, 218
    peritus, 212, 215, 218
Villa Stillman, 206-208
Ligutti, Napoleon, 1, 3
Ligutti, Pietro, 151
Ligutti, Spiridione, 1, 3, 44
Ligutti, Teresa, 1
Ligutti, Teresa (nee Ciriani), 1-4, 10, 16, 17, 18, 23, 24, 26, 44, 56, 88, 295
Likert, Rensis, 311
Lincoln, James, 312
Liturgical Conference, 72-73
Lodge, Cabot, 150
Loftus, Msgr. Eugene, 96
London *Daily Worker*, 163, 269
Tablet, 89
Long Island *Catholic*, 279
Los Angeles *Tidings*, 9, 23
L'Osservatore della Dominica, 207
L'Osservatore Romano, 214, 246
Lourdusamy, Archbishop Simon, 287
Lovejoy, J. E., Company of, 35
Lowell, James, 8
Lucey, Archbishop Robert, 303

Lucker, Dr. Alberta, 74
Lunding, Franklin, 312

McCann, Archbishop Owen, 190
McCarran-Walter Act, 129-144
McCarran, Sen. Patrick, 130, 133, 134
McCarthy, Sen. Eugene, 91
McCloskey, Jack, 99, 128, 186
McConnell, Dr. Charles, 71
McCormack, M.H.M., Fr. Arthur, 227
McCormack, Paul, 135
McDermott, Fr. Patrick, 17
McDougall, Frank, 232-233, 239, 240, 241, 246
McEntegart, Bishop Bryan, 128
McGeough, Msgr. Joseph, 123
McGowan, Fr. Raymond, 68
McGrath, C.S.C., Archbishop Marco, 162
McGuire, Dr. Constantine, 131-132, 140, 142
McGuire, C.M., Fr. Frederick, 83, 159
McIntyre, Cardinal James, 258
McMahon, Msgr. T., 103
McMillen, Wheeler, 160
McNabb, O.P., Fr. Vincent, 89
McNicholas, Archbishop John, 74
Magnet, Alexander, 163
Mahon, M.H.M., Very Rev. Gerald, 226
Main Street, 24
Malone, Fr. H., 25
Malta, Church finances, 281-285
Management Record, 311
Mangers, Bishop James, 88
Manifesto on Rural Life, 53, 57, 71, 179
Mannix, Archbishop Daniel, 52, 201
"Man's Relation to the Land," 67
Maranta, Archbishop Edgaro, 193
Marasco, Msgr. Paul, 27, 36, 82
Marella, Cardinal Paul, 215
Marling, Bishop Joseph, 81, 83, 84, 115, 206, 207
Marshall Plan, 119, 239, 245
Mater et Magistra, 223, 269-270, 271
Mayo, Dr. Elton, 307-308
Mazzuchelli, O.P., Fr. Samuel, 8
Medeiros, Cardinal Humberto, 288

Meier, Joseph, 312
Meisner, Joseph, 80
Mentz, Admiral George, 99
Metzler, Rev. John, 70
Mexico, Land of Volcanoes, 149
Meyer, Cardinal Albert, 76-77, 216
Michel, O.S.B., Dom Virgil, 12-13, 56, 73
Miconi, Fr. Leonard, 80
Mikolajczyk, Stanislaw, 163
Miller, Dr. Raymond, 109, 160, 188, 255, 307
Miranda, Cardinal Raimono, 171
Mohler, Bruce, 131, 134, 135, 140-141
Montemayor, J., 286
Montini, Cardinal Giovanni, 66, 71-72, 80, 82, 83, 90, 92, 99, 105, 106-107, 118, 121, 122, 123, 125, 159, 161, 169-170, 174, 195, 212, 216, 217, 218, 224, 227, 228, 231-232, 236, 237-238, 241, 246, 247, 253-254, 262, 266, 272, 275-276, 279, 285, 288, 290, 293
Moody, Sen. Blair, 132, 133
Mooney, Cardinal Edward, 93
More, Br. Thomas, 291
Morino, Msgr. Claude, 220
Morrison, Msgr. Joseph, 9, 73, 89, 151, 159, 160, 178, 260, 270
Morrow, Bishop, Luigi, 203
Muench, Cardinal Aloysius, 44, 52-54, 55, 56, 57, 65, 91, 93, 94, 97, 121, 187, 240
Muhm, Donald, 49
Mulroy, Msgr. John, 96
Mulloy, Bishop William, 54, 57, 76, 81, 82, 142, 187, 240
Mundelein, Cardinal George, 74, 91, 99
Munitir da Tire, 89

Natalini, Msgr. Terzo, 287, 289
National Catholic Resettlement Council, 118
National Catholic Rural Life Conference,
    finances, 77-81
    first episcopal president, 53
    founding, 51

National Catholic Rural Life
  Conference, (cont.)
    Ligutti, Msgr. Luigi G., 51, 52,
      56, 57, 58, 60, 63, 71-72,
      76-81, 82, 84, 105, 117, 152
    philosophy, 65
    publications, 51, 53, 54, 57, 61,
      73
    silver jubilee, 51
National Catholic Welfare
  Conference, 55, 57, 68, 78, 80, 91,
  92, 96, 98, 99, 102, 118, 121, 123,
  128, 131, 132, 134, 135-137, 139-
  143, 151, 168, 181, 186, 203, 222,
  228, 239, 240, 242, 258, 288
National Recovery Act, 33
Nesbit, Wilbur, 31-32
New York *Times*, 21, 159, 163
New Yorker, 40
Nixon, President Richard, 67, 146-
  147, 153, 166
Nohs, O.S.B., Abbot Lawrence, 149
Norris, James, 96, 99, 121-128, 222,
  223-224, 229
Nuesse, Dr. C., 304
Nugent, Fr. Joseph, 7-8
Nunn, Henry, 312

O'Boyle, Cardinal Patrick, 91, 128,
  134, 173, 223, 225
O'Connor, Edward, 96
O'Connor, Archbishop Martin, 257,
  281-282, 284
O'Connor, Fr. Michael, 193
O'Dwyer, William, 150
O'Grady, Msgr. John, 12, 32, 123,
  124, 133, 134, 135, 141, 143, 155,
  190, 241, 245
O'Hara, Bishop Edwin, 19, 20, 51,
  52, 53, 55, 61, 65, 108, 109, 110,
  159, 160
Olson, Dr. Karl, 277
Operare, 311
Orate Fratres, 12
O'Rourke, Msgr. Edward, 83, 84, 240
Ottaviani, Cardinal Alfredo, 99
Our Sunday Visitor, 39, 79
Overboss, Joan, 290

Pacem in Terris, 223
Pastore, Sen. John, 145

Patterson, Albion, 162
Patton, James, 268
Paul VI, Pope, *See* Montini, Cardinal
  Giovanni
Pavan, Msgr. Pietro, 82, 83, 105, 108,
  109, 188, 190, 208, 209, 210, 211,
  214
Pearson, Lester, 235
Pelikan, Dr. Jaroslav, 73-74
Perkins, Frances, 37
Perlman, Phillip, 136
Pernicone, Bishop Joseph, 144, 161
Persegati, Walter, 83, 116, 206, 207,
  220, 256, 290, 292
Piazza, Cardinal Adeodato, 257
Pigata, C.S., Fr. Remigio, 144
Pillai, O.M.I., Fr. Peter, 203
Pius X, Pope St., 1, 6, 19
Pius XI, Pope, 31, 270, 299
Pius XII, Pope, 71, 90, 92, 93, 99,
  102, 103, 106, 109-110, 112, 119-
  125, 159, 197, 237, 239
Point Four Program, 100, 149, 189
Populorum Progressio, 232, 279
  Fund, 170, 277
Prayers and Blessings of the Church,
  54
Price, Gwylim, 312
Primeau, Bishop Ernest, 83, 92, 99,
  188, 216, 290
Pro, S.J., Fr. Michael, 51
Purcell, S.J., Fr. Theodore, 304
Pursley, Bishop Leo, 79, 81

Quadragesimo Anno, 270
Quadri, Bishop Santo, 209, 211
Quebec *Conference Report*, 235
Quinn, Fr. John, 99
Quintero, Cardinal José, 269

Raimondi, Archbishop Luigi, 93
Ramacher, Fr. Edward, 76, 79
Rava, Paul, 130
Rawe, S.J., Fr. John, 57
Ready, Msgr. Michael, 57
Reh, Bishop Francis, 216, 257
Reisner, Dr. John, 107, 254, 255
Rerum Novarum, 42, 44, 302, 303
Reynolds, prayer of, 60
Rink, O.M.I., Fr. Othmar, 286

Ripley, Dr. S. Dillon, 173
Ritter, Cardinal Joseph, 129, 133, 134, 135, 142, 143
Rockefeller Foundation, 158, 271
Rodhain, Msgr. Jean, 222
Rodino, Rep. Peter, 145
Roling, Leo, 5
Romano, Joseph, 4, 193
Rome *Daily American*, 281
Romualdi, Serafino, 301
Roosevelt, Mrs. Franklin, 36, 38, 40, 233
Roosevelt, President Franklin, 32, 37, 40, 41-42, 51, 233
Roosevelt, President Theodore, 153
Rosenthal, Edward, 5
Rottenberg, Dr. S., 164
Roy, Cardinal Maurice, 227
Rural Life Prayerbook, 61
Rural Roads to Security, 57
Ruttenberg, Harold, 311
Ryan, Msgr. John, 41, 68
Ryan, Bishop Vincent, 53-54, 56, 57, 84, 179

St. Isidore, 72, 87, 100, 101, 103, 104, 105-106, 110, 178, 182, 204, 267, 268, 291
Saint Isidore's Plow, 61
St. John's Abbey and University, 12, 28, 67-68, 155
St. Maria de la Cabeza, 87, 106, 110, 204
St. Mary's Seminary, 7
St. Raphaelsverein, 122, 123
Salazar, President Antonio, 169
Samore, Archbishop Antonio, 159, 224, 229, 246
Santamaria, Bob, 104-105, 201
Santos, Archbishop Rufino, 197
Sauer, Dr. Elmer, 305
Scalabrini Fathers, 144-146, 187, 207, 257, 263, 291
Scalabrini, Bishop Giovanni, 257
Schauff, Dr. Johannes, 119-127
Scheidler, Fr. Russell, 96, 99
Schirber, O.S.B., Fr. Martin, 68
Schlarman, Archbishop Joseph, 54-55, 69, 73, 85, 110, 149, 151, 160, 178, 180, 240, 270

Schmidt, Fr. Hans, 14
Schnepp, S.M., Br. Gerald, 304
School Reading by Grades, 5
Schultz, Dr. T., 305-307
Schutte, Fr. Johannes, 290
Schwartz, Harry, 163
Second International Congress on Rural Life, 158-160
Secours Catholique, 101, 222, 250
Sen, Dr. B., 259-260, 276
Servé, S.J., Fr. Joseph, 101, 104, 157
Shadeg, S.V.D., Fr. Norbert, 202
Shanahan, Fr. William, 5, 11
Shanley, Bishop James, 53
Sharing a Business, 312
Sharp, Fr. John, 9
Sheen, Archbishop Fulton, 211
Sheil, Bishop Bernard, 74
Shipstead, Sen. Henrik, 132
Sigismondi, Archbishop Pietro, 246, 257
Silverstein, Saul, 311
Siri, Cardinal Giuseppe, 311
Sixth International Congress on Rural Life, 270-271
Skillin, Edward, 91, 304
Sklar, Ben, 309
So Bold an Aim, 234
Social Principles of an Industrial Civilization, The, 308
Soenneker, Bishop Henry, 55
Soil Conservation Society, 63
"Song of the Plow, The," xvi, 13, 100
Spellman, Cardinal Francis, 93, 198, 225, 292
Speltz, Bishop George, 55, 164, 213
Staffa, Archbishop Dino, 215
Sternberg, Dr. Hilgard, 156
Stillman, Chauncey, 78, 79, 80, 81, 82, 105, 175, 206-207, 291-292
Stritch, Cardinal Samuel, 73, 93
Sturzo, Don Luigi, 52, 89, 91-94, 99, 103, 179
Subsistence Homesteads Division, U.S. Dept. of Interior, 33, 35, 38
Suenens, Cardinal Leo, 213, 214
Sullivan, S.J., Fr. John, 154

Index 323

Swanstrom, Bishop Edward, 78, 96, 121, 123, 124, 128, 129, 133, 135, 143, 146, 222, 225-226, 239, 240, 288

Taft, Sen. Robert, 66-67
Tale of Two Cities, The, 4
Tanner, Msgr. Paul, 133-134, 142, 143
Tessarolo, C.S., Fr. Giulius, 263
Third International Congress on Rural Life, 161-162
Tisserant, Cardinal Eugené, 216
"Tither's Creed, A," 20-21
tithing and stewardship, 20, 26-27, 210, 219-221, 223
Toffolini, Fr. Nino, 99, 187, 204
Tonini, Don Justiniano, 1
Tonna, Fr. Benjamin, 281-282
Tramontin, Mr. and Mrs. James, 91
Treacy, Bishop John, 85, 187, 216
Truman, President Harry 131, 133
Tucci, S.J., Fr. Robert, 214
Twenty-Five Years of Crusading, 51

Umberto I, King, 194
United Nations,
  FAO, 60, 75, 77, 80, 85, 90, 106, 107, 109, 111, 117, 165-166, 174, 178, 179, 186, 187, 189, 195, 196-197, 206, 210, 212, 214, 215, 220, 222, 229, 248-260, 262-266, 268, 270, 273, 275-276, 277, 279, 282, 288, 289-290, 291, 292
    anniversaries, tenth, 234, 237
      twenty-fifth, 238
    budget, 235, 259
    established, 231-236
    membership, 254-255, 259
    praise by popes, 236-238
    principles and objectives, 231-236, 244, 259
    Vatican observership established, 239-247
  founded, 74-75, 231, 245
Urbani, Cardinal Giovanni, 214

Vaccari, Vittorio, 311
Vagnozzi, Archbishop Egidio, 197, 210

van Kersbergen, Dr. Lydwine, 74
Vatican,
  Food and Agriculture Organization, *See* Ligutti, Msgr. Luigi G., Vatican observer to FAO
  Migration Bureau, 101
  Pontifical Commissions,
    Bishops and Government of Dioceses, 215
    Justice and Peace, 217-228, 229, 265, 279
    Lay Apostolate, 208-211, 214, 217, 218, 220, 221, 286
    Schema, 13, 215
  Second Council, opening, 211
Vekemans, Fr. Roger, 162
Veronese, Vittorino, 105-106, 188, 190
Villa Stillman, 176, 206-208, 210, 212, 213
Villot, Cardinal Jean, 257, 273-274, 284-285
Vizzard, S.J., Fr. James, 71, 76, 79

Wakely, Ray, 37-39
Wallace, Henry, 33
Walsh, Fr. James, 7
Walter, Rep. Francis, 130, 136
War Relief Services, *See* National Catholic Welfare Conference
Ward, Barbara, 222, 224
Ward, Maisie, 89
Warren, Louis, 207, 292
Washington *Post*, 166
  Times-Herald, 136
Weber, Msgr. George, 83, 84
Wehrle, O.S.B., Bishop Vincent, 56
Weisblat, Dr. A., 271-272
Weiss, Fr. Jacob, 50
Weiss, Jake, 23
Weller, George, 36, 105
Welsch, "Lizzy," 5
Wesley, John, 177
Whalen, Fr. John, 173
Wheeler, Walter, 312-313
Whole Man Goes to Work, The, 312
Whyte, William, 307
Wilson, M., 33, 34, 35, 106
Witte, Br. Raymond, 51

324   *The People I Love*

Woodbine *Twine*, 21
Woodruff, Douglas, 89
Works of Horace, The, 6-7
World Council of Churches, 73, 167-168
Wosnicki, Bishop Stephen, 80-81

Yates, P. Lamartine, 234
Yu Pin, Cardinal Paul, 221

Zuroweste, Bishop Albert, 108, 109, 139-140, 142, 159, 160, 220, 221, 285